AF560481

India-Pakistan

The Intractable Conflict and the China Factor

India-Pakistan

The Intractable Conflict
and the China Factor

Maj Gen Virender Singh Budhwar

Title: India-Pakistan: The Intractable Conflict and the China Factor
Author: Maj Gen Virender Singh Budhwar

ISBN: 978-93-92210-73-0

Published by:
JGS Enterprises Pvt Ltd
Imprint: The Browser

Publisher's Address:
SCO 14-15, FF, Sector 8-C, Chandigarh 160 009

Website: www.thebrowser.org
Email: service@thebrowser.org

Printed in India

© Layout and Cover Design by 99 beagles
99beagles.com

*Dedicated to my father Abhay,
an officer and a gentleman who fought in the Second World War
in Burma. A salute to the officers and men who fought
in the Kargil War.*

Contents

Ch 8: Intransigence and Reconciliation

List of Annexures

List of Abbreviations

ADB	Asian Development Bank
A2/AD	Anti-Access/Area Denial
AD/CE	Anno Domini/Common Era
AFPAK	Afghanistan and Pakistan
AGPL	Actual Ground Position Line
AI	Artificial Intelligence
AIB	Asian Infrastructure Bank
ALCM	Air-Launched Cruise Missile
AMRAAM	Advanced Medium-Range Air-to-Air Missile
ANA	Afghan National Army
APHC	All Party Hurriyat Conference
APTTA	Afghan Pakistan Transit Trade Agreement
ASEAN	Association of South Eastern Asian Nations
APT-10	Advanced Persistent Threat-10
AWACS	Airborne Warning and Control System
BLA	Baluchistan Liberation Army
BARC	Bhabha Atomic Research Centre
BC/BCE	Before Christ/Before the Common Era
BSF	Border Security Force
CACTSA	Countering America's Adversaries Through Sanctions Act (USA)
CAA	Citizens Amendment Act (India)

CARs	Central Asian Republics (Includes Turkmenistan, Kyrgyzstan, Uzbekistan, Tajikistan, and Kazakhstan, all of whom were part of the former Union of Soviet Socialist Republics)
CENTO	Central Treaty Organization
CENTCOM	Central Command (USA)
C-in-C	Commander-in-Chief
CFL	Cease-fire Line
CIA	Central Intelligence Agency (US)
COAS	Chief of Army Staff
CPEC	China-Pakistan Economic Corridor
CRPF	Central Reserve Police Force (India)
CSEL	Cyber Security Auditing and Evaluation
DBO	Daulat Beg Oldi (named after a trader who passed away on his way to Yarkand on the Silk Route)
DCC	Deployment Control Committee (Relates to Pakistan's nuclear weapons)
DGMO	Director General of Military Operations
ECC	Employment Control Committee (Pakistan's decision-making body on employment of nuclear weapons)
EEZ	Exclusive Economic Zone
FATF	Financial Action Task Force
FCNA	Force Command Northern Areas (Pakistan)
FATA	Federally Administered Tribal Areas (Pakistan)
GDP	Gross Domestic Product
GID	General Intelligence Division (Saudi Arabia)
GLOC	Ground Line of Communications
GHQ	General Headquarters

GOC	General Officer Commanding
HAWS	High Altitude Warfare School
HQ	Headquarters
HEU	Highly Enriched Uranium
HM	Hizbul Mujahideen
IA	Indian Army
IAF	Indian Air Force
IB	International Border
IAEC	Indian Atomic Energy Commission
ICBM	Intercontinental Ballistic Missile
ICTP	International Center for Theoretical Physics
IAEA	International Atomic Energy Agency
IED	Improvised Explosive Devices
IMF	International Monetary Fund
IoT	Internet of Things
IPC	Indian Penal Code
IPKF	Indian Peace Keeping Force
ISI	Inter-Services Intelligence
ISIS	Islamic State of Iraq and the Levant
IT	Information Technology
ISPR	Inter-Services Public Relations (Pakistan Army)
JCPOA	Joint Comprehensive Plan of Action (Agreement with Iran)
JeM	Jaish-e-Mohammed (Jihadist group Pakistan)
JeI	Jamaat-e-Islami
J&K	Jammu and Kashmir (Union Territory in India)

JKLF	Jammu and Kashmir Liberation Front
JKSDMI	Jammu and Kashmir Self-determination Movement
JIB	Joint Intelligence Bureau (Pakistan)
KRL	Kahuta Research Laboratories/Khan Research Laboratories (Pakistan)
LAC	Line of Actual Control
LeT	Lashkar-e-Taiba (Jihadist group Pakistan)
Lt Gen	Lieutenant General
LOC	Line of Control
Maj Gen	Major General
MAD	Mutual Assured Destruction
MBRL	Multi-Barrel Rocket Launcher
MIRV	Multiple Independently-targetable Re-entry Vehicle
MFN	Most Favoured Nation
MOU	Memorandum of Understanding
MP	Member of Parliament
MTCR	Missile Technology Control Regime
MTPA	Metric Tonnes Per Annum
NATO	North Atlantic Treaty Organization
NADRA	National Database and Registration Authority
NDB	New Development Bank
NE	North-east
NEFA	North-east Frontier Agency
NLI	Northern Light Infantry (Pakistan)
NWFP	North-west Frontier Province
NCA	National Command Authority (Pakistan)

NW	North-west
NRC	National Register of Citizens (India)
NSC	National Security Council (Pakistan)
NSG	Nuclear Suppliers Group
NPT	Nuclear Non-proliferation Treaty
NTRO	National Technical Research Organization (India)
OIC	Organization of Islamic Cooperation
Ops	Operations
ORBAT	Order of Battle
PAEC	Pakistan Atomic Energy Commission
PAF	Pakistan Air Force
PLA	People's Liberation Army (China)
PDP	People's Democratic Party (J&K)
PLO	Palestine Liberation Organization
PML	Pakistan Muslim League
POK	Pakistan Occupied Kashmir
Pp	Printed Pages
PPP	People's Party of Pakistan
PNE	Peaceful Nuclear Explosion
PSA	Public Security Act (India)
PTI	Pakistan Tehreek-e-Insaf (Political party in Pakistan)
PW	Prisoner of War
Quad	A diplomatic partnership between Australia, India, Japan, and the United States committed to supporting an open, stable, and prosperous Indo-Pacific that is inclusive and resilient
RAW	Research and Analysis Wing (Indian Intelligence Agency)

RCEP	Regional Comprehensive Economic Partnership
R&D	Research and Development
RITES	Rail India Technical and Economic Service
RODRA	National Database and Registration Authority (Pakistan)
RR	Rashtriya Rifles (India)
SAARC	South Asian Association for Regional Cooperation
SE	South-east
SEATO	South-east Asia Treaty Organization
SEZ	Special Economic Zone
SIPRI	Stockholm International Peace Research Institute
SFF	Special Frontier Force
SLBM	Submarine Launched Ballistic Missile
SLCM	Submarine Launched Cruise Missile
SPD	Strategic Plans Division
SPO	Special Police Officer
SSG	Special Service Group
SSW	Sub-sector west
SW	South-west
TNFJ	Tehreek Nafaze Fiqhe Jafariya
TEP	Tehreek-e-Taliban (Jihadi group in Pakistan)
TPG	Theoretical Physics Group
TPNW	Treaty on the Prohibition of Nuclear Weapons
TTP	Tehreek-e-Taliban Pakistan (Jihadi group in Pakistan)
TV	Television
UAE	United Arab Emirates

UCLA	University of California, Los Angeles
UN	United Nations
UNCIP	United Nations Commission India and Pakistan
UNHRC	United Nations Human Rights Commission
UJC	United Jihad Council
UK	United Kingdom
UNMOGIP	UN Military Observer Group in India and Pakistan
UNSC	United Nations Security Council
UNCLOS	United Nations Convention on the Law of the Sea
US	United States
USA	United States of America
USSR	Union of Soviet Socialist Republics

Glossary of Foreign Words

Azadi	freedom
Ad nauseam	refers to something that has been repeated so often that it has become annoying or tiresome
Akhand Bharat	undivided India
Azad	free
Caliphate	a Muslim tenet of having one government in which political and religious leadership is united under a head of state (caliph)
Casus belli	an act or situation provoking or justifying war
Dhar	mountain
Dar es Salaam	haven of peace
Fauji	person employed in the armed forces or connected to the armed forces
Hadith	a collection of traditions containing sayings of Prophet Mohammad, which account for daily practice, and constitute the major source of guidance for Muslims
Hartals	industrial action or strikes
Hatf	deadly
Hurriyat	freedom
Imam	Muslim religious teacher
Islamist	following the Salafi form of Islam
Izzat	reputation, prestige
Jihad	holy war fought to safeguard Islam
Jihadis	fighters who wage war in the name of Islam
Kashmiryat	ethno-national, social consciousness, and cultural values of the people of Kashmir
Khilafat	opposition

Kuffar	a non-believer or infidel
Khutbah	a formal method of teaching the Muslim tradition
Looting	theft
Maidan	open ground
Madrasa	religious seminary for Islamic studies
Minar	tower
Muhajir	emigrant in general
Mukti Bahini	brotherhood of freedom fighters
Mujahideen	freedom fighters
Namaste	a respectful form of greeting meaning 'I bow to the Divine in you'; same as namaskar
Paltan maidan	garrison ground
Panchayat	elected council of a village having five to seven members
Raison d'etre	the most important reason or purpose for something's existence
Sadbhavana	goodwill
Sangars	temporary fire position made for protection using stones and rocks
Tianxia	All under heaven, a Chinese concept associated with civilisation and order. In the present it relates to the rejuvenation of the Chinese nation.
Urs	death anniversary of a saint

Preface

Only a soldier knows the trepidation, the fear, the excitement, and the raw emotions before and during a war, battle, or a military operation.

The subject matter and analysis in this book are based on experience gained during thirty-eight years of service in the Indian Army and an extensive and continuous study of the subject since 1971. I am sanguine that I have endeavoured to put into perspective the unremitting hostility that has bedeviled relations between India and Pakistan since 1947, and between India and China since 1962. I examine issues that prevail and project these views candidly. I may seem hawkish, but I strive to be forthright in my approach. I have attempted to ensure that I do not hurt sentiments and religious leanings of anyone. My aim, as far as possible, is to remove misconceptions, anomalies, incorrect information, and doubts. It has taken considerable time and effort to gather my thoughts and study the works of professional authors, scholars, learned elite, diplomats and journalists, armchair analysts, and editorials to formulate a comprehensive account on this subject. The research, coupled with personal experience, has afforded me a wealth of knowledge and perspectives.

For most of my life, I have lived in India and closely observed the dynamics in the South-Asian subcontinent. I have witnessed the 1965 Indo-Pakistan war and participated in the 1971 Indo-Pakistan war. I commanded an Infantry battalion as part of the Indian Peace Keeping Force (IPKF) in Sri Lanka from 1987-89. In 1999, I was the General Officer in Commanding (GOC), 3 Infantry Division, the Indian Army formation responsible for the defence of the Ladakh Sector of Jammu and Kashmir (J&K). The responsibility of GOC 3 Division was immense as this Division was uniquely tasked to counter threats from two inimical neighbours, China and Pakistan. This Division was defending area along the Line of Actual Control (LAC), which included areas in Eastern Ladakh, Aksai Chin, Tibet, and Xinjiang against China an estimated frontage of 883 kilometers(kms) and the Siachen Glacier Sector, the Soltoro Mountain Range, also referred to as Actual Ground Position Line (AGPL), LOC including Mashkoh, Dras, Kargil, Batalik and Turtuk Sectors over 400 kms, against Pakistan.

While serving in J&K for over five years, I had the opportunity to interact with common Kashmiri folks in the Valley-citizens of Kargil, Ladakh, and nomads. Each tenure in the region was exciting, challenging, and eventful and gave me an insight into life in J&K. In my first tenure, I found the local population had no ill will or hostility towards Indian troops or towards India. In my second tenure, the situation had changed, the Kashmir Valley had radical elements who were clearly anti-India. The peace in this area was now disturbed largely because of foreign mercenaries and terrorists from Pakistan, who had infiltrated the state of J&K. By carrying out terrorist attacks, destroying public property, targeting the original inhabitants of the state, and creating fear and terror, it was their aim to spoil the equilibrium of normal life. More alarmingly, a section of the Kashmiri population was also being radicalized.

Kargil and Ladakh were peaceful areas until the intrusion by Pakistan in 1999 across the LOC, which perpetrated the Kargil War. The area of the Jammu sub-division has remained peaceful, except for trans-LOC firing, shelling, and stray incidents of terror. The Ladakh border is no longer peaceful as a result of Chinese actions which led to a deadly confrontation between India and China in 2020.

Regrettably, ordinary Kashmiris have found their lives and privacy being violated by both terrorists and Indian Security Forces during counterinsurgency and anti-terrorist ops. Terrorists who manage to infiltrate J&K seek refuge, shelter, food, medicine, money, and operational support from locals. In an ethnic cleansing of the most heinous kind, the terrorists have evicted the Kashmiri Pandits from their homes in Kashmir and made them refugees in their own land since the late 1980s. The terrorists merged into the local population using sheer force and by inflicting terror. India contended definitively with the situation as it escalated. Without strong intervention, terrorists would continue to inflict more damage to infrastructure, cause further casualties, and radicalize and subvert the population. The Kashmiris do not want war and are embittered by the terrorists, especially the foreign mercenaries.

Information forthcoming from the locals on the presence of terrorists has helped the Indian security forces to continue to launch counter-terrorist ops. Extremism and terrorism are not a phenomenon unique to Kashmir. But in this region, the Kashmiri population is without a doubt, enduring a sustained terrorism effort by Pakistan.

Terrorism perpetrated by Pakistan is not limited only to Kashmir, but the whole of India has been subjected to Pakistan's dastardly acts. Terrorists attacked the Red Fort in Delhi on 22 December 2000 and audaciously attempted violence at the Indian Parliament in New Delhi on 13 December 2001. There cannot be a worse affront to a democratic country than an attack on its seat of power. What could have been a massacre of the members of the Indian Parliament (MPs), was prevented by the timely and determined action of the Indian security forces as they eliminated the terrorists before they entered Parliament House. Previously, terrorist attacks in Mumbai on 23/11 had also resulted in the massacre of innocent civilians. There is ample proof of Pakistan's involvement in the planning and execution of these operations. These are all well-known incidents highlighting a mindless cult of violence executed by terrorists under the direction of their mentors in Pakistan.

To prevent any ripostes for its terrorist attacks, and as a preemptive measure, Pakistan has often articulated the nuclear threat it poses. Without any provocation, India has repeatedly suffered such attacks within its boundaries and has shown restraint in the past. However, the policy of the Indian government changed in September 2016 when IA special forces conducted an operation across the LOC into POK. This was a surgical strike in response to the terrorist attack on the administrative base of the IA in Uri in which 19 soldiers were killed. Thus, India had established new red lines that the LOC would no longer inhibit any military action against terrorists. On 14 February 2019 an attack on Indian soil was perpetrated by a Pakistan-based terror proxy, Jaish-e-Mohammed (JeM), which is controlled by Pakistan's Inter-Services Intelligence (ISI). The JeM was audacious enough to claim responsibility for this attack in India, from their location in Pakistan. In this deadly aggression by the JeM, an Indian police convoy was targeted in the Pulwama district of J&K, leading to the deaths of 40 police personnel. This violent attack changed the Indian policy further, and instead of restraint came a resolve to counter such mindless terror attacks on Indian soil by striking at terrorist centers in Pakistan's mainland. Within a few days of this attack, Indian Air Force was deployed to strike the terrorist training center of JeM at Balakot in Pakistan. This response into mainland Pakistan indicated that henceforth, attacks by Pakistan and its proxies on Indian soil will not go unpunished. The uneasy peaceful situation had been shattered once again by terrorists on 22 April 2025 when they murdered 26 innocent civilians near Pahalgam in J&K. In a short war that lasted over four days commencing on 6 May 2025, India targeted nine terrorist establishments inside Pakistan. The Pakistan armed forces came to the support of the terrorists by escalating the conflict. They launched relentless streams of armed drone swarms, missiles and their air force to attack civilian and military targets inside India. The Indian armed forces defended its airspace making the strikes ineffective. In retaliation India attacked and made 13 military airbases inside Pakistan in-operational. This short war displayed India's resolve to defeat military action and terrorism by inimical nations against India by whatever means necessary. By taking the bold action of striking deep inside Pakistan's heartland, India has called this country's bluff of the threat of nuclear weapons. India has clearly stated that any terrorism against it will be treated as an act of war.

With this ongoing tension as the backdrop, this book examines threat perceptions, the worsening of relations, and periods of relative peace between India and Pakistan. China is a part of this equation since it has willfully and consistently supported Pakistan's claim on J&K. It had forcefully occupied Aksai Chin, and a part of Eastern Ladakh that is claimed by India. In a unilateral border settlement, China was also bestowed the Shaksgam Valley in northern Kashmir by Pakistan. This makes China party to the Kashmir dispute. China is now undertaking the construction of a major infrastructure project in northern J&K through the area occupied by Pakistan. It has already set in motion its string of pearls projects in the Indian Ocean, which is detrimental to India's security, United States (US) interests in the region, and world trade. Relations between India and China have soured, with China unexpectedly upping the ante in eastern Ladakh. In an incident on 20 April 2020, there was a dangerous stand-off between Indian and Chinese forces. Chinese troops had challenged India's assimilation of Sikkim. China has also occupied select areas of Nepal across the Himalayan watershed, it has laid claim on Bhutan's north-eastern (NE) region and on India's state of Arunachal Pradesh. President Xi Jinping has disregarded Prime Minister Modi's attempts to establish friendly relations. It is apparent that China is deeply embroiled in South Asian geopolitics as it pursues the larger objective of becoming a regional and global superpower. India is dealing with a belligerent and aggressive China and an inimical Pakistan operating conjointly against Indian interests in the region. With a power-hungry China and Pakistan's efforts to up the ante since the late eighties, the situation in this region is extremely complex. These incessant hostilities against India, a turbulent and radical Afghanistan in the North-west (NW), the rise of communism in Nepal, an independent Islamic state with a stand by government in Bangladesh having anti-India overtones that was established after the over throw of Sheikh Haseena, the Prime Minister, and the financial crisis in Sri Lanka all play a part in this regional conundrum.

In its tumultuous history, India has had to contend with bitter rivalries, lack of trust, violence, and division that has ensued in the South Asian region since independence from the British in 1947. Pakistan rose as a sovereign nation from the ashes of India's independence, but it is now a diminished country led by power mongering elites and the army who consistently put their own interests first. A very populous country, Pakistan struggles to find its way as it navigates poor economic policies, lack of infrastructure, ideological fragmentation, lack of modern education, a drift towards radicalism, a goal to establish a friendly government in Afghanistan, and an intractable conflict with India.

What are the possibilities that one day India and Pakistan, both nuclear powers, will reconcile and cooperate with each other? How will this intractable conflict between India and Pakistan be resolved? Will India and Pakistan begin to treat Kashmir as an area of friendship instead of a zone of conflict? How does India manage an inimical and self-serving China? These are complex but important questions with no easy answers. Today, there is a lack of trust between India and China, and between India and Pakistan. However, if there is a political will, it is possible to defuse tensions by adopting a change of attitude followed by meaningful dialogue. Resolving this conflict is possible only through dialogue and a mutual spirit of reconciliation.

There are parochial attitudes, behaviours, and complexities in India-Pakistan relations and in the role played by China. As I attempt to capture these nuances in this book, to substantiate my point of view and to provide a wider perspective on the subject, I cite works of scholars and authors, more literate and erudite than me. I gratefully acknowledge their contribution to the depth of knowledge and information in this book.

What motivated me to write this book was an impression that not many within India and the developed world are aware of the complex, intertwined realities that exist in the South Asian region. Friends and colleagues in the Indian Army and associates across the world have encouraged me to write this narrative to spread such awareness. Their enthusiasm to support this project has been highly motivating. Post retirement from the Indian Army, while working in the corporate sector, I continued to study this topic and deliver lectures on Indo-Pakistan relations at various forums. These included the threats from China, and other related subjects. Having gleaned much material on the situation in South Asia and by experiencing it first-hand, I find that the existing literature-books, magazines, newspaper articles, published works, and present-day visual and social media have addressed the subject piecemeal and not entirely adequately. In some cases, there is an information void, at times there is a blatant bias. Hence, an all-encompassing account was felt necessary.

I most thankfully acknowledge the support of my family, especially my wife Indubala, for encouraging my efforts and giving me wise counsel as I undertook this project. My daughter Amrita helped edit the script and my grandchildren always kept me motivated to complete this task. I am grateful for the understanding and patience shown by scholars and colleagues who answered my questions and for those who have inspired me to make this book a reality.

Virender Budhwar

Introduction

Pakistan was created by the British, when they divided India into two with a separate homeland for the Muslims. This division of the country was not a simple journey. Prior to Independence from the British, Mohammad Ali Jinnah and his party, the Muslim League, had initially wanted an equal representation of Muslims and Hindus in the Parliament of India. This was despite the fact that the Muslim population was only a fraction of the overall population of undivided India.[1, 2] While asking for this disproportionate representation, Jinnah did not take into consideration the wishes of other religious denominations in the country, such as Buddhists, Christians, Jains, Jews, Persians, Sikhs, Sindhis, Zoroastrians, miscellaneous sects, and scheduled castes and tribes. Jinnah's only concern was that Muslims would be dominated politically by Hindus in undivided India. However, any concession or preferential allocation of seats in the Constituent Assembly to the Muslims alone would have set a negative precedent.

Jinnah's demand was considered unreasonable and unacceptable to the other mainstream political party, the Indian National Congress, which was a party with secular credentials. The Congress, in its ideology, believed that all Indian citizens were equal, with equal rights, irrespective of caste, creed, or faith.

Jinnah had developed an uncompromising and intransigent attitude supported by some members of the British establishment who wanted to break up India into several sovereign states. The British felt that these principalities, would remain tied to Britain as independent dominions. This

1. *The Warrior State* by T. V. Paul, printed pages (pp) 39
2. *The Struggle for Pakistan* by Ayesha Jalal, pp 28

suited the ambitions of the Muslim League, as a fragmented India with independent kingdoms would give Pakistan a preeminent position in the subcontinent. The British schemed to get opinions of representatives of each province to confirm their wish to remain in the central Constituent Assembly or as independent states. As per this plan, in Bengal, the legislative assembly was required to have two parts, one representing Muslim majority districts and the other representing the rest of the religious communities. A similar arrangement was envisaged in Punjab. Meanwhile, in the North-west Frontier Province (NWFP), a referendum was to be conducted to ascertain whether the resident population there favoured the partition of India. In the case of Baluchistan, the members of the assembly would exercise their option under the aegis of the rulers. With regard to the numerous princely states, the proposal was that when the paramountcy of the British ended and India was granted independence, all rights surrendered by them to the British would be restored to these states. They would then be free to join either of the two parts of divided India based on whatever they considered best in the interest of their people.

This plan, if it has been enacted, would have divided India into 500 or more sovereign units. When Lord Mountbatten, the last Governor General of India, shared this plan with Jawaharlal Nehru, the leader of the Congress, Nehru rejected it totally and vehemently. A revised plan was then prepared, and the Chief of Staff to Lord Mountbatten, Baron Hastings Ismay, who had arrived in India with the original plan, was sent back to the United Kingdom (UK) on 2 May 1947 to present the revised plan to the British Parliament. Hastings returned to India after nearly a month with an amended partition plan for India that was subsequently accepted on 3 June 1947 with some reluctance by the Congress and the Sikhs. Jinnah and his Muslim League also accepted the partition plan with some misgivings because they desired a larger area for their new country. The plan envisaged the division of India into two dominions, but it still retained the provisions that the princely states had the choice to accede to either India or Pakistan or to remain sovereign. With this proviso and in pursuance of his desire to gain more territory out of India, Jinnah tried to lure away the Maharajas of Jodhpur and Jaisalmer, which were Hindu majority states ruled by Hindu Princes, to join Pakistan. This was contrary to Jinnah's initial premise of obtaining a separate homeland for Muslims. The two Hindu states did not accept his proposal and chose to remain in India.

The partition of India was poorly supervised by the British. It brought upheaval and mayhem and resulted in the largest migration of the Hindus,

Sikhs, and other minorities from Pakistan to India and a reverse migration from India to Pakistan. The unplanned and unsupervised movement of the population, an estimated 15 million on both sides, led to violence, animosity and extreme brutalities. Mob attacks, mass murders, hangings, burning, looting, kidnapping, and rapes occurred. With no law and order, every kind of heinous crime was perpetrated in a frenzy of violence by both sides. Hatred and revenge took over all human sensibilities and in Pakistan, no actions were taken to deal with the carnage, as a post-imperial vacuum existed. An estimated one million people perished in the carnage and after such a brutal origin, the deep divide between the people of the two countries was created.

The India Independence Act was passed by the British Parliament only on 4 July 1947. This late decision created problems, which were exacerbated by the decision of the British to prepone their departure from India from June 1948 to 15 August 1947. The decision to leave India early was, to an extent, influenced by large-scale communal rioting, which had already started taking a toll on human lives. There was also a mutiny in the Royal Indian Navy, in February 1946 which added to the unease in the minds of the British that India was becoming ungovernable. Besides this, after the Second World War, the British economy was in a failing state and could not financially sustain holding on to their various colonies and dominions.

The Indian National Congress and Mahatma Gandhi were not in agreement with the plan for partitioning India. However, when the situation in the country began to deteriorate, when Indians were turning against their own countrymen, they relented in an attempt to stop the bloodshed. India was partitioned. Most of the princely states joined either of the two countries except for J&K, Hyderabad, and Junagarh. Jinnah had written to the Maharaja of J&K, asking him to cede to Pakistan, but the ruler of this state remained undecided. The Maharaja was Hindu, though the population in the state had an overall majority of Muslims. The Kashmir Valley had a Muslim majority, the Jammu Division had a Hindu majority, and Ladakh was predominantly Buddhist. The Maharaja wanted time to consider the proposal by Jinnah and entered into a standstill agreement with Pakistan. Showing no patience for the Maharaja's will, Pakistan violated the standstill agreement and launched operations in October 1947 to annex the state forcibly. Hordes of tribals and demobilized Army soldiers with support from the Pakistan Army reached the outskirts of Srinagar, the capital city of J&K. Resorting to looting, murder, and rape enroute, these forces made slow progress in reaching Srinagar. This gave the Maharaja some time to assess the imminent threat to his honour and to his people. Given the abrogation of the standstill agreement by Pakistan, the Maharaja of J&K ceded the state to India on 27 October 1947.

Pakistan also laid claim to Hyderabad on the basis that it was the home to the oldest Muslim dynasty. This state was larger in area than Punjab, and at that time, Jinnah and his colleagues considered it more important than Kashmir. Located in India's fertile Deccan Plateau, this princely state had a Hindu majority population. In September 1948, the state was merged into India thereby causing another blow to Pakistan's expansionist aims. The Nawab (ruler) of Junagarh, a Muslim, had decided to cede to Pakistan. This was opposed by the Hindu majority population in the state. Facing the vehement opposition from his subjects, the Nawab decided to abdicate and migrate to Pakistan. This state thereafter voluntarily joined India. The Indian Union was thus, consolidated. On 26 January 1950, the Constitution of India was promulgated, and India became a democratic republic.

Pakistan was created based on the Two Nation Theory, which advocated a separate homeland for Muslims of undivided India.[3] It is to be noted that not a single member of the Muslim League was ever jailed by the British even as Nehru and Gandhi were imprisoned repeatedly. Without much resistance, the British awarded a separate country to Jinnah and the Muslim League and divided India, forever. It is to be noted that even after the migration of people, at the formal independence of Pakistan, on 14 August 1947, India continued to retain more Muslims than the entire country of East and West Pakistan put together. The fact that so many Muslims chose to stay in India is a tragic and ironic reminder that the bloody partition of India did not achieve a complete separation of the Muslim population into one state, as was envisioned by Jinnah. Pakistan received 23 per cent of the area, and 18 per cent of India's population, which included a smaller Muslim population than India. Jinnah in his myopic view assumed that Hindus and the rest of the minorities would live in one country and all Indian Muslims would choose to live in their own separate nation. Jinnah's Two Nation Theory was a failure from the start.

Since partition, Pakistan has insecurities which likely manifest for two reasons. First, their ideology of the Two Nation Theory that must be

3. *The Story of the Integration of the Indian States* by V. P. Menon, pp 116–118

defended at any cost against the purported designs of India to dominate the region. Pakistan continues to propound the theory that India has not come to terms with its separate existence and is therefore a constant threat. This theory has not been substantiated with any evidence and India has shown no designs to annex any Pakistani territory. But clearly, the view is different on the Pakistani side of the border. The second reason for Pakistan's insecurity is related to its western border with Afghanistan, where demands for a separate state of Pashtunistan have risen from time to time. In Pakistan's strategic assessment, if Afghanistan is inimical to their interests, it would pose another existential threat to the country, from Northwest (NW).

The International Border (IB) between Afghanistan and Pakistan is the Durand Line, it is 2430 kilometers (kms) long and is largely inhabited by Pashtuns on either side. The boundary between India and Pakistan is the Radcliffe Line. These active borders are porous and prone to infiltration, smuggling, and present-day terrorist ops. Easy movements across the border facilitate espionage, subversion, smuggling, sabotage, and a sub-conventional war. Infiltration and exfiltration of intelligence and military personnel, terrorists, mercenaries, smugglers, and refugees across the border continue to occur. In Afghanistan, Pakistan has been an active participant in the jihad against the Soviet forces in the eighties and in recent times, it provided support to US and allied forces in Afghanistan while continuing to re-organise the jihadists.

On the front with India, Pakistan has always sought opportunities for upping the ante, ensuring a continuous belligerence. The India-Pakistan warlike status quo has become even more precarious, as both countries are now overt nuclear powers. The nuclear dimension is discussed in Chapter 1.

To pose an impediment to illegal access from Pakistan across the border, India has fenced and electrified the entire IB on its side, from the state of Gujrat to the state of J&K. This border fencing is illuminated at night to maintain surveillance and manned by pickets and patrols of the Border Security Force (BSF). These measures have proven some-what inadequate as terrorists from Pakistan manage to cross over into India using the rugged terrain, under the cover of darkness, or when visibility is impaired. In J&K, Pakistan resorts to firing artillery, mortars, and small arms to suppress physical observation and intervention by Indian troops to support infiltration by their proxies. The Director General of Military Operations (DGMO) of both armies, however, jointly announced a cease-fire along the IB and LOC, to be effective from midnight 24 February 2021. Terrorists from Pakistan circumvent this ceasefire by managing to sneak through the restive border and even by flying to Nepal and entering India across the open India-Nepal IB. This ceasefire between the countries is no longer holding after the terrorist action in Pahalgam in April 2025. A temporary stopping of fire has been agreed upon once again by the DGMOs of India and Pakistan.

The ongoing pattern of hostilities perpetrated by Pakistan continues despite the many agreements to de-escalate the situation, which have been signed by both India and Pakistan. Agreements include the Karachi Agreement of 27 July 1949, signed under the auspices of the United Nations (UN) in which the Cease-fire Line (CFL) between Indian and Pakistani troops was defined, delineated, and signed by both countries. The Shimla Agreement of 2 July 1972, due to which the LOC between India and Pakistan came into being. The LOC is mutually delineated on maps, agreed upon on the ground, and both countries are signatories to the agreement. The Lahore Declaration of 21 February 1999 and the ceasefire agreement on the LOC of 23 November 2003 are also other globally recognized agreements between India and Pakistan. With all these agreements in place, even with international denouncements of Pakistan's subversive actions, there has been no letup in the cross-border violence by Pakistan. In addition to this omnipresent threat, India faces the challenge posed by China to its territorial integrity and sovereignty, because of an undefined IB. China is also known to actively support insurgencies in NE India.

In the West and the world at large, perhaps shortsightedly, there was a lack of awareness of the strife because of terrorism in the India-Pakistan dynamic. In May 1998, India and Pakistan, demonstrated their nuclear capabilities overtly. Once they became nuclear-armed states, the world had to take notice. However, since then, the two nations have been on a different trajectory. India's economy is on an upward trend, and it is flexing its power across the world with a vision that includes rapid infrastructure development, modernization, self-reliance, poverty alleviation, education, manufacturing and economic growth. While India is a nation to be reckoned with as its immense economic power grows, Pakistan has fallen into instability and decline. This marked difference no doubt rankles on the sentiments of the Pakistani establishment.

It is among the many reasons that Pakistan continues to have animosity towards India. Pakistan has not overcome the hatred of India that was sparked at the time of independence and has passed this hatred on to successive generations even through the school curriculum. This extreme vitriol is exacerbated by their politicians who garner supporters by showcasing their animosity and inimical behaviour towards India. This political posturing has provided Pakistan's Army opportunities to manipulate policy and governance, become all powerful and an inextricable part of politics. For many leaders in Pakistan, 'to bleed India through a thousand cuts' is an existential reality. They seek revenge for India's help in forming the country of Bangladesh. They still despise India for including Kashmir, and other Muslim princely states in its territory. They have not reconciled to the fact that a very large number of Muslims chose India as their homeland and not Pakistan. The animosity and need for retribution in Pakistan is deep rooted and visceral.

It is well known that the Pakistan Army has played a dominant role in the governance of their country. It began usurping power from political leaders and the bureaucracy after the assassination of Prime Minister, Liaquat Ali Khan in October 1951. The Army has been in power and governed Pakistan for 33 years since Independence. In the remainder of the years since independence, the Army has continued to dominate and dictate terms to the elected government. It has also imbued a sense of insecurity in the minds of their population to justify disproportionate allocation of funds for itself from the country's Gross Domestic Product (GDP).

Since independence, Pakistan has raised, trained, and employed proxies and terrorists to wage war both in Afghanistan and India. As part of its Afghanistan policy, Pakistan has attempted to have a friendly government installed there with hopes to defuse tension on its borders to the NW. The desire to have an amicable government in Afghanistan began in late fifties, when Zulfikar Ali Bhutto, Foreign Minister of Pakistan, initiated training of irregulars from Afghanistan to fight against the Afghan government, which was aligning with the Soviet Union. The Afghans were seeking a greater Pashtunistan, which would include areas of Pakistan inhabited by Pashtuns and Baluchis. Bhutto feared that if the Pashtuns were allowed to come together with their tribes in Afghanistan, then Pakistan may, one day, lose control of this area and become truncated. With a peaceful Durand Line, Pakistan had possibly planned to relocate parts of its XI and XII Army Corps deployed there, to augment its strength against India. This transition is unlikely under the existing circumstances, as tensions exist on its borders with Afghanistan and Iran and the present Taliban government in Afghanistan has not been entirely beneficial to Pakistan.

During British rule, Russia had expanded its domain up to the northern Afghan border. Given the implications of this, the British had also assessed that having a friendly government in Afghanistan was necessary to prevent further expansion of the Russian Empire. The British were apprehensive of the possible threat and wanted a protective buffer between British India and Imperial Russia. This buffer was created by demarcating the Durand Line between Afghanistan and their realm in India. In this process, they divided the Pashtun-inhabited areas between Afghanistan and India. The British also appreciated that the area of Gilgit-Baltistan in the princely state of J&K could also be utilised as an avenue of ingress to extend the Russian Empire towards India. A map of the princely state of J&K is in Annexure 1.

Annexure 1

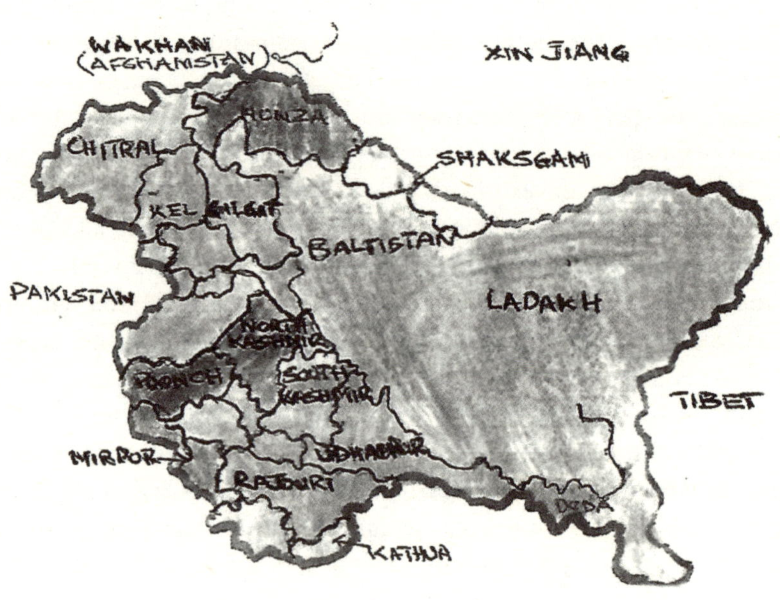

Map of Jammu and Kashmir – 1947

Notes

1. The map is a rough impression of the princely State of J&K prior to India's independence.
2. The location of Shaksgam is to be noted as it was ceded by Pakistan to China in 1963.

3. J&K borders Xin Jiang and Tibet in China to the east, Afghanistan (Wakhan Corridor) to the north and Pakistan to the west. It provides access to the Central Asian Republics (CARs) across the Wakhan Corridor from south.
4. During the period of the cold war, the communist threat from Soviet Russia had morphed into a larger threat augmented by the communist takeover in China. Gilgit-Baltistan was a buffer between these expansionist Communist countries and India.
5. J&K and Pakistan derive their strategic importance from their location.

The British had posted an officer in Gilgit in J&K and established an intelligence outpost there in 1868 to surveil the Russian Empire's advance. They established a political agency there in 1877. In 1913, the British raised the Gilgit Scouts. Colonel Calvin, who was the British advisor to the state, was able to lease the Gilgit Agency from the ruler of J&K for the British in 1935 for 60 years. This was done with the provision that the ownership of the area remained with the Maharaja, and it would revert when the lease was terminated or ended. The British continued to play their geo-politics, even after the partition of India, by favouring Pakistan in the context of the erstwhile princely state of J&K. They terminated the lease and reverted Gilgit-Baltistan to the Maharaja of J&K when Pakistan gained independence on 14 August 1947. The British officer in Gilgit, Major William Brown, enabled the Gilgit-Baltistan Agency to declare independence and, after another fourteen days, influenced the Agency to self-cede to Pakistan in complete violation of the lease agreement with the Maharaja of J&K.

All these actions were taken when Lord Mountbatten was the Governor General of India, under the directions of General Frank Messervy, the Commander-in-Chief (C-in-C) of the Pakistan Army. It is noteworthy that in his reply to Maharaja Hari Singh's letter of accession of J&K to India, Lord Mountbatten, accepted the accession, but made a mention of ascertaining the will of the people to join India or Pakistan. Mountbatten reiterated this during his visit to Pakistan at Lahore on 2 November 1947, stating that a plebiscite should be conducted in Kashmir. This assertion was made without consulting the Indian Prime Minister, Jawaharlal Nehru, and the Home Minister, Sardar Vallabh Bhai Patel. These Indian leaders were informed of his unilateral offer for a plebiscite on 2 November 1947, only on Mountbatten's return to Delhi. This shows that the British did not stop meddling with the affairs of India even after Independence and only accentuated the already tenuous situation.

There is further evidence of the British maleficence even after the partition of India. The United Nations (UN) was founded in 1945 by 51 countries committed to maintaining international peace and security. The allied powers, victorious after the Second World War, ensured that they acquired a major influence in the functioning of the United Nations Security Council (UNSC). These selected countries had arrogated to themselves the veto powers in the UN charter. Pakistan, as mentioned earlier, had launched operations to annex J&K by force in October 1947. This aggression by Pakistan was referred to the UN on the advice of Lord Mountbatten. As the UNSC failed to declare Pakistan as the aggressor in J&K, Nehru and the Indian government discerned a decisive bias from the UNSC and the Western powers. With his British education and manipulative ways, Jinnah had always endeared himself to the colonial masters. Hence, it is likely that the British continued to influence matters in Pakistan's favour in the UN and influenced the United States to do the same. This support for Pakistan became even more apparent after the Western democracies started opposing the expansionist Communist powers, while India chose a path of neutrality.

These developments had a bearing on Afghanistan's strategic importance. As mentioned earlier, Afghanistan together with Gilgit-Baltistan, was a buffer from the expansionist Soviet Union towards India and the Arabian Sea. The Pakistani leadership and their Army also desired Afghanistan to be a fallback area for their country if ever their country was overwhelmed from the east by India. The threat from the north did materialize when Soviet Russia invaded and occupied Afghanistan in the late seventies. The threat from India has never manifested after the CFL came into being in July 1949. Another major reason for Pakistan to have a favourable government in Afghanistan was to ensure that India does not have undue influence in that country. This view persists in the Pakistan Army's threat perception even today. With this imagined threat perception, Pakistan justifies maintaining an Army of half a million regular troops supported by paramilitary forces, reservists, and numerous militant groups.

It is well known that Pakistan had played a duplicitous role during Operation Enduring Freedom when it was launched in Afghanistan by the US and allies on 7 October 2001. General Pervez Musharraf, who was in power at that time, also held the position of COAS of the Pakistan Army. Publicly, he indicated Pakistan's support for the US and its allies while in fact his regime continued to revive and unleash the Taliban and Haqqani militants to fight the allied forces and weaken the elected government in Kabul. In this conflict, Pakistan provided the US and its allies a Ground Line of Communication (GLOC) for the movement of troops, goods and services, and logistics for the maintenance of troops in Afghanistan. The US had assessed that under the prevailing circumstances, this was the best and most cost-effective method to support their forces in Afghanistan. An alternative for logistic support from the North had been tested and could be organized through Central Asian Republics (CARs), but this proved to be far more expensive. Under the guise of a US ally, Pakistan's covert support to the Taliban and Al Qaeda did not allow Afghanistan to stabilize as a democracy. In good faith, the US continued to provide financial support to Pakistan despite its subversive plot to destabilize the region. In May 2018, President Donald Trump highlighted the duplicity of Pakistan and withdrew any US financial grants.

Other self-serving and duplicitous actions by Pakistan are commonly known. The most prominent one is the provision of a safe haven to Al Qaeda's most-wanted leader Osama bin Laden. The elimination of Osama bin Laden, on 2 May 2011, by US special forces caused great embarrassment to Pakistan and its Army. However, to avoid admitting to the safe sanctuary provided to Osama bin Laden, in close proximity to their Military Academy in Abbottabad, the Pakistan Army went into a denial mode. They professed a complete lack of awareness of his location in the prominent compound where he was found. This lack of accountability and subterfuge is a regular feature of the Pakistan Army's modus operandi. Ralph Peters, a retired Lieutenant Colonel of the US army, had served in the US embassy in Islamabad and later was a Fox News analyst till 2018. He wrote in his article 'Spies, Lies and Terrorists, in (not much) Disguises', about Bin Laden being provided sanctuary by Pakistan. He opined that Bin Laden was hidden purposefully by Pakistan and would have been unleashed to their advantage when required. An undetected Bin Laden guaranteed continuing billions of dollars in aid while the world searched for him. Peters asks the question, 'What do you do with an ally that hides your most wanted enemy from you, actually helps to kill your soldiers, uses terrorist attacks on the world's largest democracy, India, tries to destabilize the Afghan government, aligns with China, and employs terrorism as an essential tool of strategy for war?' The Pakistan Army may have planned to trade Osama bin Laden to seek further largesse and weaponry from the US. Pakistan's actions have showed that it would seek money and compensation from wherever and by any means, like a mercenary. Al Qaeda, perhaps, became aware of the possibility that Pakistan may sacrifice Osama bin Laden and tried to assassinate General Musharraf for this reason. He survived two assassination attempts. Musharraf has written in his book, *In the Line of Fire,* that the plotters of the assassination attempts were Al Qaeda, and the supporters of the terrorists were from their Special Service Group (SSG). In stark contrast to this, in a statement in Pakistan's Parliament in June 2020, Imran Khan, then Prime Minister, had called Osama bin Laden a martyr.

Besides the sub-conventional war with India, Pakistan perpetrates terror elsewhere as well. It has been proven time and again that people of Pakistani origin or foreigners, trained in Pakistan have supported, may resort to and been responsible for terrorist acts in Europe and the US. It is necessary to understand the reason why Pakistan pursues this dangerous path. Javed Ahmed Ghamidi, a moderate cleric and philosopher from Pakistan who lives in Dubai, ascribes this behaviour to the religious teachings in seminaries and religious institutions. The main tenets of these teachings are: apostasy in Islam, or for anyone renouncing the religion, the punishment is death. The seminaries also propound the theory that all non-Muslims are subordinate to Muslims, no non-Muslim can rule, and Muslims will forcibly subjugate other religious denominations if and when they have the power. They also promote the ideology that there should be one government of Muslims or the Caliphate. Lastly, they promote the belief that all nation states are an aberration and anti-Islam.

On September 11, 2018, Mubarak Haider, a journalist on an independent Pakistani TV channel, delved into some thought-provoking aspects of the Pakistani psyche. In his report, he was covering Pakistan's Defence Day 2018. There was gratitude expressed by well-rehearsed voices in Pakistan's media on how their Army had defended the people against India, the eternal enemy. Haider questioned whether India was in fact the eternal enemy of Pakistan and asked if there was any evidence that India was trying to overrun Pakistan. He further stated that some 50,000 Army personnel, civilians, and militants had been killed in the fighting between their Army and the terrorist organization Tehreek-e-Taliban Pakistan (TTP). This is more than the number killed in the four wars with India. In 2009, General David Petraeus, C-in-C of US Central Command (CENTCOM) had made a similar assessment at a Senate hearing. He stated that 'Pakistan needs to change its threat perception, which is focused on India, and instead needs to be refocused on the western borders where Taliban and Al Qaeda activists operate. Frankly, in Pakistan the biggest threat to their country's existence is the internal threat rather than the threat from the east'.[4]

After the 1965 Indo-Pakistan war, Air Marshal Asghar Khan, the Pakistani Chief of Air Staff, had gone on record in a post-retirement interview on a Pakistani news channel. This interview is available on YouTube and Khan states that his country had started all four wars between India and Pakistan, and in each of them, Pakistan had been defeated. Despite these four wars and numerous attacks by terrorists on India, the gains made by Pakistan are, at best, negligible.

Mubarak Haider further states that Pakistan has never called any militant group, including Al Qaeda, Taliban, and others, as their enemy. Even though the Taliban and Al Qaeda have been hosted, revived, supported, and protected by them, these groups have never been condemned by Pakistan. The emergence of the anti-state Punjabi Taliban has created an unstable internal situation for the country. Attacks by this militant organization on the Pakistan Army HQ and the Marriot Hotel in Islamabad are examples of this defiance. Militant attacks continue unabated in Pakistan, and Haider indicates that the paranoia vis-à-vis India and the infatuation with medieval order has given Pakistan no glory. His opinion is that affairs in this regard have not gone well for Pakistan, and his advice is that the process of religious radicalization has to end.

Even though the Shimla Agreement of July 1972 outlines that all pending issues between India and Pakistan be resolved peacefully and through dialogue, Pakistan has never reconciled to encouraging peace with India. If peace is manifested, the terrorist groups cultivated specifically for attacking and carrying out subversion in India would have no reason to exist. The troubling fact is that the days may come when the Pakistani establishment is no longer able to rein in these organizations as they become too unhinged and are hard to control even for the Pakistan Army.

As indicated previously, the Pakistan Army has played the role of a spoiler when the elected governments in their country have shown an inclination to work towards reconciliation with India. The Indian government has tried many times, in various ways, to resolve disputes with Pakistan. Dialogue has been offered and started formally, and also through what is referred to

4. *The Most Dangerous Place: Pakistan's Lawless Frontier* by Imtiaz Gul, pp xii-xiv

as track two diplomacy. Representatives of both countries have met and shared their viewpoint and concerns. However, every time this diplomacy began or was proposed, the Pakistan Army, through the covert actions of the ISI, have launched terrorist attacks on India. The result is that the negotiating process is called off and tensions are exacerbated.

When Imran Khan took over as Prime Minister of Pakistan in September 2018, he proposed talks with India to resolve disputes. In an inexplicable concurrence, at the same time, Pakistan launched a postage stamp with the face of a known terrorist, who had been killed by Indian Security Forces in J&K. Pakistan also glorified this individual in other ways. The excuse offered for this contradiction was that the stamp was published and printed two months prior to the election in August 2018. After taking office, Imran Khan reiterated that he could work with Narendra Modi, the Indian Prime Minister to resolve bilateral matters. However, in January 2019, soon after Khan's comments, Pakistan's terrorist group JeM attacked an Indian Police convoy in J&K, killing 40. Once again, the sincerity of holding peace talks with India seemed like mere rhetoric.

Terrorism and the militancy that Pakistan inspires, is a malaise that is proliferating. Terrorist attacks in various part of the world are indicative of an increasing cult of violence. This is now a major global concern and countering terrorism is a key responsibility for leaders across the world. The 7 October 2023 attack by Hamas on Israel is a stark reminder of an intractable conflict in the Middle East and how deadly terrorism has far-reaching and devastating consequences. Similarly, for India, the continuous acts of terrorism generated by Pakistan maintain the intractable conflict in that region. In Mumbai, the financial hub of India, two major terrorist attacks have occurred over recent years. Both were carried out by Pakistani terror groups, and many innocent civilians and foreign visitors were killed and injured. On 26 November 2008, an attack was carried out by a terrorist squad that traveled to India by sea from Karachi to Mumbai. Understandably, the Indian government will not proceed with negotiating peace when their country is being bled by Pakistan's retrograde actions and Pakistan is constantly devising new plots to cause harm to India. The long history of devious and dishonest interactions by Pakistan, accompanied by violent attacks on the Indian public, does not augur well for peace in the future between the India and Pakistan.

The nexus of power is a complex situation in Pakistan, which impacts everything including the country's messaging. The military's hold on the tightly controlled media adds fire to the strained situation. Media helps Pakistan's Army to shroud facts and encourages bombastic political rhetoric. With clever manipulation and false information, Pakistan's media provides limited meaningful and constructive analysis of India-Pakistan relations. In fact, media establishments out do themselves in their anti-India rhetoric. By manipulating the messaging and disseminating propaganda, Pakistani media ensures that public opinion is influenced, and sympathy is garnered in other Muslim countries. This is a concerted effort at spreading animosity and negativity towards India. On rare occasions, some media coverage, if not censored, has highlighted India's growth and democratic governance in contrast to their own country's plight and poverty. But this is a rare occurrence.

The Inter-Services Intelligence (ISI) in Pakistan is the agency that controls and directs the actions of terrorist groups against India. The Hurriyat Conference in J&K State, the World Sikh Youth Forum, Babbar Khalsa in the UK, Sikhs for Justice in the US, and Canada, and other fringe groups of Sikh and Kashmiri separatists in these countries, are supported by Pakistan. They are a very negligible vote bank in their respective adopted countries and since they are no longer Indian citizens, there is no logical reason for these groups to pursue an anti-India agenda, unless they are being coerced by an outside source. The ISI continues to collaborate with such easy targets to carry out its anti-India agenda by proxy. The Pakistan Army and ISI will not encourage peace with India as this would diminish their all-powerful role in Pakistan. They are the Deep State in their country. They know that by repeatedly articulating that India poses a threat, Pakistan obtains financial and other aid to fund their vast defence and nuclear assets from friendly countries. With their single-minded focus to retain power and be a thorn in India's side, the corrupt Army and ISI in Pakistan have neglected the development of their country and its public infrastructure, especially in impoverished regions such as the NWFP. This province includes the Federally Administered Tribal Areas (FATA), and Waziristan and renamed Khyber Pakhtunkhwa. Psychological factors, Deep State, and terrorism are discussed in Chapter 2.

In the early eighties, Sikh separatists, some of whom were trained in Pakistan, created an insurgency in Punjab, one of the most progressive states in India. The separatist militants, supported by the ISI, spread terror in this prosperous Indian state. Under the guise of religion, the militants also built up an arsenal and fortified themselves inside the holiest of Sikh shrines, the Golden Temple in Amritsar city. The assessment by

Indian authorities was that the separatists were on the verge of declaring independence from India. Pakistan would have recognized their call for independence and coerced other nations to follow suit. If Pakistan had decided at that juncture to become operationally active across the Punjab border in support of the separatists, the situation could have morphed into a serious cross-border conflict challenging the integrity of India. To quell the militancy and separatist movement, India launched *Operation Blue Star* to rid the Golden Temple of the armed extremists. It is outside the purview of this narrative to go into details of the pre and post of this operation, however it concluded in restoring the sanctity of the shrine and the militancy was upended. Indian authorities have since become extremely cautious about the continuing attempts of the ISI to regenerate a separatist movement in Punjab. The Sikh population of India have not forgotten the terrible carnage at the time of partition of India when thousands of Hindus and Sikhs were uprooted from their homes and subjected to the worst crimes. Today, most of the Sikh community in India is progressive, affluent, and proud citizens of a united country. They want no part of a separatist movement.

Of note is a slow demographic change that has been occurring in India. There has been an influx of Muslims from Bangladesh seeking a better livelihood. Domestic help, and daily wage labour originating from Bangladesh are employed in urban areas all across India. Madrasas and mosques have come up in the Terai region, the foothills of the Himalayas in Nepal, abutting the Indian border. In 2018, a large number of Rohingya from Myanmar took refuge in India. These refugees have merged with the Muslim population of India, and some have managed to move as far north as Samba and Jammu districts in J&K State. Approximately 750,000 people have also migrated from Pakistan, POK, and Gilgit-Baltistan into India during and after various wars. Ethnic cleansing of 600,000 Kashmiri Pandits (Hindus) from the Kashmir Valley was also enacted by radical terrorists in the 1980s. Pakistan, although not entirely responsible for all the above, may choose to exploit these changes in demographics. Confirmation of this intent is apparent in the posturing of Pakistan's political leaders, its media, and pronouncements by its foreign office.

No analysis on this topic is complete without discussing the importance of Kashmir in Indo-Pakistan relations. Indian and foreign scholars have recounted detailed versions of the history of Kashmir, from ancient times. It is suggested that as per Hindu mythology, Kashmir was the abode of Saraswati, the Goddess of knowledge, music, art, wisdom and nature.

This land was, perhaps, the keystone of Indian heritage. Emperor Ashoka ruled the Indian sub-continent for 40 years till 232 BCE. He established the city of Srinagar, the capital city of Kashmir. Historically, Islam, Hinduism, Buddhism, Christianity, and Sikhism have coexisted peacefully in the state of J&K. It was known to be a secular and peaceful region, where many diverse people have thrived. The present reality is very different. Today, the erstwhile princely State of J&K stands divided between China, India, and Pakistan, even though its ruler ceded the entire area of the State to India. This was done formally as per provisions of the India Independence Act in 1947. The map of the divided J&K region is in Annexure 2.

Annexure 2

Map of Jammu and Kashmir Showing Areas Occupied by China and Pakistan

Notes

1. The area under Indian control is the state of J&K. This state has been divided into two union territories, namely J&K and Ladakh by Government of India.
2. India has published revised maps showing areas occupied by China and Pakistan as part of these union territories based on the accession of the state to India by its ruler.
3. The China-Pakistan Economic Corridor is being developed through the Pakistan-occupied part of the state of J&K.

4. The map is not to scale, and the boundaries marked are approximate.

The recent history of the region is also well documented and not disputed. After the British established their rule over most of India, they sold J&K to Gulab Singh, who became its ruler, under provisions of the Treaty of Amritsar in 1846. It was the attempt to forcefully annex the State by Pakistan in October1947, that caused the Maharaja of J&K to cede to India. The events that followed, including the ceasefire under the aegis of the UN and subsequent resolutions on Kashmir, are also well documented. To consolidate its territories after partition, India dispatched its forces to assimilate the princely state of Hyderabad, in the heart of the Deccan Plateau, to make sure that an independent state did not exist in the middle of the country. Further consolidation occurred when the Portuguese were evicted from their Indian colonies of Goa, Daman, and Diu. These colonies were ruled by Portugal since the eighteenth century.

After J&K was ceded to India, Pakistan has continued to launch operations and wars to acquire more area in J&K by use of force. Their most recent, major attempt at this was what led to the Kargil war of 1999. In violation of the Lahore Declaration of 21 February 1999, this audacious offensive operation across the LOC caused Pakistan to suffer another defeat at the hands of the Indian Armed Forces. Details on the J&K situation, new realities, and the Kargil War are discussed in Chapter 3.

Afghanistan is also an area of concern, especially since it figures prominently in Pakistan's regional strategy. In retaliation to 9/11 attacks by Al Qaeda, the US launched Op Enduring Freedom in 2001 to defeat the militant groups in Afghanistan and bring about a change in the governance in this country. After nearly 20 years of combating insurgency the US realized that the Afghan war had become an open-ended conflict and the Trump administration made the decision to extricate US troops. The US signed an agreement with the Afghan Taliban on 29 February 2020 to withdraw from Afghanistan in the next 18 months. The Afghan government was excluded from these negotiations and this withdrawal was completed in August 2021. Over the years, the ongoing support provided by Pakistan to anti-government mujahids, and the failure of Afghanistan's elected governments to effectively administer the country have led to the Taliban establishing their stronghold on the country once again. The instability in Afghanistan has an impact on the strategies that India and Pakistan adopt. China is a new entrant in the affairs of Afghanistan as it has established diplomatic relations with the Taliban government. The Afghan conundrum is discussed in Chapter 4.

Pakistan's prominence as a strategic partner to the West came about when the US had accorded Pakistan the status of a frontline State against an expansionist USSR. The US and UK, being allies pursued similar strategies, and acted in tandem in most cases brought to the UN. Pakistan, an ally of the West, joined the South-East Treaty Organization (SEATO) in 1954 and the Central Asian Treaty Organization in 1955 (CENTO). It also established friendly relations with communist China. The above treaties were created by Western powers to prevent forcible expansion by the Soviet Union and China. Pakistan also played a role in facilitating a dialogue between US and China that enabled the visit of President, Richard Nixon, to China on 21 February 1972. India, meanwhile, had become a founding member of the Non-Aligned Movement and was pursuing a non-aligned stance, which was unacceptable to the West in the Cold War era. Pakistan played the part of an amicable partner and frontline state to contend with the expansionist USSR and became a willing ally of the US. Pakistan's leadership further cemented this relationship by stating that communism was not acceptable to an Islamic nation.

The establishment of friendly relations with China was a matter of strategic convenience for Pakistan. China had fought a war with India in 1962, and ever since, it has remained inimical to India. Pakistan saw the opportunity to cultivate a relationship and to establish a strategic partnership with China. In Pakistan's assessment, China's rising power could in the long-term help to build Pakistan's Armed Forces and assist in acquiring nuclear capability. After signing a border agreement on 2 March 1963, this liaison developed further. In this agreement, Pakistan ceded the Shaksgam Valley, abutting the Siachen glacier area, to China in exchange for retaining the area of Hunza that China claimed. Both these areas were part of the princely state of J&K and these agreements were in violation of Indian sovereignty.

Then began the construction of the Karakoram Highway through the Northern Areas of J&K, connecting the Chinese province of Xinjiang with Islamabad, Pakistan's capital. On its completion, the highway facilitated trade and the movement of strategic materials. The Belt and Road Initiative (BRI) and the String of Pearls, a brainchild of Xi Jinping, have found a willing partner in Pakistan. China has gained a larger stake in the area by launching its mega project known as the China-Pakistan Economic Corridor (CPEC). An inimical China will continue to use Pakistan as a proxy against India. Some aspects of the challenge that China poses, and its BRI are discussed in Chapter 5 and later in this narrative.

A new dimension that impacts the stability of this region is the use of information technology (IT) and cyber warfare. Any nation with expertise in IT can resort to cyberattacks and spread its influence through the Internet and social media. Server hacks, Artificial Intelligence (AI) generated imagery, and fake news are already being used as tools to sway and influence public opinion. Agitation and unrest are being propagated via social media. In assessing the cyber threat, India must consider China as Pakistan partners closely with China in this regard. Under Xi Jinping's leadership, China considers itself equal to the US economically and even technologically. AI, quantum computing, the Internet of Things (IoT), robotics, drones, autonomous weapons, and related technologies will continue to become pervasive and influence any conflict in this region.

As yet, there is limited control on the growth of AI except in a few countries such as China, Indonesia, and Russia. AI is now entrenched in defence applications such as air defence, ground weapons and drone ops. It is being used in the ongoing conflict between Israel and Hamas/ Hezbollah, in the Ukraine war, and in the stand-off between India and China. Israel has used AI to counter missile and rocket attacks from Hamas and Hezbollah and for precision targeting of purported terrorist hideouts. Similarly, Ukraine has been able to defend its vital assets from the missile and drone attacks launched by Russia with AI-controlled air defence systems received by them from North Atlantic Treaty Organization (NATO) countries. The use of autonomous weapons is reaching a new level of sophistication. The possibilities in this arena are immense and not fully explored.

China maintains its independence with its own Internet, with government controls to safeguard its IT systems and ensure security. China intends to create an impregnable cyber defence system and is vying to lead the world in IT. The People's Liberation Army (PLA) of China has announced plans to develop cyber forces and has developed its own network defence to defeat cyber-attacks. The restrictions that were imposed by the US on the export of advanced technologies like electronic chips, have forced China to conduct research and produce these at home. China is spending large sums on research and development (R&D) and its scientists are finding new breakthroughs in technologies. A sum of US $150 billion is earmarked for use over a decade to design advanced microprocessors. Advances in quantum computing could facilitate Chinese intelligence services to create highly encrypted and secure communication channels and also breach most conventional encryption.

In 2016 Russia's attempts to influence the US presidential elections made the world aware of how the Internet could be used to manipulate the outcome of important elections across the world. The Internet provided Russia's intelligence services the unprecedented ability to reach millions of American voters through Facebook, Twitter and other social media platforms to propagate false information. In Canada, interference by China in the last federal elections has been purported. Cyber-attacks are an addition to the arsenal of a technologically superior military and provide the ability to perpetrate disruptive attacks from afar. Cyberspace and IT systems are becoming a domain of intense competition and information warfare. More on this is discussed in Chapter 6.

With three nuclear-armed nations China, India, and Pakistan, the South Asian region is an area of concern for the world at large. A resurgent China is pursuing the ambition of dominating Asia, Europe, Africa, and Latin America. It is leading the charge by making large investments, by tapping into large mineral deposits of rare earth minerals, funding infrastructure projects, expanding trade and increasing its IT spending. China is shrewdly seeking domination without waging war. In its sights, China has plans of negating the influence of the US by becoming the largest economy in the world and an IT and military superpower. What will China's role be in Pakistan's proxy war against India? Can it encourage Pakistan to commence negotiations to restore peace? Will Pakistan continue its policy of unremitting hostility towards India and up the ante through a sub-conventional war? These topics are discussed in Chapter 7.

With its new status as a union territory, the situation in J&K is slowly undergoing a change for the better. However, terrorist action by Pakistan's proxies can create deadly incidents at any time that would be detrimental to peace. China's continued support to this country and quest for domination poses serious challenges to India's security and territorial integrity. To ensure peace in the region, the government of Pakistan should try and dismantle the terrorist groups it nurtures. After the short war in April-May 2025, India has laid out new red lines that any terrorist attack would be considered an act of war. An analysis of these topics and the external forces that influence matters will indicate how the leaders of India, China and Pakistan will likely steer the conflicts in this region. Is there any reason to be optimistic that trust can be generated between India and Pakistan and with China? Is there a light at the end of the tunnel? This is discussed in Chapter 8.

CHAPTER 1

The Nuclear Dimension

Background

With many nuclear states across the world, in the conflict ridden present, there is legitimate global concern about the proliferation and the possible use of weapons of mass destruction. Nuclear proliferation is the spread of nuclear technology facilitating the construction of nuclear weapons and their means of delivery. It includes the direct or indirect transfer of nuclear technologies from one nation to another. It also implies the vertical increase, advancement, and modernization of holdings and types of nuclear weapons in the inventory of a nuclear-armed country. Proliferation and use of weapons of mass destruction have been a global concern which have risen to the fore once again with the Russia-Ukraine war, the resurgence of North Korea, the Hamas-Israel war and the quest by Iran to be a nuclear power. In an effort to monitor and control the rampant spread of nuclear technology and weapons, nuclear treaties and controls have been established, but some nations have violated these agreements to suit their interests, and this continues to be an ongoing conundrum.

The reasons that led to India and Pakistan's nuclearization begin with China. Since its independence from the British in 1947, India has been a non-aligned and non-violent nation. Matters relating to weapons of mass destruction were considered abhorrent by Indian policymakers. Even the pre-independence freedom movement in India was led by those who were against the use of violence in any form as propounded by Mahatma Gandhi. At the time of independence, India was an impoverished nation. It had neither the technology nor the finances to start investing in nuclear technology, even for peaceful purposes. Hence, Indian leadership paid little attention to acquiring nuclear technology in the initial years after India became a free country. Indian policymakers continued to insist that international problems should be solved peacefully and through dialogue. The non-aligned movement (NAM) was the face of this policy.

Jawaharlal Nehru, the first Prime Minister of independent India, set up the Indian Atomic Energy Commission (IAEC) on 10 August 1948. He was knowledgeable about the positive and negative aspects of nuclear sciences. His vision was to ensure that India acquired knowledge of nuclear sciences and used it only for peaceful purposes. Meanwhile, the nuclear standoff between Western powers and the Soviet Union achieved a strategic balance and prevented a third world war. It was evident to Indian leaders that possession of nuclear weapons provided a physiological advantage against all opposition. It gave power and status to the countries that possessed nuclear weapons. China was a late entrant to the nuclear club and on 16 October 1964 the Chinese conducted their first nuclear test at Lop Nur in South-East (SE) Xinjiang province. The test site was established in October 1959 with Soviet assistance. China's first nuclear weapons test underscored the strategic advantage that it achieved by becoming a nuclear power. The Indian military was not ambivalent about the necessity and advantages of possessing nuclear weapons. But perhaps, their opinion was not strong enough to sway the civilian government at that time about their stance on national nuclear policy. Under Nehru's leadership, India began a modest nuclear program for research into the peaceful uses of nuclear technology, for electricity generation, and for making radioisotopes and medicine with the collaboration of the US. Despite his antipathy towards nuclear weapons and other means of mass destruction, chemical and biological, Nehru knew the discriminatory nature of the International Atomic Energy Agency (IAEA) safeguards that were proposed for India's nuclear reactors. The safeguards, he felt, impinged on India's sovereign rights and, hence, were not acceptable. Even so, the production of nuclear weapons by India was not a priority and not in Nehru's mind.

As mentioned above, it was the Chinese nuclear test in 1964 that brought to the fore the implications of an openly inimical power possessing nuclear weapons. It made the Indian establishment examine the possible courses needed to counter this emerging threat. After Nehru's death on 27 May 1964, his successor, Lal Bahadur Shastri, approved an underground peaceful nuclear explosion (PNE). This was the beginning of the research and development (R&D) in the field of nuclear weapons in India. The proposed experiment was intended to demonstrate India's ability in this scientific field. The PNE was delayed because of the untimely demise of Prime Minister Shastri and Dr Homi J. Bhabha, the architect of India's nuclear program. At one point of time in 1964, India was willing to give up its quest to produce nuclear weapons, but it was conditional on the provision of a nuclear umbrella by countries who were keen to keep India out of the nuclear club. PM Shastri had suggested this to the British knowing full well that Britain had no independent standing or means to provide a nuclear umbrella. A nuclear guarantee, in any case, would be meaningless unless the technical and military means were in place. A formal treaty would be required, as well as the means for early warning, detection, anti-aircraft and anti-missile defence, and a retaliatory strike capability with nuclear weapons suitably deployed.

A dichotomy existed in the minds of the Indian leadership at that time as India was unwilling to give up its non-aligned status. Under the circumstances, it was difficult to fathom how a defensive nuclear pact could be achieved without giving up the non-aligned stance. Thus, it became clear to India that in a world where nuclear weapons and military strength had gained much importance in diplomacy, it would be prudent to rely on one's own weapons and strength to ensure national security. The Chinese developments in the nuclear field notwithstanding, India's policymakers were not reconciled as yet to turning India into a nuclear power, as this would be at the cost of economic development. At the same time, India did not want to give up its right to produce nuclear weapons, as this was crucial to its national security imperatives. To begin a foray into nuclear energy, India established safeguard-free nuclear facilities in the 1950s, which started with Canada India Utility Reactor Services (CIRUS), a 40 mega-watt research and power reactor with a re-processing plant at Trombay.

At that time, China was the only nuclear power inimical to India. Even though China led India in all fields of the power matrix, including economic and military strength, India chose different priorities. It was striving to become a country that possessed modern, intellectual and technological prowess and therefore established world-class schools, colleges, and institutes of higher learning. The Indian leadership also realized that economic upliftment was essential to improve the country's standing in international relations. Modernization of India's Armed Forces was also steadily taking place within its limited means. The Chinese, in the meantime, expanded their nuclear capability, started resettling their citizens from their mainland into Tibet, extended their lines of communications onto their perception of LAC/IB, and tried to create a psychological ascendency over India. The most compelling means for India to deal with the imbalance created by the forces of China and Pakistan was to strengthen the Armed Forces and acquire nuclear capability. India conducted the peaceful nuclear experiment (PNE) in May 1974 at the Pokhran nuclear test site in Rajasthan. This project was called the Smiling Buddha and was the fruition of Prime Minister Shastri's vision. India's developing expertise in nuclear technology was thereby displayed to the world.

Having suffered defeat in the 1965 war with India, Pakistan understood that in a future war, India would always be at an advantage due to the numerical strength of its conventional forces and the ability to escalate the conflict to the entire Indo-Pakistan border. This assessment led to the belief in the Pakistani military that India's advantage could only be neutralized with nuclear weapons. An essential motivating factor was the insatiable, perhaps self-deluding desire in Pakistan to be India's equal, whatever the means. The setting up of safeguard-free nuclear establishments by India and the go ahead for the PNE indicated to Pakistan that this was one more strategic area in which India had taken the lead over their country. Foreign Minister Zulfikar Ali Bhutto's observations in the UNSC, a month after the end of the 1965 Indo-Pakistan war, bore testimony to his way of thinking. He stated, 'If India builds the bomb, we will eat grass and leaves for a thousand years, even go hungry, but will get one of our own. The Christians have the bomb, the Jews have the bomb, and now the Hindus have the bomb. Why not Muslims, too, have the bomb.' In Pakistan, the Army had acquired a dominant role in politics, and this did not go unnoticed by Indian political leaders. Indian politicians and administrative services continued to ensure that there was a separation of the political establishment and the Armed Forces in India. Even today, the Armed Service HQs are not part of the top government structure in India.

The Indian Army (IA) Chief of Army Staff (COAS), General (Gen) K Sunderji, recognized the imperative of possessing nuclear capability for the defence of the nation. Sunderji assessed that China posed a nuclear threat in addition to the conventional threat to India and this threat analysis was projected to the country's political leadership in 1984. At that time, India's defence minister, Arun Singh, was amenable to military advice. The assessment made by General Sunderji bore in mind the comments by Robert McNamara published in the *New York Times* on 15 September 1963. McNamarra had said, 'Nuclear weapons serve no purpose whatsoever except only to deter one's opponent from using them.' This was a simplistic explanation, however, it implied that an opponent can be deterred from using nuclear weapons only by possessing nuclear weapons. The devastating effects of nuclear weapons could, by inference, deter conventional war. The assessment by General Sunderji evoked considerable debate in the political leadership, and India undertook a serious re-examination of its nuclear options.

The Islamic Bomb – Pakistan's Path to Nuclearization

Zulfikar Ali Bhutto's emotional rants in the UNSC in 1965, as mentioned above, were taken seriously in Pakistan. In October 1965, Bhutto met with Munir Ahmed Khan, a Pakistani nuclear scientist who was a director at the nuclear power and reactor division of IAEA, in Vienna. Bhutto was briefed about the Indian nuclear program and the research ongoing at its Bhabha Atomic Research Centre (BARC). Munir Khan asserted that a nuclear India would further undermine and threaten Pakistan's security, and for its own survival, Pakistan needed its own nuclear deterrent. When the proposal was put forward to President Ayub Khan, he reportedly rejected the proposal, stating that when and if Pakistan needed the bomb, it could acquire one off the shelf and therefore did not need to develop one from scratch.

Pakistan's pursuit of nuclear weapons appears to have gained impetus from the desire to regain prestige after its ignominious defeat in the 1971 war with India. Zulfikar Ali Bhutto became the Prime Minister of Pakistan after this war. At a meeting of the UNSC in 1972, he drew a comparison between the surrender of Pakistan forces to India in 1971 to the Treaty of Versailles, which Germany signed in June 1919. Bhutto vowed never to allow defeat of this nature to be repeated. He planned to ensure that Pakistan would become the first nuclear-armed state in the Islamic world and gain the concomitant prestige associated with that. To garner support from Islamic countries, Bhutto insisted on calling a Pakistan developed nuclear bomb, the Islamic bomb.

To pursue this strategy, Bhutto called a meeting of nuclear scientists on 20 January 1972, in Multan, Pakistan, to discuss how to proceed further with the nuclear plans. He invited prominent Pakistani nuclear scientists serving overseas to the meeting and exhorted them to do some good for their home country. He gave the example of Raziuddin Siddiqui, an Indian of undivided India who had contributed immensely in the early 1940s to the Manhattan Project at Los Alamos, New Mexico. The Multan meeting gave impetus to their nuclear program. Pakistani scientists working at the IAEA and International Centre for Theoretical Physics (ICTP) in Italy were asked to return to their home country to work on the nuclear projects. Experts in theoretical physics and computerized numerical controls, including Munir Ahmad Khan, volunteered to come back to Pakistan, while others were coerced into doing so. Scientists from local institutes in nuclear physics were recruited, and hundreds were sent abroad for higher education in nuclear technology to create a pool of trained scientists. Pakistan was thus preparing to play the long game.

Munir Ahmad Khan, after returning from the IAEA, was appointed by Bhutto as the head of the Pakistan Atomic Energy Commission (PAEC) and the Theoretical Physics Group (TPG). The project was slow to achieve results, and it was only in 1977/78 that they managed to prepare a design for an implosion-type of weapon. It was much later, on 11 March 1983, that Munir Khan and his team were able to carry out the first sub-critical test, which was named Kirana-I. There were 24 other cold tests conducted between 1983 and 1994. Their research adopted the plutonium route for an implosion device. After the PNE conducted by India at the Pokhran test site in 1974, Pakistan had advanced the timeline to achieve its proper nuclear capability to 1976.

Meanwhile, Abdul Qadir Khan, a nuclear scientist of Pakistani origin working for the Urenco Group in the Netherlands, contacted the Bhutto government in 1974 and convinced them that he had the expertise in making Highly Enriched Uranium (HEU) for the eventual assembling of nuclear bombs. He had, on his own accord, started purloining centrifuge plans and offered them for Pakistan's nuclear program. Subsequently, the Kahuta Research Laboratories (KRL) were set up and A.Q. Khan was made head of the program and facilities at KRL. In recognition of his services, it was later renamed Khan Research Laboratories. A.Q. Khan, with the support of successive Pakistani leaders, namely Prime Minister Zulfikar Ali Bhutto, President General Muhammad Zia ul Haq, and Prime Minister Benazir Bhutto, was able to pursue his objective with no impediments. He had developed business links with over 50 dealers of nuclear components in European countries and was able to import the necessary components for fabricating nuclear weapons. Khan even sold these components to other countries that were willing to acquire nuclear technology. All such businesses controlled by Khan were clandestine, independent of each other, and profitable. He established a covert acquisition and nuclear proliferation ring that operated through Dubai. Components were purchased at prices quoted by middlemen and multiple agents were employed to obviate breach of secrecy. This clandestine proliferation of nuclear technology was done with no qualms about violating international norms and with no consideration of future consequences for the world at large.

It is impossible to believe that A.Q. Khan acted alone in proffering nuclear technology to select countries, as purported by General Pervez Musharraf in his book, *In the Line of Fire.*[1] Musharraf made this observation to build the grounds to pardon Khan as there was pressure from the US to indict Khan for his clandestine actions, as mentioned above. The military elite and political leaders in Pakistan clearly drove their nuclear program as was proven later.[2] Centrifuges for uranium enrichment, triggers, rotors, and other related parts were sold through Khan's covert organization with no questions asked. Such subterfuge could only be successful with the blessing of the Pakistan government, its Army and the ISI.

Thriving under the auspices of the Pakistan government, the underground trade for this sought after technology continued at extortionate prices under A.Q. Khan. Using his contacts, Khan was able to circumvent any existing international controls and sell nuclear enrichment technology and components to Iran, North Korea, and Libya. He also tried negotiating the sale of this technology to Iraq and South Africa. The brokers, dealers, manufacturers, and even the governments of countries from where Khan ordered and purchased the sensitive components for nuclear weapons were complicit in this indiscriminate, dangerous trade in nuclear technology.

It is likely that the production of HEU was achieved at KRL in 1984. Pakistan demonstrated its covertly acquired nuclear capability to the world at the Chagai-I tests on 28 May 1998. Achieving nuclear capability in totality is not a simple achievement. It requires a minimum quantity of weapon-grade fissile material, assembling of warheads, delivery means, controls, triggers, security measures, storage, and safety. Once means of delivery are available, then nuclear warheads must combine with these, the electronic controls, and triggers. Finally, the safety protocols require considerable expertise and organization. It is very remarkable how Pakistan somehow acquired all these prerequisites to ensure its own nuclear capability and was

1. *In the Line of Fire* by Pervez Musharraf pp 289–296
2. *No Exit from Pakistan* by Daniel Markey, pp 88

also complicit in the proliferation of nuclear technology to other nations. This is mentioned by Mathew Kroenig in his book.[3,4]

Proliferation of Nuclear Weapons Technology by Pakistan

In July 1977, General Mohammad Zia ul Haq, COAS Pakistan Army, ousted the civilian government of Zulfikar Ali Bhutto. Zia jailed Bhutto and approved his public hanging on 4 April 1979. In December 1979, the Soviet Union invaded Afghanistan, and because of its geographic and strategic location, Pakistan emerged as a frontline state for the US against the expansionist communist USSR. Zia was a clever negotiator and was able to extract billions of dollars from the US and Saudi Arabia to modernize and build the Armed Forces of his country. He used the aid from these countries to train, expand and equip the Mujahideen to fight the Soviet Forces and to prevent further advance by the USSR towards the Arabian Sea. The US government and its Central Intelligence Agency (CIA), and the British government and its MI6 were no doubt aware that simultaneously, efforts were being made by Pakistan to acquire nuclear weapons. It was an inconvenient truth, which they chose to ignore. With billions of dollars of aid for Pakistan from the US, it can be posited that the US was indirectly funding the Pakistani nuclear program. For a weak economy such as that of Pakistan, it would have been impossible to internally finance the huge nuclear industry and to develop the nuclear weapons that exist there today. Since Pakistan was an ally of the US to counter the occupation of Afghanistan by the USSR, this alliance perhaps diluted the requirements of US policies on non-proliferation in relation to Pakistan.

After the sudden demise of Zia in an air crash on 17 August 1988, Benazir Bhutto took over as Pakistan's Prime Minister. A very staunch follower of her father's policies, it was under her guidance that the Lashkar-e-Taiba (LeT) and JeM terrorist groups were raised. Bhutto also provided enhanced support for Pakistan's quest for nuclear technology. She actively assisted A.Q. Khan in the transfer of sensitive nuclear technologies to North Korea, Libya, and Iran in return for economic benefits. She was hands on in obtaining

---

3. *Exporting the Bomb: Technology Transfer and the Spread of Nuclear Weapons* by Matthew Kroenig

4. *Global Security Watch-India* by Amit Gupta, Air War College, Maxwell Air Force Base, Alabama, USA

missile technology from North Korea and Iran. On a visit to Pyongyang, as Prime Minister of Pakistan, she carried compact discs containing details of uranium enrichment technology in her overcoat.[5] This was disclosed by Benazir Bhutto herself in an interview with Shyam Bhatia, an author from India. However, she reneged from this admission in a later interview. Shyam Bhatia mentions this in his book *Goodbye Shahzadi*, a political biography of Benazir Bhutto published in 2008.

Benazir had visited North Korea in 1993 to obtain missile technology of the Nodong-1 Missile, and for swapping scientific data for making the bomb. When the serving Prime Minister is directly involved in the conspiracy, it can then be unequivocally stated that Pakistan was a reckless proliferator of nuclear weapons technology. It is no coincidence that North Korea's nuclear plant at Yongbyon has plans and layouts similar to those of the Kahuta plant in Pakistan. A. Q. Khan is known to have sold PI and PII centrifuges and other critical parts to North Korea. He also provided training and teaching material to the North Koreans.[6]

General Musharraf, as President of Pakistan, had A.Q. Khan arrested under pressure from the US. This proved to be a token measure because, on the same day of his arrest, Khan was released and pardoned by Musharraf on the pretext that he was the father of Pakistan's nuclear bomb. Thereafter, Pakistan did not allow Khan to be interviewed by anyone, including the IAEA. The activities of A.Q. Khan since his release, were kept completely secret. It would not be unreasonable to assume that he once again secretly began working for Pakistan's nuclear program. While deliberately staying out of the public eye, Khan did an interview on Al Jazeera television network on 30 May 2016. During the interview, he continued to boast about Pakistan's readiness to engage India with nuclear weapons. He stated that with the press of a button, Pakistani nuclear missiles could target Delhi within five minutes and destroy India's capital city. A.Q. Khan died on 10 October 2021.

It is evident that in the process of development of nuclear weapons by Pakistan, the role played by the US has been somewhat of an enigma. In all likelihood, Pakistan's nuclear efforts were unquestioned as a *quid pro quo* for Pakistan's involvement and cooperation in Afghanistan against Soviet occupation. Pakistan had also succeeded in convincing the US government,

5. *The Warrior State: Pakistan in the Contemporary World by TV Paul;* pp 59–60

6. *In the Line of Fire* by Pervez Musharraf; pp 296

with the help of the Pakistan lobby in the US, that their country was far from achieving nuclear capability. In the West, Pakistan's nuclear program was also assessed to be India-focused, unlike that of Iran or North Korea. This was their public perception even as Pakistan imported Kryton nuclear weapon triggers from Texas, USA, which was a completely illegal export from the US perspective. Even before the authorities in the US became aware of this violation, Pakistan had already received these deliveries. Pakistan's plans had no anti-US implications at that time, and hence, the US turned a blind eye to it.

The US has made efforts to undo the nuclear proliferation in Iran and North Korea. The latter, as is well known, has conducted nuclear tests and has test-fired ballistic missiles that can reach Canada and the US. Missiles have been test-fired by North Korea across Japan into the Pacific Ocean. President, Donald Trump began the process of dialogue with Kim Jong Un, the North Korean dictator, with the aim of persuading North Korea to dismantle its nuclear capability. In exchange, Western nations would lift sanctions against North Korea. President Trump was optimistic after he met Kim Jong Un at the demilitarized Zone between North and South Korea on 30 June 2019 and when the two met once again in Singapore. These summits between the two leaders failed to make any progress and despite Trump's optimism North Korea has continued with its nuclear weapons program. It is to be noted here that China is averse to any reconciliation between the US and North Korea or between the South and North Korea. The Chinese leadership is blatantly aware that if the two Koreas merge into one country, US influence would then spread up to the Chinese border, much to the detriment of the latter.

China's role in nuclear proliferation to Pakistan is also very pertinent. It is known that Pakistani scientists and A.Q. Khan himself could not technically analyze or make use of the designs of nuclear centrifuges that he had stolen from the Dutch at Urenco. This technology is specialized and related to ultracentrifuges, a fast process of enrichment of uranium. For the practical use of the stolen expertise, Pakistan therefore requested China's help. In exchange, Pakistan was willing to share the technology stolen from Urenco. China was obviously willing to oblige on acquiring the blueprints of the ultra-fast centrifuges, it was successful in developing an advanced method of uranium enrichment. With this advancement in its nuclear program, China provided Pakistan with a functional bomb design and gifted Pakistan 50 kg of weapon-grade enriched uranium, enough for two nuclear weapons. Chinese scientists had been visiting

Pakistan for liaison and to obtain details of the technology obtained from Urenco by A.Q. Khan. He had boasted that Pakistan had sent 135 plane loads of C-130 Hercules aircraft for construction of the nuclear plant at Hanzhong to China. If this bears truth, it shows the close cooperation that had developed between China and Pakistan in the transfer of nuclear and missile technology.

Emboldened by its growing nuclear prowess, in 1987 belligerent Pakistani leader Zia ul Haq warned India's Prime Minister, Rajiv Gandhi, that if India crossed Pakistan's borders by an inch, Pakistan would annihilate India's cities. Pakistan had carried out a cold test in 1983 under PAEC and was possibly successful in making highly enriched uranium (HEU) in 1984, as mentioned earlier. In this process of acquiring nuclear capability, it is also alleged that China allowed or conducted a test of a Pakistani nuclear device in 1980 at Lop Nur, but this has not been conclusively proven. It seems entirely plausible that China, while working on the design of the Dutch centrifuge enrichment process to make it functional, may have also conducted the alleged test for Pakistan in a quid pro quo.

Pakistan's nuclear projects comprise some 20 laboratories at various sites. To sustain the weapons program and continue its vertical proliferation, Pakistan requires more and more fissile material, concomitant technology upgrades, multiple means of delivery, security of its establishments and stockpiles and, an inflow of finances. The fissile material is produced at the Nilore, Kahuta, and Khusab nuclear complexes. Pakistan appears to have adequate uranium ore deposits located near Dera Ghazi Khan. A plant to concentrate uranium, which washes the ore, has therefore been built there. An estimated four tons of ore are processed per day in preparation for nuclear enrichment. Pakistan's scientists have developed a miniature plutonium warhead that could be delivered by a short-range ballistic missile, which may be Hatf IX. Technology for this has been obtained from North Korea. The Hatf system and warhead fall into the category of a tactical nuclear weapon. Such weapons were deployed by the US in Western Europe at the height of the Cold War. They were meant to thwart Soviet designs into objectives such as the Fulda Gap in Germany. Pakistan openly displayed its nuclear capability on 28 and 30 May 1998, subsequent to India conducting its nuclear tests a few days earlier. These tests gave credence to earlier disclosures by A.Q. Khan, and the rhetorical threats from Zia, that Pakistan had achieved what it desired in the field of nuclear technology. It had made the Islamic Bomb!

The US, on many occasions, has protested and even confronted China regarding the sharing of nuclear technology with Pakistan. China, of course, has denied such allegations every time.[7] In 1992, the US had adequate proof that China had violated the Missile Technology Control Regime (MTCR), but once again, China denied any knowledge. China is a known nuclear power, but details of its stockpile, storage, type of nuclear weapons, the availability of fissile material and means of delivery are not accurately known. China continues to multiply its stockpile and poses a challenge to other nuclear powers. Pakistan initially pursued the plutonium route for producing nuclear warheads under the aegis of their PAEC. The Khushab Nuclear Complex near Joharabad, where a heavy water reactor was set up, became operational in the early nineties. It could produce 8–10 kgs of plutonium each year. Plutonium warheads, being lighter, would be easier to deliver with short-range ballistic missiles. China desires parity with the US and Russia and continues to bolster Pakistan's capacity to enrich uranium.[8]

Nuclear Threshold and Emerging Threats

The Pakistan Army, with assistance from the US, had demonstrated the success of the sub-conventional proxy war against Soviet forces in Afghanistan. With this training ground, Pakistan is adopting a similar strategy against India. It pursues a sub-conventional war through terrorism and poses a nuclear threat. A very dangerous combination. Under the bravado of its nuclear umbrella, there is a possibility that Pakistan may become more reckless in the future and take even more bold, unprovoked risks to attack India. What form these provocations will take is always a wild card given the fragile political state and unpredictable leadership in the Pakistan Army top brass. India has called Pakistan's bluff of sabre blackmail by refusing to succumb to terrorism as displayed in the operations in May 2025. More on this operation later.

Successive US administrations under presidents Ford, Carter, Bush, and Reagan have made attempts to dissuade Pakistan from acquiring nuclear weapons. It was only after the withdrawal of Soviet forces from Afghanistan that the George Bush administration finally took stock of developments and evoked action under the provisions of the Pressler Amendment. The US froze over half a billion dollars in annual military and developmental

---

7. *Washington Post*, 13 November 2009

8. *China-Pakistan Nuclear Deal* by Glenn Kessler; *Washington Post*, 14 June 2010 *Pakistan's Development of Nuclear Weapons*, by J. Cirincione

aid. Twenty-eight F-16 fighter aircraft sold to Pakistan were put in storage in the Nevada Desert. This was done in response to intelligence estimates at that time that Pakistan had acquired the bomb.

The above measures notwithstanding, Pakistan and USA resorted to collaboration once again when Operation Enduring Freedom was launched by the US and its allies in Afghanistan in 2001. The US needed Pakistani land routes to manage logistics and use its airspace to support ops and engage targets in Afghanistan. Also, and more importantly, the US desired that Pakistan impose controls on militant groups supported by the ISI to stop them from operating against the allied forces. General Pervez Musharraf, who had ousted the Nawaz Sharif government, was presented with a choice to either support the US and its allies in the war in Afghanistan or be subjected to US offensive action and face large-scale devastation. Musharraf made the choice to assist the US, and he describes the reasons for his decision in his book, *In the Line of Fire*.[9]

In brief, the reasons were: Pakistan's military did not have the capacity and means to contend with the threat enunciated by the US leadership. The country's economy was in a terrible state, it would have collapsed under the expenditure of war, and politically, there were divided opinions in Pakistan about whether to support the US. Another argument that influenced this decision was that if Pakistan opted not to assist the US-led coalition, as an alternative, the US may have sought assistance from India. In which case, Pakistan would have been in the enemy camp with Afghanistan for revitalizing the Taliban and for providing safe sanctuary to Al Qaeda and the Taliban. The entire region of Afghanistan and Pakistan (AFPAK) would then be engulfed in war and Pakistan's nuclear assets would have become prime and priority targets. Having achieved nuclear capability, Musharraf was unwilling to let this triumph be diminished and his country be devastated by war. However, despite publicly reaching a compromise to ally with the US, Musharraf continued to play a duplicitous role. It is known well that during that period, Pakistan continued to assist the Taliban in reorganizing and supporting the groups that the US and allied forces were fighting in Afghanistan.

The US and their allies have been myopic in their approach to Pakistan and over time their indulgence has allowed Pakistan to have a free hand. The US neglected to counter and stop Pakistan's cooperation with China

9. *In the Line of Fire* by Pervez Musharraf, pp 224

and other nations in its quest to become a nuclear power. At the same time, the US propped up the Pakistan economy by providing them billions of dollars for military and civilian aid. The result of all this is that Pakistan has emerged as a nuclear power and brought further instability to the region. However, this power has proven to be a double-edged sword for Pakistan.

It would not be too unrealistic to imagine a scenario where Pakistan's political establishment lose their tenuous control over their country, or it becomes a country severely divided between radicals and moderates or if the country implodes. Their nuclear set up would then be in jeopardy and may fall into the hands of those who desire to convert Pakistan into a caliphate. A far more dangerous Pakistan would then emerge, even as it already continues to harbour and abet the world's most dangerous terrorists.[10] Such an unstable Pakistan would create many crises for the world at large. Its illicit proliferation and continuous support to terrorists, while perpetrating violence, would have devastating impacts. As of now, because of its weak economy, Pakistan must seek grants or loans to ensure the security of its sensitive nuclear establishments. If financial aid is not forthcoming, then these establishments may no longer remain secure.[11] A very grim possibility indeed.

The nuclear capability of India and Pakistan was not seriously acknowledged in the global strategic equation until May 1998, when the two countries simultaneously conducted successful nuclear tests. Shortly after, during the Kargil War in 1999, it was established that Pakistan had actually deployed missiles in the Deosai plains in Gilgit-Baltistan in POK. These were probably the missiles supplied by China and moved along the Karakoram Highway. With a range of approximately 300 km, these missiles would have targeted most areas of J&K as well as the road and rail communication into J&K from Punjab. In the areas of Pathankot, Madhopur, and Samba in J&K, the communications on the Indian side of the IB pass through a bottleneck and are vulnerable to disruption. Today, Pakistan's nuclear capability is an ongoing clear and present danger. There are notable threats that have come to exist in the world as a consequence of nuclear proliferation by Pakistan. An emboldened and nuclear equipped North Korea is the foremost. Despite the two meetings that President Trump had with Kim Jong Un in February

---

10. 'Pakistan's Nuclear Arsenal' by Richards Hass, *Foreign Affairs* November– December 2014

11. *The Most Dangerous Place: Pakistan's Lawless Frontier* by Imtiaz Gul

and June 2019, North Korea has not abated the development of its nuclear weapons and missiles. Neither has it made any effort to dismantle any of its nuclear enrichment facilities. It carried out tests of short-range missiles in February 2020 and carried out further tests in 2022–23.

Iran is another nation that has obtained Uranium enrichment technology from Pakistan. This occurred even as Iran's nuclear R&D was already quite advanced. The US and allies, assessing that a nuclear-armed Iran would pose a threat to Saudi Arabia, Israel, other Sunni Arab states, and also to US assets and bases in the Middle East, negotiated an accord with Iran on 14 July 2015. In an assessment by Wendy R. Sherman, who was the team leader of American and allied diplomats who negotiated with Iran to curb its nuclear weapons development, she stated that Iran had 19,000 centrifuges at its facilities in Natanz and at the underground facility at Fordow.[12]

During the Obama administration, under the provisions of the accord with Iran, the US and its allies lifted sanctions and compensated Iran by giving it access to $7 billion frozen funds. In exchange, Iran was expected to restrict its uranium enrichment program and make all its nuclear establishments available for inspection and safeguards by the IAEA. There were, however, suspicions that Iran could violate the deal and continue its program for uranium enrichment in a clandestine manner. Based on these assessments, President Trump withdrew the US from this accord in May 2018. Trump decided that he could not certify to Congress that Iran was not pursuing its nuclear ambition. Other signatories to the accord – China, Russia, France, Germany, and the UK, had decided to continue with it, but lately, the accord has become defunct.

It is apparent that Pakistan's unchecked activities in acquiring and selling nuclear secrets, technology and materials, has contributed to the conundrum in the Middle East. The implications of Iran's quest to achieve nuclear weapons capability are considerable. If Iran carries on with its nuclear weapons development program and manages to create a nuclear weapon, then it surely will pose a grave danger to the region as mentioned previously. If Iran, a largely Shia nation, acquires nuclear weapons, then Saudi Arabia, a largely Sunni nation, would aspire to have their own deterrent. In this case, they could be provided with a nuclear umbrella by friendly nations, or they may purchase their own nuclear weapons,

---

12. 'How We Got the Deal' by Wendy R. Sherman, *Foreign Affairs* September– October 2018, pp 189

whatever the cost. Prince Mohammed bin Salman of Saudi Arabia had stated in 2019 that if Iran develops a nuclear bomb, then his country will surely follow suit. In this quest to be nuclear armed, one of the obvious sources to acquire nuclear weapons, along with multiple delivery means, may prove to be Pakistan. The other rich Gulf States may also get into this reckless game of proliferation. Hence, the events in Iran and other countries in the region need constant surveillance.

Pakistan's attempts to play broker in this dangerous game also led to Libya under Ghaddafi having ambitions of becoming a nuclear power. Due to extreme pressure from the West and a lack of technical know-how, Libya could not pursue this quest. Iraq's ambition to have weapons of mass destruction was neutralized when the US and its allies launched Op Desert Storm to oust Saddam Hussein. The Iraqis did have an operational nuclear reactor in 1980, which France had supplied in exchange for the supply of oil at concessional rates. However, this reactor was damaged by Israel in an air raid. South Africa was also offered nuclear technology by A.Q. Khan, but they did not wish to deal with Pakistan on such sensitive matters.

It is to be noted that even though the possession of nuclear weapons was considered a deterrent to war, the nuclear capability of India and Pakistan failed to discourage Pakistan from launching the Kargil War in 1999. Ever since this war, there have been further advances made in nuclear capability both by India and Pakistan. It is therefore necessary to ascertain and highlight their different strategies. The Indian establishment is patently aware that Pakistan has acted without caution in launching earlier wars and terrorist attacks against India. In addition, Pakistan's quest to continue to multiply and advance its nuclear weapons and delivery means needs careful attention and monitoring by the world.

While Pakistan plays the dangerous game of nuclear arms broker, the world has observed that unlike Pakistan, India has never proliferated nuclear weapon technology to any other nation. Given this reality, the US, through the nuclear accord of 18 July 2005, made an exception for a non-signatory of the Nuclear Non-Proliferation Treaty (NPT), thereby restoring India-US relations, which were not very amicable prior to this. The US removed sanctions against India with the aim of letting their nuclear industry re-establish itself in India. This was necessary as India intended to replace its coal-fired power plants with other renewable means of energy to reduce its carbon footprint. Even though India is making considerable investments in solar and wind power, it will still need nuclear power to meet its growing requirements. After the Bhopal gas tragedy in 1984, the

Government of India had enacted the legislation termed Civil Liability for Nuclear Damage. This legislation had prevented the purchase of nuclear reactors from the US and other Western nations as these countries were wary of the conditions imposed by this act. The exception is that India does import reactors from Rostom, the Russian State Corporation.

The US also tried to promote an agreement between the Nuclear Suppliers Group (NSG) and India in 2008. Such an agreement was to allow India to import nuclear technology and raw materials for its nuclear needs. Membership of the NSG for India was vetoed by China at that time. China, along with three other countries, out of a total of 48 members of the NSG, again turned down India's request to become a member in October 2021. As mentioned previously, China had already helped Pakistan with proven designs for nuclear weapons, gifted 50 kg of weapon-grade uranium, ring magnets for enriching uranium, dual-use diagnostic equipment, and an industrial furnace to produce components for nuclear weapons. In direct retaliation to the constructive relationship between the US and India, China also agreed to supply two second-hand nuclear reactors to Pakistan. Thus, the circuitous nexus between Pakistan and China continues.

The Nuclear Doctrine

Pakistan's own nuclear strategy remains somewhat ambiguous. What is known is that Pakistan has chosen to retain the option of a first strike. In contrast, India's policy has been that it will not use nuclear weapons first and will retaliate in kind if subjected to a nuclear attack. To launch a counterstrike, India has to ensure that it has an adequate number and types of nuclear weapons that are dispersed, concealed, and secured to survive a first strike by Pakistan or China. In addition, it has to have an effective and foolproof AI-based air defence system to destroy all incoming missiles, rockets, drones, and aircraft carrying nuclear warheads launched by adversaries against India. The weapons that India launches for a second strike must be effective and should be able to penetrate the defensive measures of the aggressor nation. Underground and under water capability with hardened shelters/silos, dispersion, mobility, and having a triad of weapon delivery means, including land, air, and submarine, will be necessary to ensure survivability. India's doctrine states that it will launch a second or retaliatory strike if necessary. This strike would be so potent that it ensures large-scale degradation and defeat of the aggressor nation. The intention would be to destroy the enemy's will to wage war, creating circumstances similar to the Japanese surrender in the Second World War after the US nuclear strikes on Hiroshima and Nagasaki.

India released its draft nuclear doctrine in August 1999. The doctrine considers a triad of nuclear strike systems as the basis of its force structure. The intent of this may have been misunderstood because it was presumed that the doctrine advocated a large nuclear force structure. It seemed like India had changed tracks from a previously self-restraining doctrine. In his analysis, a Rand Corporation scholar and senior fellow at Carnegie Endowment for International Peace, Ashley Tellis, commented on the doctrine, stating that it was sober, enlightened, and, under the existing geostrategic scenario, it was proper.

In a nuclear environment, defence against nuclear attacks requires an air umbrella or protective measures over the air space of a country. The first requirement is to deploy a foolproof and effective early warning system. All incoming threats are discerned, and their destruction is planned and executed in real-time. This is achieved by the use of Artificial Intelligence or AI, extending control over all air defence measures, which are an array of air defence missile clusters. The defensive system discerns the incoming missiles, drones, and/or aircraft immediately on launch or being airborne. The air defence missiles are then launched within seconds, utilizing AI guidance to destroy specific incoming targets in the air. The US Patriot missile system, Iron Dome and Spider systems deployed by Israel are examples of defensive systems. These have protected Israel from short-range missile attacks launched by Hezbollah and Hamas by destroying 90 per cent of missiles fired onto the country in mid-air. In the mass attack by Hamas on Israel on 7 October 2023, quite a few rockets (out of a reported 5,000 in numbers) did manage to penetrate the air defence of the latter, causing considerable casualties in Israel. A similar strategy is being adopted by Ukraine, utilizing the air defence systems donated to it by the US and NATO allies. This is to counter and defeat sustained efforts by Russia attempting to engage value targets in this country. The result has been that the damage caused by Russian missile and drone attacks has been minimized.

India had perhaps negotiated with Israel for the transfer of technology to enable the manufacture of air defence systems in India and the purchase of a ready system, for $2 billion. India had also signed an agreement to purchase an S-400 surface-to-air missile system from Russia for $5 billion, the delivery of which commenced in 2021. This purchase from Russia had initially subjected India to sanctions by the US under their law for buying sensitive weaponry from rival nations. India had, after due negotiations, been granted a waiver by the US for purchase of this air defence system. A point to note here is that India can afford to purchase $7 billion worth of air defence weapon systems in addition to two squadrons of Rafale fighter aircraft from France and other military hardware. It has the financial ability to upgrade its Armed Forces further. The additions to India's defence arsenal will augment the existing early warning and air defence systems that are deployed indigenously. The existing systems are AI based and encompass an array of some 600 air defence missiles or more, under India's Ballistic Missile Defence Program to defend against potential Chinese or Pakistan's missile attacks. These numbers need to be augmented based on assessments of threat of missile, drones and combat aircrafts emanating from these countries.

Known as a powerhouse of scientific minds, India's achievements in aerospace technology are demonstrated to the world regularly. Its probe reached Mars and in January 2019, India launched 194 satellites in a single launch, an unmatched accomplishment. India's early warning systems and surveillance capability is also indigenous and based on geostationary satellites, the Nav IC, which is last known to be eight satellites in space. This early warning system can detect and track missiles from as far away as 5000 km.[13, 14] The acquisition of Airborne Warning and Control System (AWACS) aircraft and air refueling tankers aircraft by India has added range and monitoring capability. India has a sizeable lead in surveillance systems which it develops, whereas Pakistan is dependent on China and other nations for its capabilities. In the wake of the standoff on the LAC with China, an agreement has been signed between India and the US for sharing satellite intelligence. This has been termed the Basic Exchange and Cooperation Agreement. It would facilitate the sharing of nautical and aeronautical data for better accuracy of missiles and drones. In 2018, the Communication Compatibility and Security Agreement was signed between the two countries, which provides for interoperability between forces.

Ashley Tellis had carried out a methodical analysis of the prevailing dynamic in the South Asian region in 1999, in the wake of the Kargil War. He established that Indian nuclear weapons were meant for deterrence and to ensure that India was not put at a disadvantage politically or militarily.

---

13. '*Chinese Nuclear Proliferation*' by Susan Turner Haynes
14. Analysis of India's Nuclear Doctrine by Ashley J. Tellis, Rand Corporation 1999

India's nuclear weapons were, therefore, to become her political strength and reinforce her commitment to non-violence and hence contribute to peace in the region. In another analysis on the subject, Stephen Cohen of the Brookings Institute stated that the nuclear equation in the region is growing more complex. India's security really depends upon the Pakistanis. The latter's weakest link is their chain of command for their nuclear weapons. The wild card is that their least informed, but most powerful decision maker who is at the helm of affairs may be their most extremist general. And alongside, it could be that their most rabidly anti-Indian politician is leading Pakistan's decision-making. This is a possibility that has grave implications and has come to pass previously. This kind of irresponsible catastrophic event can be perpetrated by Pakistan. A possibility of this is well understood by India. In the short war in May 2025 there appears to have been a leak and spread of fallout from the Kirana nuclear complex in Pakistan. The Indian minister of defence calling Pakistan a rogue state commented that all nuclear weapons held by Pakistan be placed under IAEA scrutiny. This is because Pakistan has failed to give reason for the possible nuclear leak, whether it occurred or not.

During the India-Pakistan Kargil War in 1999, the US administration had conducted an evaluation on the possible deployment of nuclear weapons by Pakistan. It was presumed that Pakistan would do so to counter an all-out war, if the conflict had been expanded by India. For such an escalation, India would also have kept its nuclear options open in readiness. Hence, in the assessment of the Clinton administration, a very dangerous situation was emerging in South Asia during the Kargil war. At that time, in a meeting between President Clinton and Prime Minister Nawaz Sharif, Bruce Riedel, the senior director for South Asia in the Clinton administration, was present. While working at the University of Pennsylvania, three years later, he wrote an article, quoted by Robert Wirsing in his book.[15] In this article he indicated that when Prime Minister Nawaz Sharif was at the White House on 4 July 1999, he was confronted with evidence about the deployment of nuclear weapons by Pakistan. Sharif was apparently taken aback by this evidence, almost as if it was a surprise or he was unaware of it. It can therefore be conjectured that Pakistan's deployment of nuclear-tipped missiles, to target India, in the Deosai Plains and elsewhere, may actually have been done without the approval of Nawaz Sharif, the political

15. *Kashmir in the Shadow of War* by Robert G. Wirsing, pp 50

head of Pakistan's government at that time. It can also be posited that in Pakistan, such violations of the chain of command can be expected, where the head of the government is kept out of the loop when nuclear weapons are deployed. This sets an incredibly dangerous precedent.

To add to the dangerous rhetoric, Pakistan's politicians and the media have been saber-rattling about their nuclear weapons time and again. This bombastic expression of bravado is not taken lightly by Indian decision makers. From November 1986 to January 1987, India conducted a major combined arms military exercise of the Indian Armed Forces called Operation Brasstacks. The operation took place near the Pakistan border and included a series of exercises to simulate the operational capabilities of the Indian Armed Forces. It was the largest mobilization of Indian forces in the Indian subcontinent, involving the combined strength of two Army Commands – almost 500,000 troops – a large portion of the Indian Army. As India demonstrated its military might, a nuclear threat was conveyed by Pakistan. Their minister of foreign affairs communicated this threat to S.K. Singh, the Indian ambassador in Islamabad, which was not the first instance of Pakistan upping the ante.[16] As mentioned earlier, General Zia had already conveyed a similar threat to the Indian Prime Minister Rajiv Gandhi, and A.Q. Khan had also expressed the same on Pakistani media. The Pakistani Foreign Minister, Sahibzada Yakub Khan, also put across this sobering threat to the Prime Minister, V. P. Singh during a visit to India. This heightened danger of a possible nuclear attack was defused by Robert Gates, the US Foreign Secretary, on a visit to Islamabad, during which he advised Pakistan to restrain their warlike ambitions. Pakistan had clearly achieved nuclear capability by the late eighties or early nineties. Despite many historical defeats in conflicts with India and despite America's attempts to quell their belligerent ambitions, once Pakistan achieved a nuclear deterrence, the country was audacious enough to launch the Kargil War. Another blatant, unprovoked aggression against India! More on this is discussed in Chapter 3.

Pakistan's rationale to become a nuclear power can be attributed to the intractable desire it has to be at par, if not stronger than India. Pakistan demonstrated its nuclear capability in May 1998 with different yields of warheads. It is assumed that a higher number of warheads and delivery

16. Report of the Kargil Review Committee: Executive Summary

means creates more options for them. Pakistan's nuclear arsenal includes land-based and air-deliverable systems. Its land-based nuclear weapons are mobile by road and rail. Additional protective measures such as silo hardening, steel tunnels, storage underground and concealment in Chagai and Kirana hills and mountains have been undertaken to ensure survivability. It is reasonable to assume that nuclear weapons deter conventional and nuclear attacks. However, these weapons do not deter the sub-conventional proxy war that Pakistan continues to wage against India as it builds its stockpile of various types of nuclear weapons. The only constraint to this deadly ambition is economic. It is assessed that Pakistan will soon overtake France in the number and type of nuclear warheads in its possession. With its increasing arsenal, Pakistan has professed a new doctrine, calling it 'Full Spectrum Deterrence', likely initiated around 2012. At a seminar, the subject of which was *Defence Deterrence and Stability in South Asia*, Lt Gen Khalid Kidwai, adviser to Pakistan's National Command Authority (NCA), shared that this doctrine encompasses all three: strategic, operational, and tactical nuclear weapons, with full coverage of the Indian land mass and its outlying territories.[17] In addition, Kidwai stated, 'Pakistan should have appropriate weapon yields to deter the adversary's policy of massive retaliation.' The last element of the policy emphasized by Kidwai was regarding the liberty of choosing from a full spectrum of targets, including counter value, counterforce, and battlefield targets. Kidwai further reiterated, 'Because of Mutual Assured Destruction (MAD), there is the unlikelihood of a hot war or conventional war, and therefore the conflict has shifted to sub-conventional.'

India had also evolved a new doctrine called 'Cold Start'. It aimed at a rapid retaliatory offensive by specially constituted task forces to seize vital targets while the rest of the Indian forces mobilized. This was to be deployed in response to sub-conventional attacks by Pakistan-based groups. The rationale behind this doctrine was to prevent Pakistan's regular Armed Forces from seizing the initiative as done in earlier wars because of shorter interior lines of communication; this action by Indian troops intended to put Pakistan at a disadvantage. While considering this doctrine, India also assessed whether Pakistan could use nuclear weapons on its own territory in response to incursions by Indian troops. This is still a matter of debate, but Pakistan's full spectrum deterrence allows flexibility to deal with such

17. 'Full Spectrum Deterrence', *Dawn* newspaper, Pakistan, 7 December 2017

kinds of threats with tactical nuclear weapons. These weapons give options to planners as they would not be forced to use strategic or operational nuclear weapons as a first response to India's conventional force. India has since shelved the Cold Start doctrine. The country has evolved other methods to carry out punitive action in response to a terrorist attack by Pakistan. Pakistan's doctrine of first use and full spectrum deterrence has definitely impacted India's conventional options. At the time of operational exercise Brasstacks, when both India and Pakistan had mobilized their forces, it was thought prudent by the Indian leadership that more was to be gained by not attacking Pakistan than the converse.

While analyzing the nuclear equation in South Asia, China figures prominently. Even in conventional ops where China initiates an intrusion, counter-intrusions are one method to deal with their belligerent actions under a nuclear umbrella. China definitely also figures in the nuclear threat evaluation for the US and Russia. What needs analysis is China's perception of India's nuclear capability. China knows that India has the option of deploying nuclear weapons in case its vital interests are threatened. India, meanwhile, is speedily enhancing its conventional capability and will likely modify its nuclear doctrine if it is forced into an adverse situation by China alone or in a combined offensive with Pakistan. A change in India's doctrine of *No First Use* has been alluded to by the Indian Defence Ministry, in reference to a larger conflict with Pakistan. The ultimate outcome of the border issue between India and China, and the direction of related policy, will be determined by interactions on many issues including Tibet.

Stockpile of Warheads and Delivery Means

It is difficult to know definitively the types and numbers of nuclear weapons and their means of delivery that India, Pakistan, and China possess. These facts are kept ultra secret. Each country has its own threat assessments, deterrence strategy, and options to deploy nuclear weapons. However, an assessment can be made about how much inventory is necessary for each nation. This estimate is based on strategic perspectives, threat analysis with a focus on imperatives of national security, finances, availability of ores, capability in the enrichment of ores to weapon-grade, technology to assemble nuclear weapons, delivery means, storage, and security apparatus. In an article published in *The Hindu*, a daily newspaper in India, Shyam Saran, former foreign secretary to the Government of India, provided an assessment. He had stated that Pakistan's expanding nuclear capability is no longer driven solely by its oft-cited fears of India but by the paranoia of attacks on its nuclear assets by the US and or Israel. This observation was made over a decade ago and threats to nations keep changing over time. Pakistan may in fact be endeavoring to increase the effective range of its missiles to deter such threats for the long term. In 2018, Pakistan's intercontinental missile, Shaheen-III, had achieved a maximum range of 2,750 km. By all accounts, Pakistan's quest may have evolved to include building missiles with longer ranges to reach nations further afield.

The developments in the Middle East also impact Pakistan's strategy in this regard. Saudi Arabia and Iran have been involved in sectarian conflicts in the Middle East. Iran, largely a Shia nation, has created the Hezbollah in Lebanon and Hamas in Gaza and West Bank. It supported Bashar al Assad's regime, which has been toppled, in Syria and Houthi rebels in Yemen. All these groups are opposed to the Sunni nations and also Israel. In Iraq, where both Sunnis and Shias reside, there is sectarian support from Saudi Arabia and Iran, respectively. Iran has developed links with China and North Korea and is friendly with Russia. To reiterate, if Iran continues its nuclear ambitions and clandestinely acquires nuclear weapons, then the outcome would be a Shia nuclear-armed state. Since Saudi Arabia is Sunni, it may not be too far-fetched to conjecture that they country will acquire nuclear weapons as a deterrent to a nuclear-armed Iran. Sunni, being the majority Islamic sect in Pakistan, suggests to some analysts that Pakistan's nuclear capability is controlled by the Sunnis. They can very well choose to provide the same capability to Saudi Arabia. In fact, it was, perhaps, Saudi Arabia that advised the US to not club Pakistan with Afghanistan in the once-considered AFPAK scenario in the war against Al Qaeda and their host Taliban. Saudi Arabia's influence over Pakistan is considerable and there is a mutually beneficial relationship between the two nations. Pakistan has provided troops to guard and protect the Saudi royal family, who find these guards to be more trustworthy than their own personnel. The Saudis can, therefore, seek nuclear guarantees or nuclear weapons capability from Pakistan. Saudi Arabia also has another angle to explore in this regard. The amicable relationship with the US, especially under President Trump, has emboldened the Saudis to want a defence treaty with the US, perhaps as their shield against nuclear attacks. Saudi Arabia already has nuclear power plants that produce 52 gigawatts of electricity, and its first nuclear reactor is under construction. However, this reactor has not been under the IAEAs watch and no other international monitoring agency has imposed any scrutiny over it.

Pakistan is not a signatory of the Non-Proliferation Treaty (NPT) and MTCR possibly because India is not a signatory to these controls. Hence, it is not restricted by any international controls. As it faces a continuing financial crisis, this may force Pakistan to resort to nuclear proliferation once again. Some of the motivations for Pakistan's ongoing vertical proliferation are as follows:

a. Pakistan assesses that India remains a major security threat and hence the need to have the preponderance of nuclear power to deter India.

b. Pakistan claims that they have achieved full spectrum deterrence vis-à-vis India. It claims to have developed tactical nuclear warheads, possibly plutonium-based, to tip short-range missiles. Pakistan may also be in the process of developing nuclear warheads for heavier artillery weapons. The threat created by these is expected to deter India from crossing the IB or LOC with ground forces.

c. To provide a nuclear umbrella to friendly countries such as Saudi Arabia, if required. Pakistan needs to earmark and store additional nuclear weapons and deploy these if and when needed.

d. Pakistan continues to develop its expertise in missile technology to perhaps achieve longer ranges with its missiles. This is based on Pakistan's evolving threat perception, availability of technology, and funding.

e. Pakistan builds its stockpile to have a psychological upper hand over its adversaries and have adequate weapons available for a second strike.

f. The nuclear arsenal Pakistan has accumulated is meant to deter all types of attacks against its geographical area.

The likely scale of Pakistan's nuclear weapons program is immense. A report published in 2007 in Pakistani media quoted Brigadier Feroz Khan, previously the second-in-command of the Strategic Arms Division, confirming that Pakistan had 80–120 nuclear warheads. A fusion-type nuclear weapon requires approximately 20 kg of enriched uranium for its core. In the case of a fission weapon, only 2–4 kg of plutonium is needed to produce a similar effect. Tritium, a by-product of uranium enrichment, if added to the latter, will increase the yield three to four times. There are about 10,000–20,000 centrifuges in Kahuta, which could produce 75–100 kg of HEU every year. Since Zia ul Haq threatened India with dire consequences in 1987, it can be deduced that HEU production at KRL has been ongoing since 1986. Except for the stoppage imposed in the period 1991–1997, KRL has now been producing HEU for nearly 30 years. With the technology that Pakistan possesses, they would have produced approximately 2,500–3,000 kg of HEU, sufficient to produce approximately 150 nuclear warheads. In addition, Pakistan has proceeded with refining of plutonium to weapons grade. Pakistan's actual capability with the plutonium nuclear warhead was only demonstrated in the sub-kiloton test in Chagai on 30 May 1998. The number of warheads already produced, stored, and those ready for use cannot be ascertained, and neither is it known whether they have successfully added Tritium to increase the yield. According to estimates in the fifty-fourth edition of the *Stockholm International Peace Research Institute* (SIPRI) yearbook, published in January 2023, Pakistan has a stockpile of 170 nuclear weapons and India has 164. It is also known that Pakistan had three reactors at Khushab, and a fourth was commissioned in 2015. This fourth reactor, if taken into account, will mean that these reactors can produce 11–15 kg of refined plutonium each year for miniature nuclear warheads. New construction is ongoing at the site. It has not yet been confirmed via satellite imagery or by other means whether this is an additional reactor or some other laboratory or installation.[18] The above estimates would no doubt be impacted by the availability of finances to continue Pakistan's nuclear program. Indications are that Pakistan is in pursuit of a larger stockpile, but is restricted by the country's economy, which is in a morass. A summary and timeline of known nuclear tests conducted by Pakistan is as follows:

a. 28 May 1998, Chagai-I. Five nuclear devices exploded underground in the Ras Koh Hills of Chagai District, Baluchistan. These were HEU devices.

b. 30 May 1998, Chagai-II. One nuclear device was test-fired underground at a site in the Kharan Desert, Chagai District, Baluchistan. This was, perhaps, a plutonium device. All tests were conducted in steel tunnels constructed in the late eighties.

There is no separation between Pakistan's military and civilian nuclear programs. This is, perhaps, the reason why many countries oppose Pakistan's

18. A report on Nuclear Tests by David Albright, 16 June 2015, Institute of Science and International Security, Washington DC

membership of NSG and also since it is a known proliferator. The NSG has even objected to China providing Pakistan with two additional second-hand reactors. One of these reactors is for gas centrifuge enrichment of uranium, and the other is a uranium plant for power generation. These are being built in Mianwali. China has also sold an advanced tracking system to Pakistan, which could boost the latter's ability to build, test, and improve missiles capable of multiple warheads.[19]

Details of the transfer of the advanced tracking system are mentioned on the Chinese Academy of Sciences website. According to Zheng Mengwai, a researcher at the Chinese Academy of Sciences, Institute of Optics and Electronics, this is a highly sophisticated measuring and tracking system, a critical component required for missile testing. Pakistan would, in all probability be endeavouring to develop multiple independently targetable re-entry vehicles (MIRVs) to improve offensive nuclear capability and to enable penetration of missile defence systems. Pakistan has a missile production center at the National Defence Complex in the *Kala Chitta Dhar* (mountains), and testing is done south of Attock using mobile launchers designed by China. Pakistan's Ababeel missile is likely being tested with MIRV warheads. In the report published by SIPRI titled, 'Trends in World Nuclear Forces 2023',[20] worldwide nuclear stockpiles have been increasing as compared to earlier data. Pakistan has continued to expand its fissile material production, enabling an increase in weapons inventories. It has also been aspiring to develop a sea-based nuclear force. On 9 January 2018, Pakistan officially announced that it had tested, for the first time, a nuclear-capable submarine-launched cruise missile (SLCM), the *Babur-3*.[21]

The increasing capability of China in submarine ops in India's coastal waters need also be noted. India test-fired a Submarine Launched Ballistic Missile (SLBM) in early 2016 from its submarine, the INS *Arihant*. As per an article published in the *Dawn* newspaper in May 2016, the development of this submarine and missile system is considered an enhancement of threat from India by Pakistan's Strategic Plans Division (SPD). Pakistan's development of an SLCM, if true, will provide it with a second-strike capability, augmenting deterrence and related threats. China is also

19. 'Advanced Tracking System', a report published in the South China Morning Post, 22 March 2018

20. 'Trends in Nuclear Forces 2023', a report published by SIPRI

21. 'The Indian Ocean Waters Will Get Roiled with Babur-3', article by C. Bhasker, *Economic Times*, New Delhi, 21 January 2018

expected to supply eight Yuan class submarines to Pakistan, which will be SLBM-capable. When these submarines become available, they will boost Pakistan's nuclear capability significantly.

India's nuclear policy makers are carefully monitoring the situation as China continues to share nuclear technology with Pakistan. With an ever-evolving threat perception, India has had no choice but to remain outside the NPT to retain its sovereignty and options for defence. It also must maintain nuclear deterrence in light of the strategic challenges posed by China and Pakistan. India has been scrupulous in ensuring that its development of nuclear weapons, materials, and related technology is safeguarded and that there is no possibility of illicit or accidental export to other countries. Owing to this responsible behaviour by India, the non-proliferation regime has not been punitive against the nation. In 1992, in an effort to expand the participation in NPT, the NSG decided to prohibit all nuclear trade with nations that had not agreed to the full scope of safeguards. This pre-condition required countries to join the NPT, including non-nuclear states, if they were to participate in nuclear commerce. This pre-condition left India at a great disadvantage as it was prohibited from purchasing nuclear ores from the members of the NSG. India has, however, been able to meet its requirement of ores through friendly nations and indigenous production. To recall, the NPT came into being on 1 July 1968, but it became effective on 7 March 1970, with 190 nations becoming its members. This treaty denied non-nuclear states the right to acquire nuclear weapons. India's PNE was conducted on 18 May 1974. The NSG was founded soon thereafter in May 1974, in response to India's PNE. On 6 September 2008, the NSG granted India a waiver from its guidelines that require international safeguards as a condition for nuclear trade. This gives India access to low-cost, clean energy, which is useful for reducing emissions from fossil fuels and tackling air pollution. India, for various reasons, did join the MTCR.

As mentioned earlier, Pakistan has continued to strengthen its nuclear capability and delivery means. Summarized below are its estimated weapon systems and means of delivery.

Land Systems

Over time, Pakistan has been able to develop a variety of missile systems with ranges of up to 2,750 km. Some of these are propelled by solid fuel, and some by liquid fuel. Technology for these has been received from China, Iran, and North Korea. A summary of the weapons is given in Annexure 3.

Annexure 3

Pakistan's Missile Systems			
Missile	**Range**	**Maximum Payload**	**Introduced In Service**
Hatf 1	170–100 km	500 kg	1992
Hatf 2 (Abdali) (probably nuclear-tipped)	200 km	200–400 kg	2015
Hatf 3 (Ghaznavi)	290 km	700 kg	2004
Hatf 4 (Shaheen)	750 km	1,500 kg	2004
Hatf 9 (Nasr) (under development)	60 km		
Hatf 5 (Ghauri 1)	1,500 km	100 kg	2009
Ghauri 2	1,800 km	not known	
Ababeel	2,200 km	not known	
Hatf 6 (Shaheen 2)	2,500 km	10,00 kg	2014
Shaheen 3	27,500 km	1,500 kg	
Hatf 8 (Ra'ad) (air-to-surface, under development	350 km		

source: SIPRI

Notes

1. It is not known whether all the above inventory is nuclear-tipped.
2. 'Hatf' is an Arabic word which means 'target or aim point'.

Air Systems

In the initial stages, while Pakistan was acquiring missile technology, it had developed the means to carry nuclear weapons on board fighter bomber aircraft, to be tossed onto an area target. Two squadrons of aircraft were prepared for this purpose. These squadrons of F-16 fighters were acquired from the US. It is known that Pakistan had formally asked the US whether they could carry out modifications to make their F-16s nuclear-capable. The US had reportedly given Israel permission to modify its F-16 aircraft. Similarly, it is presumed, that they may also have consented to Pakistan's request. The JF-17 fighter was also procured by Pakistan from China. Pakistan assembles these fighter aircraft at their Kamra Aeronautical Complex. They are originally of Russian Mikoyan design, a first-generation fighter aircraft. Two squadrons of these had been modified to carry nuclear weapons, namely 16 Squadron Black Panthers and 26 Squadron Black Spiders. Pakistan had also modified Mirage III fighters of French origin to carry air-launched cruise missiles (ALCM), namely Hatf 8 (Ra'ad).

Sea Systems

Pakistan has developed a seaboard variant of Hatf 7 (Babur), which was initially only a land-launched cruise missile. In addition, Pakistan may be working to tip C-802 and C-803 anti-ship missiles with plutonium warheads. It is not known whether research is ongoing on other sea-based weapon systems. Pakistan had announced plans to build its own nuclear submarine in 2012. It was assessed that it would take an estimated eight to ten years for a project of this nature to be completed after it is launched, if adequate technology and funds are available and with no roadblocks.

As already mentioned, with the ranges shown in Annexure 3, the Pakistani missiles cannot reach Israel, since it is likely out of range for the present. This is a temporary reassurance to Israel, whom Pakistan considers an enemy, albeit purely on religious grounds. Pakistan, however, can arm inimical organizations with missiles, in Israel's neighbourhood, thereby augmenting the threat to the country.

Pakistan's deterrence capability thus far caters mostly to India. In comparison, the Indian systems are designed for longer ranges and can cover the whole of China, the Middle East, and parts of East Asia. Details of Indian Missile systems are given in Annexure 4.

Annexure 4

India's Missile Systems			
Missile	Range	Payload	Introduced
Short Range			
Prithvi-I	150 km	500 kg	1994

Prithvi-II	250 km	100 kg	2004
Prithvi-III	250 km	500 kg	
	350 km	100 kg	
	750 km	350 kg	
Medium Range			
Agni-I	750/1,200 km	1,500 kg	
Agni-II	2,000/3,500 km	1,500/2500 kg	
Agni-III	3,500/4,000 km	2000 kg	2011
Intermediate Range			
Agni-IV	4,000/4,500 km	1,500/2000 kg	tested
Agni-V	5,500/8,000 km	1,500/2000 kg	tested
Inter-Continental			
Agni-VI	8,000/10,000 km		under development
Cruise			
Brahmos	300 km	300/450 kg	in service under development tested
Nirbhay	10,00/1500 km		
Shaurya	Hybrid Cruise Missile	not known	

Notes

1. SIPRI states that the availability of reliable information on nuclear arsenals and capabilities of nuclear-armed states varies considerably.
2. Discussion on a treaty called 'The Treaty on the Prohibition of Nuclear Weapons (TPNW)' was opened for negotiations under a mandate of the UN General Assembly at the end of 2016. The ultimate aim of this treaty was complete nuclear disarmament.

Command and Control of Nuclear Forces

When General Musharraf was President, Pakistan had established a proper hierarchy of checks and controls over its nuclear weapons. The apex body in Pakistan that makes decisions about the employment and posturing of nuclear weapons is the National Command Authority (NCA). The chairman of this body is the President and nuclear force planning is done by the NCA. The NCA has two wings: the Employment Control Committee (ECC) and the Development Control Committee (DCC). The ECC has the foreign and defence ministers as deputy chairmen. This body defines the nuclear strategy and criteria for the employment of strategic forces. It also includes the three service chiefs of the Army, Navy, and Air Force as members. Its main functions are:

a. Review strategic threat perceptions.

b. Monitor the progress of weapon development. Decide on response to emerging threats.

c. Issue guidelines for effective command and control against accidental or unauthorized use of nuclear weapons.

d. Under the NCA, the SPD is responsible for the security and protection of the country's nuclear arsenal and establishments.

Details of the NCA are given in Annexure 5.

Annexure 5

National Command Authority, Pakistan

Chairman: President

Members: Prime Minister

Key Federal ministers

Military chiefs and senior scientists

↕

ECC ← SPD → DCC

Strategic Force Command: Army, Navy, Air Force

Source: *In the Line of Fire*, Pervez Musharraf

Note: The strategic forces command of the three military services have been delegated control over tactical nuclear weapons. It is not clear who will ultimately authorize their use and under what circumstances.

Pakistan has previously taken considerable actions to safeguard its nuclear assets to obviate the chances of any breach of security of these assets. The US had taken a role in this and assisted in the specialized training of personnel to provide necessary safeguards to Pakistan's nuclear establishments. Pakistan claims that its security measures are the best in the world. This claim may not be truthful as shown by events in May 2025 in Kirana area. Accidents, though, can happen just like they have happened in the US and in the erstwhile USSR. Anti-national activities generated by greed or radical zeal can be an internal threat. There are various reasons why the security of nuclear assets can be compromised. Some possibilities are as follows:

a. Terrorists may manage to acquire a complete weapon in connivance with the security establishment. Such a weapon will require storage, safety, triggering, and delivery means, which the terrorists will also need to organize.

b. Just as AQ Khan had done from URENCO, an employee could gradually smuggle enough material and data to sell nuclear designs and plans.

c. Fissile material and components could be taken away in a clandestine manner to make a nuclear weapon, if storage containers to house the bomb and a triggering device are also sourced. The miniaturization of warheads and weapons adds to this risk by making them more portable.

d. While marrying up nuclear devices with delivery means, triggers and controls the system can go awry unless stringent measures are adopted.

Despite its inimical attitude and constant threats, Pakistan has come to some understanding with India on nuclear matters. These measures are not well known as they tend to get obfuscated by more prominent worries about proliferation, terrorism, proxy war, disregard of international norms, repeated violation of treaties, and one-upmanship. The accords between India and Pakistan on nuclear matters that are of consequence are:

a. In 1991, India and Pakistan entered into an agreement not to attack each other's nuclear installations.

b. On 1 January 1996, India and Pakistan exchanged lists of their respective nuclear installations, which each side would not attack.

The agreement in this regard is being adhered to, and the list is updated on 1 January each year.

c. In February 1999, Prime Minister Atal Bihari Vajpayee and Prime Minister Nawaz Sharif signed the Lahore Declaration, in which they agreed to a bilateral moratorium on further nuclear weapon tests.

d. In 2004, a hotline was established between Delhi and Islamabad to warn each other of an accidental firing of missiles that could be mistaken for a nuclear attack.

e. In March 2005, an agreement was also signed between both countries that they would alert each other about any ballistic missile tests being conducted.

There is a hotline between the DGMOs of the Indian and Pakistan armies. In some instances, when contacted, the Pakistan Army has not answered this hotline, probably to stall or gain time or to figure out a suitable response, especially after a terrorist action by Pakistan on Indian soil. An additional hotline was established in 2004, as mentioned above, to convey information about accidental missile launches. This was done essentially to reduce the risk of war breaking out.

The above measures notwithstanding, no meaningful dialogue has ever taken place between India and Pakistan about sharing information on nuclear accidents and capping of nuclear capability or on mutual nuclear weapons limitations. India will continue to maintain in future negotiations that its capabilities need to expand to balance the increase in Chinese nuclear arsenal. India will also highlight its need to counter the cooperation between China and Pakistan in the field of technology, including weapon delivery means, sophisticated test equipment, stealth technology, offensive and defensive measures in cyber warfare, and help in conventional armaments. Similarly, China and Pakistan's assessment of India's capability will include the defence cooperation between India, the US, Israel, Russia, and the Quad.

India and Pakistan's nuclear missile inventories can reach each other's value targets within a maximum of five to ten minutes of launch. The distances to value targets from launch sites are short, and warning times are limited. In the existing hostile scenario, both countries must remain on alert and maintain surveillance to obtain early warning of such attacks. Any nuclear war in South Asia or, for that matter, anywhere in the world will have a larger adverse impact. Numerous assessments have been carried out by analysts for such a scenario as the effects of a nuclear explosion are long-lasting. In Japan, over seven decades after the nuclear attack by the US, even today, many babies and cattle are born with deformities in and around Hiroshima and Nagasaki. If India and Pakistan used their nuclear weapons, given the density of population in both countries, the damage would be long-term and probably devastate both countries. Radioactive fallout will steadily spread and permanently damage vast areas. With this sobering knowledge, India has clearly stated in its doctrine that it will not be the first to use nuclear weapons.

In a stark contrast between the leadership styles of India and Pakistan, the Indian polity has control over its Armed Forces whereas, in Pakistan, the Army controls the foreign and defence policies in their country. Pakistan's army has, perhaps, been delegated the authority to use tactical nuclear weapons and it is more than likely that the Army in Pakistan will never relinquish its supreme status. Meanwhile, India will continue to be haunted by the threat of terrorism and nuclear attacks by its inimical neighbour. Despite the original intent, these weapons of mass destruction have not deterred war and the use of terrorism as an instrument of state policy in this region. This Pandora's box cannot be closed, and their scourge is here to stay. Terrorism is discussed in the ensuing chapter.

CHAPTER 2

Psychological Factors and Terrorism

Psyche

The founder of Pakistan, Muhammad Ali Jinnah, gave a well-meaning and somewhat generic motto to his new country: 'Faith, Unity, Discipline'. On 11 August 1947, he addressed the Constituent Assembly of the future State of Pakistan and stated, as quoted in the Independence Day supplement of the *Dawn* newspaper published from Karachi on 14 August 1947, 'You are free; you are free to go to your temples, you are free to go to your mosques or any other place of worship in this State of Pakistan. You may belong to any religion or caste or creed – that has nothing to do with the business of the State. Now I think... you will find that in course of time, Hindus would cease to be Hindus and Muslims would cease to be Muslims, not in the religious sense, because that is the personal faith of each individual, but in the political sense as citizens of the State'.[1, 2]

With this public statement, after the partition of India, Jinnah, perhaps, expected India and Pakistan to settle into a peaceful relationship as should exist between two good neighbours such as the US and Canada. Even Mahatma Gandhi had expressed that India should treat Pakistan as a member of the family setting up a new home. Despite these secular

1. *No Exit from Pakistan: America's Tortured Relationship with Islamabad* by Daniel Markey, pp 49

2. *The Struggle for Pakistan* by Ayesha Jalal, pp 53

thoughts and Gandhi's expectations, the divisive and hate ridden manner in which the partition of India took place, laid the foundation for an intractable and enduring rivalry between India and Pakistan. Subsequent statements made by Jinnah, while addressing various forums, were at variance with his initial message and, as such, created doubts about his intent and sincerity. After his death on 11 September 1948, Pakistan has not demonstrated any will to uphold the ideals of Jinnah's initial address to the citizens of the country.

At the time of Independence, the non-Muslim population in Pakistan was 24 per cent. This included Hindus, Christians, Sikhs, Sindhis, Parsis, and various other sects of non-Islamic minorities. In 2019, the population of Hindu and other minorities in Pakistan was assessed to be between 1–2 per cent. What has become of the other 22/23 per cent Hindus and other minorities? Some are known to have migrated to India during and in the wake of the Indo-Pakistan wars; some of them converted to Islam, and others cannot be accounted for. Jinnah's words that Hindus will not remain Hindus have become an ironic reality.

The followers of Islam worldwide, are 1.9 billion or about 24.1 per cent of the world's population. In this population, an estimated 7 per cent are hardcore Islamic radicals, and another 25 per cent are in immediate contact with the hardliners because of familial ties, fear of reprisals, religious tenets, and other relationships influenced by radicals. The radicals are sometimes also called jihadis, those who wage war in the name of Islam. Some of these are also referred to as Islamic terrorists. Despite their common religion Muslim blood is being shed in internecine conflicts in many areas of Africa, the Middle East, and Southeast Asia. The jihadis believe that Islam is under threat and must be defended at any cost. Anyone not supportive of their beliefs is not considered a true Muslim, is an infidel, and hence the enemy. These radicals believe that Muslims have been subjugated in various parts of the world. This is their motivating factor for jihad and for liberating the subjugated. They believe that only the true devout Muslims are meant to rule the world, and the world must be subservient to them. In a way this kind of theocracy aims at gaining power, wealth and dominance. In the words of Jinnah, Pakistan, founded as a modern democracy for Muslims and non-Muslims alike, was to be the moderate face of Islam. This has not turned out to be true, as Pakistan has discriminatory laws against minorities. The vanishing Hindu and Sikh population and violence against Christians prove this. Even the Shia and Ahmadiyya populations within Pakistan are being subjected to sectarian violence.

Various analysts and leaders voice strong reminders that the religion of Islam does not in fact encourage violence. A few voices articulate these thoughts, including from nations with a majority Islamic population. These peaceful exhortations however do not mask the more violent face of Islam that is brought forth every time there is a terrorist attack perpetrated by radical Islamists. Today, the proliferation of terrorism and extreme religious beliefs are of concern worldwide. It has become apparent that countries such as Afghanistan and Pakistan propagate extremist ideology and have nurtured extremist groups to enforce it. Since India has been repeatedly subjected to terrorism, this is of grave concern and relevance to India. After over seven decades of independence, four wars with India, separation of its eastern wing, loss of several thousands of lives, and massive expenditure on its Armed Forces, Pakistan has achieved little and made negligible gains from its unrelenting terrorism against India. Terrorist groups such as LeT, JeM, Hizbul Mujahideen (HM), and others were raised and are supported by Pakistan as they continue to carry the sub-conventional war into India and spread their ideology and violence from safe havens in Pakistan. The Taliban and other terrorist groups also brought the sub-conventional war into Afghanistan. Al Qaeda, under the leadership of Osama bin Laden carried out terrorist attacks on US assets in various parts of the world, including in the USA. As is well known, bin Laden was living in Pakistan when he was finally tracked down. He was a known and most wanted terrorist and Pakistan knowingly provided him safe haven. His son Hamza bin Laden is now working to strengthen Al Qaeda in Afghanistan. Another terrorist group that has gained prominence is the Islamic State of Iraq and the Levant (ISIS). It is active in various parts of the world including Afghanistan and finds support in Pakistan. Clearly, the involvement of Pakistan is a theme that is repeated in all the above instances.

With serious differences within the religion of Islam, its teachings have not been able to curb the ethnic divide within Pakistan. The Muslims who migrated from India to Pakistan are known as Muhajirs or immigrants. Even today they are treated as inferior by the resident population. In contrast, the Muslims who stayed on in India, comprising approximately 14 per cent of India's population, the second largest in the world not so long ago, have had a much more peaceful and progressive life of freedom and are largely assimilated in society. In the history of the Indian subcontinent, there have been various invasions from the Northwest (NW), over many centuries. The earliest Muslim invasion was in 712 CE when Muhammad bin Qasim, a general from the Umayyad Dynasty in Saudi Arabia, fought the first war with Raja Dhir of Sindh, a Hindu king. For many centuries, the invasions continued intermittently. The main aims of the invasions were to raid and plunder riches from India, forcibly convert people to Islam, desecrate and destroy places of worship, and overall, subjugate the population.

Over time, the Islamic invaders knew the advantages of conquering parts of India to establish their rule. The Mughals were the last of the dynasties that ruled parts of India. The Mughal Dynasty was established by Zahir-ud-din Babur and lasted till the eighteenth century. Over the extensive period of their rule, the Mughals and other Muslim invaders were unable to take control over the entire subcontinent. Strong opposition by Indian states ruled by Hindu kings thwarted their attempts to expand their area of control. Some rulers did align their realms with the invaders due to their own reasons. However, some strong Jat, Marathas, Rajput, and Sikhs rulers extended and maintained their princely states over large parts of India even during the Mughal rule. Unfortunately, these rulers were parochial and did not unite to defeat the aggressions from the NW or to contend with the British who ruled India after the Mughals. India was fractured by the ruthless will of the invaders over several centuries.

In Pakistan some have the skewed belief that their country is a successor of the millennia-old Muslim rule in India. The Mughal empire plays a significant role in this thinking and in the history-books taught in Pakistan's schools. As a country created on the basis of religion, Pakistan zealously protects and proliferates Islam. It is constantly gravitating towards a more aggressive and radical form of Islam and some of the Pakistani population, have even declared allegiance to ISIS. These affiliations are growing even in neighbouring Afghanistan as well. ISIS is targeting Shia and other minorities with impunity. This is even though the Taliban has regained power in Afghanistan.

Pakistan struggles with internal strife in various regions of the country. It has not been able to bring the Federally Administered Tribal Areas (FATA) under the control of their central government. These areas have been merged into the province of Khyber Pakhtunkhwa. An estimated 3.7 million refugees from Afghanistan had made this area their home, and efforts are now on to ensure their repatriation to Afghanistan. The Tehreek e Taliban Pakistan (TPP) is a militant group that has been formed by dissident jihadis to create terror inside the Pakistani State. In February 2023, they led a suicide attack on a mosque in Peshawar, inside a secure area manned by police. In this attack, 101 people were killed and many more injured, highlighting that internal terrorism now haunts Pakistan. The Baluchis and Pashtuns are split between Afghanistan, Iran and Pakistan. These tribes are rebellious with nationalistic ambitions, and even Sindh has simmering discontent as it desires an independent state called Sindhudesh. The Baluch Liberation Army has been more active than others and resorts to multiple attacks against Pakistan's forces on a regular basis. The radical elements have slowly and steadily made inroads into Pakistan communities. While facing this growing internal turmoil, Pakistan still continues to nurture terrorist groups as proxies for extremism.

Pakistan is a democracy, and elections are held at the provincial and federal levels from time to time. The country also has a written constitution. However, elected governments have proven to be self-serving and led by politicians who have acquired wealth disproportionate to their positions and earnings. Elected governments in Pakistan also must contend with the guardians of Islamic tenets, the Ulama, who intervene in the functioning of the government. The Ulama are usually propped up by one political party or another to garner their support and to appease them. To add to the power struggles, the Pakistan Army has steadily become a power center, as it takes advantage of the tenuous political situation. The Pakistan Army maintains a hold on the country's foreign and defence policies and ensures a disproportionate allocation of the GDP for itself.

As a society, Pakistan does have an educated and progressive middle class. With liberal religious beliefs these citizens aspire towards a prevailing peace and for the country to be led towards development and progress. However, successive governments in Pakistan have failed to meet these aspirations, including their hopes of a life secure from internal threats. The country's police force is known to be corrupt, heavy-handed and often ineffective. Their courts are similarly corrupt and partisan, and in some areas, such as the Swat district of Khyber Pakhtunkhwa province, Sharia law had been enforced. Given the chaotic state of the administration, the radicals, warlords, and corrupt government officials have maintained their hold over ordinary citizens. This complicated reality does not hold promise for a future that is progressive or peaceful.

Partisanship and Ethnic Divide

During the vast and complicated history of India, the Muslim rulers were not able to convert the majority of Hindus to Islam. A few benevolent Muslim rulers did not force conversions but instead learned from the customs of other religions or followed a more secular style of governance. All of these influences make India what it is today – a mix of culture and history percolating down from ancient times. With a shared history, the people of India and Pakistan are in fact not dissimilar in their heritage. The people of Pakistan are also a product of the teachings of the ancient Hindu texts, the Vedas and Puranas. Their ancestors also lived through the Maurya Dynasty, a Hindu empire which extended from Afghanistan and beyond to present day Myanmar. Hindu monuments found as far away as Baku on the Caspian Sea are evidence of this pervasive dynasty. People from both countries still have common surnames, speak a similar language, have customs, food, arts and culture that overlap and are indicative of their shared ancestry and heritage. In fact, most Pakistanis have more in common with an Indian than with an Arab, Turk or Persian, except for their religion. Tragically, the divisions that exist today surmount these intrinsic similarities.

An abridged account of reasons that contributed to the establishment of Pakistan as a separate country is essential to understand the background of the inimical nature of the relationship between India and Pakistan. Consequent to 1857, the First War of Independence, also called by the British as the Sepoy Mutiny, the Indian population began seeking freedom and self-governance. For the British, however, India was the 'Jewel in the Crown', a key part of its colonial empire. After the mutiny of 1857, India was converted to a garrison state. Approximately 40–50 per cent of revenue was spent on expanding and maintaining the military and the rest on running the administration, famine relief, transport, irrigation projects, and education. India bore the yoke of an undisguised dictatorship by the British, who treated Indians as coloured people who were inferior and only worthy of scorn and disrespect. The British were arrogant, self-serving, and demonstrated no sense of responsibility toward the indigenous population. Over their 200-year rule, the British deliberately ensured that Indians remained illiterate and poor. Under their rule the Indian population was gripped with hunger and neglect and was subject to what can be called a colonial holocaust.[3]

The world is aware of the holocaust suffered by the Jews in Germany and Poland but is, perhaps, unaware that under British rule, Indians were also

3. *Crusade and Jihad* by William R. Polk, pp 248-249

subjected to discrimination, poverty and deaths in the millions over a long period of time. There were 24 famines in the period that India was under British rule. During this period, one out of ten Indians starved to death out of a population of 240 million. At the time of independence, only about 3-4 per cent of the population of India could read and write, of which only one-fourth could read and write English. During their rule over India, the British took away immense wealth and natural resources from the country. They exported raw materials from India to make manufactured goods in Britain and exported these products back to India and elsewhere, making huge profits. Any infrastructure they created was largely for the ease of governance and to support the war effort. The local population enjoyed minimal benefits from the revenue generated off their backs.

India provided a million and a half troops in the First War and two and a half million troops in the Second World War to fight for the British and their sovereignty. The British were forced to take a softer view towards Indian political affairs during the first World War as Britain was vulnerable and desperately needed Indian troops to blunt the German offensive into Belgium and northern France. Out of the million and a half Indian troops deployed in the Great War, over 50,000 were killed and over 75,000 wounded. They fought in Flanders, where British troops were heavily outnumbered by Germans, in Ypres, Loos, and Nouveau Chappelle. While the wars were fought overseas, millions of Indians at home had to endure near starvation and famine as food shortages occurred, being driven by wartime exports and droughts. Oblivious to their plight, the King of England at that time, George V, exhorted Indians to fight for the Crown in the Great War. On 23 August 1914, he stated, 'I look to all my Indian soldiers to uphold the *izzat* (honour) of the British Raj against an aggressive enemy. I know with what readiness my brave and loyal Indian soldiers are prepared to fulfil this sacred trust on the field of battle shoulder to shoulder with their comrades from all parts of the Empire. Rest assured that you will always be in my thoughts and prayers. I bid you to go forward and add fresh luster to the glorious achievements and noble traditions of courage and chivalry of my Indian Army, whose honour and fame are in your hands.'[4]

After the end of World War I, the British Prime Minister, David Lloyd George, referred to the Indian Army soldiers and stated in the British Parliament, 'We owe them a great debt'. The contributions of the Indian

4. An article published in the *Vancouver Sun*, British Columbia, Canada on 10 November 2018

Armed Forces in the two world wars are still not fully known and certainly not given due recognition by Britain to this day. These contributions are, however, proven by the graves of Indian soldiers maintained by the Commonwealth War Graves Commission in various parts of the world. India contributes to the yearly budget of this Commission till today. This notwithstanding, it was under the aegis of the British that the divisive partition of India was enacted. A brutal partition of a peaceful nation was the fate of the 'Jewel in the Crown.'

The British came to India as traders along with other seafaring European nations. They established the British East India Company, which steadily expanded and grew in strength with a mercenary force and emerged as an entity that steadily established its rule over parts of India when the Mughal empire's rule was waning. The last Mughal rulers failed to provide satisfactory governance, as a result of the competition for the throne within their dynasty. The latter part of the Mughal Dynasty was led by debauched rulers who lacked moral authority. Aurangzeb (1658–1707) was the last strong ruler, and Bahadur Shah II (1837–1857) was the last Mughal ruler. After the death of Aurangzeb, the Mughals steadily lost power over the regions they once ruled. As mentioned earlier, at that time India was not united as a nation. In fact, it was divided and led by ruler of various princely states. For the British East India Company, this was their opportunity to gain control over a fragmented country. They spread their influence in India, especially after the so-called Battle of Plassey on 23 June 1757. These supposedly accurate historical accounts are whitewashed by Britain's version of events; hence they are 'so-called'. Robert Clive and his much-touted victories at Plassey and Buxar were actually achieved through successful negotiations between the East India Company and Indian princes with the help of power brokers. These were not triumphs of arms and valour on the battlefield as the imperial propaganda later made them to be.[5] The British cleverly played princely Indian states against each other and, thus, steadily made them subservient. They posted resident advisors in the court of each princely state as monitors, slowly integrating themselves in the day-to-day functioning of these states. The gameplan of the British was always to divide and conquer and they were very successful at it. When they came into power, the British governed India with an iron hand and adopted the policy of divide and rule. They were entirely responsible for creating the conditions for partitioning India.

5. *Return of a King* by William Dalrymple, pp 25

India continued under the yoke of British rule for decades till the country and its citizens began to rise in protest, which led to the Indian Rebellion of 1857. At the same time, there was an awakening of Muslim interests in political affairs in India. Syed Ahmad Taqvi, a civilian clerk in the British administration in India, inspired the movement to generate separatist tendencies in the Muslim population. He was a devout Muslim and a Salafi. The War of Independence in 1857 made the British wary of local uprisings and they brought India directly under the Crown. A Viceroy was thereafter appointed to govern India. Syed Ahmad wrote a largely fabricated account of the reasons for the Sepoy Mutiny of 1857 to promote Muslim interests. His aim was to influence the British in their favour. The British awarded him a knighthood in 1869 for his loyalty to the Crown, an affiliation which he clearly demonstrated in his thinking and writings.

Under British rule, employment in government services was considered prestigious as there were very few other avenues of employment except for the Armed Forces. The Muslims were at a disadvantage, being more focused on religious learning, they were unable to compete for the limited employment opportunities because of a lack of higher education. An education commission was set up by the British in 1882, which came up with conclusions that favoured Muslims. The findings of the commission, supported by the educated-Muslim elite, encouraged their population to seek a separate path for themselves in the Indian milieu. The British formed the opinion that Hindus were seditious while Muslims were loyal to the Crown and hence acquiesced to Muslim demands, much to the chagrin of the rest of the population. Reservation was granted to Muslims in certain constituencies and in municipal and provincial councils. This led to a hardening of the communal fissure.

Thus, the British consciously divided their preferences within the Indian population – Muslims on one side and Hindus and the other religious beliefs, on the other. This fissure was created despite Queen Victoria's promise in 1858 that, 'Indians would be freely and impartially admitted to office in our service.' The divisive tactics of the British failed to quell the rising unrest in India. Six more major uprisings against British rule occurred after 1857. The British repressed the dissent with maximum and brutal force, paying no heed to the growing movement towards India's independence.

The Indian National Congress (INC), a broad-based political party, was founded in 1885 by Allan Octavian Hume, a retired British officer. He created the party as a platform for civic and political dialogue among educated Indians. The INC supported competitive examinations for securing positions in the Indian Civil Service and promoted equal opportunities for all Indians. In 1906, once again, Muslims leaders demanded further reservations and weightage in government service and even higher levels of reservations in representative bodies, more than the British had previously granted to Muslims. This was an attempt to increase Muslim representation from the district level to the governing Council of the Viceroy. The British accepted their recommendations, as they seemed to be pleased by the unwavering loyalty to the Crown displayed by Muslims. Reservations and weightage were granted formally in the Indian Council Act of 1909 and repeated in acts passed subsequently by the British Parliament in 1919 and 1937. They also set up political norms of having separate electorates for Hindus and Muslims. This undid whatever unity that was forged between Hindu and Muslim leaders in the First World War. Communal relationships started to become polarized, exacerbating the movement for separatism and freedom from British rule. Communal clashes were engineered by Muslim leaders to counter the growing popularity of the Congress, resulting in a widening fissure between the communities. The effort to divide and rule was working for the British.

In 1927, the British government sent Sir John Simon to work out constitutional reforms in India even as no Indian leader was allowed to participate in this commission. Indian political leaders, instead, convened a conference on their own to work out constitutional reforms for self-governance, which were to be articulated to the British. At this conference, Jinnah represented the Muslim League. He had understood that there would be considerable devolution of powers to Indian politicians by the British. He proposed that reservation and weightage be given to Muslims in a united confederation of India with more power to provinces and a weaker center. The proposal meant that districts and provinces with Muslim majority populations would have Muslim governance with the power to exercise a veto over the central government, which was likely to have a Hindu majority. The Congress had refused to accept Muslim communalism in the all-party conference based on the belief that all citizens of India, irrespective of their caste, creed, or religion, were equal. It was the Muslim League that evoked Muslim nationalism because it did not want a common nationhood with Hindus. In 1940, the Muslim League passed a resolution for a separate Muslim state in NW India.

As the opposition to British rule grew, in 1942, the Congress, led by Mahatma Gandhi, introduced the Quit India Movement. This was at a critical time globally, as Germany was threatening Britain with an invasion in the Second World War. The Muslim League did not support the Quit

India resolution. The British had unilaterally declared war on India's behalf, on the Axis powers and the country was forced to join the Second World War without any consultation with Indian political leaders. In response, the Congress organized a countrywide agitation against this decision. To quell this dissent and to thwart efforts towards independence, the British Prime Minister, Winston Churchill, ordered tens of thousands of Congress leaders to be imprisoned. Mahatma Gandhi and Jawaharlal Nehru were among those jailed till the end of the war. Jinnah, the leader of the Muslim League, was never imprisoned.

As stated earlier, 2.5 million Indian troops were deployed in the second world war to fight in North Africa, Europe, Asia, and the Middle East against the Axis Powers. This participation by Indian troops contributed greatly to the successful war effort. At that time, the Japanese had fought their way through Southeast Asia and had reached the borders of India in their campaign. The Indian and British troops were able to defeat the Japanese in the jungles of Manipur and Nagaland States and were successful in pushing them back into Burma. Approximately 87,000 Indian troops were killed in action in the war. Yet again, because of the diversion of food supplies for the war effort, about six million Indian citizens died of starvation. Field Marshal Claude Auchinleck, C-in-C of the Indian Army, asserted that Britain could not have succeeded in both world wars without the support of the Royal Indian Army. In addition to the military deployment, industrial materials and supplies from India formed a crucial logistics component of the British campaign against the Axis powers.

In 1946, after the war, elections were held in India under British auspices. Candidates of the Muslim League were elected to quite a few Muslim-majority constituencies. They reiterated their demand for greater autonomy to Muslim-majority provinces, with less power to the central government. The Congress once again rejected the proposal for reservation, and weightage for Muslims. It was promoting the ethos and spirit of one India, and its leadership intended to consolidate India into one nation for all citizens. Contrary to this, in August 1946 Jinnah declared a direct-action day by Muslims, demanding a separate country. Since the British had decided to leave India within a year, Jinnah used the opportunity to pressurize them to agree to a separate independent Muslim State. He already knew they were partial to the cause. Communal riots and strife were unleashed to mount the pressure, and India was torn apart on communal lines. The subcontinent was partitioned, and Pakistan was created as a separate country on 14 August 1947.

It is clear that the British were instrumental in creating the circumstances for the division of India. The divide was impossible to undo because they favoured Muslims outright and their systematic policy of divide and rule had caused indelible fractures in Indian society. A division of India was favorable to them as with Pakistan's creation they could retain their influence in the region. Victory over Germany in the Second World War was achieved with the massive participation of Indian and other allied troops and with the assistance and participation of the US. After the costly and devastating war, the British had effectively no finances to support the governance of dominions of their Empire. The pressures to grant freedom and independence to the dominions and colonies were far too strong to oppose and they finally quit India. When the British Raj ended in India in August 1947, they left the country in shambles, impoverished, and underdeveloped, with very few educational institutions, little infrastructure and industry. This was their payback to India, their prime dominion, which they reluctantly exited. The British plundered India and left the country with empty coffers and a complicated, divided and uncertain identity.

The degree of animosity displayed within India during partition never abated, and the divisiveness continues to this day. Pakistan's rallying point and the reason for its creation was Islam and a separate homeland for Indian Muslims. The unreasonable quest for political power and ambitions of the Muslim leaders, supported by the British caused the partition of India. Today, instead of a cohesive, prosperous Muslim nation, Pakistan is rife with divisive conflicts between different sects of Islam, differing religious beliefs, and sectarian conflict in various regions in the country. The Punjabis consider themselves the elite in Pakistan. Their step-brotherly treatment and disdain for other religious minorities, created a chasm with Bengalis, and led to East Pakistan breaking away to become the independent nation of Bangladesh. In the NWFP of Pakistan, Khan Abdul Gaffar Khan, known well as 'Frontier Gandhi', was the de facto leader of the Pashtun and a close friend of Mahatma Gandhi. Till the end, he was very vocal in sharing his belief that India should not be partitioned. But that was not to be.

In many parts of the developed world, religious tolerance together with quality and scientific education has contributed to progress in the lives of citizens and to flourishing economies. In Pakistan, tolerance of other faiths, progressive education and peaceful co existence with its neighbouring countries remain imbalanced equations. Since partition, Islamic education has proliferated in Pakistan with the aim of promoting nationalism. The Pakistani State has failed to further develop and expand the means of modern education commensurate to the growth in population. This has been partially responsible for the bourgeoning of religious seminaries throughout the country.

Madrasas and Growth of Terrorism

The madrasa is a seminary where religious teachings dominate the curriculum. Most madrasas teach Islamic subjects such as tafseer (interpretation of the Quran), hadith (sayings of prophet Muhammad), figh (Islamic law) and Arabic (language of the Quran). Some seminaries do supplement religious teachings with non-Islamic subjects such as logic, philosophy and mathematics. It is estimated that at the time of India's partition in 1947, there were 137 madrasas in Pakistan.[6] This number grew dramatically during and in the period following the rule of General Zia ul Haq. Estimates suggest that there are close to 40,000 such schools in Pakistan and in some parts of the country, madrasas outnumber the regular public schools. It would be safe to infer that some seminaries have proliferated with financial support from vested interests, and some are run as commercial enterprises by the Imams, or Muslim clerics. Many of these schools get direct financial assistance from Saudi Arabia and other Gulf states and perhaps, from rich donors overseas. At the madrasa, some of the teachings profess that Islam is threatened and it is the duty of every devout Muslim to protect the religion and take measures to ensure its predominance in the world. In some cases, the students are urged to protect Islam, promote war, terrorism, or encourage belligerence against non-Muslims. An estimated three million students graduate from madrasas in Pakistan each year, which is a significant number of young people. This proliferation of madrasas is known to exacerbate the jihadi culture and widen the chasm between the moderates and radicals as well as the educated and the illiterate. It also means a large portion of the population is growing up with no access to progressive, scientific education and their understanding of the world is based on the somewhat archaic teachings imparted at a madrasa.

It is known that the Pakistan Army and the ISI nurture and provide active support to jihadi/terrorist groups. Army recruitment depends on the available pool of manpower, including the large numbers of youth studying at madrasas. There are indications that radicalized youth from

6. Nasr, quoted in *The Warrior State: Pakistan in the Contemporary World* by T.V. Paul

madrasas are being recruited selectively into lower ranks in the Army. These young men fall within the age group for selection and meet the criteria of the minimum qualifications required for recruitment and military discipline and training make them professional soldiers, irrespective of their beliefs. Each jihadi organization is known to have its own seminary. The Haqqani network has one in Attock, and the LeT has one in Muridke. The JeM has one in Bhawalpur and a terrorist training centre in Balakot in Khyber Pakhtunkhwa. The HM has a training center at Mahmoona near Sialkot. These and other fringe terrorist organisations have established holding areas or launch pads in proximity to the LOC/IB for terrorists to be inducted into India. The TTP has its madrasa in Quetta in proximity to the corps HQ of the Pakistan Army.

The madrasas are an accepted norm in Pakistan and are entrenched in society. To be clear, all madrasas do not produce extremists. Some of them are affiliated with local mosques, which take care of and educate underprivileged children. The curriculum in such madrasas is liberal, but their teachings enforce a staunch obedience to the faith in the students. This is an alternative method of education, which is parochial and perhaps denies children basic modern-day education and a broader view of a globalized world.

Since September 11 in 2001, when terrorists flew passenger aircraft into the World Trade Center and the Pentagon in the US, terrorism has proliferated widely and has become a global phenomenon. One of the major reasons for this increase is that in some populous countries, a lot of young people have inadequate access to education and no skills to pursue a career. Without skills and training, this young and impressionable cohort has limited opportunities to aspire towards lives of prosperity. With poor employment prospects and, in some cases, a lack a purpose in life, these young people are easy targets for extremist indoctrination and are being recruited by terrorist organizations. Leaders who promote religious fundamentalism, in some cases, give these young individuals an avenue and a purpose in life, even if it is terrorism and an extremist ideology. As they get radicalized, these vulnerable young people are willing to sacrifice their lives for glory, for promised riches and a better life, which they are told will be achieved by becoming a jihadi.

Some other reasons for an impetus for terrorism in some countries are – indifferent and uninspiring leadership coupled with a poor system of governance. Societal challenges like feudal structure, corruption, dictatorship, autocratic governance, rampant unemployment, a lack of human rights and liberties, and no incentives to uplift individuals out of the mire of poverty, all serve to drag ordinary individuals into a desperate, extremist ideology. Regions with a predominantly Muslim population or its sects have seen extremist movements born because of displacement and territorial disputes. Gaza and Afghanistan are two such examples. The people of Palestine and the Gaza Strip have been under constant duress, because of which the Palestine Liberation Organization (PLO) and Hamas were raised. In Lebanon, the Hezbollah or the 'Party of God' came into being for similar reasons. In the case of Pakistan, they raised the Islamic Movement of the Taliban and its affiliates to fight in Afghanistan and gave refuge to Al Qaeda. To create insurgency and separatism in India, Pakistan raised the LeT, JeM, HM, and other such groups. These groups have created affiliates within India to pursue the proxy war. In most circumstances where it is not possible to launch a major campaign against a more powerful adversary, subversive terrorist attacks and a sub-conventional are pursued.

Exacerbating the move towards radicalization is human displacement and refugee flow. Those caught within a conflict zone are forced to move to safer places, giving up their homes and hearth, and this is a psychological blow. The ordeal and suffering of the people in a conflict zone generates sympathy and, in some cases, this has led to war or armed intervention. Strife is also caused by armed and or political opposition to the authority in power or due to sectarian religious persecution. The reasons are many and complex and have no single solution.

Power struggles have dominated the daily lives of many in countries where long-running conflicts persist. Some opportunists and mercenaries who have no agenda beyond themselves, have joined insurgencies positioned as 'freedom fighters.' These are not freedom fighters; they are self-serving individuals and groups who cause havoc in the name of religion! General Musharraf, as Prime Minister of Pakistan, said terrorism and radicalization in the Indian State of J&K was akin to the independence movement generated by freedom fighters. This false narrative obfuscates the real issues. In actual fact, those who call themselves freedom fighters are carrying out extortion, looting, home invasions, ethnic cleansing, abduction for ransom, dishonouring local women, and committing murder. These people gain power from the guns they carry and have no value for human life. They make entire populations live under the threat of terror and force people to live in fear. Destabilizing a region and causing mayhem in a perfectly stable society, ethnic cleansing, and committing crimes against humanity cannot be recognized as the work of freedom fighters.

Minority groups have on occasion risen to fight and to stop extreme cruelty and unmitigated oppression. In such circumstances, world bodies such as the UN and international alliances have recognized their ordeal and offered help. However, conflicts continue across the world and any political grandstanding further exacerbates the situation.

In the state of J&K, India has always encouraged people of this region to live freely and integrate with the entire country. However, the Deep State of Pakistan has consistently perpetrated terror in Kashmir which is an intrinsic part of India. This interference by Pakistan is at the root of the long-running conflict between India and Pakistan, which is similar to the conflicts between Saudi Arabia and Iran, and Israel and Palestine. India and Pakistan's continuous impasse has ramifications for the entire region since Afghanistan, China, and Iran are bordering states and because both India and Pakistan possess nuclear arms. In contrast, the conflicts between Saudi Arabia and Iran, and Israel and Palestine generate international attention because of the religious denominations that come into play. For Israel, countering terrorist threats is a matter of survival since it is a Jewish country surrounded by Islamic nations. Besides the terrorist threat from Gaza, Israel is constantly on guard against Muslims who are radicalized and have low tolerance for other religious beliefs and in some cases even treat other sects of Islam as their enemies. As with the Taliban in Afghanistan, the practice of Wahabi Islam has led to regressive beliefs, a dislike of foreigners, and a need to oppress women.

In Kashmir, it was assessed by the Indian Home Ministry in 1999 that out of the 2,300 hardcore terrorists operating there, nearly 70 per cent were foreign mercenaries. The proof for this is that nearly half of the seven hundred or so militants killed in the Kashmir Valley were foreigners. A report published by J&K Police in January 2023 stated that 186 militants were killed in 2022, out of which 86 were foreigners. A further report suggests that about 150 trained terrorists had managed to ingress into J&K in 2024. After many encounters some of these would have been eliminated. Did these foreigners have any business in J&K? Were they visitors or tourists? Did they contribute anything to society there? With no indication of any legitimate reasons for these individuals to be in Kashmir, it was proven that they were terrorists sponsored by Pakistan. In the history of this region after India's partition, there is ample evidence that terrorists supported by Pakistan have inflicted indiscriminate violence against Indian civilians who are supportive of the democratic process of India. Extremists have also attacked Indian security personnel to create a climate of internal conflict, chaos, and insecurity.

Pakistan has demonstrated time and again that it has every intention of keeping the Kashmir issue alive, through every means possible.

In 1989–90, an ethnic cleansing of Kashmiri Pandits (Hindus) from the Kashmir Valley was perpetrated, a fact that is not well known. During this period, an approximate 600,000 Kashmiri Pandits who resided in the Kashmir Valley and adjoining mountain regions were either killed or forced to flee the area. They were made refugees in their own country and were subjected to the most heinous and staggering brutality by Islamist extremists. Thousands of Hindus were murdered by strangulation, hanging, impaling, branding, burning alive, lynching, bleeding to death, dismemberment, drowning, and other barbaric methods. They were practically ordered to leave the area, leave their young women behind, or be killed. Most of the Hindus left the state at that time. Some were killed others forced to become refugees. The region of the Kashmir Valley, which had a population of about seven million, now has 97 per cent Muslims. This brutal and merciless ethnic cleansing has converted a peaceful and progressive community to one that endures displacement, torture, and genocide. In doing so, the radical extremists wanted to obliterate knowledge of the historical past, of their ancestry, and of their connections to the rest of India.

The shocking events in the Kashmir Valley were covered in an exposé by *India Today*, a reputed media company. In their television broadcast on 27 May 2018, they provided proof of state sponsored terrorism by Pakistan-based terrorist groups with the aim of making it a profitable industry in the Kashmir Valley. It was reported in this broadcast that Syed Shah Geelani, erstwhile head of the separatist organization, the APHC, remained in contact with Hafiz Saeed, the head of LeT in Pakistan. Geelani received ₹700 million from Saeed to perpetrate anarchy in Kashmir. The terrorists had managed to destroy about fifty school buildings and set fire to railway train stations, a few local governing council (panchayat) offices, and some police stations. Stone throwers were hired and directed, primarily through social media, to come out in large numbers into the streets at short notice, to create mob violence and pelt stones at security forces/police patrols, vehicles, and even picquets. Bitta Karate, a known terrorist, and his gang were given ₹100/200 million to stir up unrest and hire stone throwers for six months.

Pakistan's claims that there is a separatist movement in Kashmir, is a mere facade. It is, in fact, mercenary violence generated through the efforts of the APHC, the agents of Pakistan and other terror groups paid for and directed by the ISI. The operation mentioned above was exposed by an

India Today journalist, Shuja ul Haq, who was operating undercover. His report proved that the Hurriyat is a hardcore terrorist proxy of Pakistan. This extremist group was raised to provide a united political direction to the Kashmiri separatists, but instead, it has degenerated into a terrorist faction.

The IB and the LOC require considerable deployment of Indian troops to prevent the ingress of terrorists from across this very active border. This deployment also serves to prevent any misadventure by the Pakistani Army. Within J&K, a large force comprising paramilitary forces, police, and the Army, are needed to prevent subversion, damage to essential services, government installations, and institutions and to make the lives of peace-loving citizens and visitors more secure. For India, this has been a concerted effort to bring about normalcy in the state. To outsiders, and perhaps the world at large, during the height of insurgency, the large number of armed forces deployed made the Kashmir Valley appear to be an area under siege. This perspective was myopic and did not explain the situation and the reason why security forces were present in such imposing numbers. India took necessary and appropriate actions to address the situation to secure a part of the country. More on Kashmir is discussed in a subsequent chapter.

Proxies and Wars

It is well known that a large number of militant organizations have been raised in Pakistan to wage sub-conventional wars in Afghanistan and India under the aegis of its intelligence agency the ISI. Zulfikar Ali Bhutto became the Foreign Minister of Pakistan in 1963, and it was then that the country began organizing dissident Afghans into militant groups to fight the pro-Soviet government in Afghanistan. At that time, in the border areas of NWFP and Baluchistan, the Pakistani government had limited control. The local government officials had their heyday, making money smuggling drugs, human trafficking, and gunrunning. At that time, the pro-Soviet government in Afghanistan had started raising the issue of Pashtunistan. The Pashtuns inhabit both sides of the IB and the Durand Line and share culture, language, and national identity. From October 1963 onwards, dissident Afghans were brought onto the payroll of the frontier constabulary in Pakistan. The more zealous were given commando training at the Pakistan Army's SSG training centre located at Cherat, 80 km from Peshawar. They were provided adequate funds, armed, and were motivated to influence public opinion in favour of Pakistan and against the Soviets. There was also a larger aim to all this. It was to orientate the population towards religious indoctrination. This idea was pursued by General Zia ul Haq from 1977 onwards when he deposed Bhutto in a coup and took over as the President of Pakistan. Stephen Cohen, in his book *The Idea of Pakistan*, states, 'For Zia, a more truly Islamic Pakistan would have the moral qualities to stand up to India since its scientists, generals, and politicians would be strengthened by Islam'. Pakistan had thereafter unleashed mayhem in Afghanistan and later pursued the same agenda in India through a proxy war.

In Afghanistan, Mohammad Daud, the first cousin of King Zahir Shah of Afghanistan, overthrew the King on 24 August 1973. He was of the view that the British had been unfair in demarcating the Durand Line border between his country and British India since it divided the Pashtun nation. As the Pashtuns were divided on either side of the border, demands for uniting the two parts and forming a greater Pashtunistan had commenced. To eradicate the threat of Afghanistan trying to wean away Pashtun-inhabited areas from Pakistan, Zulfikar Ali Bhutto and others felt that it was necessary to have a friendly government in Afghanistan. Pakistan was threatened because Mohammad Daud had started to obtain military aid, including armaments, equipment, training facilities, and some financial support from the erstwhile USSR. Western nations, after the end of the second world war, had decided to counter the expansionist policies of communist countries and the Cold War had become a reality. The USSR invaded Afghanistan in December 1979 and an existential threat was created towards the Arabian Sea through Pakistan. Millions of Afghans fled their country and sought refuge in Pakistan where camps were established to accommodate these refugees. Seminaries mushroomed in Pakistan, catering to the needs of the refugees, and also served as indoctrination and training centers for mujahids to be employed to strike back at the occupying Soviets in Afghanistan. In addition, religious mercenaries came to Pakistan from other countries to be trained and equipped to take part in the jihad. To augment the effort, the US decided to contest the occupation of Afghanistan by the USSR. Pakistan therefore emerged as a frontline state to prevent further expansion by the USSR.

Earlier in July 1977, on taking power in his hands, General Zia brought in Salafi / Wahabi preachers from Saudi Arabia to spread the more radical form of Sunni Islam in Pakistan. Concomitantly, the expansion of the mujahideen cadre, their training, and outfitting were started on a regular basis. Aided by Western powers, the plan was to embroil the USSR in an insurgency and eventually defeat them. Parallels can be drawn between US operations in Vietnam and their eventual disengagement from there. General Zia negotiated with the US and was able to extract $5 billion for training and equipping the mujahideen and an additional $5.7 billion of direct military assistance for his country to strengthen its Armed Forces. This aid was granted to make Pakistan strong enough to contend with any further offensive by the Soviets towards the Arabian Sea. Saudi Arabia decided to match the amount of aid provided by the US to augment the effort. A Joint HQ comprising the ISI and Saudi General Intelligence Division (GID) was established in Peshawar. Al Qaeda arrived in Pakistan and participated in the war and the US supported the war through its CIA. Their operatives had no direct contact with the mujahideen, it was the ISI who directed the ops and utilized the grants from the US. As the war progressed, the ISI established its operating bases inside Afghanistan to direct the war. The mujahideen became a potent force equipped with modern weapons. The relentless effort mounted by the Pakistan Army and its ISI through its proxies began to take a toll on the Soviet troops in Afghanistan. Eventually, the Soviets were forced to withdraw on account of mounting casualties and based on an assessment that the war could not be won. This was hailed as an achievement for sub-conventional warfare. It became a template for pursuing such wars in the future by Pakistan and others to engage and defeat an adversary and to achieve larger political or religious goals.

Under Zia's rule, Pakistan had an internecine proxy tussle initiated at the behest of Saudi Arabia, a Sunni nation, and Iran, a predominantly Shia country. Both these countries provided millions of dollars to raise Sunni and Shia seminaries in Pakistan to assist in strengthening their respective religious ideologues. All of this contributed to the Islamization of Pakistani society and the divisive animosity in the country's Islamic sects.

The US had limited interest in the area after the Soviet withdrawal from Afghanistan and therefore kept its distance. The mujahideen groups organized by Zia in Afghanistan eventually transformed into the Taliban. By 1979, the Taliban and Al Qaeda had some hundred thousand mujahideen who followed the Wahabi form of Islam. They had become a strong enough force to wage war to gain control of Afghanistan and Al Qaeda established a global network of terror in the coming years. Once the Soviets left, some foreign mercenaries went back to their respective countries to pursue jihad there. Some joined other terrorist groups outside Pakistan, and some stayed back in Pakistan either to settle down or to fight the proxy war against India. Pakistan had achieved success, and the ISI emerged as a force to be reckoned with.

Given the major role played by ISI, its evolution and rise to prominence needs to be analyzed and understood. In 1948, Major General Robert

Cawthorne, a British Army officer, created the ISI while serving as Deputy Chief of Staff in the Pakistan Army. At inception, the main role of the ISI was to gather intelligence. Ayub Khan, the second President of Pakistan expanded the role of the ISI in the 1950s, to include counterintelligence. During General Zia's regime, the ISI grew to 20,000 operatives and later to 40,000, with a budget of $1 billion. The ISI still maintains contact with the Saudi GID. With its pervading presence in Pakistan, the ISI has grown to be the strong arm of the Pakistan Army. Its roles are assessed to be the following:

a. Collect foreign and domestic intelligence.
b. Maintain surveillance over foreigners serving in or visiting Pakistan.
c. Manage and control the media.
d. Maintain dossiers on politicians.
e. Oversee political activities and manipulate elections.
f. Watch over and deter the activities of foreign diplomats accredited to Pakistan. Conduct surveillance over Pakistan's diplomats serving outside the country.
g. Intercept and monitor communications.
h. Conduct covert offensive operations.
i. Manage all militant groups supportive of the policies of the Army.
j. Establish intelligence agents, terrorist cells, and links in foreign countries to facilitate terrorist ops or direct ops there and participate in these if required.
k. Serve in Pakistan embassies/high commissions overseas to carry out intelligence functions.

The above roles of the ISI are not exhaustive in detail. The Chief of the ISI is supposed to report to the Prime Minister (PM) and is appointed by the PM by selecting a candidate from the serving Lt Gens of the Pakistan Army. This notwithstanding, in reality, the head of the ISI works for their COAS. The ISI is staffed by military officers drawn from the three services – Army, Navy, and Airforce, hence the name, Inter-Services Intelligence (ISI). The HQ of the ISI is in Aabpara, Islamabad. From what is known about this covert organization, its SS directorate is responsible for covert, hostile propaganda, and planning and directing offensive actions outside the country. One of the sections of this directorate deals with Kashmir and one with Afghanistan. The Joint Intelligence Bureau (JIB), one of its subsections, is devoted to conducting ops in India. It also has the Joint Signals Intelligence Bureau, which maintains communications with Kashmiri terrorists. One more subsection supports the International Sikh Youth Federation, and other separatist organizations abroad, and separatists in India.

The ISI, it was reported but not proven, had created three mints to produce counterfeit Indian currency notes. These counterfeits were purported to be circulated by terrorists infiltrating into India through Nepal and Bangladesh or a third country. Some reports suggested that large sums of fake Indian currency bills were sent to Dubai to be exchanged for hard currency. After demonetization of the ₹1,000 and ₹500 currency notes by the Government of India on 8 November 2016, this nefarious activity was brought to a halt. What is known for a fact is that a large number of counterfeit currency notes were in circulation in India prior to 2016. There are indications that Pakistan ISI was attempting to counterfeit the Indian ₹2,000 currency note but was unable to copy all of its security features. To eliminate a parallel economy that existed through cash transactions and black money, these bills had also been ordered to be demonetized by the Reserve Bank of India with effect from 1 September 2023. Since the entire organization of the ISI is super-covert, it can only be conjectured that it has interests in various other countries besides India and Afghanistan. The ISI does have a section dealing with Uyghur affairs and the Xinjiang Province in China. It is also known to direct the spread of Islamist ideology through its appointed Imams in mosques and affiliated seminaries, especially on the India-Nepal border within Nepal's Terai Region. Radical Islam is also being promoted in Bangladesh and Sri Lanka. The SS directorate as mentioned above, is the planner, selector, trainer and it maintains control over the execution of cross-border terrorism. They are in constant contact with sponsored militant organizations and their madrasas. ISI officers meet terrorist leaders, assign missions, coordinate their specialized training for the missions, equip the terrorists, and support specific operations. They had also provided the Taliban and Haqqani network with funds, vehicles, weapons, ammunition, explosives, communications, fuel, logistics, and aviation support, while they were operating in Afghanistan. It is also known that the ISI deputed a retired Army officer to supervise matters connected with Osama bin Laden. His role was independent of anyone else to prove deniability.[7]

In Pakistan, the ISI has been most active in ensuring that the civilian government toes the line of the Pakistan Army. Through large-scale bribery

7. *The Wrong Enemy: America in Afghanistan* by Carlotta Gall, pp 92

and payoffs, they ensure that their chosen candidates are elected to office. Entire communities, because of the bondage of a feudal society, are thus swayed and made to support the ISI's favoured candidates. This effort is organized by the political wing of the ISI. Quite simply, the ISI keeps an eye on the activities of the various political parties and stirs up trouble to their detriment if required. It has in the past devised and propogated false propaganda against candidates who were considered unsupportive of the Army. The M wing of the ISI controls and manipulates information that is projected internally and to the world. Those journalists who do not adhere to the directions of the ISI are threatened, coerced and, in some cases, have disappeared. Quetta, the provincial capital of Baluchistan, houses the HQ of Pakistan's Army XI Corps and their corps troops. This city also had the Taliban leadership as part of the Quetta Shura residing there. Journalists based there could have exposed the presence of the Taliban, Al Qaeda, and other jihadi outfits and highlighted their close relationship with the ISI, but they did not do so. When ops are being conducted to eliminate the threat of terrorists and other inimical groups, information about such ops by the US and allied forces in Afghanistan and by Indian Security Forces in Kashmir was being conveyed to the terrorists and jihadi organizations. The ISI itself supported these groups by providing them information in real-time, to evade capture and to employ improvised explosive devices (IEDs), ambushes, suicide attacks, and other hit-and-run tactics to cause casualties.

With the assistance of the ISI, the Pakistan Army has raised and deployed terrorist proxies ever since the country became independent on 14 August 1947. Soon after independence, demobilized soldiers were employed to train tribal jihadis from the NWFP. This was the invading force launched to annex J&K in October 1947. It was raised, directed, supervised, and officered by the Pakistan Army. The tribal invaders had reached the outskirts of Srinagar and its airfield at Badgam, both of which were under imminent threat. At this critical juncture, the Indian Army airlifted its units onto Badgam and were immediately launched into action to subvert the Pakistani invaders. With this offensive, Kashmir had its first experience of the onslaught of tribal invaders who resorted to looting, indiscriminate murder, rape, and abduction. Even the Catholic nuns at St Joseph Convent High School, Baramulla, were not spared. The tribal invaders were however, defeated, and the Pakistan Army was forced to fall back. While the ops to oust the Pakistanis from J&K were in progress, Prime Minister Nehru was advised by the Governor General of India, Lord Mountbatten, to refer Pakistan's aggression to the UN. The UN instituted an immediate ceasefire but failed to declare Pakistan as the aggressor. It is to be clearly understood that the entire princely state of J&K was now a part of India. Its ruler, Maharaja Hari Singh, had signed the papers of accession in favour of India. The accession was final and indisputable. Sheikh Abdullah, the only prominent political leader in Kashmir at that time, supported the accession to India. A copy of the Instrument of Accession signed by Maharaja Hari Singh of J&K and accepted by Mountbatten, the Governor General of India, is shown in Annexure 6.

Annexure 6

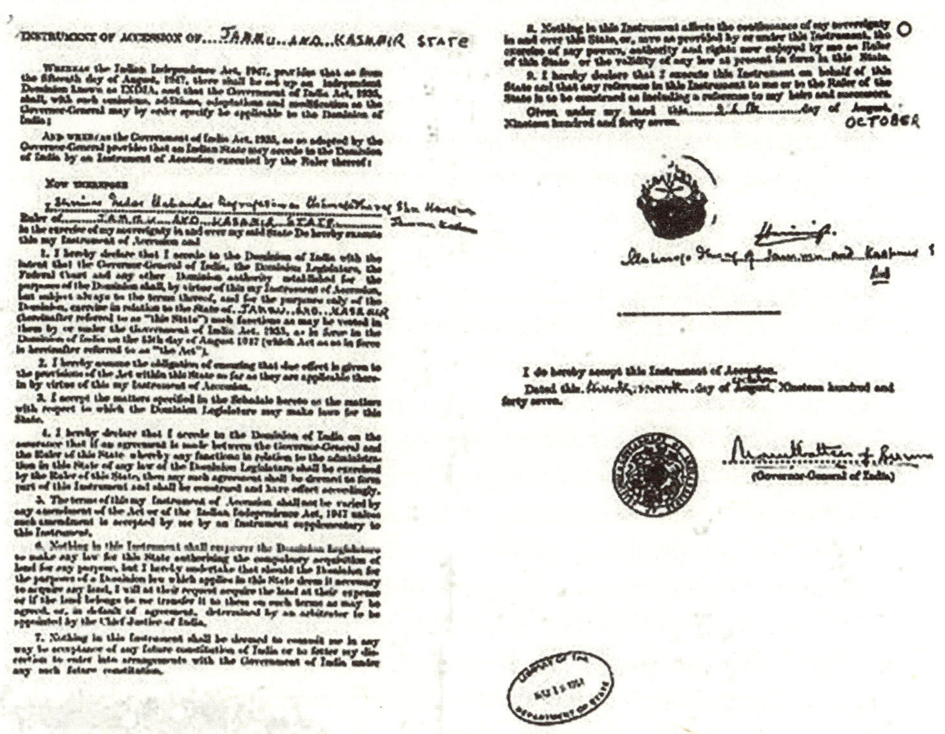

INSTRUMENT OF ACCESSION OF....JAMMU..AND..KASHMIR STATE

WHEREAS the Indian Independence Act, 1947, provides that as from the fifteenth day of August, 1947, there shall be set up an Independent Dominion known as INDIA, and that the Government of India Act, 1935, shall, with such omissions, additions, adaptations and modifications as the Governor-General may by order specify be applicable to the Dominion of India;

AND WHEREAS the Government of India Act, 1935, as so adapted by the Governor-General provides that an Indian State may accede to the Dominion of India by an Instrument of Accession executed by the Ruler thereof;

NOW THEREFORE

I [illegible] Ruler of ......JAMMU...AND...KASHMIR...STATE...... in the exercise of my sovereignty in and over my said State Do hereby execute this my Instrument of Accession and

1. I hereby declare that I accede to the Dominion of India with the intent that the Governor-General of India, the Dominion Legislature, the Federal Court and any other Dominion authority established for the purposes of the Dominion shall, by virtue of this my Instrument of Accession, but subject always to the terms thereof, and for the purposes only of the Dominion, exercise in relation to the State of ..JAMMU..AND..KASHMIR (hereinafter referred to as "this State") such functions as may be vested in them by or under the Government of India Act, 1935, as in force in the Dominion of India on the 15th day of August 1947 (which Act as so in force is hereinafter referred to as "the Act").

2. I hereby assume the obligation of ensuring that due effect is given to the provisions of the Act within this State so far as they are applicable therein by virtue of this my Instrument of Accession.

3. I accept the matters specified in the Schedule hereto as the matters with respect to which the Dominion Legislature may make laws for this State.

4. I hereby declare that I accede to the Dominion of India on the assurance that if an agreement is made between the Governor-General and the Ruler of this State whereby any functions in relation to the administration in this State of any law of the Dominion Legislature shall be exercised by the Ruler of this State, then any such agreement shall be deemed to form part of this Instrument and shall be construed and have effect accordingly.

5. The terms of this my Instrument of Accession shall not be varied by any amendment of the Act or of the Indian Independence Act, 1947 unless such amendment is accepted by me by an Instrument supplementary to this Instrument.

6. Nothing in this Instrument shall empower the Dominion Legislature to make any law for this State authorising the compulsory acquisition of land for any purpose, but I hereby undertake that should the Dominion for the purposes of a Dominion law which applies in this State deem it necessary to acquire any land, I will at their request acquire the land at their expense or if the land belongs to me transfer it to them on such terms as may be agreed, or, in default of agreement, determined by an arbitrator to be appointed by the Chief Justice of India.

7. Nothing in this Instrument shall be deemed to commit me in any way to acceptance of any future constitution of India or to fetter my discretion to enter into arrangements with the Government of India under any such future constitution.

8. Nothing in this Instrument affects the continuance of my sovereignty in and over this State, or, save as provided by or under this Instrument, the exercise of any powers, authority and rights now enjoyed by me as Ruler of this State or the validity of any law at present in force in this State.

9. I hereby declare that I execute this Instrument on behalf of this State and that any reference in this Instrument to me or to the Ruler of the State is to be construed as including a reference to my heirs and successors.

Given under my hand this......[illegible]......day of ~~August~~ OCTOBER Nineteen hundred and forty seven.

[illegible]

(Governor-General of India)

I do hereby accept this Instrument of Accession.

Dated this [illegible] day of ~~August~~ [illegible] Nineteen hundred and forty seven.

[illegible]

(Governor-General of India)

Instrument of Accession Jammu and Kashmir State

When the ceasefire was instituted by the UN on 15 August 1948, and was adopted on 5 January 1949, the incursion by the Pakistan Army had not been completely evicted from J&K. The area that Pakistan had illegally occupied in 1947–48, remains under their occupation to date. This is about a third of the entire area of J&K. This occupation is in defiance of the UN resolution which directed Pakistan to withdraw its Armed Forces, both regular and irregular from J&K, while allowing India to maintain minimal force within the state to maintain law and order and to enable a plebiscite to be held. More on the Kashmir issue is discussed in Chapter 3.

Thwarted in its first attempt, Pakistan took to the offensive once again in 1965. Irregular forces were employed to infiltrate into J&K and perpetrate a war with India. These irregular forces were deployed prior to conventional ops being launched. This action was code-named Op Gibraltar. Pakistan specifically chose this name from an op launched by Muslims from the port of Gibraltar into Spain. The Gibraltar plan was conceived under the patronage of Zulfikar Bhutto, the Foreign Minister of Pakistan, Aziz Ahmed, the Foreign Secretary, and GOC Pakistan Occupied Kashmir (POK) under the directions of their Army HQ. Pakistan calls the area of Kashmir that it occupied, Azad Kashmir. Whereas India refers to it as Pakistan Occupied Kashmir or POK. General Ayub Khan was the President of Pakistan at that time. He was convinced by Bhutto that the local population in Kashmir would support the operation and 7,000 to 10,000 specially trained jihadis were infiltrated into the Indian state of J&K. The outline of Pakistan's plan was that these insurgents would sabotage military installations and disrupt communications. This incursion was to be followed by the distribution of arms and ammunition to the dissident Kashmiri population who desired independence. It was envisaged that a guerrilla movement would then begin. It was also expected that counter offensive by Indian Security Forces to flush out the intruders would inevitably cause collateral damage and harassment of the civil population. This would alienate the population, and support for the infiltrators would grow. In their planning for this op, the Pakistani hierarchy, perhaps, assumed that India had not recouped sufficiently from the 1962 war with China and that India would not be able to widen such a conflict or even sustain it. Pakistan's assumptions were incorrect. Once again, a ceasefire was declared following diplomatic intervention by the Soviet Union, the US and UN. The conflict ended with a strategic and political defeat for Pakistan.

Being an ally of the US, Pakistan had received free grants, armaments, and munitions to strengthen Pakistan to counter an expansionist USSR. In armaments, it received new Patton tanks, anti-tank missiles, fighter aircraft, attack helicopters, and 155 mm guns. Pakistan, thus, had the misconception that its Army and air force had qualitative superiority in armament to offset India's quantitative superiority. These assumptions were ill-conceived and proved to have a disastrous outcome. The Indian Armed Forces took on the challenge posed by Pakistan in 1965 and within three days of the start of the war, Ayub Khan realized the folly. He called President Johnson of the US, seeking his intervention to institute a ceasefire with India. The population of J&K did not support the intruders and instead helped identify them. The Pakistanis had started conventional ops with pre-emptive strikes at a few Indian Air Force (IAF) bases. They launched an armoured attack on J&K, in the plains sector, in the area of Chamb-Jourian, with the aim of severing the road axis towards Poonch. This thrust failed to make headway and was blunted and beaten back. In the Uri Sector of J&K, the Indian Army captured the Haji Pir Pass through which the Uri-Poonch Road passes. They were poised to link up with Poonch, which was held by troops of the Indian Army's XVI Corps. India also expanded the war along its western border. Indian Army thrusts were launched toward Sialkot and across the Rajasthan border in the Barmer Sector. In Punjab, the Indian Army was threatening the city of Lahore within a few days of the commencement of war by Pakistan. A bridgehead was established by the 3rd Battalion of the Jat Regiment, commanded by Lt Col Desmond Hayde, across the Ichhogil Canal, an anti-tank obstacle, at a place called Burki. This was on the axis of Lahore. Pakistan was forced to withdraw troops from POK to deal with the Indian offensive in their Punjab Province. In a later statement, Pakistan's Chief of Air Staff at that time, Air Marshal Noor Khan said that 'The 1965 war was a self-inflicted wound. Within three days of declaring war on India, President of Pakistan, General Ayub Khan knew that a terrible mistake had been made. His plea to President Johnson of the US, requesting him to intervene, was made in the hope that the war would end honourably and without too much of a debacle for Pakistan.[8] President Johnson called Kosygin, President of the USSR, requesting him to use his influence with Prime Minister Shastri of India, urging him to call for a ceasefire.

The war in 1965 did end in a fiasco for Pakistan. A ceasefire came into effect after 17 days of fighting and by that time Pakistan had exhausted all means of continuing its offensive. In J&K, the Indian Army had captured areas of significant tactical importance. Most of the intruders were either captured or killed and just a few managed to escape to Pakistan. Neither the US nor China came to Pakistan's assistance, which was contrary to what Pakistan's leadership had expected. No international support was

8. *'Let's Forget about Kargil'*, an article by Air Marshal Noor Khan, published in *The Kasheer*, Muzaffarabad and reproduced in *Border Affairs*, Volume 1 Number 1, October–November 1999, New Delhi

forthcoming for Pakistan because of the unprovoked aggression that it had initiated. After the dust settled, Kosygin invited Lal Bahadur Shastri and Ayub Khan to Tashkent for a meeting in January 1966. At this meeting, the Tashkent Agreement was signed by the two rival leaders. In his magnanimity, Shastri agreed to return 15010 square kms of area captured by the Indian Army, restoring the borders/LOC to the status quo. During the meeting at Tashkent, in a conciliatory gesture, Shastri suggested to Ayub Khan that instead of going to war, their countries should be fighting poverty, hunger, and illiteracy. General Ayub Khan concurred with Shastri and a slim hope of peace emerged. However, tragically, Shastri passed away that night due to heart failure. Ayub Khan's gesture of lending his shoulder to Shastri's coffin when it was being carried to the IAF aircraft at Tashkent was a token of respect for the departed Prime Minister of India. With Shastri's passing, a possible bid at peace between India and Pakistan was summarily concluded.

Another momentous event in the fraught India-Pakistan history is the war of 1971. This was a very significant episode which resulted in the dismemberment of Pakistan as it led to East Pakistan becoming Bangladesh. This was a momentous event, a major embarrassment and bitter pill to swallow for the Pakistan leadership. The events that led up to the formation of the independent nation of Bangladesh are relevant here. In the months and years prior, the parochial and overbearing policies of the Pakistani military and politicians had begun to alienate the people of East Pakistan. The ruling Punjabi elites of West Pakistan always considered the Bangla population of East Pakistan as inferior and neglected this region of the country and the people who resided there. On 2 November 1970, when a deadly cyclone and tidal wave struck the coastal areas of India and East Pakistan, matters came to a head. In this natural disaster, 500,000 people perished, and there was considerable loss of livestock and property. Such massive losses due to natural disasters had never occurred in that part of the world. Despite the magnitude of the devastation, the response of the Yahya Khan government to this disaster was perfunctory, and hardly any aid was forthcoming for East Pakistan. At this vulnerable moment, the population of East Pakistan was disillusioned and felt abandoned.

Pakistan held national elections shortly after this, in December 1970. The National Awami League, the major political party in East Pakistan led by Mujibur Rahman, emerged as the winner with 160 seats in Pakistan's Constituent Assembly or Parliament. In West Pakistan, Zulfiqar Ali Bhutto's party, the Peoples Party of Pakistan (PPP) won 81 seats. Bhutto and the elites in West Pakistan who held the Bengalis of East Pakistan in disdain, were not ready to accept a Bengali as head of the government. They were definitely not ready to accept the popular Bangla leader Mujibur Rahman as their potential Prime Minister because they felt that he would have a conciliatory approach towards India and dilute Pakistan's bid for Kashmir. After the election, Bhutto visited East Pakistan and suggested to Mujibur Rahman that he should head the assembly for East Pakistan while Bhutto headed West Pakistan. This was unacceptable to Mujib and the Awami League. On Bhutto's advice, General Yahya Khan, the President, abrogated the elections and chose to suppress dissidence in the Bengali population. The Pakistan Army co-opted Jamaat-e-Islami (JeI), a radical group of West Pakistan, to enforce the dictates of their President and Commander in Chief (C-in-C). The Army and JeI resorted to the targeted killing of the intelligentsia in East Pakistan and inflicted extreme human rights violations. Indiscriminate killings, mass rape, looting, curfews, control of media, and blocking of communications resulted in ten million citizens fleeing to India as refugees. Mujibur Rahman was detained and put in jail in West Pakistan.

The repression that the population endured in East Pakistan was undeniably reprehensible. The Bengalis were dishonored and treated with brutality. The fracture created between the people of East and West Pakistan became untenable. India had to bear the burden of ten million refugees from East Pakistan with some help offered by other countries. As a result, an independence movement was born in the Bengali population of East Pakistan. They declared independence on 26 March 1971 and established a provisional government in Calcutta. They also organised themselves into the *Mukti Bahini*, a guerrilla resistance group in East Pakistan which consisted of members of the military, paramilitary and civilians. This movement was led by Bengali officers of the Pakistan Army who had defected and had crossed over to India. Indira Gandhi, the Prime Minister of India, travelled to major countries, including the US, giving detailed information on Pakistani atrocities against their Bengali population and highlighted the plight of the refugees. She sought help to manage the humanitarian crisis. Senator Edward Kennedy of the US visited the squalid refugee camps in India in August 1971 and saw their plight first hand. Having been pushed to the wall diplomatically, Pakistan declared war on India on 3 December 1971.

The outbreak of war began with pre-emptive strikes by Pakistan on Indian airfields. The Indian Navy had deployed on 3 December 1971 to isolate East Pakistan from the sea. The Indian Air Force (IAF) had established air supremacy over East Pakistan within 48 hours of the commencement of ops. With these advantages, the Pakistan Army's defeat was only a matter of time. In an op lasting only 13 days, the Pakistan Army was crushed, and Indian formations were closing in rapidly on Dhaka, the capital of East Pakistan. General SHFJ Manekshaw, the Indian Army Chief, through broadcasts on radio and television, implored the Pakistan Army to surrender or face dire consequences. As better sense prevailed, they did surrender, all 93,000 of them and India declared a ceasefire. A formal surrender ceremony was conducted in the Paltan Maidan in Dhaka. Lieutenant General AAK Niazi signed the document of surrender on behalf of General Yahya Khan and Pakistan and Lt Gen JS Aurora on behalf of India on 16 December 1971. The outcome of this offensive was a crushing blow for Pakistan. Their Air Force Chief at that time, Air Marshal Asghar Khan, acknowledged that, 'this was the darkest day in our history'.[9] After the surrender by Pakistan, the Army and the Government of India treated the Pakistani Prisoners of War (PPW) humanely, and as per the Geneva Convention. Indira Gandhi was gracious and considerate even as India celebrated its victory, and her diplomacy and decisive leadership solidified her place as a prominent world leader.

Politically and morally, the differences between West Pakistan, which was generally dominated by Punjabis, and East Pakistan, mainly Bengali, had reached a breaking point. Bangladesh emerged as a separate nation for the Bengalis as reconciliation was not possible. After a laudable victory, the Indian Forces withdrew from Bangladesh within a few months of the signing of the Shimla Agreement. The lessons that Pakistan learned from this ill-planned war and the carnage inflicted on the population of East Pakistan that resulted in their separation, have been extensively researched. However, the failure of the Pakistan Army after this fiasco was obscured by their leadership and so were the details of the origin of Bangladesh. Instead, the myth was propagated that India's role in the division of Pakistan was because India had not reconciled to the partition of 1947. This narrative was manifested to save face for the Pakistan Army after its major and embarrassing defeat in an offensive that it launched unilaterally. The propaganda machine in Pakistan has ensured that the uneducated

---

9. 'Pakistan's War for a Ceasefire', an article by Air Marshal Asghar Khan, published in *The Kaseer*, a daily newspaper of Muzzafarabad (POK) and reproduced in Border Affairs, Volume 1 Number1 1999, New Delhi

population in Pakistan still believe that East Pakistan broke away because of India's actions, through no fault of Pakistan. After the devastating loss in this war, Pakistan has endeavored to become stronger militarily and to achieve parity with India. The concepts of strategic depth and forward defence have evolved over time in the Pakistan Army. These now play a prominent role in the Pakistani military operations as they plan future aggressions against India.

Pakistan's Deep State

A Deep State is comprised of a country's powerful government service, bureaucrats, the military, and/or an intelligence agency to covertly pursue their specific aims and agenda. This term is conspiratorial and has clear, negative connotations. In a democratic form of government, administrative agencies provide continuity in policies and accordingly have their own planned mission and objectives. Based on this, budgetary allocations are made. These agencies work in concert with the policies evolved by political leaders. In Pakistan, a Deep State has existed for years. As stated by Shashi Tharoor, Member of Parliament (MP) in India and erstwhile Deputy Secretary-General of the UN, 'the Pakistan Army has a country and in contrast, India as a country has an Army'. Simply put, the Deep State in Pakistan exists to influence and control the policies of the legitimately elected government of the day.[10] It is evident that the powerful elites within the Pakistan Army dictate terms to the elected government of the day. This state of affairs exists even when the Pakistan Army does not hold the reins of power. Military leadership in the country has become so powerful that they are regularly consulted on defence, economic affairs, and foreign policies. Whenever Pakistani politicians or even the Prime Minister have attempted to exercise control over the Army, they have been forced to exit from office or backtrack. The existential threat of a military coup always looms large and instils fear in politicians. The ISI maintains dossiers on politicians, senior bureaucrats, and even officials in their own organizations. The information in the dossiers provides useful fodder for the media and the judiciary to slander and defame individuals when deemed appropriate. Over the years, this method of exposing corrupt individuals and criminals has created the impression in the minds of the public that politicians are

10. 'Trump and the Deep State', an article by Jon Michaels in *Foreign Affairs* September-October 2017

untrustworthy. Conversely, it is repeatedly proclaimed in various forums that only the Pakistan Army is trustworthy.

Wielding an unquestionable power, the Pakistan Army has traditionally been allocated a large slice of the national budget for its maintenance. This has been at the cost of other national priorities such as education, poverty alleviation, business development, and so on. Grants and military assistance coming from friendly nations are similarly absorbed by the Army. Pakistan has received financial aid, military hardware, and training assistance from the US over the years, as a signatory to anti-communism treaties. These grants from the US, those from Saudi Arabia and other Muslim nations, have largely kept the Pakistan economy afloat. Pakistan however uses most of this aid to strengthen its Armed Forces, build its nuclear arsenal, continue to challenge and bleed India, perpetrate strife and to enable a favourable dispensation in Afghanistan, and breed and maintain terrorist organizations that execute their designs worldwide. Military expenditure in Pakistan is shrouded in secrecy as there are no statements of expenditure or audits. It is reported that large sums are purloined by the military elite for self-aggrandizement, with no identifiable caps. The ISI ensures that no debates or discussions are conducted by politicians on the budget and the requirements of the armed forces. Civil agencies or elected politicians do not question the military about expenditure. If they did, formidable consequences hang over their heads like the Sword of Damocles.

To remain relevant and maintain its superiority, the Pakistan Army must maintain the impression that the country is at a perpetual state of war. A state of undeclared war with India must, therefore, always exist. To pursue its aim, the Line of Control (LOC) with India must be transgressed with one means or another and terrorist actions perpetrated from time to time to keep the situation alive. After Pakistan became a nuclear power, their Army has become even more belligerent. They force the elected leaders and media to resort to saber rattling as a stark reminder of the nuclear threat that their country poses. The Pakistan Army has unabashedly and disingenuously managed to depict make-believe victories after clear defeat in wars by India. The world acknowledges that Pakistan has repeatedly suffered defeat at the hands of India in the various wars launched by Pakistan. However, Pakistan's leadership, including that of the Army, have justified these defeats by propagating the notion that a status quo has been maintained.

The vested interests of the Pakistan Army have not allowed peace to be ushered in with India. Despite the defeats in various wars and their negative impacts on the country's economic and social prosperity, Pakistan continues to up the ante against India through clandestine hostilities. It is as if any improvement of relations will eliminate the benefits that accrue from highlighting India as an existential threat. Pakistan's continued threat perception has drawn the sympathy of oil-rich Islamic nations who have been willing to provide monetary support to prop up another Islamic country. Pakistan works this sympathy to its advantage by propagating the theory that if it is threatened, Islam is threatened.

In Pakistan the Deep State – the Army and the all-pervasive ISI, continue to maintain their hold on the country and an elected government holds very little sway. There are numerous examples of Pakistani politicians trying to gain control over the Pakistan Army. Benazir Bhutto made a few such attempts, but her government was dismissed by President Leghari at the behest of the Army. Nawaz Sharif tried to bridge the gap by appointing General Musharraf, as the COAS, but this out of turn promotion also failed. There was also a very audacious rebuke of the peace process by Pakistan that began in February 1999. In an attempt to normalize the strained relations between India and Pakistan, Prime Minister Vajpayee of India and Prime Minister Nawaz Sharif of Pakistan signed the Lahore Declaration after Vajpayee's visit to Pakistan. For India, the aim of this accord was to encourage an environment of mutual confidence. For Pakistan it was only a sham, conducted only for optics. The world is witness to the fact that soon after the signing of this agreement, paying no heed to its spirit and tenor, General Musharraf set in motion Pakistan army's intrusions into India, setting off the Kargil war.

Despite the duplicitous and overconfident attempt by Pakistan to attack India and capture Indian territory, the Kargil war was a disastrous failure for Pakistan and ended in their defeat. Pakistan's politics underwent a dramatic turn of events after the failure of the Kargil war, as the Army once again asserted itself. General Musharraf took over as the Chief Executive of Pakistan in a bloodless coup and Nawaz Sharif was jailed and tried for treason. With the influence of friendly countries, Nawaz Sharif escaped execution and was sent to exile in Saudi Arabia. Another failed attempt to rein in the Pakistan Army was made by Asif Ali Zardari, when he took over as President on 9 September 2008. In a conciliatory gesture, Zardari planned to send the ISI Chief, Lt Gen Shuja Pasha, to India after the terrorist attack in Mumbai on 26 November 2008. The news of this planned but secret trip somehow became public knowledge. It was flashed on TV and radio channels in Pakistan and highlighted with such poor optics, that the peacemaking trip was cancelled. In another instance, during a visit to

London, Prime Minister Gilani announced that the ISI would be placed under the Interior Ministry. Not amenable to this, the Army intervened, and Gilani had to reverse his decision. Some leaders like Imran Khan began their tenure as moderate leaders of the country. Khan did not last long and was ousted from his position as the Prime Minister for falling out with the then Army Chief, General Bajwa, after a no confidence vote in parliament. With no regard to the serious embarrassment that the country and the elected President and/or Prime Minister of Pakistan have endured in each of these instances, the Pakistan Army has reaffirmed its supremacy and reinforced that it cannot be dictated terms by any elected government or by bureaucrats.

Politicians who understand how the ISI and the Pakistan Army operate know that these organizations are draining large amounts of the country's budget and carry an undue influence on the polity. During the period when Ayub Khan, Yahya Khan, Zia ul Haq, and Pervez Musharraf were in power, a total of 33 years of military rule, the Army cultivated the support of influential civilians, including scholars, journalists, analysts and scientists, providing them selective access to Army institutions. These individuals were expected to highlight the positive features of the Army and project that it was a benign force. They were to emphasize the Army's importance in national life, and how it was contributing to National Security by dealing with external threats and internal strife. Those individuals who went against this policy were subjected to punitive measures, denied further privileges or their family members were threatened. In some cases, some of these individuals have vanished or were never heard of again.

The Army and ISI propaganda mills have also ensured that India was always declared the aggressor by Pakistan at the outset of each of the wars they have launched. They also always falsely projected that their military had the upper hand in the wars. After each war, when a ceasefire came into effect, the facts and any adverse coverage was ruthlessly curbed. After the Kargil War, Najam Sethi, a very senior and respected journalist and the Chief Editor of the *Friday Times* in Pakistan, had gone on record on YouTube to condemn the war and the Army for launching this most unnecessary intrusion across the LOC because of which Pakistan lost face across the world. He was arrested and jailed for his analysis, which was viewed as derogatory to their Army. As a journalist of repute, he was finally released on orders of the Supreme Court of Pakistan after he had undergone weeks of internment. Such acts of retribution bring out the ruthless nature of Pakistan's Deep State. In today's information age, this kind of reprisal is being exposed, and comments of mature journalists, such as Sethi, are now being conveyed over various social media platforms. This is a new dimension of opposition for the Deep State to contend with.

An examination of elections in Pakistan reveals how the army is an intrinsic part of the process. The Pakistan Army has steadily acquired the power to promote their candidates to win the general elections. Candidates opposing their policies are ignored by the media or maligned by information leaks and adverse publicity. The Army has even ensured that supporters of opposition candidates are detracted and even physically prevented from voting. There is vote-rigging, and ballot boxes are stolen. Irregularities and criticism of the election process are suppressed and not allowed to be broadcast. In the general elections in August 2018, Imran Khan and his party Pakistan Tehreek-e-Insaf (PTI), emerged as the winners with the largest number of seats. Some in the media attempted to examine how, in this election, Imran Khan's party was supported and backed by the Army, voting was orchestrated, and vote-rigging took place. This led to a complete blackout of media coverage being enforced on the subject. Then curiously, in the election in 2024 Imran Khan was jailed to prevent him from participating in the general elections. In stark contrast to this farcical election process in Pakistan, India has conducted many free and fair elections. In May-June 2024, it held the largest democratic election in the world and this marked contrast in politics has been highlighted by private media channels in Pakistan.

It is evident that the Pakistan Army is all pervasive and is inherently a part of fabric of society in the country. The Army has been able to establish itself as a corporate entity with its Fauji/Army Welfare Trust, Shaheen Foundation, and Baharia Foundation. The Army HQ uses these foundations ostensibly for the welfare and resettlement of retired officers and soldiers, an estimated three million of whom now own businesses. Major holdings of these foundations are in real estate, cement, fertilizers, oil, gas and agricultural industries. Land allotments are made to officers based on their rank on retirement and lower ranks are absorbed into business ventures. General officers and bureaucrats ensure their re-employment or re-settlement because of the power they wield. After retirement from the Army, many of them are now rich businessmen running successful enterprises. They have cultivated links with foreign and domestic companies and are often appointed to the board of directors.

For retired soldiers, the Army provides loans with favorable terms to purchase vehicles. Some of these retirees have created a large trucking enterprise for the transportation of goods, known as the National Logistics Cell. In times of operational requirements, these vehicles are pooled together to lift and mobilize the Army units and formations for war or for deployment to their op locations, thus serving a dual purpose. The Army runs many institutions, such as military schools, colleges, language institutes, and the National University of Science and Technology. The Fauji Foundation runs other educational and healthcare institutions. The Army Medical Corps runs many hospitals for serving and retired defence personnel and civilians. In this manner the Army certainly looks after its own and has become a corporate entity with its tentacles in all aspects of life.

An assessment of the Pakistan Army's full involvement in the country's affairs is difficult as their businesses are concealed, and there is no reliable avenue to gain an accurate insight. The civilian population has steadily become aware of the Army's business activities, which are projected as legitimate enterprises for rehabilitating Army personnel and as some of the Army's establishments also provide benefits to the civilian population. Educational institutions and hospitals are a few such examples. The Army ensures good relations with the banking sector, which is necessary for managing the funds of their various commercial ventures. It also establishes a benign image for itself by helping in disaster relief during floods, earthquakes, fires, and even during man-made crises such as bomb blasts. The Army is also employed in infrastructure development and protection of key installations. Undeniably, the Pakistan has become an immutable and inextricable part of the fabric of the country.

Security and Expansionism

Another cause for the disharmony that rose during the partition of India was that Jinnah felt that Pakistan was granted a smaller area than what he expected. In actual fact, the population ratio and area given to Pakistan was proportionately much larger than anticipated. Pakistan has since been a security-seeking state with an incessant, heightened threat perception and a need to expand its territory. Soon after gaining Independence, as early as the 1950s, a threat perception had developed in Pakistan that India would threaten its sovereignty. On the Western border, it had to deal with Afghanistan raking up the issue of Pashtunistan and a strong separatist movement of the Balouch.Afghanistan had often-articulated the intention of merging the Pashtun-inhabited areas of Pakistan into their country. This border dissent along with the existential threat from India were fears that were escalated by Pakistan's politicians and the Army. At the same time, its geographical location was exploited by Pakistan's leadership for politico-military gains. Pakistan became an ally of the US and other Western nations as a result of the Cold War and the threat of expansionist communist nations. As is well known, these alliances have proved useful to Pakistan in obtaining grants, aid and the means to strengthen its Armed Forces.

Conversely, India has been caught in a triangle of animosity with two of its neighbours, Pakistan and China. Pakistan's leaders have taken every opportunity to enhance its security through mutually beneficial treaties and agreements to try and to maintain an upper hand vis-à-vis India. As mentioned earlier, Pakistan signed a border agreement in 1963 with China and in a border settlement gave away the Shaksgam Valley. Pakistan and China have collaborated to maintain a combative relationship against India, as two adversaries. As discussed previously, China and Pakistan also had a mutually beneficial cooperation in developing nuclear weapons technology. Pakistan shrewdly articulated its anti-communist vitriol to elicit monetary assistance from the US and even requested $2 billion in aid in the mid-fifties, a very substantial sum at that time. In comparison, the US had allotted only $13 billion under the Marshal Plan for the reconstruction of Europe, devastated after World War II.

Pakistan's participation in the treaties of SEATO in 1954 and CENTO in 1955 led to it receiving military assistance to continually equip its Armed Forces. This aid was provided by Western powers to make Pakistan's Armed Forces ready to counter and resist any expansion by the USSR and China towards South Asia and the Arabian Sea. This support only emboldened Pakistan to pursue its expansionist policies against India. In 1959, the US gifted Pakistan twelve F-104 fighter aircraft in exchange for access to the Badaber Air Force Base at Sargodha near Peshawar. This base was utilized by the US for U-2 spy plane ops over the USSR. On 1 May 1960, when the U-2 plane flown by Major Gary Powers was shot down while flying a mission over Sverdlovsk, now in Ukraine, the USSR threatened Pakistan with airstrikes if the flights did not cease. Pakistan taking no accountability, responded that the US flights were flown from Peshawar without its knowledge or permission.

During the Second World War, the British Indian Army underwent a massive expansion. After the war, even though there was large-scale demobilization, at the time of the partition of India, the Army was still very large. Pakistan received one-sixth of the British Indian Army as its share. To justify the large strength of their Army, they had to engender a threat perception. The only threats that did exist at that time were the internal struggles of post-independence. The animosity that was generated at the time of India's partition could not be diffused by politicians in either of the two countries. Instead of abating this enmity and stabilizing the nation, the Pakistan Army utilised the situation and began training tribals from the NWFP and demobilized soldiers. The aim was to annex J&K by force.

With only rudimentary training, the Pakistan Army trained and deployed tribal irregulars to annex J&K. Their ops started in October 1947, just two months after Pakistan became an independent country. Mutinies were instigated in the J&K State Forces garrisons. With brutal intent, Hindus serving in the State Forces of J&K were overpowered and massacred in a heinous campaign by their own Muslim colleagues. Communal hatred was fueled with the intention of encouraging rebellion and dissent. After Pakistan occupied the POK area and after the capitulation of the Gilgit garrison, the siege of Skardu in Baltistan was undertaken by their mercenaries and their Army. There were 300 civilians, including women and children, who had sought refuge with the Skardu garrison. The garrison bravely continued to withstand attacks from the Pakistan Army until 14 August 1948. It was then overpowered and the local governor, Brigadier Ghansara Singh was also imprisoned.[11] With single minded focus, the assault from Pakistan was merciless, ruthless and devastating.

At that time, the Pakistan Army had also employed an infantry battalion to hold the Zoji La Pass. This pass is strategically located in Ladakh on the erstwhile track linking Srinagar-Dras-Kargil-Leh. To open this link to Leh, a motorable road was developed by Indian Army engineers in the face of Pakistani opposition. 7 Cavalry, equipped with Stuart tanks along with two infantry battalions, the 1st Battalion of the 5 Gorkha Rifles and the Patiala Infantry (now 14 Punjab), were deployed to evict the Pakistanis from Zoji La. Pakistan thus suffered another setback in this operation, and the road to Kargil and to Leh was cleared by the Indian Army.

The 1947–48 war was the first India-Pakistan war. It could be considered the last nail in the coffin of the brotherhood between India and Pakistan. To find a more non-violent and lasting solution to this aggression, India had taken the decision to refer Pakistan's actions to the UN. This decision had implications. Tactically, the Pakistani intrusion had been evicted from the Kashmir Valley. The road access from Srinagar to Leh was opened and

11. *Field Marshal KM Cariappa: His Life and Times* by Brigadier C. B. Khanduri, 1993

secured, and it was hoped that the rest of J&K would also revert back to India under the aegis of the UN. Strategically, the seceding of J&K by Maharaja Hari Singh to India, a genuinely legitimate action in accordance with the India Independence Act legislated by the British, became a dispute. The J&K State, having been legally ceded to India, was now divided. The areas of South-West Kashmir, Gilgit, Baltistan, Chitral, Hunza, and Nager in Northern Areas, renamed as Gilgit-Baltistan, came under Pakistan's illegal occupation and remain so to date. This entire area is known as Pakistan Occupied Kashmir (POK).

As a result of this illegal occupation, Pakistan and China became neighbours since Gilgit-Baltistan adjoins Xinjiang. POK and Gilgit-Baltistan also separate the Indian state of J&K from the Wakhan Corridor in Afghanistan to the north, thereby denying a possible land route between India and Afghanistan. It also denies India a land route beyond to the Central Asian Republics. The development of the Karakoram Highway through this area of J&K occupied by Pakistan was, thus, facilitated. This highway is important in the development of the China Pakistan Economic Corridor (CPEC).

As is known, the geographic location of Pakistan gave it strategic importance during the Cold War. The Western Allies trained selected officers from the Pakistan's Armed Forces and provided fairly advanced weapon systems and equipment to Pakistan. The Soviet occupation of Afghanistan further augmented Pakistan's strategic importance. At the launch of Operation Enduring Freedom by the US and NATO forces in Afghanistan in October 2001, Pakistan once again gained strategic importance for providing land routes for the movement of logistics to Afghanistan and to utilize its air space for air ops by the US and allied forces.

Pakistan, emboldened by its strategic advantage and the nexus of partnership with China, continues to demonstrate expansionist tendencies. Over time, it has created separatist movements in various states within India. J&K has been their main, ambitious target, but there has also been insurgency and extremism abetted by Pakistan in Punjab and parts of Northeast India. By perpetrating separatist movements in various parts of India, Pakistan aims to destabilize and weaken the country, perhaps with the aim of assimilating and encroaching on more of its territory. This is a pipe dream as no matter what the circumstances, no government in India will allow any of its states or territories to break away. While addressing the Indian Parliament, Dr Manmohan Singh, the erstwhile Prime Minister of India, had stated that India's borders are not negotiable, and India will not accept any changes to its borders. This is, in principle, the ideology that

India follows. India had fought the insurgencies in Mizoram and Nagaland for decades until a political solution was reached for each of them. India is currently dealing with a communist insurgency in a few of its states, known as the Naxalite Movement. Additional police forces have been deployed in these areas and measures to bring the Naxalite insurgency to an end are being enacted including via democratic rule, development, and the spread of education and employment schemes.

For the world at large, the events following 9/11 provided an insight into the mindset that drives decision making in Pakistan. Pakistan was in a dilemma whether to join the US-led op against Al Qaeda and the Taliban in 2001 because it was providing sanctuary to these jihadi groups and their affiliates in the country. Supporting the US-led ops would mean sacrificing the interests of their proxies – the Taliban and their allies, Al Qaeda, the Haqqani network, and others. Musharraf, who was in power at that time, overtly chose to support the US but covertly continued to support these clandestine organizations. This deception is a fundamental part of Pakistan's strategy and continues even as the world is patently aware of this duplicity.

With successful launch of ops by US and allied forces after 9/11, an estimated 100,000 militants had been forced to withdraw from Afghanistan and had sought shelter in Pakistan's tribal areas. These militants augmented the strength of Jalaluddin Haqqani and other anti-US terrorist leaders. Some remained loyal to Mullah Omar, the Taliban leader, who also had sought refuge in Pakistan and died there a few years later. In the case of Osama bin Laden, Pakistan has continued to maintain a policy of denial till today. Earlier, when a democratic government was in place in Afghanistan, Major General Zahir Azmi, the spokesman for Kabul's defence ministry, had aptly stated, 'If the Pakistani intelligence agency does not know about a home located a few hundred metres away from its National Academy where, for the last six years, the biggest terrorist in the world is living, how can this country take care of its strategic weapons?'

In a narrative written by a Pakistani author, Imtiaz Gul, he states that during a visit to the ISI HQ in the mid-1990s, Prime Minister Benazir Bhutto was given a presentation by the Kashmir cell on how the mujahideen were being trained and infiltrated into Indian Kashmir. Gul's account suggests that Bhutto seemed unaware and somewhat taken aback by the extent of these covert efforts and said, 'Are we really doing this?'[12] This

12. *The Most Dangerous Place: Pakistan's Lawless Frontier* by Imtiaz Gul, pp 156

statement of surprise by Bhutto, if true, is incredulous since it was under her leadership that terrorist groups were raised specifically to fight in J&K and create an ongoing insurgency there. This contradiction requires further examination as it is well known that Benazir Bhutto continued to pursue her father's adversarial policies in relation to India. She was no doubt, absolutely aware of what the Pakistan Army and the ISI were working towards, against India.

With the iron hand of the Deep State dictating politics in Pakistan, it is evident that the country's political leadership has shown little or no success or consistency in its efforts to bring about peace with India. Because of political expediency, they have on occasion agreed to hold talks to reduce tensions and mend relations. Such attempts have likely been just for positive optics and mere rhetoric. On every occasion when talks were proposed or when the leaders of the two countries have met, Pakistan has concurrently launched unprovoked terrorist attacks on Indian citizens or on its establishments. The Deep State in Pakistan will not allow peace between the two nations to be considered even a possibility. A few examples of the major terrorist attacks launched by Pakistan on India are given below in Annexure 7.

Annexure 7
Terrorist Attacks by Pakistan on India

12 March 1993

In this major terrorist operation, 12 bombs exploded across Mumbai, killing 350 and injuring approximately 1,200 innocent civilians. The attack was coordinated by Dawood Ibrahim, head of a crime syndicate known as D-Company, and propped up by Pakistan. Aslam Bhatti and Dawood Jatt were Pakistani smugglers who perpetrated this terrorist attack. Indian intelligence services assessed that these lead figures had links with the ISI. Dawood has been given refuge by Pakistan ever since, and he now lives in Karachi or in Dubai. He is most wanted by India, whereas Pakistan still denies knowing his whereabouts.

1 October 2001

Militants rammed an explosive laden vehicle into the J&K state assembly killing 35.

13 December 2001

Six terrorists attacked the Indian Parliament. The attack was thwarted by Indian forces. All terrorists were killed.

11 July 2006

Train bombings took place on Mumbai's commuter train killing 174.

7 March 2006

Bombings in Varanasi took the lives of 28 people and over a hundred were injured. Indian police arrested six Islamic terrorists belonging to a group called Lashkar-e-Kahar including a cleric who was head of Harkat-ul-Jihad al-Islami, which had strong links with Pakistan's ISI.

25 August 2007

Two bombs exploded in Hyderabad, Andhra Pradesh, in which 42 people were killed and 54 were injured. This, too, was linked to the ISI.

10 March 2008

Bomb blasts were carried out near the J&K State Secretariat, in which five civilians were killed and three were injured.

7 July 2008

The Indian embassy was bombed in Kabul. US intelligence communication intercepts confirmed Pakistan was behind this attack.

26 November 2008

Mumbai was attacked by ten terrorists of the LeT who travelled by sea from Karachi to Mumbai. Nine terrorists were killed, and one was taken prisoner. The prisoner divulged details of this terrorist plot by Pakistan. In this attack, 166 Indians and some foreign citizens were killed.

27 July 2015

Three terrorists dressed in Indian Army uniforms opened fire on a bus and attacked Dinanager Police Station in Gurdaspur, Punjab. Three civilians, four policemen, including a superintendent of police, lost their lives, and 15 others were injured. All three attackers were killed in the op. The Global Positioning System found on their bodies indicated that the terrorists had entered India from Pakistan.

2 January 2016

The Indian Air Force base at Pathankot was attacked, in which three terrorists were killed. One Indian Army special forces officer and five other personnel lost their lives in the op.

18 September 2016

Four terrorists attacked the Indian Army's administrative base in Uri, J&K, killing 21 unarmed soldiers and injuring nearly 100. All four terrorists were killed.

10 February 2018

Three terrorists attacked Indian Army family lines in Jammu, J&K, killing six soldiers and a civilian. All three terrorists were also killed.

14 February 2019

A suicide bomber and support group attacked and killed 40 personnel of the Indian Central Reserve Police Force near Pulwama, J&K.

22 April 2025

A squad of terrorists killed 26 tourists in Baisaran, six kms from the township of Pahalgam in Anantnag District of J&K. Those killed include one tourist from Nepal and one pony owner who tried to intervene on behalf of his customer. The terrorist first identified that the tourists were non-Muslim, segregated the males and shot them dead in front of their families.

The above-mentioned are just a few of the 300 or so terrorist attacks launched by Pakistan against India up to 2025. Pakistan used its proxies as the perpetrators as proven many times with proof and at times with circumstantial evidence. In these incidents civilians and security personnel have suffered casualties. Many other similar attacks were prevented and neutralized at the LOC or the IB itself.

In addition to the above planned attacks, Pakistan has utilised its tribal people, trained as irregular forces, to wage its proxy war against India. A summary of these attacks is given in Annexure 8 below.

Annexure 8
Use of Irregular Forces for Attacks by Pakistan

1947–1948

In October 1947, tribal militia and demobilized soldiers from the North-West Frontier Agency, officered by the Pakistan Army, infiltrated into the princely state of J&K to annex it by use of armed force. Maj Gen Akbar Khan of Pakistan Army was believed to have commanded the op. He was the originator of the strategy of armed insurrection and the utilization of irregulars as proxies. This intrusion resulted in the first Indo-Pakistan war, soon after partition, and at this time, it is to be noted that Jinnah was alive. The war ended with the signing of the Karachi Agreement on 27 July 1949. The CFL came into being in October 1947, and it was delineated on maps and accepted by both countries.

1965

In August 1965, Op Gibraltar was launched by Pakistan, in which thousands of Pakistan Army's Azad Kashmir regular troops and trained tribal irregulars were pushed across the CFL into the Indian state of J&K. Their aim was to cause maximum damage to Indian communication networks, disrupt logistics, and distribute weapons to citizens of the state to instigate insurgency.

1970–79

Mujahideen groups carried out ops in Afghanistan.

1984–to date

Ops by Pakistan based jihadi groups and ISI continue within J&K.

2001–2021

When Operation Enduring Freedom was launched in Afghanistan by the US and allied forces, the US obtained Pakistan's support. Of course, Pakistan played a duplicitous role as an ally on one hand and by supporting attacks by terrorist groups on the US and allied forces. This two-faced strategy undermined the efforts and success of the US and its allies and made the war unwinable.

Once the Pakistan Army achieved success against the Soviets in Afghanistan it took the lessons learned from that conflict to enhance the sub-conventional war against India. Some strategies used by Pakistan were as follows:

a. Infiltrate foreign hired mercenaries and Pakistani terrorists to carry out ethnic cleansing of Kashmiri Pandits from the Kashmir Valley and create an insurgency there to give impetus to separatism.

b. Engage the separatists trained in Pakistan for commencing an insurgency in the Indian state of Punjab.

c. Influence the fringe groups of Indian immigrants in Canada, UK, and the US to sow the seeds of an anti-India resistance and bring to bear external separatist movements. Develop links with politicians in select countries to support such activities.

d. Build up support for insurgents in Northeast India.

e. Spread Islam in the Hindu population of Nepal, especially along the Indo-Nepalese border.

f. Attempt to subvert the Muslim population in India who have been averse to radicalization and have never adopted an anti-national posture.

g. Avenge the defeat of 1971 by continuing its efforts to divide India. Create an adverse impression in the minds of the local population in the Kashmir Valley.

h. Project the Indian Security Forces as an occupying force, accuse them of human rights violations and create a mass movement demanding separatism.

i. Provoke India to retaliate so that people of Pakistan rally around their armed forces and with a larger aim to curb separatism and unify its people around an anti-India cause.

In its efforts to inflict harm on India, the Deep State in Pakistan has continued to have ambitions beyond what it can achieve. It is about time that the international community take a serious note of terrorism generated by Pakistan. Ahmed Rashid, an author and journalist of Pakistani origin, has been a correspondent for the *Daily Telegraph* and writes for other newspapers and journals. He states in his work, *Pakistan on the Brink*, 'There is no other military elite in the world whose aspirations are all-pervading for great power and regional status, whose desire is to overextend and outmatch itself with meagre resources, so outstrips reality as that of Pakistan.' He further states, 'But for propping up by major powers, Pakistan would not have been able to match India in any key dimension of power. Its desire to achieve strategic parity with India is an obsession. India is considered heretic, and hence, conflict with India is natural, and to do nothing means defeat. Hence, achieving a balance of power is essential for Pakistan. With its limited resources, it will continue with the low-cost option of fighting a proxy war.' This relentless approach has come to haunt Pakistani society, most of which is impoverished, under-developed and marginalized. General Musharraf himself wrote in his memoirs, 'I believe that our greatest oversight was to forget that when you help to organize and use people fired by the extraordinary religious or ideological zeal to achieve your objectives, you must consider that they might be using you to achieve their objectives.'[13] This becomes clear from the actions of the TTP and its offshoot, the Punjabi Taliban, who have made radical Islam their functional policy and have made a violent impact in Pakistan's society. In recent years, the bombing of the Marriot Hotel in Islamabad, the Red Mosque action, the

13. *In the Line of Fire* by Pervez Musharraf

killing of children in the Army school in Quetta, the attack on the Sri Lankan cricket team, and the attack on a mosque in guarded premises are examples of this radicalization which has gone awry.

When Musharraf agreed to side with the US after 9/11, to indicate that he was stopping Pakistan's assistance to the terrorists, he was going against more than 50 years of Pakistan's legacy of raising terror groups as proxies. At that time, it seemed inconceivable for Pakistan to give up this strategy. In fact, any such effort was a farce and mere lip service. By fostering a continued ideology of hate and division, Pakistan must now contend with the complex problems that have manifested out of its reckless policies. Amid the TTP, there exists a vicious Sunni group that is ruthless and galvanizes inimical actions towards all other Muslim sects and non-Muslims alike. This radical faction undermines the State's functioning by perpetrating violent terror attacks and continues to commit other sectarian atrocities. There are many indicators that the ISI continues to exert control over all these terrorist groups. The ISI remains the mastermind behind this divisiveness and continuously supports these operations and proxy wars. If Pakistan is to save its democratic structure and build some degree of prosperity in the future, it must contend with and quell these internal threats. This is discussed further in Chapters 7 and 8.

CHAPTER 3

Kashmir and the Kargil War

Perspectives and New Realities

The Pakistan Army's previous COAS, General Bajwa, had described Kashmir as the jugular of Pakistan and so has General Asim Munir, the current COAS of the Pakistan Army, a week prior to the dastardly killing of tourists near Pahalgam on 22 April 2025. The latter's remarks also included anti-Hindu rhetoric validating the two-nation theory that was the basis of creation of this rogue nation. Before being ousted from power, Prime Minister Imran Khan had called himself the ambassador of Kashmir. This hyperbole and these bombastic proclamations indicate that for the leaders in Pakistan there is a need, almost a desperation, to keep Kashmir as an issue at the forefront. Let's recap the geographical realities which are that POK and Gilgit-Baltistan are under Pakistani occupation since 1947–48. China had occupied Aksai Chin in the 1950s and surreptitiously moved forward in 2020, which is part of eastern Ladakh. The Chinese had also received Shaksgam Valley from Pakistan in 1963 in a border settlement. As a result of these incursions and illegal occupations, the erstwhile princely state of J&K today stands divided between India, Pakistan, and China.

To pursue its animosity against India on the world stage, Pakistan has been relentless in raising the issue of Kashmir in international forums at every opportunity. Pakistan has hoped to win the sympathy of the international community, seeking intervention in the dispute that they have created. In these exhortations, Pakistan chooses not to mention the area of Indian territory which it illegally occupies, the manner in which this occupation was enacted, and it disregards the UNSC proclamation to withdraw its forces from the occupied area to facilitate a plebiscite.

Pakistan has tried to play the 'Muslim card' to make it a pan-Islamic issue by repeatedly alluding to Kashmir as its territory at meetings of the Organization of Islamic Cooperation (OIC). The OIC is a sub-optimal body of 57 Muslim countries consisting primarily of states that are dictatorships and sundry kingdoms that need no persuasion to pay attention to the issue in the name of their religion. Most of these Nations have never allowed their own people freedom and democracy and have their own internecine struggles to contend with. In the recent past, some of these countries have broken from the fold and have suggested that the Kashmir dispute be resolved mutually through dialogue between India and Pakistan. As discussed previously, the Pakistan Army strives to maintain its supremacy and its influence in their country. It continues to foster a heightened threat perception, reiterates the threat from India and demands resources from the government in Islamabad, which the country can ill afford. The Pakistan Army and ISI must know that the Kashmir issue, created and nurtured by them, has proven to have no justifiable solution and is bleeding their country dry financially. Despite this, they continue to devise anti-India plans and zealously guard their clout in Pakistan's administration.

For Pakistan, the basic premise of the Kashmir conflict is their claim that it was an illegitimate cessation of the entire state to India. Notwithstanding this dispute on the facts, the reality is that after partition the Maharaja of the princely state of J&K wanted time to consider Jinnah's proposal to join Pakistan. The Maharaja had signed a standstill agreement in the interim, and this agreement did not in any way imply cessation to either country. Without waiting for a final decision from the Maharaja, Pakistan launched a military op in October 1947 to annex J&K by use of force. It was Pakistan that violated the standstill agreement. The Maharaja of J&K was therefore put under duress and chose to cede the entire state to India. For him, this was a fait accompli to protect the lives of his subjects, preserve his own honour and to avoid further ignominy and carnage. There is clear evidence to support this sequence of events, even as Pakistan continues to contend the veracity of how history played out.

At the end of the Second World War, numerous Muslim soldiers from the British Indian Army who belonged to Southwest Kashmir were demobilized. Prior to India's independence from the British, the Maharaja of J&K had raised taxes in his state. As a result, the population was disgruntled. With the support of the demobilized soldiers, the people of this area in J&K revolted against the Maharaja's rule and the rise in taxation. Due to this ongoing internal strife and turmoil, when Pakistan deployed its tribal hordes and its Army to the area in October 1947, it was easily appropriated by Pakistan.

After this illegal occupation, Pakistani troops did not withdraw from the area and instead called it 'Azad (independent) Kashmir'. This narrow belt of land seized by Pakistan provides depth towards their capital city, Islamabad, from the east. The straight road distance between Mirpur near the LOC and Islamabad is only 78 km. A map showing areas of POK, Gilgit-Baltistan, Aksai Chin, and Shaksgam Valley is in Annexure 9.

Annexure 9

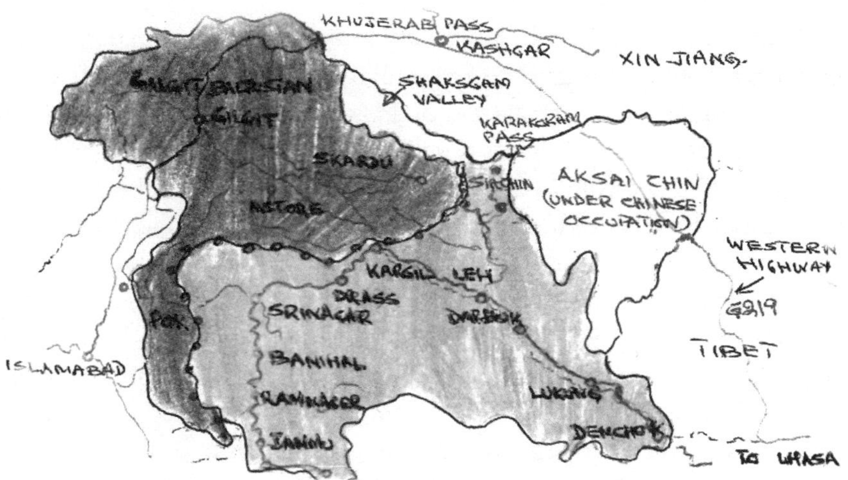

Area of Pakistan-occupied Kashmir, Gilgit-Baltistan, Aksai Chin, and Shaksgam Valley

Notes

1. The map shows the alignment of the Karakoram Highway across Khunjerab Pass. It links Kashgar in Xinjiang with Gilgit and Islamabad. The Western Highway, or G219 from Lhasa, passes through Aksai Chin and leads to Kashgar.
2. The CFL shown on the map was renamed LOC at the signing of the Shimla Agreement between India and Pakistan on 6 July 1972. The CFL, now the LOC, ends in the area of Turtuk at Zero Point and beyond this it is held by both armies on the ground. This is called the Actual Ground Position Line (AGPL). It follows the ridgeline of the Soltoro range that runs approximately south to north.

Despite the continuous animosity from across the border, India has consistently adopted policies based on goodwill and in the hope of establishing peace, even though an inimical relationship persists with Pakistan. This goodwill, however, has not overcome the intransigence in Pakistan's behaviour and attitude towards India, ever since independence. It needs to be understood that the Kashmir has become an excuse for Pakistan to continue its unremitting hostility towards India. This hostility has now become an existential need for Pakistan as it attempts to raise its profile and identity by referring to the issue internationally. This is a poorly crafted attempt to bring unity and a sense of national pride to its diverse and impoverished population.

The population of Pakistan is the second largest in Muslim nations after Indonesia. It has experienced exponential growth and is estimated to be over 240 million. The population of Pakistan has surpassed the Muslim population of India, which was estimated to be 197.5 million, in 2023. The people of POK and Gilgit-Baltistan, which have been under the occupation of Pakistan, have been ruled with an iron hand ever since Pakistan illegally usurped these territories. The communities in POK speak a dialect of Punjabi, and unlike Kashmiris, the inhabitants of this area are known as Mirpuris. Despite the high-level optics that suggest otherwise, the general population of Pakistan is not consumed by the Kashmir dispute or animosity against India as day-to-day survival and the struggles of life are omnipresent and more urgent. It is a populace that is in desperate need of leadership, basic infrastructure, and a hopeful future.

The seeds of the division, mistrust and communal disharmony that exist today in Pakistan were planted by the founders of the nation. Even prior to independence, the Muslim League and Jinnah had adopted a policy that was not conducive to the unity of India. They continued to repeatedly harp upon the notion that Muslims were at a disadvantage in India. Today's leaders in Pakistan have followed in the footsteps of Jinnah and the Muslim league and are still crying wolf about Pakistan's treatment in the Indian sub-continent. Pre-independence, Jinnah and his supporters used this ploy to obtain concessions from the ruling British and to ensure that the Indian National Congress did not gain an upper hand in Indian politics. They resorted to violence, disruption, and communal riots to keep the anarchy alive. Even after becoming an independent nation, Pakistan's leadership continued with this divisive strategy in J&K when they carried out ethnic cleansing of Hindus from the Kashmir Valley in 1947–48 and in 1989–90. Till this day, Pakistan's leaders have continued to instigate terrorism in the region. However, in the recent past, Indian politicians have been resolute about countering this nagging issue and India's armed forces have been very effective in curbing the rampant terrorism in the Kashmir Valley. Pakistan's ISI is now targeting other districts to pursue its sub-conventional war, and the Government of India has assigned additional security forces to contend with the evolving situation in the region.

To further analyze Pakistan's perspective on the matter, we need to delve deeper into the role and importance of the leadership and messaging of Muhammad Ali Jinnah, the founder of Pakistan. Historian Akbar S. Ahmed alludes that in his role as the leader of the Muslim League, Jinnah 'rediscovered his own Islamic roots, his own sense of identity, of culture and history, which would come increasingly to the fore in the final years of his life'. While Jinnah publicly advocated freedom of religion and protection of minorities, he was personally driven by Islamic teachings, and not that of a secular politician. As Balraj Puri suggests in his journal article, Jinnah, the Muslim League president, introduced the idea of partition in 'sheer desperation'. His unyielding resolve in this regard could not be undone and India underwent a fractured division.

Jinnah was in fact a supercilious, ambitious man and an opportunist with a desire to gain political power. Even as he professed secular ideals, he used Islam as the basis to carve out Pakistan as a separate country from British India. It is apropos this that the identity of Pakistan has since been strongly Islamic with an anti-India bias. Even though Jinnah instigated insecurities for the Muslim population in India, time has proven that Islam has never been under threat in India. In his efforts to establish himself as a powerful leader, Jinnah had realized that he could not become the Prime Minister of a secular, independent India. This is despite the fact that he was actually offered the role by Gandhi to maintain national unity and to avoid the country's partition. A shrewd opportunist, he knew that the Muslim representation in the Constituent Assembly of India would be inadequate to form a government and his hold on the government would be tenuous. Instead, Jinnah decided, along with the Muslim League, to create a separate country whose identity was to be a predominantly Muslim nation. It was this identity and the ambition to have a larger area for his new country that he wrote to the Maharaja of J&K to join Pakistan. It was his self-serving leadership which led India being violently torn apart.

After partition, devastating riots followed, and the two countries had to endure immense poverty and disharmony. However, Jinnah did not rest. The first India-Pakistan war was initiated by Pakistan when Jinnah was at the helm. Tilak Devasher, an Indian author, wrote about Indo-Pak relationship stating, 'As soon as India became a negative reference point for defining Pakistani nationalism, there was no way Pakistan could develop a new identity for itself or develop normal relations with India. This is the continuing tragedy of Pakistan'.[1] This statement highlights the legacy that perhaps guides Pakistan's politics till today.

A perpetual, hostile attitude and policy towards India persists in Pakistan. Continuing cross-border and trans-LOC hostilities have demonstrated this. Hypothetically, if peace were to come about between India and Pakistan, the grip of the Pakistan Army over the affairs of the state, the officials and its feudal lords who play the system, would be in jeopardy. The civilian government would then be strengthened. In the past, the Indian authorities were caught on their back foot as partisan politics of the state and central governments in India provided Pakistan an opportunity to create adverse conditions in Kashmir. Initially, the Indian response to terrorist attacks was cautious and measured. Today, India's ripostes are punitive and definitive. Pakistan continues to maintain cross-border terrorism in Kashmir, but there had been a significant drop in terrorist activities mainly due to the counteractions of the Indian security forces and the local authorities. India's policy and response to Pakistan's hostile actions are now firm and stoic and Pakistan suffers every time its clandestine efforts are thwarted. Its authorities save face by suppressing the information related to collateral damage and casualties suffered by its people and armed forces. The domestic narrative, which is dictated by their Army, prevents public disclosure of casualties as this would indicate defeat or failure and create an adverse impression and even panic in the population. In each war or terrorist action, Pakistan has obfuscated the facts and misrepresented the extent of defeat and the casualties. Despite so many setbacks, Pakistan persists in maintaining belligerence towards India since for Pakistan, the Kashmir issue remains an unfinished business. It has been the causes belli for the four wars with India. All these wars ended with Pakistan's defeat, but this still did not deter Pakistan's resolve to keep the Kashmir issue alive.

On 31 October 2019, in a significant change to the governance structure, the state of Jammu and Kashmir was split into two union territories (UT), namely, J&K and Ladakh. Each UT is now governed by an appointed Lieutenant Governor. Maps subsequently published by the

1. *Pakistan: At the Helm* by Tilak Devasher, Google Books 2018

Indian government show areas under occupation by China and Pakistan as part of these union territories. This is a clear message that India lays claim to the entire region, as was legislated in the India Independence Act by the British, and as ceded by the Maharaja of J&K, solely to India. It should be noted that the people of Jammu and Ladakh regions have always had an affinity and loyalty towards India. Prior to its division into two union territories, the state of J&K had five major regions, each with different ethnic, linguistic, and religious identities. Three of these regions include the Muslim-majority Kashmir Valley, the Hindu-majority Jammu region, and the Buddhist-majority Ladakh uplands. These regions now form part of India's union territories of J&K and Ladakh. The other two areas, POK and Gilgit-Baltistan, are under the occupation of Pakistan. The areas of Gilgit-Baltistan were largely tribal, sparsely populated, with a few Shia and Ismaili Muslims. These include Gilgit, Chitral, Hunza, Nagar, Shigar, Baltistan and a few other areas. Out of the original population of these northern areas, some have migrated, and those who remain have probably been reduced to a minority because Pakistan has resettled people from other areas of their mainland to these areas. These new settlers are mainly veterans and some civilians from Punjab and some from the NWFP. Historically, the Gilgit Wazirat (district), as it was designated then, had been leased by the Maharaja for ₹75,000 to the British for sixty years in 1935. The British had leased the area to maintain surveillance on the North and Northwest (NW) region to discern and counter any attempts being made by the Soviet Union to expand southwards. At the independence of India, Lord Mountbatten, the last British Governor General, terminated the lease on the advice of the British agent in Gilgit. The British role, thus ceased, and the area reverted under the Maharaja, and he subsequently ceded his entire state to India. All these developments are well documented and should not be under dispute.

On 10 November 2010, President Obama addressed the Indian Parliament and made the unambiguous declaration that safe havens for terrorists in Pakistan were unacceptable. This statement once again shone the world's spotlight on Pakistan's support for terrorism. Closer to the LOC, Pakistan has established many bases to launch terrorists into the area of J&K. Frequent attempts are made by terrorists to infiltrate the Indian territory from the area occupied by Pakistan. Some of these infiltrators are ISI operatives, who fan the fire of separatism and terrorism through the JeI, sleeper cells and other proxies. The infiltrators include members of LeT, JeM, HM and a few home grown terrorist jihadist groups within J&K affiliated to these groups , which are being sustained by Pakistan. Approximately 100 local youth were recruited by Pakistani terrorist groups from the Kashmir Valley in 2022. This is the lowest number in the last four years and most of these detractors have been neutralized by Indian Security Forces. In Rajouri District in the Jammu division, there have been a few attacks on the resident Hindu population. This appears to be yet another attempt at ethnic cleansing as once again, a peaceful community is targeted with mindless violence.

No honourable nation would willfully violate agreements that are recognized internationally. However, it would seem that Pakistan's leaders cannot help themselves as they continue to violate the trust and efforts at building peace in the region. There are many instances of Pakistan violating agreements and international treaties to serve its own interests and to pursue its own agenda unilaterally. The Karachi Agreement between India and Pakistan was signed on 27 July 1949, under aegis of the ceasefire brokered by the UN, ending the first war between the two countries. At that time, the CFL was demarcated in J&K as per the actual position of opposing forces on the ground and it was agreed upon by the two countries. Pakistan has since violated the Karachi agreement twice by launching the 1965 and 1971 wars. Then, the Shimla Agreement was signed between India and Pakistan on 6 July 1972, and it established the LOC. Pakistan blatantly violated this agreement by intruding into the area of J&K across the LOC in Kargil District in 1999. This aggression by Pakistan led to the Kargil War, and it also went against the Lahore Declaration of the same year. Pakistan has stated in May 2025 that it abrogates the Shimla agreement in the wake of India's decisive retaliatory action against its mainland.

Pakistan's misadventures include their ploy to usurp the Siachen area located in North J&K. This was the unfortunate consequence of an anomaly created in the US when they published maps of the LOC. The US mapping agency was required to print maps of the US Air Defence Info Zone to show boundaries for air traffic control. At that time, the geographer, Robert Hodgson, noted that the LOC ended at the coordinates NJ9842. Beyond this point, he marked the LOC by drawing a straight line approximately Northeast (NE) to the Karakoram Pass. This line mistakenly linked the Aksai Chin area occupied by the Chinese with Gilgit-Baltistan and included the Siachen Sector as a part of Baltistan held by Pakistan. The remainder of the LOC, beyond NJ9842 had not been demarcated because at that time it was deemed to lie in difficult and hazardous high-altitude terrain. The Karachi agreement clearly states that the CFL, now the LOC, will run North along the glaciers. This is the approximate alignment of the Soltoro range of mountains, which the Indian Army now defends. In a fortuitous incident, an Indian Army officer procured a copy of a US map showing this inaccurate extension of the LOC towards the Karakoram Pass and raised the issue of its error. How this came to pass is a curious story as explained below.

Colonel Narender Kumar was the Commandant of India's High Altitude Warfare School (HAWS) located at Gulmarg in Kashmir. He was approached by German travelers Voler Stallbohm and Jarsolav Poncar, to consult on their planned rafting expedition on the Nubra River, which originates at the Siachen Glacier. These outdoor enthusiasts carried a map printed in the US which showed the unilateral and unexplained extension of the LOC. Colonel Kumar purchased a copy of the said US map from the explorers. He immediately brought this anomaly to the notice of Army HQ in Delhi, who in turn informed the Government of India. An official objection to this extension of the LOC was then lodged with the US. George Demko, the Chief Cartographer at that time, accepted India's contention and the line extending the LOC beyond NJ9842 was erased from US maps. Meanwhile, Pakistan had also identified the inaccuracy in the anomalous US maps, and seeing the opportunity to appropriate more Indian territory, Pakistan used the US map as a guideline to publish its own new maps showing the extension of the LOC to legitimize the error. This was yet another disingenuous attempt by Pakistan to usurp more of J&K territory.

Until 1984, Pakistan had allowed international mountaineer ing expeditions into Baltistan and the Siachen area as this is the location of some of the most pristine and challenging mountains, such as Broad Peak, Nanga Parvat, K2, Teram Kangri, Sasir Kangri, and Gasherbrum. By allowing foreigners access to these areas, one of Pakistan's aims was to create an international impression of its rights over the area. The access to this area by foreign expeditions was detected by Indian Army patrols operating in the Siachen area and Colonel Narender Kumar himself led two patrols in 1983 and 1984 to gather intelligence on the situation. Indian intelligence reports also indicated that Pakistan was procuring tents, equipment, and clothing from European suppliers in bulk, for use in extreme cold conditions. It was also detected that Pakistan Army troops were being trained to occupy the Siachen Glacier area. Observing the Pakistanis on the move, India pre-empted the occupation of the area and took control. In an operation code-named Op *Meghdoot*, Indian troops were ferried by helicopters in ones and twos and moved on foot to occupy the Soltoro range to prevent any ingress by the Pakistan Army. Indian army soldiers are currently deployed at this location along the AGPL, that remains un-demarcated. Some positions occupied are at altitudes of over 18,000 ft above mean sea level. This is a rugged and inhospitable area where more casualties occur because of elevation, crevasses, avalanches, and adverse climatic conditions than enemy action. An avalanche in 2019 buried and caused casualties to an entire battalion HQ of the Pakistan Army in Baltistan. The conflict between the two nations keeps Indian and Pakistani troops permanently deployed even in this harsh and challenging environment. The AGPL virtually extends the LOC towards the north, as mentioned in the Karachi Agreement. It follows the principle of watersheds, which is one method of demarcating boundaries between countries.

As explained earlier, in a border settlement in 1963, Pakistan donated an area of 6,993 square kms to China, known as Shaksgam Valley. This area is of importance as this valley formed part of the Shigar District in the Baltistan Region of J&K. Most of the names of places and lakes in this Valley are in Balti or Ladakhi, which are the languages spoken in Baltistan and Ladakh. A polo ground was built in the Shaksgam Valley by the royal family of Shigar, which still exists. The Rajas (rulers) of Shigar used to invite the Amir of Hotan in Xinjiang to play matches there. There is proof that the area was a part of J&K. This valley abuts the head of the Siachen Glacier at Indira Kol and is to the south of Khunjereb Pass on the Karakoram mountains. It is bounded by the Kun Lun Mountain Range in the North. China had accepted this area from Pakistan as it creates depth from the west towards the Western Highway running through Hotan to Kashgar. By negotiating with China and giving away such a large tract of J&K, Pakistan indicated their bogus ownership of this part of the state. Typical of its mercenary dealings, the border agreement that Pakistan signed with China in 1963 established its hold over areas occupied in J&K, and was perhaps done in exchange for nuclear and missile technology. The ceding of this land also facilitated the construction of the 1,300 km long Karakoram Highway linking Kashgar with Islamabad. Along this axis, China is investing $59 billion as a part of its Belt and Road Initiative (BRI). Referred to as CPEC, this project if and when completed will ultimately connect Kashgar with Gwadar Port on the Arabian Sea in Pakistan with road and rail networks. China has gauged that its sea trade passing through the Malacca Straits, a choke point, is vulnerable to interception. The CPEC corridor will obviate this and with its completion, China will gain a shorter route to access the Middle East, and it will be in proximity to the choke point to the Persian Gulf at Hormuz. China is aware that India claims the area and it is disputed due to Pakistan's illegal occupation. Despite this knowledge, China is moving ahead in developing the infrastructure under CPEC, without consulting India.

The Gilgit-Baltistan area is about 72971 square kms of rugged mountainous terrain. The occupation of this area by Pakistan in 1947 and thereafter changing its status to bring it under central government rule on 29 August 2009, was a strategic move. The area provides a vital link between Pakistan and China and to the north. According to a study in 2004 by the Geneva-based Center for International and Strategic Studies, the construction of the Karakoram Highway through the area has facilitated the movement of Chinese nuclear and military equipment, including missiles, to Pakistan. It has also facilitated overland trade between the two countries. This highway also enables faster movement of men, material, and munitions by Pakistan from the hinterland towards the LOC. It is also a support lifeline for bases of hardline terrorists that are being trained and are awaiting induction into J&K. This disputed area is also being exploited for mining by China. Some precious minerals such as gold, uranium, and rare earths, are being mined, and there are chances of oil reserves being found in the region. With the aim of snuffing separatist movements, Pakistan had resettled people from its mainland into this area. This forced demographic change has not gone well and has resulted in the indigenous population becoming more vocal in an anti-Pakistan rhetoric. They claim they do not belong to Pakistan and instead want independence.

In the late 1980s, Pakistan's separatist movement in Kashmir was failing and they needed to up the ante to keep the issue alive. Leaving no stone unturned to promote Islamic fundamentalism in J&K, Pakistan created terrorist groups, hired mercenaries, and began a sustained proxy war in the state and against India. They also created the APHC, which was, in fact, the brainchild of Robin Raphael, an Under Secretary of the US for South Asian Affairs. Raphael had visited Kashmir many times while posted at the US Embassy in Islamabad. Why a representative of the US government assisted in the raising a seditious organization in India requires a separate analysis. It took considerable diplomatic effort on the part of India through the head of the US Senate Foreign Affairs Committee to correct the damage done by Raphael. Under the aegis of the ISI, Pakistan had clearly begun to adopt the same pattern of ops and inter-community disharmony in J&K as it did in Afghanistan, using the latter as a tried and tested template. In an attempt to change the demography of the region, radicals from the Kashmir Valley and terrorists from Pakistan enacted the brutal ethnic cleansing of the Hindu, Kashmiri Pandits.

To explore these topics further, it is important to consider the politics that prevailed after J&K was ceded to India. At that juncture, Sheikh Abdullah rose as a prominent Kashmiri leader. Abdullah initially supported the decision of the Maharaja to cede the state to India, however, he also harboured nationalist thoughts and was jailed as a result. In 1953, Prime Minister Nehru came to an understanding with Abdullah and appointed him as Prime Minister of J&K. Sheikh Abdullah was able to negotiate with Nehru for granting special status to the state under an order by the President of India. The provisions were incorporated in the Indian Constitution as Articles 370 and Article 35A. At this time, the State, with the special status, had an elected government headed by a Prime Minister. This appointment was later changed to Chief Minister to conform with other states of India. Kashmir saw relative peace when Sheikh Abdullah was the Chief Minister and of note is the fact that the elected State Legislature also endorsed accession to India by a unanimous vote.

Shiekh Abdullah's son, Farooq Abdullah, took over from him as the Chief Minister. With this dynastic leadership, inertia set in, the development of the state stalled, and corruption became rampant at all levels in the state's administration. The political authorities in the State were unable to provide good governance to the people, and in this chaotic environment, radicalism and separatism began raising their head, sponsored by Pakistan. Farooq and his government were dismissed from office because of the deteriorating situation. After a period, Rajiv Gandhi who was the Prime Minister of India at the time, reinstated Farooq to his position as Chief Minister of the State. By then, a small section of the Kashmiri population was disgruntled and had become alienated from India. Some Kashmiris who had earlier joined the mujahideen to fight Soviet forces in Afghanistan, returned to form the core of the insurgency in J&K. Contributing to the alienation were the hardcore radical Islamists of JeI and groups led by Kashmiri *mullahs* (religious clerics). In the 1987 state assembly elections, vote rigging was alleged and many young politicians who were aspiring to be elected lost their bid for a seat in the State Legislature. A section of the youth was, thus, discontented and turned anti-national. Pakistan's ISI had already gained influence in the state, and it took advantage of the fluid situation by exacerbating the anti-national sentiments. More radical

Islamic fundamentalists and mercenaries were inducted into the state of J&K by Pakistan. These comprised terrorists from LeT, JeM, HM, ISI operatives, and foreigners who had volunteered to fight the government agencies in J&K. Mercenaries from Saudi Arabia, Lebanon, Afghanistan and a few other countries, perhaps those that had fought in Afghanistan and stayed back in Pakistan, were inducted by ISI into J&K to create terror and anarchy. Attacks commenced on government property, installations, Indian Security Forces, and their Kashmiri collaborators.

Some in the Pakistan Army believed that out of frustration with the relentless terrorist attacks, the Indian authorities would lose their hold on J&K. Some separatist elements in Kashmir also assumed that Pakistan would attack India to assist in their liberation. None of this came to pass. The J&K police, security forces, and the IA units deployed there, acted swiftly and with the appropriate restraint, to curb the terrorism and separatism. The Indian troops were empowered with legal authority assigned to them under the Special Powers and Terrorism Act. Most foreign terrorists were identified and eliminated within a few months of infiltrating the state. With adequate anti-terrorist measures, the Indian Security Forces were able to gain control of the situation and bring the state to normalcy. Pakistan's next ploy was to garner world opinion on human rights abuses by India. It appealed to the UN and lobbied other influential nations in the hopes of obtaining support. This effort did not yield any support for Pakistan and its agenda of imposing terror and separatism were being exposed to the world at large. In fact, the world was becoming wary of the scourge of terrorism, and most countries were unwilling to support Pakistan as it was abetting terror and extremism through its proxies and mercenaries. It was yet another setback to Pakistan's war machine.

J&K has always had many government-run and privately owned schools in rural and urban areas. The state, much like the rest of India, had a growing youth population. Over the years of political turmoil, the state's elected governments had paid little or no attention to the aspirations of the youth, even though the special status assigned to the state gave them additional powers to do so. As Pakistan's campaign of radicalization took root in the state, more madrasas were established to gain a fundamental stronghold. Imams from the Salafi sect began preaching radicalism at these madrasas. They taught the youth to denigrate all other religions and anti-India sentiments were indoctrinated in their minds. A few influential students in these madrasas were ready to serve for what they were told was 'the cause'. Many of these individuals crossed the LOC to train under the aegis of the ISI and then returned to fight in Kashmir against the Indian establishment. Islamic radicalism in Kashmir was culturally subversive and transformed a small section of the moderate Sufi society, with 'Kashmiriyat' as its philosophy, towards a radical and more polarized existence. This movement in no way improved the lives of citizens in the state. Instead, it brought division, unrest and disruption, as Pakistan had wanted.

In this complicated state of affairs, it is pertinent to discuss the will of the people of J&K, and the plebiscite that Pakistan continues to insist on. As discussed earlier, the erstwhile princely state of J&K is divided between India, Pakistan, and China. Under the current circumstances, the possibility of a plebiscite has been completely overtaken by the events that have ensued over the years, since the state was ceded to India in 1947. Holding a referendum in the Indian state of J&K, or part of it will be unjustifiable. This is because the state is now divided between the three countries and numerous demographic changes have occurred or have been forced to occur in the state. As explained, Pakistan has brought about numerous demographic changes in Gilgit-Baltistan. Ethnic cleansing of Kashmiri Pandits from the Kashmir Valley has led to changes in that population and so has forced migration into the state in 1947–48, 1965 and thereafter, from POK and Pakistan. These changes would make it impossible to determine who are the original citizens of Kashmir and who is eligible to vote in the plebiscite. The UN resolution in 1947–48 directed Pakistan to withdraw their Armed Forces from the state to facilitate a plebiscite. Since Pakistan did not adhere to this UN resolution, their machinations regarding Kashmir have no basis. However, despite these realities, it is quite clear that an unresolved Kashmir issue is conducive to Pakistan's existential quest to be inimical to India.

Given that this strategy has had little success, the leadership and the elite in Pakistan should perhaps introspect and put their own house in order. Pakistan's record of governance in POK and Gilgit-Baltistan has been poor at best. Social media and amateur journalist reporting from the region highlight the contrast between the impoverished area of J&K that is under Pakistan's illegal occupation and the Indian state of J&K, which is moving towards normalcy, progress and prosperity. There is also an expression of willingness of the people of POK to join India. The province of Baluchistan already has a separatist movement and then there is the Pashtun population who desire to have a separate Pashtunistan. Will Pakistan consider holding a plebiscite in the regions under its governance and empower those who desire a separate state? Or maybe a referendum should be held in all areas of the world where disaffection and separatism abound.

The building of the Karakoram Highway through the disputed region of Gilgit-Baltistan gave China the pretext to deny the area to India. China itself faced a separatist movement in the Muslim-majority Xinjiang province in the Uyghur Autonomous Region, earlier known as East Turkistan. This area is contiguous to Gilgit-Baltistan. China, being an authoritarian nation, had initiated strict and inhumane measures to overcome the separatist movement and repress a religious minority. Reports in Western media have indicated that China has systematically brought about a demographic change in the area inhabited by Uyghurs, similar to the demographic change it caused in Tibet. The Dalai Lama, the spiritual head of Tibet, has stated on many occasions that the Chinese now form a majority in his country. India on the other hand, cannot be accused of enacting atrocities or a demographic change in J&K state.

The rise of Pakistan's opportunist and mercenary tendencies can be understood from the writings of Rogers Brubaker, professor of Sociology at the University of California, Los Angeles (UCLA). He has researched and written on subjects such as *'Grounds for Difference'* and the *'Religious Dimension of Political Conflict and Violence'*. Pakistan's belief that it did not get a fair share of territory at the time of independence and that because of its Islamic identity, it must stake a claim on J&K, is not an authentic reason for their pursuit of Kashmir. The insurgency and terrorism, or the separatism, is not an inborn Kashmiri phenomenon. To attribute the Kashmir imbroglio to the Islamic majority in the Kashmir Valley would be too simplistic. Pakistan has in fact used Kashmir as a factor to unify its fissiparous mainland and as a reason for the existence of the terrorist groups it promotes and nurtures. Pakistan furthers radicalization and exhorts monetary and material support from willing donors and pursues an expansionist strategy while acting as an external homeland state to Kashmir.[2] Maintaining the Kashmir issue provides the ISI aims and objectives as part of their Army's directive to continue the proxy war and, of course, to remain predominant in their country.

With a concerted effort and after the many struggles since independence and partition, India has consolidated itself into a strong nation, an

2. *The Warrior State: Pakistan in the Contemporary World* by T. V. Paul, pp 170–171

economic power and a country with an incredibly compelling presence in today's world. Hypothetically, if the separation of Kashmir from India were to occur, it would have far-reaching ramifications for India and all liberal democracies in the world. Such an event would embolden Islamic fundamentalism, endangering not only the West but also liberal Muslim countries. The instability in Kashmir is therefore not a matter with only regional implications alone, in fact it is of international significance for many reasons. What needs to be clearly understood is that for the sake of a small percentage of seditious, separatist elements out of a population of 6 million Muslims in the Kashmir Valley, India cannot and will not sacrifice its unity and integrity. India will not jeopardize the interests of its 197.5 million Muslim citizens and will do everything it takes to maintain its sovereignty. Therefore, the hypothetical situation mentioned above is incredibly unlikely, if not impossible.

Despite this obvious reality, India continues to deal with Pakistani intransigence and works to prevent and defeat repeated terrorist attacks on its soil. The unfortunate reality is that terrorist actions continue to derail any peace initiatives by elected governments. Doctor Christine Fair, in her book *Fighting to the End: The Pakistan Army's Way of War*, aptly suggests that a peace initiative by Pakistan's elected government towards India, if it were to be accepted by the Pakistan Army, would tantamount to defeat. Maintaining the status quo with India also means defeat. Despite Pakistan enduring defeat in all wars, including the 1971 war, when its Eastern Wing broke away to become Bangladesh, it proclaimed victory for having disrupted the status quo.[3]

Under the special autonomous status that was granted to J&K by government of India, resentment against the State Legislature had festered in the Ladakh region, as over the years very little of the yearly budget allocation to the state was shared with this vast region. In the case of delimitation of seats for the State Legislature, successive governments had ensured the primacy of the Kashmir Valley as the bias of seats was skewed towards it. Under the delimitation rules in India, the allocation of seats is carried out based on the population in each region of every state, keeping in mind the maximum number of seats for the legislature. This delimitation is to be carried out every ten years. The last census was conducted in 1990, during which delimitation was done for the J&K

3. *Fighting to the End: The Pakistan Army's Way of War* by Christine Fair

state legislature. Since then, there has been a considerable change in the population in the three regions of J&K and ethnic cleansing of Hindus has resulted in a lowering of the population in the Valley. Further change has taken place due to the preferential allocation of land in the Jammu division by the state government to Muslim residents of the Kashmir Valley. The Farooq Abdullah government, through the state Legislature, ruled that no delimitation of seats can take place for the state Legislature until 2024. This inequity enforced by the successive state governments ensured that the elected representatives in the Kashmir Valley were always in the majority. This is clear from examining the data given below in Annexure 10.

Annexure 10

Delimitation of Seats in the J&K Legislature			
	Jammu	Kashmir	Ladakh
Population	62 million	58 million	0.2 million
Area	25.96	15.67	58.37
Indian Parliament Seats	2	3	1
State Legislature Seats	36	47	4
Jobs in Secretariat	10%	90%	-
Revenue Generation	70%	28%	2
Fund Allocation	30%	65%	5%
Electricity Supply	23 Mega Watts	350 Mega Watts	

Source: Economic Times New Delhi

The map below shows the location and importance of Kashmir Valley.

Annexure 11
The Kashmir Valley

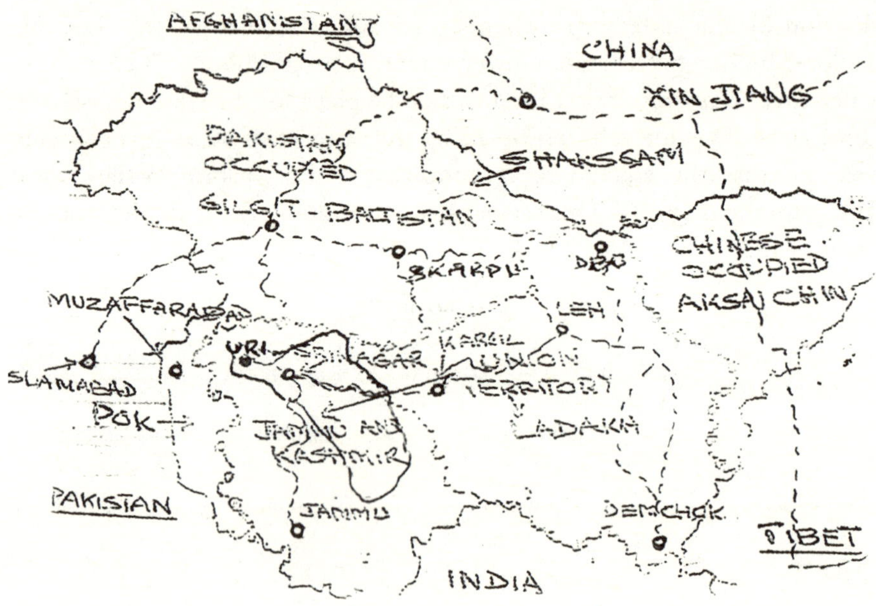

Map by Simon Ozer, Journal of Cross-Cultural Psychology, Research Gate

Notes

a. The Kashmir Valley is separated from the Jammu division by the Pir Panjal Range in the west. This Valley abuts the LOC and is vital to the integrity of J&K.

b. Access to Ladakh via National Highway 1A runs through the Zoji La. This road connects Srinagar to Dras-Kargil-Leh. Leh is the capital of the union territory of Ladakh.

c. Access to Nubra Valley and Siachen Sector is via a road through Khardungla Pass. Access to Dalat Beg Oldi (DBO) is via a road from Leh through Changla Pass and Darbuk.

On 5 August 2019, the Government of India revoked the special status, or autonomy, granted to Jammu and Kashmir under Article 370 and 35A of the Indian Constitution. This action was approved by both Houses of Parliament and its main implications are:

a. Abrogation of Article 370 takes away the right granted to the state of J&K to have its own constitution, penal code, flag, and high court and to make its own laws.

b. Abrogation of Article 35A removes restrictions on purchasing and owning property in J&K by the citizens of India, allowing Indian corporations to do the same. Prior to this, under the provisions of this section, the state government would decide who were the citizens of the state and therefore, who had the right to own property in the state. No agricultural land can be purchased by anyone from outside the union territory.

c. The state of J&K has been divided into two centrally governed union territories, namely J&K and Ladakh.

The change in status of the state has the following implications:

a. The union territories will be governed as per provisions of the Indian Constitution and at par with other states and union territories of the country.

b. The flag of J&K will no longer be flown in the union territories; instead it will be the national flag of India.

c. The Supreme Court of India will be the highest judicial authority.

d. The Indian Penal Code will apply.

e. The Auditor General of India will have jurisdiction over the union territories, and so will other central enforcing and audit authorities.

f. The police will be responsible to the respective lieutenant governors.

The aim of these decisive measures was to ensure that the corrupt and the anti-national would find it more and more difficult to pursue their vested interests. It was envisaged that there would be a steady growth in investments in the union territories and this has already begun. Many international corporations are investing in J&K and Ladakh. Several infrastructure projects have been initiated, and those that had stalled earlier have been revived by the central government in both union territories. In addition, as directed by the Election Commission of India, elections have been held in the union territory of J&K in September-October 2024 in which the electorate participated in large numbers. There is an elected government in J&K. Delimitation of seats was conducted as a precursor to the elections. The success of these measures has been evident in the large number of Kashmiri students who are studying in universities across India and who have become active participants in campus life. Kashmiris continue to be respected citizens of India with the liberty to live and pursue business opportunities anywhere in the country.

Despite the threat of terrorism, a growing number of tourists from the rest of India have been traveling to the Kashmir Valley. This may have dampened a bit after the incident at Pahalgam. In 2023, tourism numbers in the Kashmir Valley exceeded an estimated 12.8 million. Ladakh, a beautiful and unique high-altitude destination with an airport at 10,682 ft above mean sea level, at Leh, has attracted many Indian and international visitors. The population of Leh is 153,000, but as per statistics, it is visited by over 500,000 Indian and foreign tourists each year, and this number is growing. Hundreds of thousands of pilgrims visit the Hindu shrines in J&K including ancient temples such as *Vaishno Devi* and also undertake the pilgrimage to the Amarnath caves. This growth in tourism provides considerable business opportunities for the local population in terms of transportation, accommodation, tourism and guides, adventure and sports, dining and other commerce. Visitors to J&K display goodwill and solidarity with Kashmiris and enjoy the local culture and cuisine. This growth in tourism is benefitting the population of J&K immensely however this boom in tourism could become restricted if terrorism is allowed to prevail. Terrorists can create deadly incidents as has been the pattern in the past and this should not be mistaken as normalcy in Kashmir. After the reorganization of the state into union territories, there is a sea change in the behaviour of Kashmiri folk towards Indian visitors and the security forces. The population, by and large, has started to express that they are citizens of India. Children in J&K are attending school and undergoing school central board examinations. Along with these positive developments, India's security ops maintain counter terrorism ops to obviate infiltration into J&K. This includes anti-national elements from the indigenous population who operate on behalf of Pakistan based terror groups.

The abrogation of the special status and autonomy and reorganization of the state of J&K into union territories integrates them fully into mainstream India. In reaction to this administrative action by the Government of India, there had been a lot of bluster and threats from the government in Pakistan. Pakistan suspended bilateral trade and stopped the train service from Lahore to Delhi. It downgraded relations with India by recalling their High Commissioner from New Delhi and asked the Indian counterpart to leave Pakistan. Prior to raking up the Kashmir issue at the UN, Pakistan's foreign minister visited China for consultation. China had raised the issue twice at the UN on Pakistan's behest. This is the usual pattern of bilateral cooperation between Pakistan and China vis-à-vis India. When India reorganized J&K into two union territories, the erstwhile Prime Minister of Pakistan, Imran Khan, addressed the Pakistani Parliament and asked, 'Do we declare war on India, and can the opposition suggest what we should do?' The Pakistan Army held a meeting of their corps commanders to discuss the situation and concluded at that time that war with India was not an option. There is also international pressure keeping Pakistan's ambitions at bay. If Pakistan continues to aid terrorism in J&K, it will invoke action by the Financial Action Task Force (FATF). Members of the FATF met in February 2022 and continued to retain Pakistan on the grey list of countries responsible for terrorism. In August 2021, the UNSC had conveyed a new list of the most wanted terrorists and their organizations to Pakistan. To evade being blacklisted by the FATF, the Pakistani government has issued two notifications outlawing 88 members of terrorist organizations, which includes Dawood Ibrahim who is wanted for the 1993 bomb blasts in Mumbai. In October 2023 Pakistan was given a reprieve and taken off the grey list by the FATF.

The Kargil War: Revisited

India's attempts to integrate J&K into the country had led to an uneasy peace returning to the Kashmir region, and there were positive indications of progress and development. Pakistan on the other hand continues to languish and still wages a sub-conventional war against India. As a result of terrorist violence induced by Pakistan, the Indian security forces and civilians in Kashmir have suffered casualties. This status quo of sub-conventional war sponsored by Pakistan persists. India is cognizant that Pakistan's true intentions remain duplicitous and combative. This has been borne out on many occasions when peace treaties were signed between the two nations, such as the Lahore Declaration of 21 February 1999. After the signing of this Declaration, Pakistan publicly demonstrated a will to encourage peacemaking. It soon became known that in actuality, the Pakistan Army had already set plans in motion earlier that year to wage another war against India. General Musharraf was the architect of this aggression, the Kargil War of 1999. The details of the conflict, its origins and planning by Pakistan, and its resounding victory for India, are discussed hereafter.

It is understandable that the humiliation suffered by Pakistan in the 1971 war, with the surrender of its forces in East Pakistan, was a major blow to its Army's image. In this war, the eastern wing of Pakistan, despite its large population of Muslims, declared independence and became the nation of Bangladesh. Pakistan has never reconciled to this setback, this ignominy. It continues to blame India for its role in the dismemberment of the country. Besides this crushing blow, in other misadventures initiated by Pakistan, the Indian Army has also successfully and repeatedly foiled Pakistan's designs to harm India. In the Siachen Glacier Sector in 1985, India pre-emptively occupied the Saltoro Range in *Operation Meghdoot* and added to the embarrassment suffered by the Pakistan Army in the past. With a history of these defeats Pakistan's leadership understood that India could not be defeated through conventional ops. Instead, they chose to destabilize and bleed India with an insidious insurgency, sabotage, subversion, and terrorism. This is now Pakistan's modus operandi.

After the success of its nuclear tests in the late 1990s, Pakistan was emboldened and chose to up the ante against India. As insurgency was flagging in Kashmir, Pakistan made an audacious plan to launch yet another war in J&K. In May 1999, under the leadership of General Musharraf, the Pakistan army intruded across the LOC in the Kargil District of J&K. In his memoir, *In the Line of Fire,* Musharraf mentions the nuclear dimension of the Kargil war.[4] He states, 'the events of 1999 dramatically catapulted me from soldiering to leading the destiny of the nation. This also brought the two nuclear powers to the brink of war.' Later in the same narrative, he contradicts the above statement and says that, 'I can also say with authority that in 1999, our nuclear capability was not yet operational. Merely exploding a bomb does not mean that you are operationally capable of deploying nuclear forces in the field and delivering a bomb across the border onto a selected target. Any talk of preparing for a nuclear strike is preposterous.' In fact, the nuclear threat from Pakistan at that time was not preposterous. In previous years, General Zia had threatened India with nuclear strikes, so had his ministers and AQ Khan. Such a threat became

4. *In the Line of Fire* by Pervez Musharraf, pp 87 and 97–98

real once Pakistan had demonstrated its nuclear capability to the world in 1998.

In February 1999, Atal Bihari Vajpayee, the Prime Minister of India, took the initiative to attempt diplomacy between the two inimical nations. He visited Pakistan and met with Prime Minister Nawaz Sharif with the aim of diffusing tensions between the two countries. During his visit, as a gesture of goodwill, Vajpayee laid a wreath at the *Minar-e-Pakistan*, which is a symbol of Pakistan's statehood. This peace summit at Lahore generated considerable euphoria and was followed by the start of a Delhi-Lahore bus service, as an enduring symbol of peace and trust. After some deliberations, the two Prime Ministers signed the Lahore Declaration which was ratified by the parliaments of both countries. The key aspects of this bilateral agreement were:

a. Reaffirmation of India's and Pakistan's commitment to peaceful coexistence.

b. Acknowledgement of each other's nuclear status and their responsibilities to avoid conflict.

c. Settlement of all disputes between the two countries mutually as per the provisions of the Shimla Agreement.

By the end of the much-publicized summit, the leaders of both countries publicly acknowledged the need for confidence-building measures to avoid future wars. There were overt signs that the two countries were keen to work towards peace and the world was watching with hope as the summit unfolded. Well, the world soon found out the true nature of the Pakistani establishment. Even as the peace talks were ongoing between politicians, the Pakistan Army had already begun to prepare for a substantial intrusion into India across the LOC, to be launched within a few months. Pakistan showed complete disregard for the potential of the Lahore Declaration, and the opportunity to explore a path towards peace was once again stymied.

The reasons for Pakistan launching the Kargil War have been debated in various forums. The salient aspects of their motivations were possibly as follows:

a. Pakistan may have aimed to wage war to invoke international intervention in the Kashmir dispute and force India to the negotiating table with third-party mediation, thus disregarding the provisions of the Shimla agreement. The ulterior motive of occupying territory across the delineated LOC was to gain an advantage for future negotiations and possibly to relieve pressure on terrorists in the Kashmir Valley where insurgency was at an ebb.

b. The Pakistan Army could not get over the ignominy of earlier defeats by India, and decided the status quo had to be challenged with a new war effort and the hope of victory this time.

c. A plan for intrusions across the LOC in the Kargil area had also been made by General Musharraf prior to 1998, when he was DGMO. This plan was devised in consultation with the GOC of Force Command Northern Areas (FCNA). However, then Prime Minister Benazir Bhutto sensed that the plan would not work, and such an action could not be justified in various international forums. It is likely that in such an event, the UN would not only ask Pakistan to withdraw its forces from the intrusion but may even enforce the 1948 declaration for Pakistan to vacate the area of POK and Gilgit-Baltistan under their occupation. Wise counsel did prevail at that time. When General Musharraf took over as COAS, he approved the operational plan for the intrusion without considering its implications.

General Musharraf's previously conceived plan to intrude across the LOC was revived by Islamist generals in command at Pakistan's HQ 10 Corps and the FCNA. Whether the Nawaz Sharif government was taken into confidence remains a moot point. The aim was to put India in an embarrassing predicament. No doubt, the strategic importance of the Siachen Sector figured in Pakistan's plans for intrusions in the Kargil Sector, as did the need to occupy selected heights in the Turtuk Sub-Sector. The Siachen Sector lies between Gilgit-Baltistan – under the occupation of Pakistan, and Aksai Chin – under the occupation of China. Previously, India had pre-empted Pakistan's attempt to occupy the area in 1985, by establishing control over the area and occupying the Saltoro mountain range. The Saltoro range runs approximately south to north and is an offshoot of the Karakoram range of mountains. It lies to the west of the Siachen Glacier. Over the years, the Pakistan Army has unsuccessfully attempted to capture tactically important features on the Saltoro range that are held by the Indian Army.

In their 1985 op, in the initial stages, the Pakistan Army did manage to occupy perhaps the highest defensive position in the world in the

Siachen Sector, at a height of 20,523 ft. The capture of this position by the IA deserves a mention here. This position was called the *Quaid* Post, named after Jinnah. Its elevation provided the Pakistani troops with a vantage point to observe the nearby held Indian Army positions in the Bilafond La Sub-Sector, and their maintenance routes, which are supplied by porters and helicopters. Porters are a vital resource for this difficult terrain as they supplement the logistics support provided by helicopters, especially in adverse weather when helicopter flights are not possible. Light helicopters are utilized for carrying mail, special rations, medicines, oxygen sets, kerosene fuel, and other emergency supplies and for the evacuation of sick, wounded, and deceased soldiers. The efficiency of an engine reduces by about 3 per cent with every 1,000 ft gain in altitude. The load-carrying capacity of the helicopters thus reduces considerably at the super high-altitude heights that are occupied by troops in the area. When Pakistani troops occupied the *Quaid* post they could observe Indian helicopters flying in the area and target them with air bursts. Their troops also could spot the movement of patrols and logistics columns comprising porters and troops and target them. The *Quaid* Post, because of its sheer dominance, was therefore a key objective for the Indian Army. In a bold attack, Indian troops of 8 J&K Light Infantry captured this position from Pakistan on 26 June 1987. This position was then renamed *Bana* Post after Subedar Bana Singh, a junior commissioned officer of the battalion. He displayed exemplary valour during the capture of this dominating height. Bana Singh, along with his company commander, led the troops in the operation at this extreme altitude, in adverse weather and in the most treacherous terrain. This was a great victory for the Indian troops.

Maintaining a hold on the Siachen Sector is of strategic importance to India. Occupation of this area by the Indian Army has prevented Pakistan from connecting Gilgit-Baltistan with Chinese occupied Aksai Chin. Loss of this area would deny India's access to the Shaksgam Valley, ceded to China by Pakistan. The head of the Siachen Glacier abuts this valley. Indian troops deployed in the Siachen Sector maintain vigilance and defend their positions with determination and fortitude in very extreme conditions. They have thwarted many attempts by Pakistani troops to recapture *Bana* and other positions on the Saltoro range and Pakistan's aim to put India at a strategic disadvantage in the Siachen Sector has not succeeded.

As mentioned previously, despite the positive optics of the diplomacy at the Lahore summit in February 1999, the Pakistan Army had other motives. It launched ops in early May 1999 across the LOC in the Kargil

Sector, with the aim of usurping territory and occupying areas not held by either country's forces since 1947. In a two-pronged op, the Pakistan army launched intrusions and simultaneously inducted terrorists into the Kashmir Valley. These aggressions clearly violated the Shimla agreement of July 1972 and the Lahore Declaration of February 1999. It is conjectured that Pakistan expected that shortly after the intrusion, the international community would intervene to bring about a ceasefire. This hopeful prospect did not come to pass. Starting an unprovoked war and then hoping for international support was, in any event, a flawed strategy.

The planning for the Kargil War began in November 1998. Only a select few senior officers in General Headquarters (GHQ) in Rawalpindi and at HQ 10 Corps and FCNA knew of it. Even the chiefs of the Pakistan Air Force and Navy were not taken into confidence. As far as the political leadership is concerned, it is understood that Prime Minister Nawaz Sharif was given a cursory briefing in which the planned occupation of un-held areas along the LOC was mentioned. Details of the intrusion were later explained to him when the operation began to unravel in late June 1999. As described, the operation envisaged occupying dominating features across the LOC, not held since the Karachi agreement of 1949. The Pakistan Army had plans to occupy dominating positions along a frontage of over 300 km.

At that time, the area of the Kargil Sector was under the command of the Indian Army's 3 Infantry Division. Until the Kargil conflict, most people would not have been aware that the 3 Infantry Division was responsible for securing and defending this extremely sensitive part of the country. This vast area included Kargil, Siachen and Ladakh, which together form a high-altitude expanse that is over a thousand kms in frontage. To continually surveil and defend this sizeable territory is a formidable task in a very challenging, high altitude mountainous terrain. Forces deployed here are on high alert and know that they play a crucial role to defend India from two inimical, hostile nations – China and Pakistan.

The Indian Army defines high altitude areas (HAA) as those that are located at an altitude of more than 9000 ft. These HAA are further classified as Stage I (9000–12000 ft), Stage II (12,000–15,000 ft) and Stage III (>15,000 ft) for purposes of acclimatization of soldiers and personnel. To prevent acute high-altitude sickness when troops are deployed, an acclimatization schedule is followed by the Indian Army, whereby troops coming in from sea level/the plains or lower altitudes cannot be deployed until they are acclimatized. The HQ of the 3 Infantry

Division in Leh, Ladakh, was at an altitude of 11,480 feet. Therefore, it was standard protocol that any troops, officers or support staff inducted into this Division would undergo a period of acclimatization to avoid adverse health outcomes such as acute mountain sickness, high-altitude pulmonary edema and high-altitude cerebral edema. This is a reality of serving in this sector, and it is also a reason why fresh troops cannot be deployed immediately in any ops in this region. It is well known that it would take approximately three weeks of acclimatization for troops arriving in the Kargil Sector before they could be launched into operations. This was a crucial factor when weighed against the urgency to deploy troops for attack ops, as was the case during the Kargil intrusions.

The Indian Army's 70 Infantry Brigade was on the order of battle (ORBAT) of 3 Infantry Division. However, in 1997, this brigade had been withdrawn from Ladakh and deployed in the Kashmir Valley. This altered deployment of a substantial armed force had depleted the regular strength of the 3 Infantry Division in the vast Ladakh sector. It also weakened the army's defence capability in Ladakh. 70 Brigade's temporary role was to augment the counter-insurgency grid in the Kashmir Valley. However, the collateral damage of this move was that its removal from the Ladakh sector had depleted the forces required to monitor and patrol the sensitive areas of the border with China and Pakistan. The higher HQs were focused on combating the militancy in the Kashmir valley. Thereby, the defence of Ladakh was relegated to a lower priority even though it was known that without access to 70 Brigade, there were few reserves left to cater for any operational contingencies that may arise in the immense 3 Infantry Division sector.

The return of 70 Infantry Brigade back to Ladakh had become an operational imperative as Chinese troops were becoming more active on the LAC, and the Pakistan Army usually carried out forward deployment in the summer. 3 Infantry Division had requested its higher HQ to have 70 Infantry Brigade returned to its original assigned role in the Ladakh Sector. On this request, the Brigade HQ was moved back to the Ladakh Sector in November 1998. However, battalions of this formation could not move back as winter was setting in and they had to move across Zoji La pass, which would soon be blocked under considerable accumulated snow. The battalions were not relieved in time from their op responsibility in the Kashmir valley, to move across Zoji La before it was blocked for traffic. These infantry units could either be airlifted to Leh or could only be moved across Zoji La by road after it opened for motorized traffic in May 1999.

With the limited strength of forces and facing natural impediments such as adverse weather conditions in very treacherous high-altitude terrain, 3 Infantry Division continued with its directive to monitor, patrol and defend every part of the border from intrusions during the winter of 1998. Pakistan's intelligence was no doubt aware that due to the vast expanse of the area of this sector, the troops, and resources of 3 Infantry Division were spread thin and therefore it presented as an opportunity for their planned intrusion.

In his memoirs, Musharraf has made a specific mention of 70 Infantry Brigade of the Indian Army, which he claims was being deployed in Dras to undertake a possible offensive by India to capture Pakistani posts. This is an inaccurate assertion as is explained above. Pakistan did have permanent defensive posts along the LOC. In the Kaksar area their posts had observation over short sections of National Highway 1A between Dras and Kargil. They had deployed air defence guns in the ground role to fire onto these sections of the highway to engage Indian civil and military vehicles. These Pakistan Army positions were those that Musharraf assumed were possible objectives for the Indian Army. In fact, rather than plan to capture the Pakistan held positions which could engage vehicles on the highway, it was considered more prudent for the IA to develop and implement a road diversion to eliminate the risk to its civilian and military vehicles. India's Border Roads Organization (BRO) had constructed the diversion and was also working to build another road, as proposed by HQ 3 Infantry Division, branching off short of Dras through Umba La to Suru Valley and onto Kargil. This new road would be beyond the maximum range of Pakistani medium artillery guns and would be outside of visual observation from the LOC. At present a project is underway to build a tunnel under Zoji La to make the road all weather. In the Ladakh region, there is another strategic road axis connecting Ladakh with Himachal Pradesh, which is the Manali-Rohtang Pass-Karu-Leh Road. This axis is utilized by military and civil convoys for winter stocking, tourism, and adventure activities. This road is unique as it crosses over the entire pristine Himalayan range of mountains and reaches the Indus River Valley at Karu and then on to Leh. The Siachen Glacier Sector is separated from the Kargil Sector by the very high mountains of the Ladakh range. Access to the Siachen Sector and the Nubra River Valley, is via an all-weather road from Leh over Khardung La. The road crosses the pass at an altitude of 17,582 ft, which is an engineering feat, and it is maintained by the Indian BRO. There is an all-weather operational airfield at Thoise, giving access to the Nubra Valley. It is of note that any ops in the Kargil Sector would have no bearing on the Siachen Sector.

As mentioned, the forces of the 3 Infantry Division also had the responsibility to defend the hazardous and formidable Siachen Sector. The battalions earmarked for a tenure in the Siachen Sector have to coalesce by withdrawing sub-units from various deployment areas and allowing the commanding officer to prepare his troops for the impending high-altitude deployment. The turnover of battalions in the Siachen Sector involves a detailed and systematic process. It begins with bringing the unit together to prepare and re-equip for the tenure, their move to the Siachen Sector, rigorous training for a month in HA techniques and cold weather warfare, acclimatization at all three stages, induction into various locations on the glacier and Saltoro range, taking over responsibility of defending respective areas and relief of troops that currently hold the area. The de-induction and medical treatment, rest and refit of troops relieved from posts in the Siachen Sector itself takes more than a month. These facts and timelines are not well known, except by those troops who have undergone a tenure in the Siachen sector. Troops who are de-inducted after a three-month spell at such high-altitude are disoriented, afflicted with skin ailments, and suffer psychologically. They have not had a bath for over three months. Deployment of troops in this sector is a carefully managed exercise and any lack in the protocol and preparation can result in excessive medical casualties and physical distress. The deployment, well-being and effectiveness of these troops was also under the purview of 3 Infantry Division.

In early May 1999, troops of 3 Infantry Division were informed by villagers who had noticed some unusual activity in the higher reaches of the Batalik area. The villagers were part of intelligence gathering resources for the local battalion and formation. Their reports suggested that there were armed men dressed as jihadis who had come across the border into their area. As the intrusions came to light, HQ 3 Infantry Division reported this up the chain of command and put available troops on alert for deployment. With extensive use of helicopters, patrolling and deployment of troops, the extent of the Pakistani intrusion was detected. The intrusion was spread over a very wide area at various heights and remote locations. The Pakistan Army had utilized the large gaps that existed in the Indian Army's deployment of troops and occupied many positions on the Indian side of the LOC. It is to be noted that there had been no serious violation of the LOC by Pakistan since the signing of the

Shimla Agreement in 1972. This aggressive intrusion by Pakistan in 1999 across the LOC was an unprecedented event, in the shadow of the recent Lahore summit.

The intrusion across the LOC, likely put in motion soon after the 21 February 1999 Lahore Declaration, did take the Indian Armed Forces, at various levels, by surprise. Due to this element of surprise, the intrusions achieved some initial success. At that time, in India, there was a general impression that the Lahore Declaration and the diplomacy surrounding it were an indication of Pakistan's interest in easing tensions. The optics of the Lahore summit did indeed point in that direction. The Pakistan Army, however, had set the wheels in motion towards this aggression months in advance.

It soon came to light that Pakistan's plan was based on deception in various forms, from political to military. The political duplicity has been highlighted above. In terms of the military, it is known that the Pakistan Army deployed its regular troops in mujahideen attire across the LOC and referred to them as freedom fighters. This was an attempt at subterfuge by General Musharraf and his cronies, to absolve themselves of accountability. However, this plan would unravel quickly once the intrusion and its scale were detected. Positions occupied by Pakistan were contained swiftly and some were made to recoil by troops of 3 Infantry Division within a few days. These initial encounters helped the Indian Army find evidence that the intruders, dressed as mujahideen were in fact Pakistan Army soldiers. ID cards, paybooks, notebooks, letters and other accouterments on their person clearly indicated that the infiltrators were indeed Pakistani soldiers. The counter operation by Indian troops restricted the Pakistanis from gaining any tactical positions which would deny use of India's National Highway 1A. The closest position to this highway that the Pakistani troops could occupy in the Dras Sub-Sector was on a hill feature named Tololing. At this point, the Indian Army response was primarily led by 3 Infantry Division and its troops, and recapturing this peak was a priority objective.

As the scale of the intrusion came to light and Pakistan's direct involvement was highlighted, any ongoing confidence-building measures between India and Pakistan quickly dissipated and the trust and possibility of peace after the Lahore Declaration were eviscerated. This risky gamble by Musharraf and the Pakistan Army was reminiscent of their past misadventures and wars against India. Pakistan has repeatedly underestimated the risks and costs of going to war and India's capabilities and resolve of to defend itself. It is as if Pakistan's leadership is oblivious of the ramifications of war on people and politics. With no heed to the financial, economic, and logistical considerations of sustaining the war, it was an illogical gamble that led Musharraf and his army to attempt to occupy the un-held areas across the LOC. With history as a stark reminder, Pakistan should have known that the likely outcomes of this aggression were going to be of no strategic gains and no tactical advantage, would lead to a possible negative world reaction and loss of face in case of defeat.

Over the years, India has made every effort to respect the sanctity of the LOC, and the agreements signed with Pakistan. The Indian Army had assessed that in the high-altitude terrain of Ladakh, the capture of any positions held by the Pakistan Army would not be worth the effort as additional troops would be required to defend the captured area, thereby increasing the burden on the tenuous logistics system. The physical and material cost of holding picquets and maintaining them is considerable in this inhospitable area. Additional deployment carried out after the Kargil War has borne this to be true. Conversely, for Pakistan, the offensive in Kargil was an intentional plan to capture areas that were not manned by Indian troops. It was a blatant act of aggression and provoked a formidable reaction from India. The international community also denigrated the intrusion, and this combined, strong reaction was not what Pakistan had bargained for.

The Kargil War in Review

Operation Vijay was the codename for India's military operation in the Kargil War of 1999. Pakistan's intrusion was resoundingly beaten back by India during *Op Vijay*. *Vijay* means victory in Hindi, and it was indeed a huge victory for the Indian Armed Forces after which India paused to mourn the loss of the many valiant officers and soldiers who had lost their lives in this unprovoked war. The victory in this war was bittersweet, but it had rallied the nation to come together against an enduring enemy. In the aftermath of the conflict, the Government of India instituted the Kargil Review Committee. This Committee was instated to analyze the possible reasons for Pakistan launching the Kargil War and to highlight lessons that emerged from the war.

A key finding of the Committee was that Pakistan achieved an element of surprise because such a large-scale intrusion was not anticipated by India.[5] Pakistan had launched intrusions in areas which had not been

5. Report of the Kargil Review Committee

occupied since signing of the Karachi agreement, because there was a lack of infrastructure to support ops in the area, and because ops would be unsustainable on an ongoing basis. The inability to logistically build up and maintain troops in the area, especially during heavily snowbound winter months, compounds the problem. The Committee report also indicated when the intrusion began. Details were voluntarily disclosed by Pakistani prisoners who were captured by the 3 Infantry Division, and from documents recovered by Indian troops. The documents indicated that a few Pakistan Army detachments had intruded into the Dras Sector in March 1999. These smaller surveillance teams were sent in advance of the main intruding force by Pakistan, and they were not discovered by Indian Army patrols, helicopter surveillance, satellite imagery, and the limited air photograph sorties.

Between 4–6 May 1999, in the days prior to the detection of Pakistan's intrusions, the DGMO of the Indian Army visited the Ladakh-Kargil-Siachen sectors on a familiarisation visit. In fact, the DGMO visited the Kargil area just one day prior to the detection of the incursion in this Sector. This visit would have been the opportune time to discuss with the formation commanders in Ladakh, if there was any intelligence at Army HQ, that indicated a possible military action by Pakistan. However, it was business as usual, and the DGMO shared no concerns or even suggested the possibility of an intrusion by the Pakistan Army in this Sector. With no threat perception propounded even by the DGMO, it is evident that such a dire contingency was not an immediate threat perception. The Corps HQ and Command HQ for this Sector also did not identify or articulate a threat from Pakistan. In fact, there was a clear lack of intelligence, and 3 Infantry Division had no forewarning as even the higher chain of command had no inkling about the significant, impending intrusion in the Kargil Sector.

Intelligence agencies at various levels of the Armed Forces and the national level have the ability to provide an assessment of threats by analyzing available information from all sources. Without adequate intelligence, the operational commanders at various levels would have to rely solely on their own appreciation and threat analysis on an ongoing basis, based on rudimentary local intelligence. Operational commanders at regional levels have no means at their disposal to obtain intelligence from depth areas far away from their sectors, nor are they mandated to do the same. By their very nature, intelligence assessments can be imperfect and imprecise, and their veracity depends on confirmation and corroboration from various sources. Human intelligence has to carry out a serious analysis of various inputs and formulate a threat perception, and wars are often fought with this imperfect intelligence.

The lack of intelligence that led to the Indian Army being caught by surprise came under much discussion after Pakistan's intrusions were detected. The key aspects of this were addressed at the national level by the Kargil Review Committee. As highlighted above, intelligence reports were non-existent regarding the Pakistani intrusion in Kargil. On the ground, the ability of the local forces to obtain tactical intelligence from across the LOC was severely curtailed by terrain and the heavy accumulation of snow in the winter months. The capability to surveil this vast area with the reduced number of troops was also limited. Undoubtedly, the intelligence gathering effort in this sector required more hi-tech tools and more comprehensive support.

At the national level, advanced and complex technical resources and agencies gather intelligence. These resources include technical gadgetry, communication intercepts, electronic surveillance, air and satellite imagery, satellite surveillance, air reconnaissance, drones, personnel posted at foreign missions, information from allies, social media and cyberspace, signal intelligence, human intelligence, and so on. It is safe to say that the interpretation of threats and the coordination between the various intelligence organizations in India, as brought out by the Kargil Review Committee, was flawed. The lack of intelligence was acknowledged by Gen. V. P. Malik, the COAS during the Kargil conflict. He writes in his book – *Kargil: From Surprise to Victory*, 'There was not the faintest hint that the Pakistan Army was planning or preparing to send in regular troops on a large scale into the Kargil Sector.' [6]

Information about Pakistan's intrusions and intensions were obtained in real time as the intrusions unraveled. Once attack ops were launched to evict the intruders, IA troops retrieved documents and information from the captured Pakistani prisoners and from the dead bodies of their soldiers. It was ascertained that the Pakistan Army troops participating in the intrusion were trained for weeks in cold weather warfare in the area of Bunji-Gilgit. The HQ and training centre of Pakistan's NLI is located in this area. In interactions with captured prisoners, 3 Infantry Division established that extensive and specialized training was imparted to these troops in preparation for the intrusions. This included tactical training,

6. *Kargil: From Surprise Victory* by Gen VP Malik pp34

mountaineering techniques, training to counter the effects of high altitude, use and handling of special weapons and equipment, health and survival techniques, and the proper use of extreme cold weather clothing. Select personnel were also trained in radio communications and deception. Troops were trained in the use of surface-to-air missiles, rocket launchers, heavy machine guns, and directing artillery fire.

Even as India and the world discovered the scale of Pakistan's deployment in the Kargil intrusion, Pakistan denied any involvement and claimed that it was mercenary freedom fighters who were perpetrating the attack. This narrative did not hold water for long as the captured Pakistani soldiers exposed the attack being carried out by Pakistan Army troops. In his memoirs, General Musharraf once again tried to provide an alternate narrative. He described the intrusion as a defensive manoeuvre by saying, 'In the operation, the large un-held gaps in the existing deployment were to be occupied, and the troops were given special instructions not to cross the watershed along the LOC5.' In this statement he does acknowledge that it was the Pakistan Army troops who undertook the intrusion. If those were the instructions to his troops, then how does Musharraf explain the fact that the Pakistan Army transgressed the LOC and occupied areas across it?

The Kargil offensive was not a defensive manoeuvre but an act of war. Musharraf persisted and referred to the Pakistan Army troops carrying out the intrusion, as freedom fighters. It is a known fact that irregular fighters – jihadis, insurgents, and terrorists, do not capture and hold ground. That is not their modus operandi. Soldiers on the other hand are trained to capture an area, defend it and use conventional ops of war in that pursuit. This is what was enacted in Kargil, further proving that it was Pakistan Army soldiers who were perpetrating the intrusion. In the area of Zoji La, Dras, Kargil and Batalik, the local population is sparse, and most people live in small villages. Kargil is the only small town and a district HQ, and there is no other urban area. If Pakistan had inducted terrorists to start an insurgency in the district, they would have found no support from the small local population, which is aligned with India. 3 Infantry Division had conducted many goodwill gestures for the locals to maintain a degree of trust and to build an affiliation that they could rely upon. Building tangible goodwill and demonstrating an interest in the well-being of the locals is a consistent effort by the IA to uplift the areas where their forces are deployed.

This goodwill and strong affiliation between the locals and the Army in the Ladakh and Kargil Sectors, proved invaluable to 3 Infantry Division. In the Kargil Sector, the village headmen (*sarpanch*) were provided landline telephones through the Army exchange. This was done so that they could report on the presence of any intruders in these areas. These local residents were the first to inform the nearest IA battalion of the presence of intruders in the area. Even though there was no prior intelligence forthcoming from other sources the local intelligence machinery was functional, and Pakistan's intrusions were detected as they were taking place, by the most basic channels of intelligence gathering. The armed men coming across the border were no mujahideen and this was evident from the outset. In fact, it was the Northern Light Infantry (NLI) battalions that were employed for the intrusion by Pakistan. These battalions are organized like any other infantry unit in the Pakistan Army, with regular officers posted to these battalions. These units were raised in 1993 by the amalgamation of Karakoram Scouts, Northern Scouts, and Gilgit Scouts. They are specially trained in heliborne, anti-heliborne ops, commando ops, mountain and cold weather warfare. Some of them received training with the SSG. Trained as regular infantry, they have been operational in Gilgit-Baltistan for decades.

The Pakistan Army used various means of psychological warfare, disinformation, and deception to augment the overall war effort in Kargil. While conducting radio communications, to make sure their intercepts were hard to decipher, Pakistani troops used various obscure dialects, such as Balti, Shina, and Chilas and sometimes Pashto and Urdu. HQ 3 Infantry Division initially had no interpreters who could translate and understand communications in these dialects of Gilgit-Baltistan. Volunteers were soon locally garnered from Kargil town. Once again, as a result of the goodwill the Army had built in the area, civilian help was quickly forthcoming. As the conflict became public, the local population in the area was very motivated to help in any way that they could. To help expel the intrusion, civilian folks from Batalik, Kargil and Leh volunteered to carry logistic loads including ammunition to the administrative areas augmenting the effort to support troops undertaking the offensive. These porters marched on foot for more than two days and carried heavy loads to their destination bases. In the Kargil war, the many remote mountainous crags and cliffs where the counter intrusion battle was fought in May–July 1999, were only accessible by the IA and their support staff.

No reporters, no observers, no civilians witnessed firsthand, the selfless sacrifice of this high-altitude battle. This was true especially in the initial days when only 3 Infantry Division was leading the counter-offensive. The single-minded resolve and endurance that was demonstrated by the Indian

Army soldiers and officers to launch attacks and to defend the country at these extremes, was absolutely staggering. Indeed, the efforts to secure these treacherous regions need to be underscored and applauded, far more than has been done. Once the counter-offensive was launched, troops of 3 Infantry Division began to wear down the Pakistan Army's troops. They prevented the expansion of the intrusion to a greater depth and depleted the enemy resources inflicting casualties. The forces of 3 Infantry Division also prepared the battlefield for conducting eviction ops and captured/ killed some of the intruders, which provided valuable intel. Despite the initial element of surprise, the perseverance and sacrifice of the soldiers of 3 Infantry Division in preparing the battlefield, laid a solid foundation for the counter offensive that was soon launched after troops were acclimatized, briefed, prepared and rehearsed.

Patrolling in the high altitude Ladakh area in the winter months is known to be very hazardous. Commanders and their staff were aware of the grim reality that the Indian Army had lost over 100 personnel while patrolling this treacherous landscape, which was rife with avalanches and other dangers. As the height of winter abated, by early May 1999, the roads on the Pakistan side of the LOC opened to traffic, and Pakistan's intrusion began across the LOC. Pakistan's plan were to establish positions across the LOC prior to the opening of Zoji La, on the Indian side, for vehicular traffic. This plan, however, was delayed as the Burzil Bai Pass in the Skardu division and areas of Baltistan also had a heavy accumulation of snow and therefore opened later than expected for road traffic. On the Indian side of the LOC, the Zoji La was opened earlier than expected on 1 May 1999 by the Indian Border Roads. This early road access facilitated the movement of additional Indian armed forces troops and logistics convoys to support 3 Division's counter-offensive. It also facilitated the move and buildup of additional resources required for eviction of the intrusion by Pakistan.

With full knowledge of the difficulties of attack ops, soldiers and officers fought valiantly to evict the enemy. Fighting selflessly with whatever equipment that was available and no bulletproof vests, they represented the best and the brave of the country. In the initial days, 3 Infantry Division moved its tactical HQ to Kargil on 7 May and actively directed the war effort from there. The counter intrusion ops were put into top gear and the Division's senior leadership was immersed in real-time strategic and tactical planning, formulating plans for the attack ops, ordering redeployment of troops in the divisional sector, establishing contact with enemy and managing troop rotations.

Within a few days in May 1999, IA reinforcements began to arrive, and after due acclimatization, augmented the counter offensive of 3 Infantry Division. At this stage of the conflict, the forces arriving into the divisional sector were assigned missions, briefed, prepared for attack ops, given available combat support and launched into ops. It was soon assessed; after obtaining information about the extent and depth of the Pakistani intrusion, additional forces would be required to evict the enemy. Accordingly, 8 Mountain Division was inducted in stages into the sector by 1 June with the op responsibility of ousting the Pakistani intrusion from the Dras and Mashkoh sectors. 3 Infantry Division continued with its assigned defensive posture against China and Pakistan, and was responsible for eviction ops in Kargil, Batalik, and Turtuk. More infantry units were allocated to 3 Infantry Division, additional combat support arms allotted, a secure logistics chain was established and the IAF were also deployed. Additional reserve formations were available to contend with any further escalation of the war. It was a coordinated effort to make a final push to defeat the enemy.

The Turnaround

Subsequent to their defeat, the modus operandi of the Pakistan Army and its intrusion was analyzed. It became known from the prisoners captured that the participating units of the Pakistan Army had been moved to concentration areas opposite the respective areas of ingress, one to two days prior to the intrusion. These concentration areas were beyond the maximum range of Indian medium artillery guns and where physical observation was not possible. For the intrusion into the Kargil-Batalik area, troops were moved north of Olthinthang, for intruding into the Dras-Mashkoh Sectors, area south of the Burzil Bai Pass on the axis to Kel was selected, and opposite the Turtuk Sector, the Skardu-Piun-Siari axis was used with HQ at Minimarg. At the concentration areas, the soldiers' uniforms were exchanged for local attire resembling those of the mujahideen. They were equipped with the necessary extreme cold weather clothing and equipment. Task forces were presumably prepared, assigned missions, and then launched into designated areas across the LOC. The Pakistani troops occupied snow-clad areas with no resources to prepare defences. As the contact with the Indian Army troops began on and after 6/7 May 1999, both sides began suffering casualties. The initial Pakistani intrusions were contained by the troops of 3 Infantry Division, and they were forced to withdraw from their forward positions. At this juncture, it was apparent that the Pakistan Army had intruded across a wide frontage in the Dras-Kargil-Batalik Sector and would try to establish their positions on the ridges in the un-held ridge lines in Chorbatla and the Turtuk Sector.

As explained, there was a paucity of Indian Army troops in the Ladakh Sector to defeat such a large-scale intrusion. The existing forces in the Sector, which were spread throughout this vast area, were relocated and deployed to contain the incursion. Once the intrusion was detected, the immediate actions taken by 3 Infantry Division included:

a. Gaining information about the extent and depth of the intrusions and their simultaneous containment. Engaging of the Pakistani positions with available artillery and mortar fire causing casualties. In certain areas, the Pakistan Army forward elements were forced to withdraw.

b. Re-deployment in the Ladakh Sector was done to make resources available to contest the intrusion in the Kargil sector while maintaining balance in other sectors. Areas astride NHIA were secured, including the Zoji La. All key defended localities were occupied forthwith to prevent any further expansion of the intrusions.

c. Directing the build-up of additional combat troops, supporting arms, and logistics elements, the dumping of ammunition and establishment of a logistics chain. Troops were given adequate time for acclimatization, while moving enroute to deployment areas and on arrival. In the urgency of launching attacks on the intruding enemy, the need for acclimatization was a major consideration. Quick induction of reinforcements was also critical to the plan for defeating the intrusions.

d. In most areas along the steep mountainsides, gun positions had to be prepared in an unorthodox manner as there was limited space for conventional deployment.

e. A few sub-units were deployed at select locations in the existing gaps on the LOC to act as firm bases for making counter-intrusions if permitted by Army HQ and the political leadership. No violation of the LOC was done during the war by the Indian Army.

f. Extension of line communication over vast frontages away from roadheads was undertaken to establish and maintain command and control. This was time-consuming but necessary as the high-frequency radio sets available offered no secrecy and were prone to monitoring. Very high-frequency (VHF) radio sets were ineffective due to screening in the mountains.

g. Continuous efforts were made towards preparing the battlefield for offensive ops to evict the enemy. All ranks were fully briefed, motivated and geared to launch attacks to evict the Pakistani troops and defeat the intrusion.

h. Launching of deliberate multidirectional attacks with acclimatized troops commenced by the third week of May 1999.

3 Infantry Division, despite its limited personnel and logistics, launched offensive ops to evict the Pakistani intrusion, and continued its multi-faceted defensive role against the Chinese in Eastern Ladakh and the Kargil-Siachen Sectors. GOC 3 Infantry Division moved to Kargil on 7 May 1999, directing the war effort from there till victory was declared at the national level on 26 July 1999.

The identity and affiliation of Pakistani troops in the Kargil operation became known as the counter intrusion progressed. In the Batalik Sector, Pakistani troops of 5 and 8 NLI battalions and, later, 22 Sind were deployed in the intrusion. In the Mashkoh-*Tiger Hill* Sector, 12 NLI, and in Dras-Tololing-Kaksar the troops deployed were from 6 and 11 NLI battalions. In the Turtuk Sector, troops deployed were from 4 and 9 NLI. A few SSG troops were attached to these units. In addition, there were troops holding fixed defences on or in proximity to the LOC.

After years of training and operational exercises, IA troops, who had mostly never seen an active war, rose to the task and resolved to defeat the intrusion by Pakistan. The Indian Army deployed units comprising troops from J&K and other regiments. The units from Kashmir were 12 J&K Light Infantry, 13 J&K Rifles, 14 J&K Rifles and Ladakh Scouts. A coordinated counter offensive against Pakistan was launched by the IA in all sectors. All deployed forces demonstrated great bravery, national pride and a commendable performance in the face of grave danger.

Many exceptional heroes emerged, and many young officers and soldiers gave the ultimate sacrifice of their lives in the pursuit of the Nation's sovereignty and defeating the enemy. The offensive spirit, dauntless courage and confidence displayed by young leaders was exceptional. The planning and presence of formation commanders in the forward areas, to provide real-time decisions and influence attack ops, added to the motivation and high morale. With a multipronged strategy, India demonstrated its supremacy over an ill-planned Pakistani operation. While tactically, the war was being fought to evict the Pakistani intrusion, India was also prepared strategically to expand the war to the western borders with Pakistan. India also channeled its prowess in diplomacy and was able to isolate Pakistan diplomatically.

When the Pakistan Army intrusion was detected, 3 Infantry Division of the Indian Army was in situ and commenced counter-intrusion ops in areas Dras, Kaksar, Kargil, Batalik, Chorbatala and Turtuk. Deploying all forces currently available, the aim was to contain and eliminate the intrusion and re-capture areas to gain dominance. As described previously, 3 Infantry Division with its available resources had to maintain a balance continuing with its defensive role against China-Pakistan and launching the counter offensive against the Pakistani intrusion. As the conflict with Pakistan continued, it became apparent that additional troops were necessary to supplement 3 Infantry Division's response, to add to the strength of India's counter offensive and to maintain the defense of the remainder border with China-Pakistan. A larger, more concerted push was needed from India's Armed Forces to accomplish the mission to oust the Pakistan Army intrusion from the Kargil Sector. To supplement the eviction ops, 8 Mountain Division moved to Mughalpura on 1 June 1999 and took over the responsibility of Dras and Mashkoh sectors.

The Pakistani troops who had now been in battle for a few weeks could only create makeshift fire positions, called *sangars*, using available rocks and stones. In the inhospitable terrain and the cold weather, they had no overhead cover or protection. It was impossible to dig trenches in the rugged rocky terrain and stony rubble. Their positions provided limited or no protection from artillery and mortar fire and were difficult to manage and maintain. The Pakistani soldiers at these posts lacked replenishments in terms ammunition, food and water. They also lacked the means for medical aid and casualty evacuation. These posts could not have been sustained for long and were in fact being worn out by the 3 Division's offensive.

The Indian Air Force (IAF) had joined the counter offensive on 26 May 1999 adding to the psychological advantage and contributed to the attrition of Pakistani positions. Attack helicopters were used initially but were grounded when one was downed on 28 May 1999 by an air defense missile. Steadily, the pressure on the Pakistani troops grew more intense as they were unprepared for a long-drawn war. Key areas of the intrusion came under repeated attacks by both 3 Division and 8 Division of the Indian Army. Intense artillery shelling took a toll on the Pakistani troops as they had no escape and limited support. This coordinated effort by the Indian Armed Forces led to the Pakistan Army positions being steadily weakened and captured.

As the ops progressed, radio intercepts of the Pakistan soldiers indicated a low morale and a desperation to survive. After the snowmelt, by mid-June 1999, there was no water available on the mountain tops that the Pakistani troops were continuing to hold. Relentless shelling, air attacks on their positions, shelling of their maintenance routes, and lack of means for evacuation of the sick and wounded caused a collapse of morale in the Pakistan troops. A few weeks into the intrusion, an intercept of Pakistani communications by the Indian Army seemed to indicate that Osama bin Laden was sending his fighters to reinforce the intrusion area. This was an attempt at subterfuge, perhaps to boost the sagging morale of Pakistan's troops in the intrusion area. Other communication intercepts highlighted a grim picture of the condition of Pakistani troops and indicated the desperate situation they were facing. There were several injured Pakistani soldiers who urgently required medical aid, had sustained life-threatening injuries and required immediate evacuation. No help seemed to be forthcoming for them. Food and water were not available to them, and some intercepts suggested that troops were in dire straits and surviving by eating salt alone. At most of their positions ammunition had been destroyed by Indian shelling, and with no help or reinforcements coming, soldiers felt they were being made martyrs unnecessarily and felt abandoned.

By the end of June, the situation was extremely dire for the Pakistan Army troops. Their occupied positions were collapsing and were being besieged by the determined attacks of the Indian Army which had isolated them from all flanks. Yet again, the soldiers of the Pakistan army were facing the grim consequences of an unsustainable war, in which they could not have prevailed. On 10 July, a ceasefire came into effect. An act of war that began with the intrusion by Pakistan Army troops dressed in the garb of mujahideen did not lead to the desired result envisaged by the Pakistan Army leadership. With a determined and coordinated effort, the Kargil war was fought till victory, which was achieved by 3 Infantry Division, 8

Mountain Division and the Indian Air Force. This War was an ill-conceived misadventure by Pakistan, with poor strategic thought, planning and execution. The Pakistani intrusions collapsed, but it led to mindless loss of life on both sides. It also led to further mistrust and division between the two neighbouring countries.

An outline of the sequence of events that led up to the capture of Pakistani positions in the intrusion area is given in Annexure 12.

Annexure 12
Eviction of Pakistani Intrusion
(Names of places relate to Appendices A to E below)

- **4–6 May:** DGMO visits 3 Infantry Division Sector.
- **6 May:** Intrusion is reported by civilian members of the local formation's intelligence team.
- **7 May:** Tactical HQ 3 Infantry Division moves to Kargil from Leh. Patrols launched to contact intruders.
- **7–10 May:** 3 Infantry Division is mobilised.
    - Helicopter surveillance and additional patrols are launched to discern the extent and depth of Pakistani intrusion.
    - 12 J&K LI and 1/11 Gorkha Rifles are deployed in the Batalik Sector.
    - HQ 70 Infantry Brigade is assigned responsibility for evicting Pakistani intrusion from the Batalik Sector.
    - Units of this formation are ordered to move from Kashmir Valley to the Ladakh Sector as the Zoji La was open for road traffic.
    - 9 Mahar reinforces the Turtuk Sector. A company from Ladakh Scouts is deployed on the LOC, NE of Point 5140, to be prepared to make counter intrusion, if permitted.
    - 1 Bihar moved to the Batalik Sector and establishes contact with Pakistani intrusion in Juber.
    - 1/11 GR contacts Pakistani intrusion and closes in on Kukerthang.
    - 12 J&K LI moves towards the east and makes contact with Pakistani intrusion in the Khalubar complex.

- **08–14 May:** 16 Grenadiers and 60 BSF Battalion reinforce respective defended areas. Zoji La and dominating heights astride NH1A are occupied. 18 Grenadiers arrives in the Dras Sector.
- **15 May:** HQ 56 Mountain Brigade, 8 Sikh, and 1 Naga arrive in the Dras Sector. HQ 56 Mountain Brigade is assigned the responsibility for the Dras Sector.
- **16–21 May:** Additional artillery units arrive and are deployed in the Dras and Kargil Sectors, and a logistics chain is established. Troops arriving acclamatise and prepare for eviction ops.
- **22–23 May:** Eviction ops commence. 18 Grenadiers launches an attack on Tololing. The attack is unsuccessful. 8 Sikh patrols east and north of *Tiger Hill* encounter the enemy.
- **24 May:** 1 Naga launches attack on Point 5140 from east and north and on 3 Pimples from west to isolate Pakistani position at Tololing. 8 Sikh contains intrusion on Tiger Hill. HQ 76 Mountain Brigade and 17 Jat arrive and are deployed in the Mashkoh Sector. HQ 76 Mountain Brigade is given responsibility for the Mashkoh Sector.
- **25 May:** 18 Garhwal Rifles arrive in Moghalpura. Tactical HQ (I) 120 Infantry Brigade is moved to Kaksar, and HQ 70 Infantry Brigade is moved to Ganasok.
- **26 May:** Attacks by 1 Bihar, 1/11 GR, and 12 J&K LI on their respective objectives are not successful. These units are given more time to plan and prepare before the launch of further attacks. Two Indian Air Force MiG aircraft are brought down in the Batalik Sector, one due to an engine flame out and the other due to an air defence missile hit.
- **27 May:** 17 Jat progresses ops towards Point 4875 and captures Point 4540. 1 Naga makes another attempt to capture Point 5140, but the attack stalls.
- **28 May:** 1 Bihar attacks Juber and Point 4262. Attack stalls due to lack of fire support. Selected Ladakh Scouts troops under Maj. Sonam Wangchuk lifted in Cheetah helicopters, one in each sortie, to secure the area between Point 6041 and Tapkochand near Chorbatla. They encounter Pakistani soldiers climbing up an escarpment, killing six of them. The identification of Pakistani soldiers is obtained from documents carried by them.

- **29 May:** Bodies of killed Pakistani soldiers are recovered from the steep and rugged area and are evacuated to HQ 15 Corps at Srinagar.
- **30 May:** The Indian Defence Minister and COAS visit Kargil. Visitors are briefed on the assessment of Pakistani intrusion and plans for eviction of intrusion. The COAS exhorts all present to evict the Pakistani intrusion.
- **1 June:** HQ 8 Mountain Division, arrived in Mughalpura, takes over responsibility for the eviction ops in the Dras and Mashkoh Sectors.

Operations by 3 Infantry Division (See Appendices C, D, & E below)

Batalik Sector

- **1 June:** HQ 70 Infantry Brigade exploits the eastern flank of Pakistani intrusion. A company of 12 J&K LI captures Point 5390.
- **2–5 June:** Preparation for attacks in the Batalik Sector.
- **6 June:** 12 J&K LI attacks Point 5203; the attack is beaten back due to loss of surprise.
- **6–18 June:** Pakistani positions are softened with artillery and mortar fire. Additional troops are brought in for capture of Point 5203. 3 Infantry Division receives an additional regiment of 155 mm Bofors guns, which was deployed near Dah. Multi-barrel rocket launchers (MBRLs) and a regiment of 130 mm medium guns are deployed in a direct firing role. The assessed Pakistani route of maintenance is targeted with artillery fire. Ammunition stocks are built up to the desired level. Attack plans are prepared, formation and unit commanders are briefed, and rehearsals are carried out. A new deputy GOC is posted in and reports to HQ 3 Infantry Division at Kargil.
- **19/20 June:** Point 5203 is captured by troops of 5 Para and 12 J&K LI. Routes to Churbar Sispo, Padmago, Stangba, and the LOC lie open for further attacks and block Pakistani positions from the east and north.
- **21 June:** 17 Garhwal Rifles (17 Garh Rif) and 22 Grenadiers arrive in the Divisional Sector.
- **23–24 June:** 17 Garh Rif is inducted into Batalik toward the western

flank of the Pakistani intrusion, and 22 Grenadiers are moved to Ganasok towards east.

- **25–28 June:** Acclimatization and preparation for attack by 1 Bihar on Juber and 17 Garh Rif on *Kala Pathar* from the west. They move forward on foot and establish firm bases.
- **29 June:** 1 Bihar and 17 Garh Rif attack respective objectives. Both units secure footholds in proximity to Pakistani positions.
- **30 June–4 July:** The reconnaissance group of HQ 70 Infantry Brigade with Brigadier Devinder Singh is moved towards the western flank to influence ops. Brigadier Ashok Duggal, Deputy GOC, moves to the eastern flank at Ganasok to coordinate preparation for attack ops. GOC, 3 Infantry Division moves between Batalik, Ganasok and Turtuk.
- **1–2 July:** Destructive shoot is carried out with mass artillery fire on the western flank of enemy positions. A few bulletproof jackets that are received in Kargil are issued to 17 Garh Rif.
- **3–4 July:** Preparation for attack along both flanks of Pakistani intrusion. *Juber* is subjected to a destructive shoot.
- **5–6 July:** Simultaneous attacks are launched by 1 Bihar and 17 Garh Rif on the western flank. 1 Bihar captures *Juber* and Point 4924. 17 Garh Rif captures *Kala Pathar* and moves along the ridgeline towards Point 5285. Brig Devinder Singh returns to Ganasok to direct ops on the eastern flank.
- **6–7 July:** Simultaneous attacks are launched along the eastern flank of Pakistani intrusion by 12 J&K LI, 1/11 GR, 22 Grenadiers, and Ladakh Scouts. 12 J&K LI captures Point 4812, 1/11 GR captures Khalubar, 22 Grenadiers establishes a foothold at Point 5287, and Ladakh Scouts secure *Padmago*. 1/11 GR captures *Kukerthang* and exploits up to *Tharu*.
- **8 July:** 17 Garh Rif captures Point 5285. 1 Bihar links up with 17 Garh Rif at *Saddle*. Western flank of enemy intrusion secured up to LOC. Pakistani positions are routed in Batalik Sector.
- **10 July:** A ceasefire comes into effect.
- **16–26 Jul:** 70 Inf Brigade was ordered to advance up to the LOC and secure/capture the ridgeline which the Brigade accomplished. Meanwhile 14 Sikh had been inducted into Chorbatla area. After

due acclimatization the battalion took over defences in the area. The battalion pre-empted the enemy to secure Point 5310.

Sub-Sector West (SSW)/Sub-Sector Haneef (SSH)

- **7–10 May:** 27 Rajput takes over responsibility in Southern Glacier Sector. 9 Mahar allotted to 102 Inf Brigade for ops in SSW.
- **11–25 May:** Relief of troops in the central glacier.
- **1–7 June**: HQ 102 Infantry Brigade was tasked to occupy/capture the ridgeline from Point 5590 towards NW. 11 Raj Rif arrives in the area, prepares for ops. 13 Kumaon, which was de-inducted from the Northern Glacier, is concentrated at Panamik for rest and refit.
- **8–9 June:** 11 Raj Rif attacks Point 5590, the attack is repulsed. Captain Haneef Uddin is martyred. The area is redesignated as Sub-Sector Haneef (SSH)
- **10 June:** 9 Mahar recovers a large cache of small arms from the Turtuk village after obtaining information from local folks. GOC visits SSH, discusses and approves the plan for the capture of the crest line of point 5950 and point 5770 in southern glacier sub-sector.
- **12–17 June:** 11 Raj Rif displaying exceptional courage, capture Point 5950 and Point 5590.
- **18–23 June:** 13 Kumaon having been staged forward to SSH, in a series of attacks, captures Point 5810, Point 5685, and *Ring Contour.*
- **25–26 June:** 102 Infantry brigade with troops from 27 Rajput and HAWS launches ops for the capture of Point 5770 to improve dominance in the southern Siachen Sector. Troops scale a vertical ice wall, achieve complete surprise, and capture the Pakistani position.
- **1 July:** All Pakistani positions are eliminated from the LOC in the area by 102 Infantry Brigade, except the permanent defences they held prior to this war.

Kargil-Kaksar Sub-Sector

- **7–11 May:** 121(I) Infantry Brigade occupies key locations and establishes observation post opposite Pakistani fixed defences.

- **07–15 May:** Extensive patrolling and helicopter reconnaissance is conducted. Enemy positions identified and contained. The enemy in the intrusion area is engaged with artillery and mortar fire. The Bde commander is moved to Dras to coordinate action against enemy intrusion. Permanent defences are reinforced. Bde commander returns to Kargil handing over Dras Sector to Commander 56 Mountain Brigade and later moves to Kaksar.
- **18 May:** A company, each from 28 Rashtriya Rifles and from 8 Border Security Force are deployed in the area on a spur opposite Point 5280. No further progress is made in eviction ops in the area as troops were not available for attack.
- **19–27 June:** Change of command takes place in the 121 Infantry Brigade on 19 June. 14 J&K Rif is allotted to the Brigade for eviction ops. This battalion is given time to acclimatize and prepare for the attack. The new brigade commander familiarizes himself with the area of ops.
- **28 June:** 14 J&K Rif launches preliminary ops on Point 5608, Point 5280, and *Spur Junction*. The attacks were unsuccessful.
- **1Jul–4 Jul:** Further attempts were made to evict the enemy in the area. These too were unsuccessful.
- **5 Jul–9 July:** No further progress is made in the Sub-Sector due to the paucity of troops and lack of fire support.
- **10 July:** A ceasefire comes into effect. Pakistani troops withdraw from the area.
- **13–16 July:** 121 (I) 121 Inf Brigade occupies new positions along the LOC. The GOC and Brigade Commander climb *Saddle* and *Spur Junction* near Point 5280 to view new positions on the ground.

Ops by 8 Mountain Division (See Appendices A and B)

Dras Sector

- **1 June:** HQ 8 Mountain Division arrives and takes over responsibility to evict Pakistani intrusion from the Dras and Mashkoh Sectors. Two of its brigades had been inducted prior to this date and had been assigned operational missions by the GOC, 3 Infantry Division. Attacks on enemy positions commenced, as earlier stated.

- **13–17 June:** 2 Raj Rif launches a multi-directional attack and captures *Tololing*; it maintains momentum and captures *Hump*. Counterattacks by Pakistani troops are all defeated, and the battalion is reorganized on the captured objectives. Ops are resumed for the elimination of the Pakistani position on Point 5140. *Rocky Knob*, a small feature at the base of Point 5140, is captured by 13 J&K Rif.
- **18–20 June:** 18 Garh Rif, 1 Naga, and 13 J&K Rif are employed from various directions for the capture of Point 5140. Exceptional gallantry is displayed by troops of 13 J&K Rif. The Pakistanis suffer a considerable number of casualties. The objective is captured.
- **18–20 June:** 1 Naga attacks *Black Tooth*; objective is captured.
- **28–30 June:** Assessing that Pakistanis used a route through Point 4700 for maintenance, this feature is attacked and captured by 18 Garh Rif.
- **28–29 June:** The area of *3 Pimples* is captured by 2 Raj Rif.
- **30 June–2 July:** 18 Grenadiers carries out reconnaissance and prepares an attack plan for the capture of *Tiger Hill*.
- **3 July:** Indian Air Force carries out air attacks on *Tiger Hill*. 155 mm Bofors guns are employed in a direct firing role to engage the objective.
- **4 July:** The area of *Tongue* and the Western face of *Tiger Hill* are captured. This is followed by the capture of the eastern slope and the peak of *Tiger Hill*.
- **5 July:** 8 Sikh captures a hill feature called *Helmet*, which ensures the interdiction of the supply route to *Tiger Hill*.
- **8 July:** After defeating many counterattacks by the Pakistan Army, the Indian Flag is hoisted by troops of 18 Grenadiers on top of *Tiger Hill*.

Mashkoh Sector

- **1 July:** HQ 79 Mountain Brigade arrived earlier and had been geared up to conduct eviction ops. The battalions under this formation commence ops.

- **4 July:** 13 J&K Rif, who earlier gained fame, in the capture of Point 5140, launches an attack on Point 4875. A simultaneous attack is launched by 17 Jat for the capture of *Pimple* and *Whaleback*. All the objectives are captured.
- **6 July:** 2 Naga attacks and successfully captures *Twin Bumps*. 6 Para, assisted by 1 Para (SF), captures Point 4745.
- 7 **July:** 7 Para captures Point 4700.
- **8 July:** A raid on *Raki* mortar position results in the capture of three 120 mm mortars and two 81 mm mortars.
- **22–24 July:** After due planning and preparation, 3/3 GR launches ops on *Zulu Spur*, which comprised *Tri-junction, Zulu Ridge*, and *Sandow Top*. The former two objectives are captured.
- **25 July:** 9 Para (SF) captures Sando Top.

Appx A

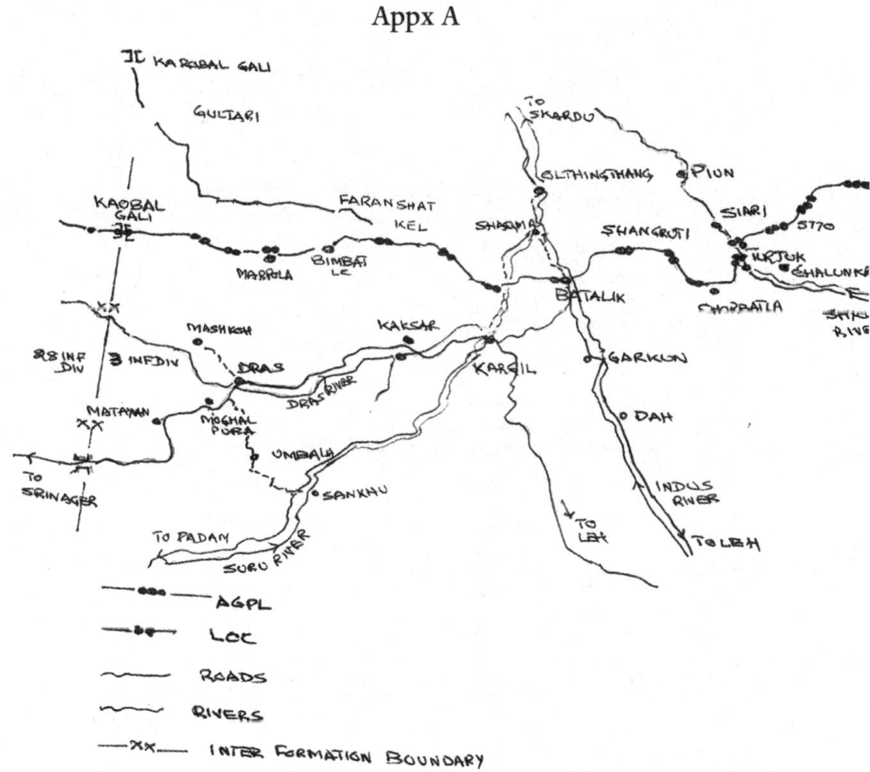

Sketch of Area of OPS: Kargil War 1999
***Note:** The sketch is not to scale*

Appx B

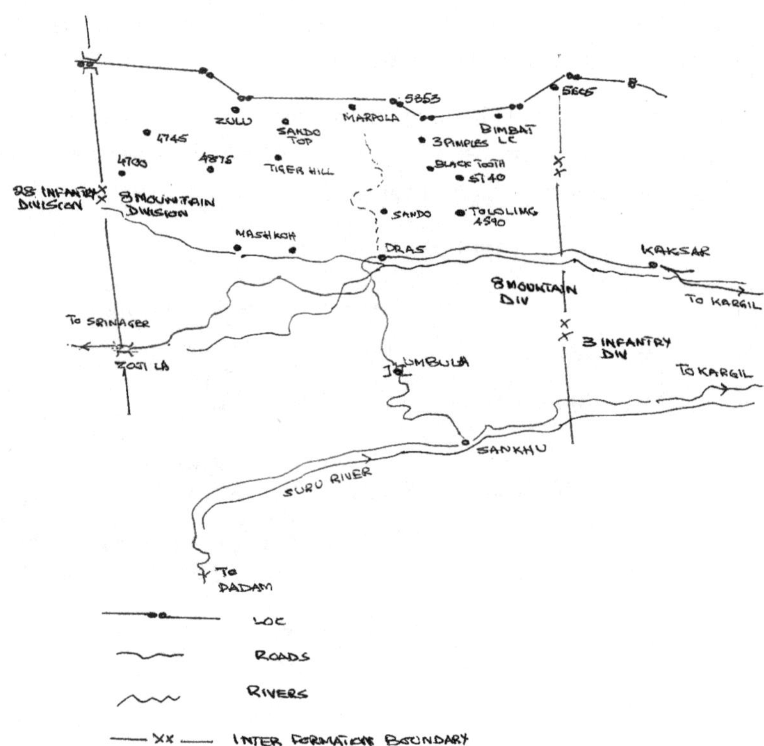

Sketch of Dras and Maskoh Sectors, 1 June 1999

Appx C

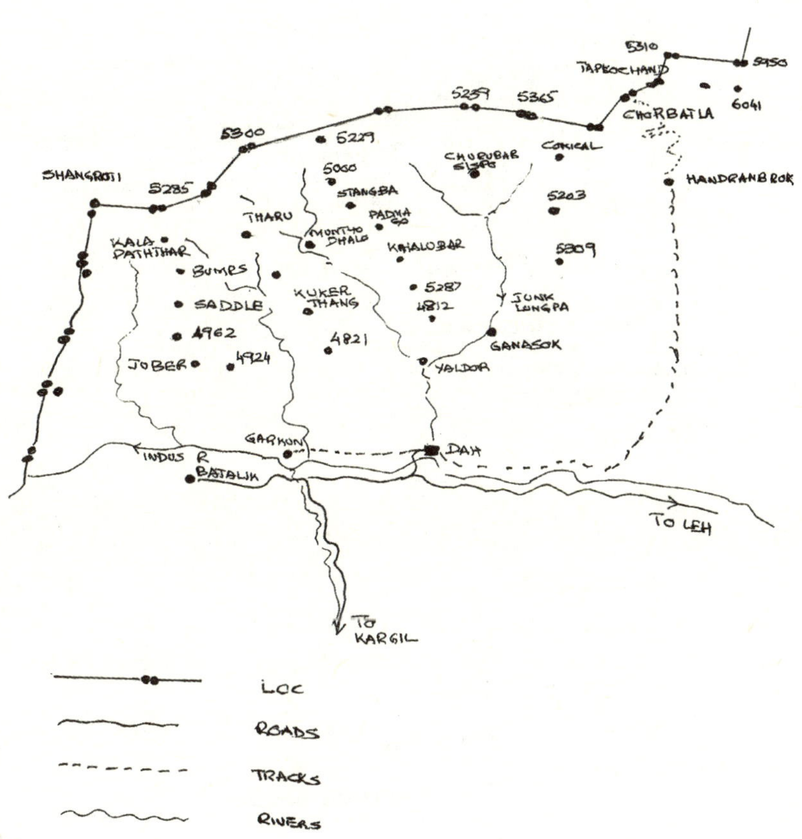

Sketch of Batalik Sector
Note: *The sketch is not to scale. All heights are in metres*

Appx D

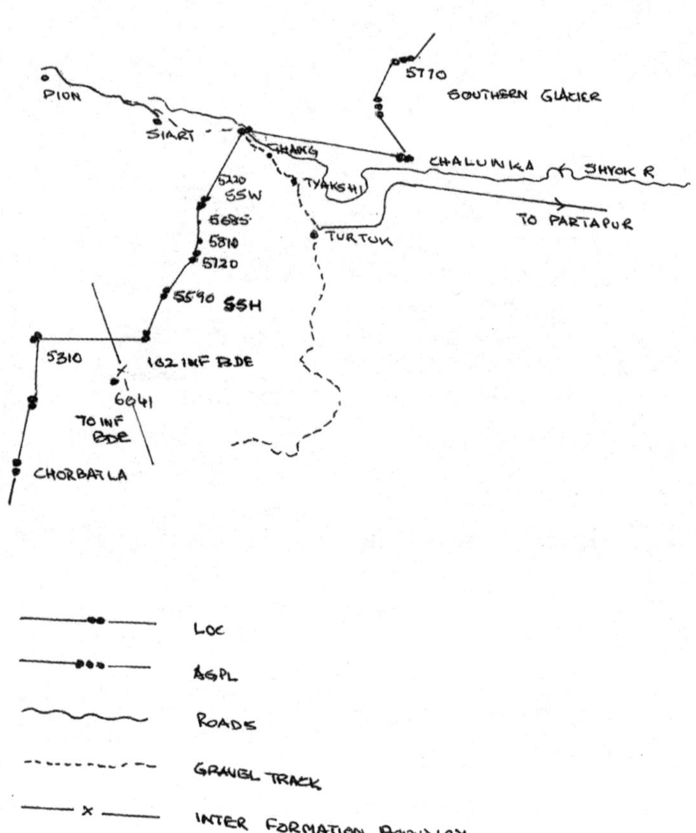

Sketch of Area Sub Sector Haneef Sub-Sector West and Southern Siachen Sector

Appx E

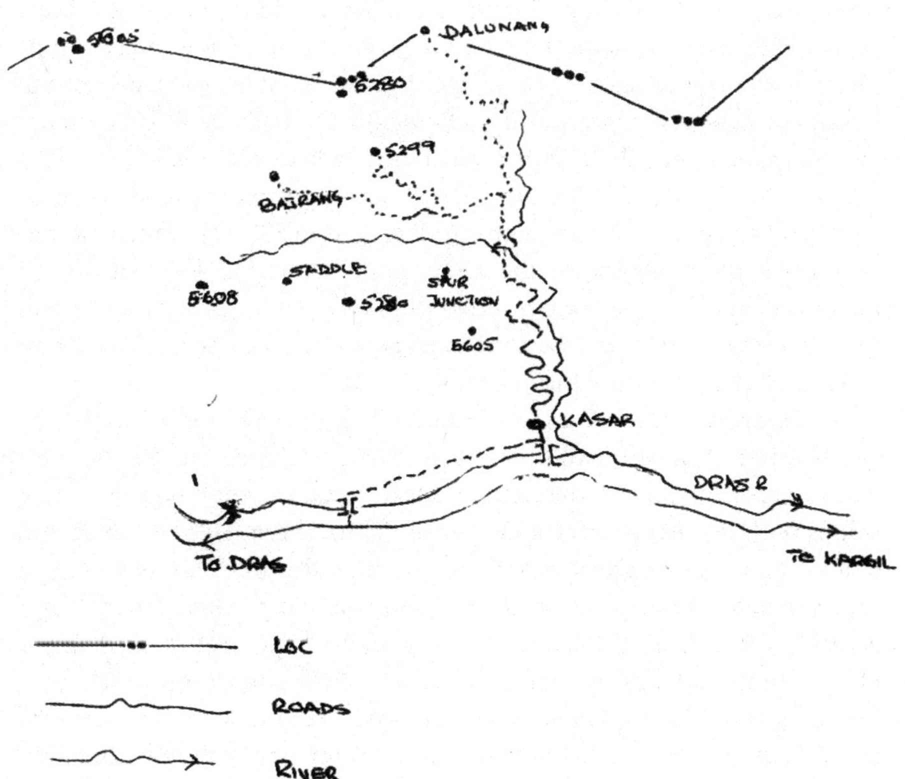

Sketch of Kaksar Sub-Sector

Note: *The sketch is not to scale. All heights are in metres.*

The Prime Minister of India, Atal Behari Vajpayee, was informed on 26 July 1999 that the Pakistani intrusion had been eliminated from Indian side of the LOC, except for three positions Pakistan continued to hold despite the ceasefire agreement. These positions were also eliminated subsequently and the mission in *Op Vijay* was accomplished.

In Sub Sector Hanif (SSH), Pakistani troops had occupied a few dominating positions. These heights had previously not been held by either side. These areas were on the LOC and provided Pakistani troops observation posts overlooking the area under the 102 Infantry Brigade of the Indian Army. There was an appreciated threat of the Pakistanis turning the flanks of the Indian permanent defences, in the sub-sector. 102 Infantry Brigade, under the command of Brig P. C. Katoch, was allotted additional resources by HQ 3 Infantry Division and the Brigade had been given the mission to attack these positions and evict the Pakistanis from all heights in SSH. This offensive was very successful as described in the outline in Annexure 12. The troops of 102 Inf Brigade gained observation across the LOC. With this win, the Indian Army now had options to attack Pakistani permanent defences from the rear and exploit this advantage further as needed.

Also worthy of mention is an exceptional local action of valour by the 102 Infantry Brigade in the Southern Siachen Glacier Sub-Sector. This daring action highlights the extraordinary feats accomplished by Indian troops with fearless bravery and resolve. In Southern Glacier Sub-Sector, point 5770 is a dominating but steep mountain feature. This location was captured in a bold surprise attack by five Indian Army troops, led by Major Navdeep Cheema of 27 Rajput, accompanied by Captain Shyamal Sinha of HAWS. In this audacious operation, a dozen Pakistani troops were killed, including the officer commanding of the post, Captain Taimur Malik of the SSG, attached to 3 NLI. At that time, Captain Malik's grandfather lived in London. On learning about his grandson's death, he made a request through the Military Advisor at the High Commission of India, in London, to have the body of his grandson, returned to Pakistan. At that time, even though the two countries were actively at war, this request was conveyed to Indian Army HQ at Delhi and was approved by the concerned authorities in India. To enable this request, a local ceasefire was brought into effect, allowing for the recovery of the body of the Pakistani officer by troops of the 102 Infantry Brigade from the treacherous heights and overhangs of point 5770. They brought the body down from the mountaintop and handed it over to Pakistani troops at Zero point on the LOC. Indian troops recognized the officer's dead body from his uniform and a letter from his father found in his pocket. Despite being subjected to Pakistan's incendiary intrusion across the LOC, India came forth with humanity and equanimity. In stark contrast to this, Pakistan returned the brutally mutilated bodies of Captain Amol Kalia and four soldiers of the Indian Army. This was indicative of the torture and medieval savagery inflicted by the Pakistan Army, in complete disregard of the Geneva Conventions. Captain Kalia and four soldiers were on a patrol on the Indian side of the LOC in Kaksar sub-sector when they were cornered and captured in a valley with no available cover having run out of ammunition. They were later brutally killed by Pakistani troops.

As described, the Pakistan Army employed troops of six to eight battalions to carry out the intrusion across the LOC. They left behind their dead at several locations while withdrawing during the ceasefire. The troops of India's 3 Infantry Division buried the remains of approximately 117 Pakistani soldiers killed in action at various locations. A similar number were buried by the 8 Mountain Division on the Indian side of the LOC. A report published in the *Economic Times*, New Delhi, on 19 December 2000, stated that the Pakistan Army, while denying its role in the Kargil War, had added the names of 453 officers and men killed in action in the war in the Batalik and Kargil Sectors to the website, *Shuhada's Corner*. The names of those Pakistani soldiers who have died in various other wars and on duty can be found on this website. The website also revealed that the name given to the Pakistani operation to occupy dominating heights on the Indian side of the LOC was *Op Koh-e-Paima,* also referred to as *Op Badr.*

By 22 June 1999, troops of 3 Infantry Division had captured Point 5203, and the eastern flank of the Pakistani intrusion lay open for further ops. The tactically important heights Juber, Kukerthang, Khalubar, Muntho Dhalo, Tharu, Padma Go and Chorbatla ridgelines were captured by 7 July 1999 in the Batalik Sector. In the Turtuk sub-sector the entire ridgeline of SSH was with Indian Army. In the Dras Sector, the dominating feature of *Tiger Hill* had been captured by troops of the 8 Mountain Division, and ops were in progress to trounce the enemy in Mashkoh. It was only a matter of time that all remaining positions held by the Pakistani troops would be captured. In light of this resounding success, the news and details of the Indian Army's victory was shared with media, visiting dignitaries, and troops at Kargil Helipad by GOC 15 Corps, Lt Gen Krishan Pal in the presence of the Military Secretary (MS), Lt Gen Inder Verma. GOC 15 Corps called it a rout of the enemy. GOC 3 Infantry Division also addressed the gathering and stated that the mission to annihilate the Pakistani intrusion across the LOC had been successful. The aim was to defeat the enemy which had been achieved. The victories achieved by 3 Infantry Division, which include the rout of the enemy in the Batalik Sector, thwarting the attempts of the Pakistan Army in the Chorbatla area, capture of the entire ridgeline in SSH and the capture of Pt 5770 in the Southern Glacier sub-sector did not get the recognition they deserved. These major achievements were not fully acknowledged even after the war ended.

During the ceasefire, India's COAS and Chief of Air Staff visited HQ 3 infantry Division at Kargil and were briefed about how the rout of the Pakistani troops was accomplished. With sober and measured decision making, the Indian Army built a numerical superiority of forces and built a logistics chain to defeat the Pakistani Forces. Preparation for war is complex, especially if the conflict is sudden and pre-planned by the enemy. The IA had to ensure concentration of force at the points of attack, degradation of objectives, acclimatization of troops, building up of ammunition stocks, deploying of heavy weapons, fool proof supply chains, set up advanced medical aid centres and equip soldiers with special clothing for extreme cold. General V. P. Malik, COAS, directed the war effort, rendered advice to the political leadership and remained in touch with formation commanders daily. The Indian Armed Forces were prepared to extend the war to the Western Sectors if needed. The Indian Army had the will, determination, and confidence to defeat the enemy. With moral fortitude and single-minded focus, despite the most daunting circumstances, they orchestrated the defeat of the Pakistani intrusion.

The Kargil War was a very significant episode for India. The country treated the intrusion by Pakistan across the LOC as a national crisis. The Indian Army's bravery and sacrifice in the war raised nationalist sentiment to a new level and every Indian had a vested interest in its success. The armed forces adapted as required and were prepared to enlarge the area and scope of the war to the western border. Such an escalation would possibly have attracted international intervention. India was prepared to defend itself by all means and the humiliating defeat for Pakistan in the mountains of Kargil was a result of the tenacity and superiority of the IA.

The formidable response from India created a crisis in the minds of the Pakistani leadership. Their military hierarchy had perhaps assumed that it would be difficult for the Indian Army to retaliate and defeat the intrusions across the LOC in the most difficult terrain in the world and over such a vast frontage. It was their anticipation that counterattacks from India would take a few days, during which Pakistan's Army troops would consolidate their positions, a ceasefire would then come into effect, and Pakistan would continue to hold the Indian territory they had occupied. Pakistan soon learned that the world was not coming to its support. Neither was India going to allow this to succeed.

As the reality of the conflict unfolded and Pakistan's defeat was imminent their Prime Minister, Nawaz Sharif, approached China to help save his country from further humiliation. China, seeing the world opinion veer in favour of India, was sympathetic but advised him to start a peace dialogue with India. Sharif then sought help from President Bill Clinton of the US. Clinton understood how precarious the situation had become and how dangerous it could become if the conflict expanded. He advised great caution and a de-escalation by Pakistan.[7] As the Indian Armed Forces battled at the war front, the Indian government was making every diplomatic effort to highlight the perfidy by Pakistan and the assault on Indian sovereignty. President Clinton had received a letter from Prime Minister Vajpayee that provided the facts about Pakistan's intrusion. He had provided an assessment of the gravity of the situation and the mounting pressure on India to retaliate in strength. While Pakistan's leaders were still denying their country's misadventure and trying back-channel diplomacy, the Indian Prime Minister visited Kargil to take stock of the situation firsthand. He visited the warzone even as artillery shelling by Pakistanis was ongoing. The PM was accompanied by George Fernandes, the Indian Defence Minister and Gen V. P. Malik, the COAS and they were briefed by the GOC 3 Infantry Division at the tactical HQ. This visit of the Prime Minister was a big morale booster for the Indian troops on the frontline.

Realizing the gravity of the situation, President Clinton had also sent the head of the Senate's Foreign Relations Committee to India, to obtain firsthand information on the events in the Kargil Sector. The Senator remained in Kargil for two days with the tactical HQ 3 of Infantry Division, 12–14 June 1999, and was briefed on the perfidious action by Pakistan and the ongoing situation in the war. President Clinton received inputs from the Senator and garnered a formal condemnation of Pakistan's armed intrusion across the LOC from the G8 countries meeting in Cologne, Germany. Clinton had earlier dispatched General Anthony Zinni, C-in-C, US Central Command, to advise Pakistan on the urgency of pulling out their troops from the intrusion across the LOC.

7. *My Life* by Bill Clinton, pp 864-65

India's diplomatic offensive and stoic resolve showed quick results and not a single country was willing to back Pakistan. Being diplomatically isolated and with a tactical defeat imminent, Sharif met the US President on 4 July 1999, the anniversary of American Independence. President Clinton had gone to great lengths to defuse the crisis created by Pakistan. He was also able to impress upon Prime Minister Vajpayee to accept a temporary ceasefire and allow Nawaz Sharif to withdraw the remaining Pakistani troops from the intrusion. Clinton's role was focused on the immediate crisis and not on the Kashmir dispute.[8] Under pressure, in view of the imminent defeat, Sharif accepted the need to restore the sanctity of the LOC. It was a face-saving solution, engineered by President Clinton for Nawaz Sharif and the Pakistan Army. The latter, while accepting the invitation to meet Nawaz Sharif, had laid out two pre-conditions.

These were – that Sharif would agree to withdraw Pakistani troops to the Pakistani side of the LOC and that he, President Clinton, would not intervene in the Kashmir dispute, especially because it was Pakistan that had launched the war and violated the Shimla Agreement. Clinton, however, stated that he would urge Vajpayee to accept the resumption of the bilateral dialogue if Pakistani troops withdrew. Sharif had no better option but to accept these terms.

To avoid further bloodshed, India was magnanimous enough to accept the ceasefire, allowing the remaining Pakistani troops to withdraw from the intrusion with effect from 10 July 1999. As per some reports, General Pervez Musharraf, who had masterminded the Kargil War, had also asked his Prime Minister to negotiate a withdrawal as a face-saving measure. In his memoirs, Musharraf has contradicted this narrative, stating that it was a surrender by Nawaz Sharif. Musharraf had to endure the fact that the political leadership in his country called the Kargil War a disaster. Thereby, they directly questioned the premise of launching the war and the professional ability of their Army. The dye was cast, and divisions between the political leadership and the Pakistan Army would result in a coup by General Musharraf just a few months later, on 12 October 1999. Ultimately, the Kargil War is a black mark in Pakistan's history and an irreparable breach of trust on the part of Pakistan. With no support from the major powers of the world, this war also highlighted Pakistan's unilateral, unprovoked belligerence towards India. The importance of the LOC was recognized

---

8. *Kashmir in the Shadow of War: Regional Rivalries in a Nuclear Age* by Robert EWirsing

worldwide and formed the basis for any further negotiations between India and Pakistan.

In Retrospect

The Kargil war began in early May of 1999. Given the sensitive nature of the events leading up to the war, initially the information flow was restricted and limited. By the time the country became aware of the severity of the situation and the media began to take interest in reporting on it, quite some time had passed, and a lot of the counter-offensive was already underway. In India, at that time a nascent and unrefined media apparatus was emerging due to the internet boom. Online news was becoming a big part of the media landscape and there was a race to break news on this very newsworthy topic. In their fervor, some journalists misreported facts, and cherry picked their stories based on the people and locations to which they had easy access. While the Army formation commanders in Kargil were consumed with war and the strategy related to it, Indian journalists scavenged for information from uncorroborated sources. Some selectively reported on the achievements of the Armed Forces while others were openly critical of the war effort with little knowledge and facts to support such critiques. Army HQ attempted to curb the disinformation by providing daily briefings, but that was not enough for some news channels. In some instances, overzealous reporters speculated on IA plans which perhaps made the enemy aware by reporting plans afoot. This was a sure sign of immature, self-serving journalism when the conflict was at a critical juncture. At a time when there was a need to demonstrate a united front to the troops and show gratitude and appreciation for their efforts, some in the media did not seem to have their back.

Some forward positions which were captured many weeks into the war, such as Tiger Hill, were lauded as key milestones by the Indian media since by then the country was following the story with rapt attention. Meanwhile other significant objectives that were captured earlier, in life threatening and heroic operations, but with little fanfare, never got reported. These include the rout of the enemy in the Batalik sector. Similarly, forward locations that were easy to access by the media or were visible from the National Highway, were reported on more frequently. This indiscriminate reporting, which glorified certain wins by the Armed Forces, led to many early successes of the Kargil war being diminished or taken for granted. To be clear, the resounding success of the Kargil war was not the result only of the achievements of some. This victory belongs to all who fought bravely, planned, strategized and led the effort against a formidable enemy. Sadly, in this momentous war, which led to the ultimate sacrifice by some, not all achievements by soldiers and commanders who led the fight are acknowledged to this day.

On 26 July 2024, India celebrated the 25th Anniversary of its success in the Kargil war. In the last 25 years, many versions of this war have been documented, and many individuals have written on the subject. Some accounts attempt to be analytical and accurate; others embellish the truth and misreport the facts. There are some, especially in the media, who still look for reprisal and assign blame till this day. These armchair warriors, who refer to themselves as investigative journalists or military experts, have never served in the armed forces. They have never lived through the pressure, the trauma, and the danger of war. These are individuals who have never been in an armed battle without a bulletproof vest or endured extreme weather with inadequate equipment, or climbed mountains covered in snow with a belligerent, armed enemy looking down from above. The Kargil Review Committee did a deep dive and declared its conclusions. And yet, these media gurus continue to critically analyze the actions of people who led the Kargil war without understanding the realities of an all-out war with Pakistan. They still dwell on petty hearsay to rake up myths that are incendiary and of no consequence. Some of these journalists raised their profiles on the back of the Kargil War and their careers still seem to depend on writing about it. Maybe it's time for them to stop obfuscating their lack of firsthand experience by pretending to be military analysts. These people are not patriots. They are a sad reflection of the disingenuous elements of Indian media.

Strong, definitive leadership certainly matters in a war. The formation commanders who led the Indian counter offensive, soon after the detection of the intrusion to the proclamation of the ceasefire, most definitely contributed to its success. In the Kargil war, the entire chain of Command from Army HQ to the Company Commanders in battalions, contributed to the victory against Pakistan. It is a fact that wars are won by armies and not by individuals. The country must therefore celebrate and felicitate all the formations and forces which together achieved the objective of defeating the enemy. If India's Armed Forces vanquished Pakistan in the Kargil War, EVERYONE[9] who fought the war honorably, deserves to be

9. Report of the Kargil Review Committee Executive Summary, para 13.1

celebrated and every one of their successes should be documented and commended. The National War Memorial in Delhi is a symbol of all their contributions and sacrifices.

As the conflict grew and the stakes for the region and the world at large became apparent, Indian and world media carried the war coverage extensively. Major international news outlets like the BBC, CNN and others were measured and somewhat unbiased in their reporting. In the Indian media, as mentioned before, this was not always the case. In the late 1990s, Indian news media had proliferated on TV, the internet and in print. Regular news outlets and new and upcoming ones were battling in a competitive landscape. 1999 was a year ripe with news and events and there was an alarming prevalence of amateur, untethered journalism to attract more viewership or readership. India had a fast-growing economy, the visit by Prime Minister Vajpayee to Lahore had taken place, national elections were due later in the year, and India's nuclear prowess along with the Kargil War were providing Indian journalists many opportunities to explore new boundaries for reporting. In such an environment, without much oversight, it was also an arena where irresponsible and rash journalism, which stretched ethical limits, was thriving. With general elections due in India, the media was partisan, and unfortunately even the Kargil War was politicized. This was to the detriment of the morale of troops fighting at the frontlines. Army HQ in New Delhi provided daily operational briefings to the media; however as mentioned, some journalists pursued their own agenda in gathering and reporting news. Various reports were based on uncorroborated sources, or on the views of pseudo military analysts who were passing judgement from the comfort of their desks. Fake news which went viral was endemic and there was a firestorm of speculation. The Army's Formation commanders also had to battle the waves of misinformation while they were engaged in an active warzone.

In fact, no journalists ventured to the forward areas of Batalik, Mashkoh and Turtuk sectors during the Kargil War. Getting to these remote regions would have involved two to three days of marching on foot from the roadhead, through areas which were under enemy observation and fire. Most of sectors were under the op jurisdiction of the 3 Infantry Division and the reality of the war in these remote areas was not covered since most of the media remained in Kargil town. There were no embedded journalists attached to formations. Only Shiv Kunal Verma remained with HQ 3 Infantry Division and accompanied the GOC on a daily basis to various forward locations, some of which experienced enemy shelling at times. Gen VP Malik, the COAS visited the critical SSH and was briefed on the success of the ops. These crucial visits got no media attention because they were not observed by journalists. Most journalists had no idea about this war's nuances, such as the need for high-altitude acclimatization. Reporters failed to understand the coordination and preparation required for the attack ops and how time-consuming they are in high-altitude terrain. Some of these 'military analysts' seem to suffer from a paralysis of analysis and are still writing books and raking up obscure, inaccurate theories about the Kargil war.

When a country is at war, the stakes are high, and national honour must be defended. At such a time, the entire country needs to be supportive to strengthen the resolve and the morale of the Armed Forces who are laying their lives on the line for the country. The role of factual, unbiased, rational and mindful reporting cannot be over-emphasized in times of war. During the Kargil War, the COAS and the chain of command had to devote time and attention to correcting the misperceptions being conveyed by the media. This diverted the attention of senior officers from the ops that were underway. Rational reporting is based on realistic assumptions, compelling logic, and evidentiary support. Some of the messages in the Indian media were blatantly incorrect but were still seen and read worldwide, thereby projecting a poor image of the country. Media does have the power to mold national and international opinion. In retrospect, it can be said that some in the Indian media, by their inconsiderate, irrational, untruthful, and irresponsible reporting, diluted the victory achieved in Kargil. The Indian media must introspect about the role they played in the Kargil War and resolve to do better.

Despite these distractions during the Kargil War, the Indian Armed Forces defended the nation and defeated Pakistan. Victory was achieved in Kargil and India's sovereignty was restored. As is well known, this was a conventional war between two nuclear-armed countries who remain inimical. The Kargil War and nuclearization have not brought India and Pakistan any closer to settling disputes. Pakistan has continued to test India's patience by launching small-scale terror attacks with its proxies, not only in Kashmir but elsewhere in India. This continues today, long after Pakistan's defeat in *Op Vijay*. India has now adopted a hard line against terrorism initiated by Pakistan and this approach is supported by the UNSC.

Kashmir is not the only issue that needs to be on the agenda between India and Pakistan. Besides discussions on peace and nuclear security, there is a need to address issues such as trans-LOC firing and infiltration by terrorists, the proxy war, violation of IB/LOC with drones, status of POK and Gilgit-Baltistan, the CPEC, the Siachen Glacier Sector, Sir Creek, drug trafficking, production of fake currency notes and their distribution, trade and economic cooperation, Indus Water Treaty, and the status of the LOC/AGPL/IB. After the terrorist attack in Pahalgam, India has adopted a hardline stance and stated that it can have a dialogue with Pakistan on terrorism and on Kashmir, how the parts of the state that are held by Pakistan will be integrated with India. Pakistan's quest to achieve a balance of power vis-à-vis India is not the consequence of India's actions. India gains nothing by being inimical to Pakistan. It is the unremitting control of foreign and defence policies by the Deep State in Pakistan that still prevents peace with India. There is also reticence in most of the world to not intervene in Kashmir because of the following possible reasons:

a. Global powers have little or no stake in the land-locked state of J&K. Most of them now understand that Pakistan has no basis to make claims on J&K, especially when it continues on the path of terrorism and sub-conventional war.

b. They view Kashmir as a dispute that is to be resolved bilaterally as per provisions contained in the bilateral agreements in place. Some nations may be sympathetic to Pakistan as it itself is marred by internal divisions and terrorism. Its location ensures major powers to maintain interest in this country as it provides some leverage and access in the region.

c. India is rising in stature in the world, it is the world's fifth largest economy, and provides opportunities for trade, manufacturing, and investment. Most nations want to maintain positive relations with India.

Today, India is perceived as a responsible and powerful nation that contributes to critical global affairs. India plays an important role in diverse issues such as the environment, disaster management and the world economy. As a key player in providing the world with vaccines during the COVID-19 pandemic, India is proactively making a positive difference to the world. Conversely, Pakistan on the other hand has a failing economy and an existential dilemma. With a population that is predominantly uneducated and at the poverty line, Pakistan is politically churlish and fails to feature on the world stage for any positive reason. More on emerging relationships is discussed in Chapters 7 and 8.

CHAPTER 4

The Afghanistan Conundrum

Insurgency and Conflict

Afghanistan has been one of the major gateways for invasions into South Asia for centuries. Its strategic importance was assessed by the British in relation to India once they saw the expansion of the Russian Empire south towards this country. The Tzars had ambitions to extend their realm further to the warm waters of the Arabian Sea through Afghanistan or even towards British-ruled India. Afghanistan had been part of the Mauryan Empire and Mughal Empire in India until the seventeenth century. It is essential to provide some background that sheds light on the present situation in Afghanistan as it relates to its neighbouring countries.

The British had an adversarial relationship with the Afghans when they had established their realm in India. Afghanistan had become a separate nation some centuries ago. To create a buffer between the fertile plains of India and the expanding Russian empire, the British had divided the Pashtun population between India and Afghanistan when they drew the Durand Line as the International Border (IB) between the two countries. The British authorities signed an agreement with the King of Afghanistan, validating the border. This was the Treaty of Gandamak signed on 27 May 1879. After the defeat of Afghanistan in the battle of Kandahar in 1880, the British appointed Abdul Rahman Khan as the Emir.[1] The treaty was ratified once again by this appointed Emir.

Another treaty was signed after the third Anglo-Afghan war at Rawalpindi on 8 August 1919, which ratified the Durand Line as the IB.

---

1. *India and Afghanistan, 1867–1907: A Study in Diplomatic Relations* by D. P. Singhal, pp 35

This border is named after Mortimer Durand, who was a British diplomat. He was responsible for delineating the IB. The British had thus created a buffer between their interests and those of Tsar-ruled Russia, at that time, as a part of what was termed the Great Game. Much later, Mohammad Daud, the first cousin of King Mohammed Zahir Shah of Afghanistan, the then Prime Minister, initiated the idea of reuniting the artificially divided Pashtuns. After the Second World War, the Soviet Union emerged as a major expansionist communist power. Daud was leaning towards the Soviet Union, and he accepted aid for his country from this communist state. This aid was provided on easy financial terms. It included economic assistance, military training, and equipment. Pakistan was concerned at these developments because a militarily strong Afghanistan would pose a threat from NW and would try and pursue the rising demand for uniting the Pashtun population divided by the Durand Line. It was in the early sixties, with the intention of curbing this Pashtun separatism, that Pakistan decided to start the mujahid operations against King Zahir Shah's regime. This marked the beginning of insurgency in Afghanistan. This was the brainchild of Zulfiqar Ali Bhutto, then the foreign minister of his country.

After Mohammad Daud overthrew Zahir Shah on 17 July 1973, the influence of the Soviet Union increased substantially in Afghanistan, including enhanced military presence in this country. The Soviet presence finally culminated in their occupation of Afghanistan in December 1979. The Afghans fought the Soviet forces occupying their country, supported by the CIA and Pakistan. The Soviet armed forces were forced to withdraw from Afghanistan after nearly a decade of conflict because of excessive casualties to men and material and realizing that their hold on this country was becoming untenable. After the Soviet withdrawal, a civil war broke out in Afghanistan, backed by Pakistan, which brought the Taliban to power. The first Taliban regime was recognized by Pakistan, Saudi Arabia, and the United Arab Emirates (UAE) only. The Taliban were medieval in their governance. They brought in radical Islam, forced women to wear the hijab and burka and closed schools for girls. They enforced Sharia law in its extreme manifestations. Flogging and even beheading were methods of imparting justice. The Taliban destroyed non-Muslim historic sites in Afghanistan and the destruction of the world heritage site, the Bamiyan Buddha monuments, led to angry protests in India and was decried worldwide. To sustain itself economically, the Taliban was generating financial resources through opium production. About 50 per cent of the Afghan economy was based on narcotics. After his retirement, General

Musharraf of Pakistan stated in an interview in London that 95 per cent of the world's demand for heroin, worth $50 billion per annum, was being processed out of Afghanistan. Whether this is factually true remains an open question, but it is indisputable that the Afghan warlords and drug producers were benefitting from this.

The nexus between Pakistan and the Taliban was plain to see on 24 December 1999. The same year that the Kargil was perpetrated, Indian Airlines flight 814 was hijacked by five Pakistani nationals, members of the Harkat-ul-Mujahideen terrorist group. This flight was hijacked after takeoff from Kathmandu Airport in Nepal and was finally brought to Kandahar Airport. The crew and passengers remained hostage until they were swapped for Pakistani terrorists who were under Indian custody. The released terrorists included Maulana Masood Azhar, Mushtaq Zargar and Omar Saeed Sheikh. The hijacked aircraft and its passengers were allowed to return to India by Taliban authorities after the release of these prisoners. This was a bruising blow for India. It was evident at the time that there would be a greater price to pay in the future for accepting the release of these terrorists in exchange for the lives of 120 Indian citizens. That prophecy did come true as after their release, these terrorists are suspected to have been involved in heinous terrorism-related incidents such as the beheading of Daniel Pearl, an American journalist from the Wall Street Journal. The 2001 attack on the Indian Parliament and other attacks on Indian soil are also attributed to these individuals.

Nation-Building in Afghanistan – India's Contribution

Operation Enduring Freedom, launched by the US and allies in November 2001, decimated the Taliban and its regime. As a result, a new regime came to power in Kabul under President Hamid Karzai and India began building ties with this new administration. During *Operation Enduring Freedom*, India offered intelligence and other forms of support to the US and the coalition forces. Over $750 million in humanitarian and economic aid has been provided by India to help alleviate the suffering of the Afghan people affected by war. India also established diplomatic relations with Afghanistan and participated in the reconstruction effort. Besides the humanitarian aid, Indian support and collaboration extended to building air links, building power plants, and investing in health and education. Indian experts have also helped train Afghan civil servants, diplomats, military officers, and their police.

India gifted three Airbus aircraft, 400 passenger buses, and almost 100 trucks and waste disposal trolleys to Afghanistan. India also contributed to the extension of power lines and oil and natural gas projects. In a literacy drive, 1,000 scholarships were granted to Afghan students to study in India, and an estimated 16,000 Afghan students are known to have studied in India. Contributing further to the decrepit education system, India constructed 200 public and private schools in Afghanistan with a contemporary curriculum. Afghan Government telecommunications, radio and television, and dozens of FM radio stations were utilizing facilities provided by Indian satellites and India also built the Parliament building in Kabul. The Indian Border Roads Organization constructed a major road in the remote Afghan province of Nimroz, connecting Zaranj on the border with Iran to Delaram, linking the existing road into the interior. This provided an alternative route for duty-free movement of goods through Chahbahar Port in Iran to Afghanistan. It was a part of India's strategy to develop transportation links bypassing Pakistan. India also rebuilt the Salma Dam on the Hari River in the Chishti Sharif District of Herat Province in Afghanistan. The Afghan cabinet, at that time, renamed it as the Afghan-India Friendship Dam. This dam provides 42 megawatts of power and irrigates 5,000 hectares of farmland. The dam was inaugurated by Prime Minister Narendra Modi in June 2016. Besides its embassy in Kabul, India had consulates in Herat, Kandahar, Jalalabad, and Mazar-Sharif. Indian doctors were deputed to serve in Afghanistan, and they provided much-needed free medical care to the population. Many Afghans traveled to India, seeking specialist medical care. These generous rehabilitation efforts brought some normalcy to Afghanistan and created much goodwill for India in Afghanistan.

Pakistan was averse to the positive impact that India was having in Afghanistan and actively tried to interfere with Indian initiatives by launching disruptive attacks on Indian assets there. It is assessed that the attacks on the Indian embassy in Kabul in July 2008 and October 2009 were orchestrated by the ISI. On 26 February 2010, an attack on Indian doctors at the Arya Guest House in Kabul killed 18 people. There were also attacks on Indian consulates. Despite these hostilities, India did not waver in its effort to assist Afghanistan in its reconstruction and continued to provide humanitarian aid.

To improve Afghanistan's access to countries in Central Asia, India invested large amounts to improve the roads going north from Kabul. There were proposals to set up iron ore mines, a steel plant with an output of six million metric tons per annum (MTPA) by the Steel Authority of India, an 800-megawatt power plant, transmission lines, and internal roads. Indian Railways, with its construction subsidiary, Rail India Technical and Economic Services, was tasked to survey a rail link between Kabul and Kandahar. Pakistan did not allow road access to India through its territory to Afghanistan, and instead India and Afghanistan established two air corridors, and India also invested in the expansion of Chahbahar Port in Iran to serve as a hub for the transportation of goods to Afghanistan, bypassing this country's territory. An estimated 3,000 Indians had been working on construction projects and in international aid agencies besides the staff at the Indian embassy and consulates in Afghanistan. These initiatives by India though less known, are significant in their impact on the Afghani population. All such projects and their planning were stalled due to increasing militant action and an altered political situation. After the Taliban takeover of the country in August 2021, the collaboration and advancements stopped completely.

The Taliban Takeover

The tenuous situation in Afghanistan underwent a rapid change after the US withdrawal from Afghanistan in August 2021. Immediately after the US withdrew its troops, the Taliban once again established control over the country. They achieved this with limited or no resistance from the Afghan National Army (ANA). The ANA was estimated to be 350,000 strong and was presumed to be well-trained under the aegis of the US. They were expected to prevent a Taliban takeover or at least to stall the process for some time. It has come to light after the rapid ascent of the Taliban in August 2021 that a large number of the ANA comprised 'ghost' soldiers. These were individuals who were on the payrolls, but did not really exist. Their pay was purloined by corrupt senior officers and those in power. This notwithstanding, when the Taliban advanced, the ANA either disappeared or surrendered with their arms and equipment. Only in very few areas was any resistance forthcoming, but that too was overcome easily by the militant Taliban. The relative strength of the Taliban was estimated to be 60,000. The speed with which the entire country fell to the Taliban was not entirely predictable. It is a moot point but worth noting that the historically, Afghans have been determined to resist foreign occupying forces. They have defeated the British, the Soviet forces, and most recently, the Americans and their allies, forcing them to withdraw from their country. Subsisting in their internal discord, Afghans tend to avoid active hostilities unless other means fail. Most resistance is overcome through payoffs and similar understandings and these arrangements tend to prevail.

After nearly 20 years of fighting in Afghanistan after the 9/11 attacks, the US signed an accord with the Taliban. The elected Afghan government was not a part of the negotiations and this deal. Besides targeting Al Qaeda and their hosts during Op Enduring Freedom, the US had planned to bring about change to Afghanistan by various means – eliminate terrorism, introduce democratic governance, infrastructure development and encourage an educated population. However, after so many years of attempting to bring about change, the Trump administration was of the impression that the war had persisted long enough and was at a stalemate. It was assessed that there would be no advantage to the US being engaged in Afghanistan any longer. The US policymakers were unwilling to seek a middle course of retaining a minimum force that would have assisted the elected Afghan government to remain in power. A few questions that remain unanswered include whether there was an unwritten deal that allowed an unscathed withdrawal of the US and allied troops, contractors, diplomats, and other assets from the country. Why did the US leave the elected government out of the negotiations with the Taliban? President Trump had set a deadline for a complete withdrawal of the US and NATO forces by 1 May 2021. When President Biden took over, it was his decision to end the US deployment in Afghanistan by the end of September 2021. It may be that the US administration was aware of the massive and undeterred corruption and the bogus reporting at various levels in the Afghan government, which falsely projected that the situation in the country would improve eventually. The decision was made to let the Afghans take care of their administration after 20 years of war and simultaneous reconstruction efforts.

Afghanistan had undergone changes to an extent during Operation Enduring Freedom. People, including women and girls, were better educated, and various infrastructure and societal developments had occurred in Afghanistan. Sceptics of the US withdrawal have expressed that like in Japan, Taiwan, South Korea, and elsewhere, the US could have maintained a presence in Afghanistan to provide stability and to preserve democracy. The dramatic events that followed the US withdrawal are well known. President Biden had declared that after the withdrawal of the US troops from Afghanistan, the only aim of the US was to make sure that this country can never be used to launch an attack on the American homeland.

The withdrawal by the US from Afghanistan was poorly executed, and as per statements by President Trump, 'it was a disaster'. After the Americans exited, the militant and regressive Taliban regime overran the Afghan security forces, entered Kabul and quickly took over the reins of the country. As per their statement, this immediate takeover was to prevent looting and anarchy. The Taliban's rapid deployment and imposing armed control of the streets did not give the US and its allies any time to process and evacuate those Afghans who served and supported them during the war. As they hastily departed, they also left behind billions of Dollars' worth of equipment and munitions in Afghanistan, which could not be gathered or repatriated. While extricating itself from Afghanistan, the US had to deploy 3,500 troops to retain control of the international airport to facilitate air evacuation of embassy staff, citizens of the US, citizens of friendly nations, and their local collaborators who could be evacuated. The Indian embassy in Kabul and staff at the various consulates had been evacuated even though it was reported that the Taliban political office in Doha had requested India not to do so. The unwavering support from Pakistan and poor governance by the elected government were also among the major reasons why the Taliban were able to re-establish their regime in Afghanistan in 2021.

As explained earlier, Afghanistan has a tumultuous history of internally warring factions, attacks by foreign conquerors and related uprisings. Located strategically, Afghanistan is the gateway between Asia and Europe and the country has been led by famous conquerors such as Mahmud of Ghazni, who in the 11th century created an empire from Iran to India. In the 13th century, Genghis Khan took over the territory, but by the late 1800s, this region had been invaded by various Arab conquerors and Islam had taken root. The British who ruled India during the 19th century, wanted to protect their empire from Russia and made attempts to annex Afghanistan, which led to various British Afghan Wars. When India gained its independence in 1947, Pakistan was formed as a country that bordered Afghanistan, and the two nations were thereby inextricably linked. Around the same time, Gen. Mohammed Daoud Khan became Afghanistan's prime minister. He was pro-Soviet Union and wanted to collaborate with the communist nation for economic and military assistance. Afghanistan's rise as a problem state began when Daud Khan abolished the monarchy, became president and established the Republic of Afghanistan, with firm links with the USSR. This was when Pakistan began to raise militant groups to fight the Afghan government that was cooperating with the Soviets and raising the issue of a greater Pashtunistan. Besides organizing the mujahideen into the Taliban, Pakistan had begun to support groups under warlords such as Gulbuddin Hekmatyar, Ahmed Shah Masood, Jalaluddin Haqqani, and others to contend with the Soviet occupation of the country in conjunction with the CIA. According to Ahmed Rashid a journalist, it is from the madrasa-educated youth that the first Taliban emerged. The Taliban, who are now in charge, are much the same, puritanical, very conservative, and driven by medieval learning and thinking.

Pakistan had to bear the burden of waves of Afghan refugees who left Afghanistan at the time of the Soviet occupation and later when *Op Enduring Freedom* was launched. After the withdrawal of the US and Allied Forces in 2021, there was another surge of refugees from Afghanistan to Pakistan. These were people trying to escape possible retribution from the Taliban. After due verification, the Pakistani authorities have forced the repatriation of most of these refugees. Relations between the first Taliban regime and Pakistan had not always been amicable because when the Taliban was in power, it refused to endorse the Durand Line border despite pressure from Pakistan. The Taliban argued that there should be no borders between Muslim brothers. Even President Hamid Karzai of Afghanistan repeated this analogy, stating, 'A line of hatred raised a wall between the two brothers.' His remarks were, perhaps, aimed at creating one nation out of the divided Pashtuns. This was a difficult proposition after more than a century of the establishment of the Durand Line border. Relations again became strained between the two countries when the Karzai Government openly accused Pakistan of using its ISI to establish a terrorist network inside Afghanistan to destabilize the country. President Ashraf Ghani, who succeeded Karzai, has gone on record to state that Pakistan has instigated an undeclared war against his country. This was after a major bombing attack in Kabul in May 2017. For the current Taliban government and for all of Afghanistan, the Durand Line has become an emotive issue because it divides the Pashtuns on two sides of the border. This is further complicated by the presence of the TTP which has support from the Afghan government.

The second Taliban government in Afghanistan is only recognized by China and Pakistan. In October 2023, China established its embassy in Kabul. The security situation in Afghanistan, as per the Taliban, has improved somewhat. However, independent reports suggest that a major part of the population lives on the brink of starvation as there are hardly any means of employment and earning. There are some visible signs that indicate that ISIS, which had morphed out of Al Qaeda initially, is showing its presence in Afghanistan by carrying out random terror attacks against soft targets and ethnic minorities, especially the Shias. Thousands of Hazara families were reportedly driven out of Daikundi, Helmand, and Kandahar in what can be called bloody ethnic cleansing. Al Qaeda has also re-emerged in Afghanistan and is being re-organised by Hamza, son of Osama bin Laden. This began after the head of Al Qaeda, Al Zawahiri, was killed on 3 August 2022 by US drones, while living in a safe house in Kabul. This targeted action also proves that the US has maintained its surveillance and intelligence links in Afghanistan.

The aim of the Taliban, as stated by their spokesman in 2021, was to establish an inclusive government representing the people of Afghanistan. This was a narrative shared only for positive public optics. No such inclusive government has ever been considered by the Taliban, and it is unlikely to come into being. The international community has, however, resigned to engage with the Taliban when necessary. The US continues to maintain contact with the Taliban through their office in Doha. The US and Russia are wary of Afghanistan becoming the incubator of terror groups once again. China is already committed to the region with its CPEC and has been sceptical about extending the BRI into Afghanistan due to the spate of violence generated by ISIS and the overall security situation. After coming to an understanding with the Taliban Government, China has decided to extend development in the country. It aims to exploit the rare earth minerals that are believed to exist there, develop infrastructure, and dissuade the Taliban from providing partisan support to Uyghur insurgents in Xinjiang. Taliban leaders had been to China for talks in August 2021 and were invited to attend the annual meeting of nations participating in BRI on 1 October 2023.

Pakistan has succeeded in its policy of establishing a Taliban government in Afghanistan. The goal is to come to terms with the Baluch and Pashtun separatist organizations based in Afghanistan, with the help of the Taliban. The TTP, has already indicated that they will not come to a compromise with the government, even as the Taliban are trying to showcase themselves as a credible political entity to the world at large. There are indications that the Taliban would like to establish political links with India and other countries. If India had retained its embassy and consulates in Afghanistan, its diplomatic presence would have implicitly recognized the newly established Taliban regime. This assessment and an overriding concern for the safety of its embassy and other staff had led India to withdraw its personnel from Afghanistan on 26/27 August 2021. Latent links established at the time of the Karzai Government may still exist between Afghanistan and India. There have been eighty Afghan cadets under training at the Indian Military Academy. Military and civilian personnel have also trained at other Indian establishments. In addition, there were many Afghans on scholarship, studying in various institutions in India. India has repatriated most of these Afghans.

In retrospect, Pakistan's priority has also been to prevent India from gaining significant influence in Afghanistan. Pakistan noted India's generous attempts to breed goodwill and influence in Afghanistan and viewed this as a direct threat to its own security. In its ever-heightened threat perception, Pakistan is aware of Shia-dominated Iran to the west, China which has invested heavily in the CPEC, is becoming increasingly overbearing but still supportive. The Gulf countries seem to be friendly with Pakistan, and some had advanced loans to this country in 2024. Some analysts in Pakistan infer that India may be involved in Baluchistan because of Pakistan's involvement in Kashmir. Intelligence sources, as per a report published in a Pakistani newspaper, mention that the Chinese, Israelis, Iranians, Russians, Americans, and Afghans have a presence in Baluchistan.

Pakistan's leadership was obviously euphoric that India had been sidelined and made to exit Afghanistan by the establishment of the Taliban regime. Pakistan wanted to take the lead in the investment process in Afghanistan. No investment has, however, been forthcoming except that by China. Pakistan has nothing to offer because its own economy is in a poor state. Soon after the Taliban takeover, Pakistan sent the head of its ISI to Afghanistan to influence government formation and to subdue the rebellious Panjshir Valley. The Pakistani Foreign Minister had also toured the Central Asian Republics bordering Afghanistan to the North to apprise them of Pakistan's role in the region. This was perhaps undertaken to seek their support and elicit loans for Pakistan. The Foreign Minister had also advised the Taliban on how to improve their standing in the international arena, which would help to facilitate recognition of their government. Most of these efforts have come to nought. The Taliban largely have ignored Pakistan's advice and have established a medieval form of governance with their own regressive policies.

Pakistan has clearly been a disruptive and revisionist neighbour, seeking leverage and depth in Afghanistan. With the Taliban in power and Al Qaeda resurgent under the leadership of Hamza bin Laden, Afghanistan is returning to medieval ways. The Taliban may even begin to reinforce radical groups that already exist in Pakistan, with the aim of extending their influence in that country. They may want to persist with the idea of uniting Pashtuns divided by the Durand Line border. It is unlikely that the Taliban will accept any request from Pakistan to take action against the TTP as this would disturb the relationship between the two groups. The friction is borne out by incidents of firing on the border between Afghan border guards and Pakistani troops. On 24 December 2024, Pakistan launched air strikes in Paktia province on purported TTP locations inside Afghanistan. The Taliban claimed that there were 61 people killed in these air strikes including women and children. Pakistan's air force encroached inside Afghanistan to engage targets, which is perceived as an act of war. This was perhaps undertaken to demonstrate its own strength and resolve in countering insurgency. Pakistan also aimed to bring caution to the minds of the TTP who have been targeting Chinese citizens working on CPEC projects. Afghanistan has retaliated by small scale attacks inside Pakistan and the relationship between the two countries is no longer amicable.

Going back a few years, after the second Taliban takeover in Afghanistan, some irresponsible statements were made by politicians of Imran Khan's party when they were in power. One statement purported that the Taliban has shown their willingness to join Pakistan to support the latter in its low intensity conflict in Kashmir. This can be perceived as mere propaganda, but some analysts suggest that the only way out of this conundrum is to mount a psychological war on Pakistan. An enhanced economic squeeze will also be useful as the entire population will feel its effect. Experts on the subject also suggest that the issue of a greater Pashtunistan be revived. Such analysis, when published in Indian media, creates the impression in the minds of Pakistanis, that India is funding separatists in its provinces, to destabilize their country.

The Taliban have now had a reasonable exposure to the dynamics of the outside world, more than they had twenty years ago. There may now be a realization that they cannot exist in isolation. This has been proven in the wake of the devastation and loss of life caused by the earthquake in Afghanistan on 22 June 2022. Due to its lack of diplomatic ties, Afghanistan did not have international aid agencies stepping in to provide humanitarian aid immediately. The affected population was still awaiting aid weeks after the quake and aftershocks. Some Afghan citizens had woefully said at that time, that if the earthquake does not kill them, then poverty most probably will. The erstwhile COAS of the Pakistan Army, General Kayani, when interviewed by journalist Imtiaz Gul, had given a simplistic reply regarding their policy towards Afghanistan, stating, 'We have been misunderstood as far as the notion of strategic depth is concerned. All we have been interested in is a stable and peaceful Afghanistan, a border that we don't have to worry about. I don't think anybody has ever dreamed of occupying and treating Afghanistan as Pakistan's surrogate.'[2] The dichotomy in this statement is quite evident. His country has assisted in the resurgence of the Taliban and the resultant turmoil in that country. It is to be noted that Saudi Arabia, the UAE, and other countries have made no comment on the events in Afghanistan.

As mentioned earlier, proxy war and terrorism at the behest of Pakistan had been ongoing in Afghanistan since the sixties. Pakistan had created circumstances in Afghanistan that seemed advantageous in the past. With the return of the Taliban, Pakistan expected an amenable environment once again. Before the first Taliban government in Afghanistan was established, Lieutenant General Asad Durrani, an ex-ISI Chief wrote a book, *The Spy Chronicles*. In his book Durrani states, 'Pakistan does not want to go against Taliban and Haqqani network as there is sympathy for them in tribal areas and in the general public for resisting US occupation.' He further states, 'Pakistan cannot defeat the Taliban and Haqqani network when a great power such as Soviet Russia could not do it. The last time that Pakistan tried to subdue these groups in 2002, it resulted in the establishment of the TTP. If they try again, something more dangerous may evolve.'[3,4]

The US had, perhaps, neglected to understand Pakistan's statecraft till very late. Perhaps they knew Pakistan's motives and neglected to pay attention to the duplicitous role it played in the region. On 21 August 2018, President Trump clearly elaborated his view, 'Pakistan provides safe haven to agents of chaos, violence, and terror. We have been paying Pakistan billions of dollars, and at the same time, they are housing the very terrorists that we are fighting. But that will have to change.' In retrospect, after the rout of the Taliban in 2001, the US had all the advantages of becoming successful in the Afghan War. The Hamid Karzai Government was popular, and many of the Taliban wanted to join the democratic process at that time. The Taliban were in contact with the Karzai Government till as late

2. *The Most Dangerous Place: Pakistan's Lawless Frontier* by Imtiaz Gul, pp 10 and 185

3. *The Spy Chronicles: RAW, ISI and Illusion of Peace* by A. S. Dulat and Lt Gen Asad Durrani, 2018, pp 159

4. *Leaving Without Losing: The War on Terror After Iraq and Afghanistan* by Mark N. Katz, pp 99–100

as 2005 for this purpose. This was not acceptable to the US, and instead, it prevailed upon the Afghan government not to negotiate with the Taliban. In the meantime, the people that Karzai appointed as governors of provinces were self-serving and corrupt. They alienated ordinary Afghans in outlying areas and the warlords emerged as power centres in the local areas of their influence. Wherever there was disaffection or neglect of local issues and corrupt officials were prominent, the people began to support the Taliban. This contributed to the revival of the Taliban. The US policymakers, perhaps, did not visualize that reverse engineering had begun. In 2011, after Osama bin Laden was killed, the US once again had an opportunity to extricate from Afghanistan. At that time, the majority of Americans felt that the US mission in Afghanistan was successful and should be over. Instead, a surge was ordered by President Obama. He was concerned about the growing strength of the Taliban and an assessment at that time that the Armed Forces in Afghanistan were not yet strong enough to deal with the resurgent Taliban. Hence, to seek an enduring and honourable outcome in Afghanistan, the US continued its endeavours in counter-insurgency ops to defeat the Taliban and its allied terrorist groups. After being elected in 2016, President Trump had started to seek a way for the US to withdraw from Afghanistan. This was the origin of negotiations between the US Government and the Taliban and the subsequent withdrawal of US forces.

Anand Gopal, an author and an Afghanistan observer, provides another perspective in his book, *No Good Men Among the Living: America, the Taliban and the War through Afghan Eyes*.[5] He writes about the importance of Pakistan's influence on the Taliban. However, he does not believe that Pakistan is the main spoiler in Afghanistan. His hypothesis states, 'Following the collapse of the Taliban regime, Al Qaeda fled the country. By April 2002, the group could no longer be found in Kandahar or anywhere else in Afghanistan. The Taliban had ceased to exist. The terrorists had merged with clans and tribes in villages. The terrorist groups had all decamped or abandoned the cause, yet US Special Forces on Afghan soil had a clear political mandate, to defeat terrorism. The question was, 'How do you fight a war without an adversary?' It was at that time the Afghan warlords were allowed to unwittingly consolidate power and wealth with American support. These warlords created enemies when there were none. They were prone to taking bribes and negotiating with the re-emerging Taliban. The result was counterproductive, as mentioned

5. *No Good Men Among the Living: America, the Taliban and the War Through Afghan Eyes* by Anand Gopal, 2014, Google Books

above. The US ops against the Taliban and Al Qaeda collaterally involved ordinary Afghans. Inadvertent casualties occurred and this further alienated and divided the people, creating conditions for the Taliban and other groups to revive and re-emerge in Afghanistan, supported by the ISI. A perfectly won victory was thus frittered away.

Prior to the Taliban takeover, the Afghan media was free and was spread across all regions of the country. Afghans had made considerable progress, especially in women's rights and education. More than a third of those who voted in the last presidential elections were women. Nearly 40 per cent of the children in Afghan schools were female. One-fourth of the members of Parliament were women, and some were being recruited by their police forces. Afghanistan's economy was growing, but the Taliban takeover has been disruptive. The country has become unstable economically. To provide relief to an impoverished population, the UN has sent food and supplies and so has India. Employment that was provided by the US and its allies, their contractors, on development and reconstruction projects, by embassies and their consulates, institutions, businesses and miscellaneous services has all but vanished. The Taliban is facing challenges internally, and there has been no recognition of their regime externally. Sectarian violence continues from time to time and those Afghans who worked for foreigners in their own country are being eliminated systematically. The Taliban has imposed a ban on higher education for girls and the female population has been subjected to other serious curbs on their freedom. Overall, the situation in the country has regressed greatly since the Taliban takeover.

With its duplicitous role in Afghan affairs, Pakistan has had a major role in preventing democracy from being sustained in Afghanistan. Pakistan has meddled in the situation and has been instrumental in making sure that the US and its allies were forced to extricate from Afghanistan. The US attempts to eradicate terrorism have failed because of Pakistan's sustained support to terrorist factions, coupled with the Afghan aversion to foreign domination.[6] Despite the US negotiations with the Taliban, the agreement that was signed on 29 February 2020 was mostly to allow for an honourable exit for the US from Afghanistan. It was a summary end to an era of major military ops that aimed to engage in nation building.

6. 'How the Good War Went Bad: America's Slow-Motion Failure in Afghanistan' by Carter Malkasian, *Foreign Affairs*, April–March 2020, pp 77–91

CHAPTER 5

The China Factor

India-China Relations

In the 1950s, Prime Minister Nehru of India had reached out to establish friendly relations with communist China under Mao Zedong's chairmanship. On 28 April 1954, China and India signed the Panchsheel Agreement, which enunciated the five principles of peaceful co-existence between the two countries. Communist China had invaded and annexed Tibet in 1950–51. India, in a conciliatory gesture, was one of the first countries to recognize Tibet as a part of China. In 2003, after India's Prime Minister, Atal Bihari Vajpayee visited China, a joint declaration was signed in which India formally recognized that Tibet was a part of Peoples Republic of China. In a reciprocal gesture China also took steps to recognize Sikkim as part of India. India had military detachments in Kashgar in Xinjiang and Yatung in Tibet, which were withdrawn when the communist government was established in China. The nationalist Kuomintang Government of China escaped the purge by the Communists and established itself in Taiwan in 1949. India was also one of the few countries that supported communist China in its bid for permanent membership of the UNSC. With these mutual efforts, Indian policymakers hoped that relations between the two countries would remain stable.

A large section of Tibetan population has sought refuge in India to escape the rigid restraints of communist rule established by China in their country. India in its magnanimity, accepted approximately 100,000 refugees from Tibet after its annexation by China. A Tibetan government in exile was established and is located at McLeodgunj near Dharamsala in India. The political and spiritual leader of Tibet, the Dalai Lama, was provided sanctuary when he arrived in India in 1959 with his followers. It is believed that hundreds of thousands, Tibetans died resisting the Chinese occupation of their country out of a total population of 6 million. China resents India providing sanctuary for Tibetans. A humanitarian gesture that is appreciated across the world is a sore point between the two nations.

India's previous friendly gestures towards China did not stop the relationship from deteriorating and communist China began to creep forward across the un-demarcated IB with India. In 1959, China's Prime Minister, Zhou Enlai, is purported to have written to Prime Minister of India, Jawaharlal Nehru, claiming areas in Eastern Ladakh, North-East Frontier Agency (NEFA), renamed as Arunachal Pradesh, and in the central Sector of the border with India. A map of the boundary as per the Chinese perception had been reportedly attached with this letter. Similar letters had been sent to the other neighbours of communist China. This claim was unacceptable to the Indian leadership as it was considered exaggerated. Incursions were thereafter started by Chinese troops across the perceived border, leading to the Indo-China War of 1962. India was defeated in the war, and this narrative does not aim to analyze the reasons why India faced a retrograde situation in this war. After the 1962 China-India war, China and Pakistan began developing friendly relations and military cooperation between the two countries commenced. They now had a common enemy. In a border settlement in 1963, Pakistan ceded the Shasksgam Valley, a largely uninhabited mountainous tract, to China.

The first nuclear test at Lop Nur on 16 October 1964 added yet one more serious threat dimension from China. There were further skirmishes between India and China in the areas of Nathu La and Cho La mountain passes in Sikkim during *Op Savage* in 1967. The Chinese had opened unprovoked fire on unarmed Indian troops, who were laying a barbed wire fence in the open area on the Indian side of Nathu La, killing 88 and injuring 163. After the initial setback, the Indian Army inflicted considerable damage to Chinese military infrastructure and caused casualties to their troops. Ever since its communist rule was established, China has pursued expansionist policies against all its neighbours by making wrongful territorial claims. In 1969 China fought a prolonged war with the Soviet Union in the disputed Ussuri River region in Manchuria. Clashes also occurred between the two countries on the border of Xinjiang. These are examples of China's policy of occupying areas and consolidating their hold on the disputed areas. China has not reached a settlement of its borders with India and Bhutan, which keeps the border issue in limbo. In this manner they continue to maintain a hostile stance and perhaps seek further opportunities to expand their area of occupation.

In the four wars between India and Pakistan, China has adopted an overtly non-partisan stance by not actively participating in the wars in collaboration with Pakistan. China did however, resort to minor incursions on the border and display a show of force. China also provides military hardware, advice, moral and diplomatic support to Pakistan. In comparison to Afghanistan and Pakistan, it is China that has greater implications for India's security. This has been proven time and again by their intentions and overtures on the LAC. In the Ladakh region, China had surreptitiously occupied the Aksai Chin area in the early 1950s and constructed their Western Highway through the area after occupying Tibet by force. This area is claimed by India. China does not recognize the McMahon Line drawn as the border between British India and Tibet in 1914 even though, at the time of signing the border agreement between the British and Tibet, a representative of the Chinese government was present. The original version of this agreement likely exists with the Government of Taiwan and in British Library and Records in the United Kingdom (UK). It may also reside with the Government of India. It was understood that China had informally recognized the Macartney-MacDonald Line but then made enhanced claims to this area in 1959. In contrast to this, China does accept the extension of the McMahon line as the border between Myanmar and China. A map of the many claim lines and where the Chinese troops reached in the 1962 war in Eastern Ladakh is shown in Annexure 13.

Annexure 13

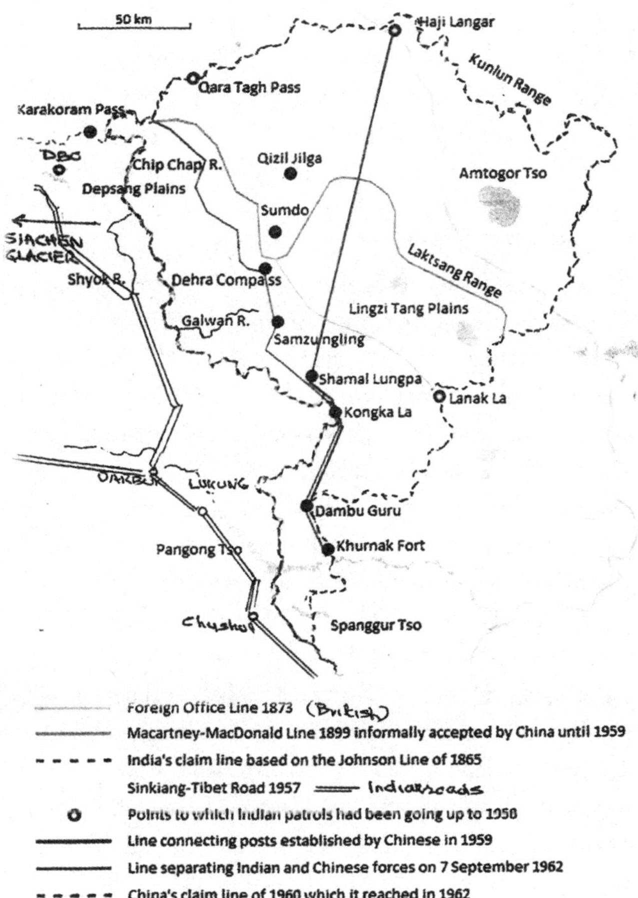

The Escalation in Eastern Ladakh

It is evident that China has kept the border issue alive with India and has made no attempts towards a resolution in order to keep India under pressure and facing a constant threat at the LAC. An incident on 20 April 2020 is of consequence since the tension on the border between China and India escalated greatly at that time. In this skirmish, Indian Army and the Chinese troops engaged at Naku La, a pass in Sikkim. The Chinese border troops told Indian troops to vacate the area, stating that this area did not belong to India. The implication of this statement was that the Naku La pass did not belong to India. The intention was perhaps for the Chinese troops to gain tactical advantage in the area. In a larger context, it could imply that China does not recognize Sikkim to be a part of India. Prior to and consequent to this incident there have been many incursions attempted by the Chinese into areas patrolled by Indian security forces at the LAC, and there has been buildup of troops on the Chinese side of the border. These belligerent actions are indicative of China's larger aims against India and its intention is to keep the border simmering as an issue between the two countries.

A famous landmark in NE Ladakh is Daulat Beg Oldi (DBO), which is about 10 km SW of the Karakoram Pass. This was an old trading post on the ancient silk route to Xinjiang. An Indian airfield is located near DBO. Further south is the area of Depsang Plains. The Depsang area is suitable for the deployment of mechanized forces. This area leads to the Shyok Valley, along which India has developed a 250 km road linking Darbuk to DBO. This axis is prone to interdiction by Chinese forces. From Darbuk, a road goes to Lukung, which is located on the western tip of Pangong Tso (Lake) and further east onto Chushul and Demchok. The Pangong Tso is a saline water, high-altitude glacial lake approximately 134 km long with a maximum width of 5 km. It is at an elevation of 14,000 ft. Two-thirds of this lake is in the area of Aksai Chin occupied by China, and the remainder is in India. China has built a bridge across the narrowest portion of this lake, approximately 25 kms from the LAC, which provides Chinese troops the flexibility to switch forces. A few attempts have been made by China to inch forward along the northern bank of this lake, to establish control up to the area of Lukung. This area has tactical significance because from here, an Indian road leads to Marsimik La and it is through this pass that the Indian posts at Gogra and Hot Springs are maintained. In the areas of the Depsang Plains and the Galwan River Valley, there have also been aggressive actions by Chinese troops. If not countered, these intrusions would have given the Chinese considerable tactical advantages, especially because the Darbuk-DBO road would become vulnerable. These forward moves by the People's Liberation Army would likely have been planned at the highest level of their government. Through such offensives, the Chinese keep advancing and changing their untenable claims across this border.

The areas of Karakoram Pass, DBO, and the Depsang Plains are of strategic importance as this area is a wedge between Aksai Chin and the Siachen Glacier, which is about 70 km to the west of the Karakoram Pass.

If the Chinese captured the area of the Depsang Plains and DBO, then they could advance and lean on to the Saser La ridgeline in the west and jeopardize the Indian defence in the Siachen Glacier area and the Soltoro range. Such an op, if successful, would establish a link between Aksai Chin and Gilgit-Baltistan. However, this is an unlikely possibility as the Indian Army has strengthened its defence posture considerably in the area. To enable safer access to the area of DBO and Depsang, an alternate road is being developed by India connecting the Nubra Valley through Saser La to DBO.

China has never clearly detailed its version of the border on maps except maybe in the central sector. Their perception of the alignment of the border is, perhaps, based on the 1959 claim mentioned earlier. On 7 September 1993, India and China signed an agreement to maintain peace along the LAC. In this agreement, the Indian Ministry of External Affairs and the Chinese counterparts did not come to an understanding on the alignment or the perception of the border of each country. Solving such a complex issue cannot be accomplished unilaterally if the other is unwilling. At that time, the Chinese stated that the resolution of the border could be left for later. In the past, Chinese troops have not established a permanent presence in the area whenever they have conducted an intrusion. They stayed in the intruded area only for a few hours to a few days. The exception was the standoff in Doklam in 2017, which is near the Bhutan-India-Tibet tri-junction. On an ongoing basis, numerous instances of forward patrolling by both sides keeps the dispute alive and result in tense confrontations. With only a few metres separating the Chinese and Indian troops, belligerent eyeball-to-eyeball contact has occurred. When weapons were not involved, there was pushing, shoving, and hand-to-hand violence between the opposing sides.

A few incidents that show the blatant belligerence of the Chinese deserve a mention here. In the village of Demchok, on the Indian side of the LAC in the Indus Valley, the Chinese have moved forward a few times and threatened the local villagers. In the same area, Indian shepherds were told to keep their yaks, pashmina goat, and sheep away from a nearby valley, which had been the traditional grazing area for their animals. This could be because the crest line in the area provides observation into the area held by the Chinese. The Chinese in reality have no *locus standi* in the area, as the inhabitants have been Indian citizens for centuries. Demchok is important, as it is the last Indian habitation close to the border. From there, about 50 km towards the east is Ngari on the Chinese Western Highway or G219, where they have developed an Air Force Base. From Demchok, a gravel road goes to Ngari.

In May 2020, approximately two divisions or more of Chinese troops assembled in Tibet on the pretext of military exercises. They moved forward in Eastern Ladakh and occupied areas that were not held by Indian troops but were patrolled periodically up to designated points. In the area of the confluence of the Galwan and Shyok rivers, the Chinese intended to establish posts in proximity to this area that would enable them to threaten the Indian road connecting Darbuk-DBO. Capture of the Depsang Plains would also cut off this axis to DBO and isolate Karakoram Pass, and it would result in the loss of the airfield. In the area of Pangong Tso, the Chinese troops had moved forward with the tactical aim of denying a few areas that were patrolled by Indian troops since the 1962 war. A series of talks had since taken place between local military commanders to prevent further escalation of the conflict and to bring about disengagement at the points of contact. Virtual talks had also taken place between the Indian National Security Advisor, Foreign and Defence Ministers and their Chinese counterparts. After the first talks between local corps commanders on 6 June 2020, it was reported that the Chinese agreed to withdraw to their previous positions in the Galwan Valley. On 15 June 2020, an unarmed Indian patrol led by the commanding officer of an infantry battalion went to verify whether the Chinese troops had removed their tents and temporary structures and withdrawn as discussed. The patrol found that the Chinese troops had not withdrawn and with no provocation physically assaulted the unarmed commanding officer and his patrol. The Chinese troops were in larger numbers and had used mallets, rods, and even rods with nails and spikes, and barbed wire rolled over wooden sticks to cause bodily harm. The Indian troops soon reinforced the patrol and retaliated. Indian authorities declared that 20 of its soldiers, including the commanding officer were killed in the skirmish. The Chinese, too, suffered casualties, but they did not disclose them as the high attrition would reflect poorly on the PLA and on Xi Jinping's prestige. The US and Indian intelligence estimated that the Chinese had 35 killed and a large number of wounded. The Russian news agency TASS reported on 11 February 2021 that 40 Chinese soldiers were killed in this skirmish. The Chinese did finally acknowledge that they had four dead as a result of the skirmish. This deadly encounter brings to the fore the state of distrust and animosity between the two countries. A stark contrast to the friendly overtures that India has been making towards China since the early 1950s.

Much like Pakistan's reaction, the Chinese had also objected to the changed status of J&K, which now divides it into two union territories. They took an exception to the maps published by the Indian Ministry of Home Affairs in December 2019 that show the areas of Aksai Chin and the Shaksgam Valley, under Chinese occupation, as Indian territory. In retaliation perhaps, the Chinese foreign ministry spokesman in a statement, claimed the whole of Ladakh. China continues to object to the development of infrastructure by India, such as roads and communication networks, in proximity to the border. In contrast to this, China continues to develop its infrastructure in the areas occupied and in Tibet, and Xinjiang. This infrastructure gives China the flexibility to build up and switch forces anywhere along the LAC. China has developed the Karakoram Highway through Khunjerab Pass into Gilgit-Baltistan. This area is part of the erstwhile princely state of J&K and is claimed by India. Reports indicate that another road is being planned to connect Yarkand in Xinjiang to Skardu in Gilgit-Baltistan through the Mustagh Pass. A railway line is also planned to link Hotan with Xigazê from the existing railway to Kashgar. The Chinese military's aim for a border buildup is perhaps to reiterate their 1959 claim to the area. Their political aim is to prevent India rise as a regional power and prevent it from acting against Chinese interests in collaboration with other countries, especially the US, in the Indo-Pacific region. China is surrounded by nineteen countries, some of which are inimical. Xi Jinping and the Chinese Communist Party (CCP) policymakers believe that China must recover those territories that it purportedly lost during a century of humiliation, prior to the communist takeover. With the aim of pursuing revisionist policies, China intends to enlarge its security perimeter by controlling most of the South China Sea and the East China Sea, integrate Taiwan and consolidate its hold on Tibet and Xinjiang. Adopting 'wolf warrior' diplomacy, a resurgent China has also displayed aggressive behaviour and belligerence in international forums and in global negotiations. Chinese leadership does not accept or even tolerate any challenge to their ideology, doctrine, way of life, and point of view.

Narendra Modi, India's Prime Minister, has had one-on-one summits with Xi Jinping on two occasions to obviate belligerence at the un-demarcated border. Troops from both armies carried out a joint exercise after the meetings between the leaders, but the skirmish at the border in 2020 occurred even after these reconciliatory measures. This is a clear indication that China cannot be trusted by India or, for that matter, by any other nation. Very similar to Pakistan's disingenuous intentions at the Lahore Summit and the subsequent Kargil War, China's actions show that despite treaties, diplomacy is not adequate to resolve disputes when one of the participants maintains an intractable attitude. Chinese policy makers have likely noticed India leaning towards the US by actively participating in military exercises as part of the Quad, holding summits with President Trump and signing treaties. This may have been interpreted by China as duplicitous diplomacy on the part of India.

A Resurgent China

Over the last few years, China has become more combatant in its dealing with Hong Kong, Taiwan, the South and East China Seas, the Senkaku Islands, Australia, India, and the Philippines. China is in direct competition with the West and is increasing its influence as an authoritarian power. It has resorted to sanctions against countries that go against its interests. As an example, it imposed sanctions on Norway to ban the import of salmon after the Norwegian Nobel Prize Committee awarded Chinese dissident Liu Xiaobo. China is also undertaking strategic expansion of its capabilities. It is making massive investment in research and development, targeting the acquisition of select foreign companies, undertaking a systematic program of industrial espionage and making widespread use of state-controlled hacker attacks. China is forging new relationships with India's South Asian neighbours, and with Iran and Russia. China is actively supporting Russia without itself physically participating in the Ukraine war. It is country that has gained considerable strength in the global south with its BRI and alliances in BRICS and SCO.

As China asserts itself, its national interests clearly override personal relationships between leaders. Trade and commercial ties do not always lead to the maintenance of peace and its alliances are purely transactional. India has been active in the BRICS and SCO along with China and other member nations of these organizations but has refused to join the Chinese BRI. The offensive posture by China in Eastern Ladakh does not threaten India's vital interest, but it impacts the latter's strategy of pursuing an independent policy in international relations. The politico-military challenge from China is real. The standoff on the LAC did not occur because Chinese interests were threatened by India, it has larger implications. China's unsubstantiated claim over Ladakh, on the Indian State of Arunachal Pradesh, areas in the Central Sector, and Bhutan show the serious nature of the border dispute which have led to violent border incidents. This is part of the Chinese strategy of expansionism and domination that it wants to achieve in the world. An example of China's undefined claims is the stand-off in the Doklam plateau, mentioned earlier, from 16 June to 28 August 2017. It was a serious provocation by China. In this incident, despite having agreed to withdraw and having done so, the Chinese returned to the area and built infrastructure opposite their point of incursion inside Tibetan territory. They built a dual-use village and positioned troops there. Reports indicate that China is creating bases for missile deployment opposite Naku La in Sikkim and on the Doklam plateau opposite Bhutan Army positions. They have started to occupy dominating heights in the area in proximity to the border, increasing their defence potential, and have constructed dual-use villages close to the border to cement their hold on the area. In addition, in recent times, China has been trying to win Bhutan over by offering financial aid and infrastructure development. Chinese tourists are visiting Bhutan in large numbers. These visitors could be gathering intelligence on terrain, communications, defence forces, their plans, and so on. Alongside the above, China is also exerting pressure on Bhutan by laying a claim to the NE part of the country. Unsubstantiated claims on territory, financial coercion, and military threats and even aggression, are indicative of the ongoing Chinese strategy. After the overthrow of the Sheikh Haseena government in Bangla Desh the Chinese have been wooing the interim administration in that country. Bangla Desh has established new relationship with Pakistan and with China.

There have been 21 rounds of negotiations between India and China since the 1950s. Despite this, the border issue remains unresolved. This is the strategy that the Chinese pursue, which facilitates their unilateral, surreptitious, and in strength, creep forward to consolidate their hold on territory and change their claims posing an enhanced threat. With this tactic, China diverts attention from contentious matters such as the Shaksgam Valley and its exploits in Gilgit-Baltistan for CPEC. India has well understood the Chinese strategy. It has had to deploy a larger number of Indian defence forces on the border to defend its soverignty.

China has large investments in various private enterprises in India and the South Asian Association for Regional Cooperation (SAARC) countries. It has financial and trade linkages with most of the world. As a rising superpower, China's relations with the US and a few other countries have been tenuous. The Chinese media and their foreign ministry spokesman have been restrained in their comments on the relations with India.

Their defence ministry spokesman has, however, stated that India should understand the bigger picture. The bigger picture seems to be to achieve geo-political domination of most parts of the world, including South Asia. It is also seeking to eliminate the US sponsored world order and its influence in the Asia-Pacific region. China has both the capacity and intent to reshape the international order, displacing the US and its democratic values. The geo-political contest between China and the US is real. The growth in nuclear weapons, as seen from the construction of silos in Xinjiang province and elsewhere within their mainland, are indications of an increasing nuclear capability. Their capability in this field is growing and China is estimated to have 1,000 nuclear warheads by 2030. This advance is unlikely to stop there as China aims for parity with the USA and Russia in nuclear weapons. The significance of this requires a separate analysis since it has implications.

The China-Pakistan Nexus

Of concern to India is China's sale of military hardware to Pakistan and other countries in South Asia including Bangladesh, Myanmar, Nepal, and Sri Lanka. China's strategic infrastructure projects on land and sea in these countries, which would be used for military purposes, are also worrisome. Reports have indicated that the Chinese helped Pakistan make up deficiencies in weapons, ammunition, and equipment at the time of the Kargil War. It has supplied Pakistan with 80% of its military hardware in recent times. This support, however, did not have an impact on the outcome of the war after the Pahalgam terrorist attack. This short war was named as *Op Sindoor* by India.

Over the years, China has become Pakistan's largest arms supplier. China and Pakistan had signed agreements on co-development and co-production of weapon systems, including the JF-17 fighter aircraft and Pakistan's main battle tank, Al-Khalid. Pakistan has made a bid for 40 of J31 fighter aircraft. China will surely upgrade Pakistan's capabilities in the AI controlled future war against India especially after *Op Sindoor*. There are indications that China has developed a biotech research facility, similar to its laboratory at Wuhan, in Multan, Pakistan. This laboratory is publicly portrayed as a joint venture in agriculture. However, this facility needs further oversight by an international body to ensure the legitimacy of such a collaboration, which may have serious global implications.

China has continued to support Pakistan in their agenda against India. Military cooperation, including exercises with troops and war gaming, is a regular feature between the PLA and Pakistan's Armed Forces and so is political consultation. When India and Pakistan tensions are aggravated or when India implements internal administrative measures related to Kashmir, Pakistan immediately consults China to formulate a combined strategy for dealing with the issue. At the behest of Pakistan, China raised the Kashmir issue at the UNSC twice – in 1919 and 2020, on abrogation of articles 370 and 35A and the bifurcation of J&K into two union territories by India. The UNSC clearly did not consider this matter as serious, or requiring its attention, and it did not even yield a written statement. Their verbal advice each time was that Kashmir is a bilateral issue, and that it should be resolved bilaterally. In a list of disputes published by the UN, J&K has been removed from the list and Pakistan has objected to this. Based on this decision by the UN, India had wound up the UN Military Observer Group in India and Pakistan (UNMOGIP), from its side of the border.

China is extending trade and development activities in the region with its BRI. The CPEC envisages the use of Pakistan-occupied territory in Gilgit-Baltistan and their mainland to develop infrastructure, gain transit through the area up to the Arabian Sea, and exploit natural resources in the area. The infrastructure development commenced with the building of the 1,300 km long Karakoram Highway connecting Kashgar in Xinjiang with Islamabad. China has become the manufacturing base for most of the world and is rapidly becoming a military and cyber superpower. In his vision Xi Jinping has explicit aims for the BRI and the String of Pearls. The main aim is the development of Chinese trade and commerce in major parts of the world and thereby establishing China's hegemony. The Chinese leadership has the impression that the US has encircled China with Armed Forces deployed in nearby countries. The US has also formed strategic alliances with select countries in the region since the Korean War. These alliances are a source of security and a source of stability for the US and its allies. China intends to establish its own linages to contend with these.

The South China Sea and Asia-Pacific Region

China has often disregarded international laws to ensure that its interests are not threatened and to gain a strategic advantage. A case in point are the violations in the South China Sea, which have implications for the free movement of trade along waterways of the world. After three years of deliberation by the Permanent Court of Arbitration, an international body of the Hague Tribunal constituted under the UN Convention on Law of the Sea (UNCLOS), ruled on 12 July 2016 that the Spratly Islands are located within the 200 nautical miles of the Exclusive Economic Zone (EEZ) of the Philippines. This ruling was against China's claims of sovereignty over these islands. Despite having ratified UNCLOS, China ignored this ruling. It has been successful in establishing its sovereignty on these islands by occupying existing ones and creating new artificial islands in the South China Sea. These islands lie within their nine-dash lines, which were drawn unilaterally by China to show to the rest of the world the extent of their claims in the South China sea. The UNCLOS has found no legal basis for the Chinese claim to date. It is to be noted that approximately $4.5 trillion worth of trade passes through this area on commercial ships each year. There are known reserves of fossil fuels under the sea, and these waters are rich in seafood. By claiming the area of the South China Sea, China has attempted to usurp this maritime territory as their own, utilize resources therein and create a large buffer to its mainland along their littoral on this sea.

China is also furthering its strategic reach in the Indo-Pacific. A disclosure by SIPRI made with the help of satellite photographs of the Maldives shows that an artificial island is being developed there by China. The Maldives had leased sixteen islands to China in 2016 for 60 years. Out of these, the Feydhoo Finolhu Island is likely to be a military base. These islands are approximately 684 km from the southern Indian coastline. Creating an artificial island indicates that China is going to have a permanent military presence in the area. This could be a counter to Diego Garcia, which is owned by the British, and has a US base 1175 km from the Maldives. The Maldives are already reeling under the debt imposed by China and on 6 October 2019, the Chinese ambassador to Maldives had presented an invoice of $3.2 billion to the country. China has also signed a protocol with Maldives to establish a joint observation station on its northernmost atoll, Makunudhoo, in the Indian Ocean close to the sea lanes, to ensure the safety of its shipping. In Sri Lanka, on 20 May 2021, their Parliament passed the Colombo City Economic Commission Bill that effectively handed over about 43 percent of the 660 acres of reclaimed land on Colombo's waterfront to the Chinese on a 99-year lease. This acquisition follows the earlier handing over of the Hambantota port to China, where Chinese submarines are observed dropping anchor. An international airport was also constructed there, but it remains unutilized. These developments have obvious security implications for international trade that flows through the Indian Ocean. China is expanding its island-building strategy in the mid-Pacific in the Republic of Kiribati. This is a small country located on the equator at its intersection with the 180 degrees meridian south of Hawaii. It comprises small islands which are prone to flooding due to an anticipated rise in sea levels due to global warming. Kiribati has agreed to be part of China's BRI. With China's help, it intends to carry out large-scale dredging to reclaim land from lagoons and raise the height of islands/atolls. This country is located on the sea lanes between the US and Australia/ New Zealand and can be utilized by China for power projection. China has already violated the one country, two systems arrangement in Hong Kong and imposed repressive laws there. China has also made its intentions regarding Taiwan clear, claiming that it is part of their one-China policy. China, perhaps, does realize the implications of seizing Taiwan by force while simultaneously holding the US at bay. Taiwan has shown patience and ensured that it does not escalate the situation.

To achieve dominance, China intends to ensure a change in the global supply chain and logistics in its favour, secure access to energy sources, minerals, and markets, utilize financial coercion, even graft and bribery to enable this, promote its Renminbi as an international currency and replace the US as the dominant power. Xi Jinping had eliminated the constitutional provision that limits his term as Chairman of the communist party and PLA to two terms, allowing him to serve for life. He has taken charge of key committees overseeing cyber matters, economic reform, and security. One of his predecessors, Deng Xiaoping, had stated that China must hide its capabilities and bide it's time to become strong. Deng set forth goals to be achieved in agriculture, industry, defence, science, and technology. During this period of opening up the country to business led to widespread corruption and power abuse, admiration for the west and erosion of the power of the CCP. Xi Jinping had stated at the 19th Party Conference that the party must be at the vanguard of the times, and the backbone of the country. Xi has relentlessly strengthened the Party's dominance and discursive power in the ideological sphere. Xi's doctrine 'China's Dream of Rejuvenation' is projected for fulfillment by 2050. It aims to restore China to the height of power, influence and international standing. It can be assumed that Xi Jinping believes that China's time has arrived to become dominant in the world. It is, as yet, not adequately strong to project military power but is preparing for it. It has amassed considerable cash reserves and continues to add to its coffers as it has continues to manufacture goods and provide services in most of the world and its international trade is incremental and profitable. China has displayed its unmatched capability in carrying out construction work at a feverish pace, including in the construction of artificial islands. It hopes to benefit from these massive projects, as these will enhance its growth rate further and secure its supply chains. It plans to create new markets for Chinese companies, so that its financial institutions will become stronger. The growth rate in the Chinese economy has however, shown a decline in 2022-24 even as the US economy is growing slightly. China continues to utilize economic outlays and political statecraft to pursue its objectives to achieve its larger aim to seek domination over collaborating countries by making them hostage with huge debt burdens. China has been helping to modernize infrastructure in countries that cannot undertake development on their own. The infrastructure to be developed or already underway includes roads, railways, airports, deep water ports, artificial islands, fibre optic networks, communications, power, exploitation of natural resources, mining, and oil and gas pipelines.

BRI and CPEC

The BRI is a mammoth project that has considerable impact on world trade and security. In brief, it has two main parts: first is the land-based Silk Road and Rail corridors extending from mainland China to the heart of Europe and eastern Russia. The second part includes the twenty-first century Maritime Silk Route or the String of Pearls, which is a series of ports covering the South China Sea, the littoral of the Indian Ocean, the Mediterranean and perhaps around the world. The Chinese plan included building the Kra Canal, cutting across Thailand as an alternative to movement through the Malacca Straits, a choke point through which 80 per cent of Chinese shipping passes. This project has, however, not been approved by the Government of Thailand. CPEC will provide an alternative for the movement of goods and services. It will connect Xinjiang with the Gwadar Port on the Arabian Sea in Pakistan.

For India, another area of concern is the cooperation between China and Myanmar and the China-Myanmar Economic Corridor. This is estimated to have an outlay of $100 billion and is larger than CPEC. These projects are indicative of the large-scale investments that China is capable of making and these have no parallel in the world. The European Union too has not been immune to Chinese influence. China offered aid when some nations in the European Union had a financial crisis. Sixteen central and east European countries are part of the BRI. China intends to use its manufacturing and marketing power to make the world more dependent on its commerce. If it is able to gain influence in Europe this may serve to prevent a united Europe acting in concert with the US.[1]

In addition to the above ventures, China has undertaken investments in areas which are of common interest in the world. This includes rule-setting in new areas such deep seas, polar regions, outer space, and cyber space. It is estimated that large quantities of fossil fuels exist in Antarctica. Although these are at an estimated depth of 1.6 miles, an estimated 500 billion tons of coal, 100 billion barrels of oil, and 5 trillion cubic meters of natural gas are believed to exist under the ice. The 1959 Treaty on Antarctica put a freeze on all territorial claims to the continent. However, in times to come, a geo-political struggle may ensue. China has become actively involved in Antarctica, having invested $46 billion in its research programs there. It intends to build new icebreaker vessels and expand bases essential for exploring the area, which has fewer barriers and no territorial claims. Similarly, China is participating in Arctic exploration with the aim of becoming a polar power. It is already doing this exploration in conjunction with Russia.

The spread and quantum of China's investments that have been elaborated above, requires massive expenditure. To finance the projects, China has developed new institutions to support them. The Asian Infrastructure Bank (AIB), the Silk Road Fund, and the New Development Bank (NDB), previously called the BRICS Bank, are the main institutions. China had invited both India and Pakistan to join the Shanghai Cooperation Organization (SCO), a regional economic bloc, and had also encouraged Iran to join. All these nations did join the SCO and currently the SCO has ten members and some dialogue partners. India had joined this organization, but did not join the Regional Comprehensive Economic Partnership, a free trade agreement signed by 15 countries on 15 November 2020 that includes China, Japan, South Korea, Australia, New Zealand, and ASEAN members. This agreement gives China rights of access to US allies, as part of its business dealings. This could tantamount to its growing influence in the world's geographical south.

The success of BRI is contingent upon stability in the various regions, especially in the Middle East and eastern Europe. China has also passed a law that allows its PLA to participate in counter-terrorism missions abroad.

1. 'Why Invest in Kazakhstan?', an article by Arif Durrani and Gabe Kirchheimer, published in *Bloomberg Businessweek*, April 2019

This was considered essential by them to protect and act against terrorists or any other forces disrupting BRI projects and infrastructure. The US and its friendly countries have planned investments in the region in parallel with Chinese investments. The proposed India-Middle East-Europe Economic Corridor is an example of this investment. Notwithstanding the foregoing, many European nations have joined the AIB and are thus participating in BRI. China has already become a major trade partner with Europe as mentioned earlier. Overall, the influence of China will continue to rise if the BRI projects and connected businesses are successful.

Chinese state-owned enterprises run 76 ports and terminals out of 34 countries, including Greece, Pakistan, Myanmar, and Sri Lanka. China continues to make selective purchases in various countries as mentioned earlier. In Portugal, for example, it bought their electricity grid and its biggest insurance company. China intends to establish special arbitration courts for BRI projects and to use these to promote its own legal system. Besides the growing economic clout, China is increasingly seeking to introduce its political values across the globe. To achieve this, it has established and is expanding the number of Confucius Institutes and Confucius classrooms to promote the spread of the Chinese language and culture abroad. These assets, besides spreading their culture and language, intend to propagate their policies on Taiwan, Hong Kong, Tibet, the South China Sea, Asia-Pacific, and the world at large. According to an article in the *Times of India*, a national newspaper, Mandarin has been made compulsory in several private schools in Nepal after China offered to pay the salaries of teachers. Mandarin is being propagated in schools in Pakistan, Iran, and Egypt. The long-term effects of all this will become apparent in the coming years. The Chinese Government has employed its state-owned enterprises and Chinese contractors to work on the projects and invest in countries that have high risk economies in order to gain controlling stakes in their strategic assets, such as ports, navigation systems, and raw materials. The countries which are likely to face debt distress from China include Djibouti, Kyrgyzstan, Laos, Maldives, Mongolia, Montenegro, Tajikistan, Pakistan, and Sri Lanka besides other African and European nations with weaker economies.

China has provided a loan of $59 billion to Pakistan to implement the CPEC. It has already taken over the port of Gwadar in the Baluchistan province. It is also believed to be developing a Naval and Air Force base in the adjacent Jivani peninsula in proximity to the Straits of Hormuz through which oil exports move from the Gulf states. This is close to the Chabahar Port developed by India in Iran. China is investing vast amounts of money to modernize Gwadar. The CPEC is seen by China as a jewel in the crown of their BRI. Gwadar will be expanded to become a trans-shipment mega port to be built alongside the Special Economic Zone (SEZ), which is under construction, from which industries will ship their products worldwide. A web of energy pipelines and road and rail links will connect Gwadar to Kashgar in Xinjiang. In addition, there are grants of $500 million to build an airport, school, college, hospital, and badly needed water infrastructure at Gwadar. Work on these has commenced. To begin, the volume of trade through Gwadar Port was expected to be 1.2 million tons, and it was to increase to 3 million tons in 2022. China will receive 90 per cent of the revenues from the Gwadar Port till it is handed over back to Pakistan in 40 years. In 2024, China has established its envoy in Afghanistan and will likely ask Afghanistan to join CPEC/BRI and develop the infrastructure towards CARs through this country. This could facilitate the land-locked CARs to use Gwadar port for their trade and transit. The instability in Baluchistan province remains a concern for the Chinese, and they have been in talks with militant leaders for the past five years to ensure that the projects in that province are not affected by insurgency or terrorism. Similar is the threat posed by militants of the TPP.

The CPEC projects have been negotiated one-to-one by the Pakistani Government and China. If Pakistan is unable to service its debts and pay back the capital, then what would China do to complete the contracts and extract funds and debts owed by that country? The economic situation in Pakistan has not stabilized after the Shahbaz Sharif government has come to power. It still depends upon bailouts from the IMF and loans from friendly countries. Politically, Pakistan and China do not plan to discuss the development of CPEC through the occupied part of J&K State, with India. This suggests that Pakistan takes for granted that the area of J&K occupied by them is their domain, and China supports this status. In addition to the Islamic card, another reason for Pakistan to retain its hold over POK and Gilgit-Baltistan is the availability of water. The drainage from the mountains in this region flows SW through Pakistan. The CPEC plan envisages the construction of six mega dams over the Indus waterway. Diamer-Bhasha is one of them. The development of these dams is expected to eliminate Pakistan's water security concerns. These plans could be put in jeopardy in case India abrogates the Indus Water Treaty, which is held in abeyance by India after the Pahalgam terrorist attack and over a period develops necessary measures to block the flow of water or minimize its flow into Pakistan.

An estimated $33 billion is being invested by China in power generation as a part of CPEC. In the initial planning, coal-fired plants were part of the project besides hydel power. The coal-fired plants would utilize imported coal for generating 5,580 megawatts of power. Pakistan's Thar coal will be available to generate 2,690 megawatts, wind energy farms will provide 1,300 megawatts, and solar energy farms will provide 1,000 megawatts.

Since Xinjiang Province has the second highest coal reserves in China, it was to be used in the aforesaid power generation and for exports through Gwadar to Egypt and other African and Middle Eastern countries. A 500-megawatt plant requires, 1.2–2 million tons of coal per year. It is, therefore, estimated that a large number of trucks would be required to move the coal over the Karakoram Highway each day and bring Chinese goods for export. This will be a massive effort, and it will be shared with the railway once it is developed. A point worth noting is that, as per the Paris Climate Protocol, China will be closing hundreds of plants that use coal and shift to clean energy in their own country. Reports, however, indicate that the closed plants will be relocated to other parts of the world, where their coal can be exported and utilised for power generation. China will be able to meet the targets on global warming as agreed upon in the Paris Climate Protocol, thus improving the quality of air in their own country. In so doing, it may be setting up polluting industries in other parts of the world. It would, therefore, be a win-win situation for China. The return on investment is expected to be 17–20 per cent. With the exemption of duties and taxes, the return may rise to 25 per cent. These statistics will undergo changes if China takes the threat of global warming seriously and accordingly curbs the use and export of polluting plants to generate power. If it is unable to meet the ever-increasing demand for power through renewable sources then it may continue to rely on the coal fired plants.

To ensure the security of the entire CPEC, China intends to develop a system of video and Internet surveillance, like the one within Beijing. Also, in partnership with Pakistani television it intends to disseminate Chinese media. China is also training local officials in other countries to manage public opinion and the media. This is done by monitoring communications and surveillance technologies. As stated earlier, China advocates a closed Internet. This is a form of digital authoritarianism. An example of authoritarianism that is being implemented internally is in Xinjiang province. a group of nearly two million Muslims, known as Uyghurs, in Xinjiang had been forced into re-education camps/detention camps. Their training and indoctrination had aimed to improve their productivity, contribute to national unity, bring them into the mainstream, and adopt the Chinese way of life. This had been undertaken after the Chinese faced regular protests and insurgency in Uyghur predominant areas in the period 2013-2016. Some of these people were released from these detention camps in December 2019 and later, as per announcements by the Chinese authorities. The detainees, when released, do not talk about their religion anymore, and their attire no longer includes the hijab and burqa. The remainder of the Muslim population is under constant screening to discern anti-national behaviour. To achieve this level of surveillance, the entire population of Xinjiang had their biometric data, such as DNA samples and iris scans, collected in a program called Physicals for All. The citizens live in fear of the state authorities. Those discerned to have anti-national behaviour through surveillance are sent to the detention camps. Similar changes could be in the offing in the Badshah Khan district/ Wakhan Corridor of Afghanistan. In Baluchistan, China intends to bring about steady change in the minds of the local population. Indoctrination methods are being employed to curb the prevalent insurgency and terrorism. Predictably, this may not happen as the Baluchistan Liberation Front, jihadis of their liberation army, and radical Islamists will want to continue to retain their hold in the area and are fighting to break away from Pakistan. With the developing relations between the Taliban government in Afghanistan and China, the area may change. In view of the present insecure environment, the Pakistan Army has, it is reported, taken on the responsibility of guarding the CPEC.

Overall, the BRI is a massive undertaking requiring $4 trillion in investments over the next few decades. To reiterate, the BRI includes those countries that account for 70 per cent of the world's natural resources, rare earths and energy reserves. China has signed contracts with these countries to make sure that they do not default in allowing their resources to be exploited. India had also attempted to secure its sources of energy but lost in few cases to China while seeking contracts in the same countries. India did, however, ensure the availability of sources of energy and natural resources from friendly countries that have the reserves.

China, by creating infrastructure along the sea lanes in the Indo-Pacific and the CPEC in the north through Gilgit-Baltistan-Pakistan, encircles India in a way. It has brought Nepal, a Hindu country, under its influence by steadily making sure that the communist party comes to power there. Having achieved this, they had perhaps instigated Nepal to revive a border dispute with India in Lipulekh and Kalapani. A strategic road, 80 km long, has been built by India up to Lipulekh on the Tibet border to facilitate pilgrimages to the Kailash Mountain and Mansarover Lake. This road is a cause of concern to China. It gives India an avenue with options to launch ops across the border into the heart of Tibet. A few media reports indicate that China has moved a battalion of the PLA opposite the Lipulekh Pass and is concentrating additional forces in the area of Kailash. After negotiations with China, the pilgrimage to Mansarover and Kailash will be opened once again in 2025. China is believed to be conducting a study through its embassy in Kathmandu to evaluate reasons for Gurkhas from Nepal to join the Indian Army. Currently, as per information available, the recruitment by India from Nepal has been stopped by the latter as they do not wish to participate in the Agni Veer programme for soldiers. In the coming years, China may even consider recruiting these warriors into the PLA if the Government of Nepal permits. Such a move will have implications and makes it imperative for India to ensure friendly relations with Nepal.

The US administration under President Bush encouraged China to be integrated into the international order, and quite a few dialogues were held to progress this. The Obama administration also followed a similar policy and attempted to seek China's cooperation on issues connected with the region from AFPAK to North Korea and on trade and climate change because it saw China as an emerging economy. The intention was to engage China in a meaningful way to strengthen the rule-based international system, essentially a western concept, that could lead to liberalisation in that country. The US, until then, was not taking China as an equal but was only extending a conciliatory hand to a possible future rival and trade partner. This was, perhaps, interpreted as a weakness of the US by the Chinese leadership. The hypothesis that moderation with trade and interdependence would lead to more openness in Chinese society has proved to be ill-founded. Xi Jinping's policies have made sure that China becomes militarily strong, and its economy eventually becomes larger than that of the US. Xi then launched the BRI in 2013 to increase his country's global presence. The aim was to achieve domination without war. The launching of the CPEC and its projects in other South Asian countries intends to seek influence in the region and in a way, it aims to isolate India. The US is leaning towards India to provide it with the leverage to contend with China. India has also looked towards the Southeast Asian nations to gain influence there, especially in Vietnam. The situation has created an inevitable conflict of interests between India and China.

The CPEC, if and when operational, will cut down the time for the movement of imports and exports from western China to the Middle East and Africa. This will become a cheaper and more secure option as compared to shipping to and from the SE Chinese ports. Pakistan, therefore, is important for China. The CPEC will also facilitate radiating Chinese authority in the region. Pakistan's links with China have, in a way, made the US cede some of the leverage it had with Islamabad. Despite this, the US will need to keep Pakistan engaged diplomatically because of the latter's nuclear capability and its hardcore Islamist groups. The US also needs to maintain links with this country to keep politico-military affairs in Afghanistan and the Al Qaeda and other terrorist groups in the region under scrutiny. The visits by the US envoy to Gilgit and Gwadar, the important hubs on the CPEC in 2024, show that the US is closely monitoring the project and retains interest in this country.

China may even be willing to cooperate with Pakistan in AI and in technology connected to cyberspace, electronics, electromagnetic spectrum, and outer space. India, however, is no longer a weak nation it was in 1962 during the China-India war. A successful strategy in relation to China must include a credible offensive component. There should be a capability to interdict and put the CPEC out of commission, once functional, and blockade sea routes to China if the need arises. China, through its BRI, is taking measures to make itself blockade-proof and reduce the impact of sanctions against it. India should ensure constant surveillance, upgrade precision strike capability with missiles, drones, aircraft, hypersonic missiles, and space-based weapons and utilize advanced AI controlling systems. To impose a maritime blockade on China, there would be a need to augment and develop under-sea capabilities in terms of submarines and associated systems. As Chinese plans progress, and if relations with China do not improve, it can be appreciated that India and like-minded nations can cooperate to contend with Chinese aggressiveness and intended hegemony in the region. China must be made to see that an open confrontation could spin out of control and may not end in desirable advantages. This can only be achieved by bringing caution into the minds of the CCP's planners. Such a strategy must be accompanied by strong deterrents and offensive capability. Future relationships and changing dynamics are discussed in subsequent chapters in this narrative.

CHAPTER 6

The Cyber Dimension

Cyberspace is the latest dimension of conflict and warfare. It is virtual, intangible and evolves fast. The growth in worldwide cyber capabilities has led to an elevated security threat for nations from an unseen enemy. In the high-tech world of today, cyber threats greatly impact the security of a country's administration, infrastructure, and military. Technological advancements are leading to intense competition in information warfare and war in the conventional sense. The widespread adoption of AI technology conjures up infinite new possibilities in terms of already complex conflicts and it highlights new concerns for the future.

As the world adopts AI and uses high speed computing to gain a cyber advantage, China and Pakistan have also developed considerable capabilities in cyber espionage. Pakistan's growing capabilities in this sphere were established some years ago when a covert operation, *Op Arachnophobia,* which originated in Pakistan in 2013, was exposed as a cyber espionage campaign that targeted Indian computer systems. There is no accurate information on which specific organizations in India were targeted and what information was hacked. The op was identified by *Dark Reading* and *Threat Connect* which are online cyber security websites that identify threats, vulnerabilities, and technology trends. Researchers from *Dark Reading*, spotted malware bundled with spurious documents concerning Indian organizations. The curious name Arachnophobia given to the op became known when Bitterbug, a computer virus, was detected by experts. The malware contained paths leading to the Pakistani website umaraziz27 and Umar Aziz was one of the employees at Tarantulas, a Pakistani tech company. India is also reported to have launched an op codenamed Hangover that targeted websites in Pakistan. This clandestine op was uncovered by Norway-based security firm Norman. In 2024, as revealed by Check Point, a cyber security provider, it was discovered that a group associated with the Pakistani government has been hacking various important entities in India. *Op Arachnophobia* and *Op Hangover* and other follow up cyber intrusions have highlighted that the rivalry between India and Pakistan now extends into cyberspace.

Multiple countries across the world are known to possess cyber-espionage and attack capabilities. The Internet and its applications currently do not have an over-arching governing protocol. Hence, misuse of cyberspace can pose a threat to institutions, organizations, and emergency services reliant on cyber systems for their functioning. By the time a cyberattack is detected, it often is too late to take countermeasures to mitigate the effects of the attack. Information is stolen and the conduct of operations and infrastructure is affected. Often the mal effects occur before a threat is detected and in today's world, preemptive cyber security measures are an essential part of a country's security apparatus.

Pakistan has IT experts who are well known in the cyber world. Fire Eye, a cyber security firm, was founded by Ashar Aziz, a Pakistani-born IT expert living in the US. Many other firms led by Pakistanis are doing well commercially. The Pakistani community is the seventh largest in the US and is estimated to be over 700,000 in number. A US-Pakistani scientist, Riyad Ghani, is well known. He was the chief scientist in President Obama's re-election campaign. Many Pakistanis have become successful IT specialists and entrepreneurs in other countries as well and some have been employed in Afghanistan where there is a shortage of such trained personnel. The success of Indian citizens in programming, IT and innovation is also very well known. Companies such as Microsoft, IBM, Alphabet, Adobe, Cognizant and Palo Alto networks, to name a few, are all headed by people of Indian origin.

In Pakistan, the National Database and Registration Authority (NADRA), e-government services, capital markets, power grid, air traffic control, and hospital services are some of the IT enabled services. These services use firewalls to protect their systems, however terrorist and inimical organizations have found ways to attack, control, and even stop or disable Internet and technology driven services. The Pakistan Government is aware of the need to be sufficiently prepared in this field. It has provided incentives to investors to encourage advancements in the IT sector and a few years ago with Intel's assistance, 220,000 teachers in Pakistan were trained in IT. Just as Zulfikar Ali Bhutto motivated Pakistani nuclear scientists to come back to their home country in the early seventies to work on making the nuclear bomb, it is quite possible that Pakistan can, if the need arises, gather people of Pakistani origin with expertise in IT, to establish a secure Internet and to develop new technologies with cyber capabilities.

Threats

Threats to cyber systems or IT-driven systems can manifest in various ways using multiple tools. In the area of defence, the threats can be present in many other ways such as electronic surveillance, intelligence platforms such as AWACS, drones, balloons, satellites, radars, telephones taps, email hacking, radio intercepts to name a few. Communication leaks, motherboard modifications, and the introduction of innocuous mini microchips in cellular devices have been used to exploit the vulnerability of IT and communication networks. This list is not exhaustive, but it shows the vulnerabilities that a hostile nation or a terrorist organization can exploit to launch attacks. Attacks in the realm of cyberspace could potentially have a serious impact on the functioning of services, especially in the defence and government departments. Cyber-attacks also target banking services, cause election interference, steal intellectual property and personal information.

In its attempt to be a dominant player in technology, China has been at the helm of IT related espionage and theft to gain economic and military advantage. A lot of IT components and hardware are assembled in China, and there have been reported instances of products that originate in China in which microchips and spyware were introduced into a device to manipulate end user computers and communication systems. China has gone to great lengths to insert spyware and related technology into US bound products and services to gather data and maintain surveillance. It is estimated that China manufactures 70 per cent of the world's smart phones and 90 per cent of personal computers. This is an example of the manufacturing dependency of western IT firms on China. The US has banned Huawei, a Chinese company, from selling 5G technology and cell phones in the USA as this company is alleged to be spying for China. Despite the ban by the US, Chinese tech companies, including Huawei and its 5G network, have been successful in expanding their business across the globe.

The Chinese have also embedded themselves in Indian business and commerce in a very innocuous way. Chinese companies such as Alibaba, Byte Dance, and Tencent have funded at least 92 start-ups in India. These include companies such as Paytm, Byju's, Oyo, Ola, Delhivery, Dream11, Make My Trip, Policy Bazar, Snapdeal, Zomato, Udaan, Swiggy, and many more. Xiaomi smartphone handsets manufactured in China are more popular than Samsung in India and Huawei routers are used extensively in India. These are examples of an approximate $4 billion in Chinese investments in private enterprises in India. The Chinese presence is also evident in e-commerce, fintech, media and social media, aggregation services, and logistics. Some of these services are intrusive and could be used for acquiring private and confidential details about individuals and companies. These invisible assets may also be employed to spy on and obtain data and information on private or government-run organizations. This fact has been acknowledged by the Indian Government, which has assessed that Chinese software and social media are now embedded in Indian society in a very significant way. Consequent to the border altercation in April 2020 and due to China's continuing belligerence, India had banned 59 Chinese apps to obviate cyber-attacks and espionage. Some Chinese companies that have manufacturing ops in India have started to put 'Made in India' labels on their end products as an assurance. This intersection between India and China in cyber affairs and in the field of technology is a matter that requires constant assessment and policy adjustments.

Competition in Cyberspace and Grey Zone Ops

It is presumed and it has been proven that China has acquired intellectual property by illegal means and has conducted cyber espionage in other countries. Conversely, when it comes to its own cyber security, China enforces it thorough stringent regulation domestically. It aims to build an impregnable cyber defence system for itself and wants to independently govern its own path in cyber development, cyber regulation, and Internet policies. As China becomes economically and militarily stronger, it promotes sovereignty as an organizing principle for Internet governance. China has its own internet which is controlled within its geographic territory. The digital Silk Road is a technological support system for China's BRI. As the BRI initiative progresses in Eurasia and Africa, it will have its own controls, interlocking framework of laws, and standards to increase cyber security and safeguard data, enabling the collection of data and garnering information in countries participating in the project. Information is power and the installation of 5G equipment around the world also enables China to gather and collect valuable information from its host countries.

Advances in computing are enabling Chinese intelligence services to create highly secure, encrypted communication channels and the ability to break most conventional encryption. To achieve this, China launched the world's first satellite using channels secured by quantum cryptography in 2016. China is utilizing AI in the PLA with special communications and cyber security protocols. The Chinese see their technology companies as a source of economic dynamism and soft power. Chinese officials claim that their objective is not simply to protect personal information but also to protect national security. China's intention is to achieve information dominance while denying the same to rival nations.

Pakistan will tend to gain from the cyber security protocols that China wants to establish for CPEC projects and the BRI. The projects under the Digital Silk Road include fibre optic cable networks, mobile networks, satellite relay stations, data centres, and even smart cities. Most of the technological build will come from Chinese technology companies like Alibaba. The latter has already acquired Draz, an e-commerce company in Pakistan. ZTE, another Chinese company, operates in 50 of the 64 countries through which the BRI is being developed. It provides surveillance, mapping, cloud storage, and data analysis services to cities in some countries. China intends to gain political influence, if not cyber control, throughout the region. The projects that are coming up in CPEC partially make Pakistan a part of the Chinese cyber network.

The Pakistan Army has also kept updated in this cyber race. It has been known to conduct a phishing campaign against top officials in several countries. Some of the known primary targets have been the governments of Afghanistan, India, Iraq, and the United Arab Emirates (UAE), as per Lookout, a cyber security company in the US. The phishing campaign has been codenamed *Stealth Manager*. The malware, it seems, was created by freelancers who were contracted by the Pakistan Army to access Android and IOS platforms for cyber espionage. Given the advances that Pakistan is making and with the benefits of collaboration with China, it is assumed that the Pakistan Army has the advanced digital capability to maintain surveillance on politicians and other civilians in their own country as well.

With the developments in the field of cyber warfare, China has been modernizing its approach to conventional warfare. It has developed Anti-Access/Area Denial (A2/AD) capabilities to detect and overwhelm the adversary's digital systems and to inflict precision attacks. China announced its largest military restructuring in almost a decade with a new emphasis on technology driven forces. As late as 18 December 2018, the US Secretary of State, Mike Pompeo, accused China of violating a 2015 assurance by Xi Jinping that his country would refrain from hacking US trade secrets, sensitive business information, and intellectual property to benefit Chinese companies. Two well-known technologists whose activities in the field of hacking had come to be known are Zhu and Zhang. They are members of a group operating in China known as Advanced Persistent Threat 10 (APT-10) and they worked for Huaying Haital Science and the Technology Development company in Tianjin, China. Cases filed in US courts against this illegal action alleged that the APT-10 Group obtained unauthorized access to the computers of a service provider that has offices in New York State. This hack compromised the data of clients in Canada, US, UK, Brazil, Finland, France, Germany, India, Japan, Sweden, Switzerland, and the UAE.

It is quite evident that China will spare no means to continue its quest to become world's dominant economic and technological power. Not always resorting to new inventions, the Chinese are experts in reverse engineering of machines, armaments, and technical equipment from other sources. Consider the case of the US stealth Blackhawk helicopters used in the raid on Osama bin Laden's residence in Abbottabad in Pakistan on 2 May 2011. One of the two helicopters used during this operation crashed and could not be flown out, so the Seals (special forces) took the decision to destroy it in situ. After blasting this disabled helicopter, the Seals exfiltrated from Pakistani territory, carrying the dead body of Osama bin Laden in the second Black Hawk. Pakistan, enraged and embarrassed by this covert op on its soil, reportedly gave access to the demolished helicopter to Chinese technicians, before returning it to the US.[1] The Black Hawk helicopters used in this op had very unique noise suppression technology and radar absorbent material to lower their radar signature to avoid detection. Pakistan, publicly an ally of the US, allowed Chinese technicians to access the wreckage of the stealth helicopter and perhaps allowed them to carry away parts of the helicopter to reverse engineer the technology.

The assumed result is that China has been able to copy and or design radar-absorbent material (like that of the Black Hawk) and incorporated it into its own stealth fighter aircraft in 2014. The J-35, with stealth technology, was unveiled at its tenth China International Aviation and Aerospace exhibition. This aircraft is produced by Shenyang Aircraft Corporation. It is

---

1. *Relentless Strike: The Secret of Joint Special Operations Command* by Sean Naylor

purported to be a fifth-generation jet fighter. It has a striking resemblance to the US-built F-35 fighter aircraft. Some reports in the *Business Insider* had purported that China had stolen the design and engineering plans of the F-35 from the US some years ago. It has also updated its J-20, which is a carrier-based stealth fighter. There has been further advanced technology demonstrated by China in their sixth-generation fighter aircraft in 2024.

Wrongful Access – the Dark Side of the Internet

Another concerning aspect of the Internet is its use by terrorists for spreading misinformation and as a medium to enhance religious intolerance. Terrorist organizations have been making extensive use of social media and other websites for indoctrination, spreading propaganda, fake news and for recruiting jihadists. Instructions to terrorists to carry out clandestine missions/attacks against targets are sent across the dark web. Islamic Jihadists, people with medieval practices and beliefs, are now using modern technology, which is quite ironic.

In the Afghan war, internet communications were used extensively in ops against the US and allies. Indian security forces in J&K have also suffered attacks that were orchestrated in cyber space. Increasingly, India is equipped to glean and identify terrorist communications in Kashmir and thereby target anti-national cells as they arise. This system is not fool proof as yet. India has implemented strict cybercrime policies under the Information Act of 2000. This act was revised in 2008 and became effective in 2009, and cyber security has been enhanced under the National Security Council Secretariat. A national cyber security policy was developed in 2013 to secure India's cyberspace for Indian citizens and businesses. This policy encompasses protection of information, safeguards infrastructure dependent upon IT and cyberspace, and builds capabilities to respond to cyber threats. It aims to reduce vulnerabilities and minimize the damage that may be caused by actions or threats initiated by inimical nations, terrorists, anti-nationals, and cyber intrusions. Technology is also being used to negate the influence of seditious elements. The National Technical Research Organization (NTRO) is the main agency that protects critical infrastructure, obtains intelligence, and deals with cyber security incidents and attacks in areas critical to the country. An Indian Computer Emergency Response Team has been created to respond to incidents, analyze and forecast threats, and initiate alerts on cyber security issues. Similarly, Pakistan, too, has established its National Cyber Security Center at Air University in Islamabad. It aims to protect the country's cyberspace and infrastructure from cyberattacks. In addition, Pakistan is introducing legislation for the seizure of digital forensic evidence. Pakistan is expanding aspects of cyberspace security and has established a Cyber Security Auditing and Evaluation Laboratory (CSEL) under the aegis of its Army's Military College of Signals.

In the past, India has sought the help of the US to trace the origin and inception of terrorist attacks conducted against its civil population and defence establishments. It did so in the Mumbai attacks in November 2009. Indian authorities understand that weaknesses in cyber ops need to be overcome to enable the identification of terrorists, their networks, their handlers and the monitoring of their communications. In addition to this, a dedicated effort is being made in India to ensure that means of long-term monitoring or surveillance are not implanted in its networks for offensive or disruptive grey zone ops.

The applications of nefarious cyber operations are numerous, and the effects are far-reaching, however despite these threats, the world continues to be inter-connected through cyberspace. The rapid advancement in AI is adding to this complexity even as it offers exciting and infinite new possibilities. It is bringing about a rapid change in how we seek and use information. Simple tools such as GPT and other AI assistants are now commonly accessed. Businesses around the world are looking to replace, where possible, manual employment with robotics and automation. Jobs are being created in the manufacturing sector to work on automated systems. The high-speed networks and computers that are being deployed along with cloud-based computing are likely to have massive political and geopolitical impacts.

AI and Applications

The capabilities of AI and generative AI are mind-boggling. China aims to become the leader in AI by 2030 and the US has announced revised and fresh AI initiatives with an outlay of $900 million. India is not far behind in the AI revolution with a reported 60 active AI start-ups with about $8 billion in funding over the past few years. To enhance their expertise and capabilities in this area of technology, Chinese Internet technology companies such as Tencent, and Alibaba, have been using highly sophisticated imports from the US. Nvidia's graphic processing units (GPUs), the fastest and best chips to support AI development, were restricted for sale to China as the Biden administration had imposed curbs on the supply of sensitive materials such as chips to China. Despite the curbs, China has been developing its AI capabilities and recently showcased a competitor to Chat GPT, which is called DeepSeek. In May 2025, President Trump has lifted the curbs imposed. Beijing is also using AI for a massive repression campaign against its own Uyghur population in Xinjiang province, utilizing data analytics, facial recognition, and predictive policing. Vast networks of cameras are deployed across China for surveillance to detect anomalous public behaviour. China's Leon Technologies is at the forefront of this invasive surveillance and has created software to record facial expressions on digital cameras, identify the behaviour of each individual, and highlight those considered to be threatening to the state. Huawei is also operating in Xinjiang, providing digital surveillance over the Uyghurs. Chinese technology companies are also introducing new intrusive systems in countries where the BRI is progressing.

While China is implementing surveillance technology across the entire country, it is exporting this behaviour discerning technology to other countries of interest. This is a program referred to as 'safe cities' to provide high-tech surveillance and security. Chinese companies have trained government officials and members of the media from over 30 countries on this technology and Pakistan is one of those nations. Autocratic regimes across the world have acquired these technologies to use them to shape public perception and enhance their own legitimacy.

AI is expected to add $13 to $15trillion to the world economy by 2030. The prolific use of AI is also impacting decision-making in warfare, as it greatly enhances the capabilities for evaluation of and situational awareness. This has been the case in the recent war between Israel and Hamas in which Israel's army used AI to track and kill alleged militants in Gaza and Lebanon. In these efforts to destroy the militants, the number of civilians killed has also soared. This aspect has also been highlighted by India in OP Sindoor in defending itself against drone swarms and missile attacks. Clearly, these new military possibilities will require oversight and monitoring as they become more entrenched in conventional warfare. With AI, the ability to process information quicker than humans, and in real-time, is multiplied exponentially. This capability will mean that on the battlefield machines will move faster and become more lethal. Emerging technologies will enable new networks of sensors to rapidly detect enemy intentions and actions and also help in striking selected targets and eliminating threats. Those countries that do not adopt the new technologies, even though their militaries may be larger and stronger, could be overpowered by superior technologies. The Chinese termed Multidomain Precision Warfare entails the PLA's use of advanced technologies to coordinate firepower. China has developed powerful AI and Electronic Warfare systems as well. India has the lead over Pakistan in AI and space-based surveillance systems. It has demonstrated the ability to deploy space-based weapons by destroying an out-of-service satellite with precision in April 2019. In the ultimate analysis, India, Pakistan, and China can now use cyberspace for non-conventional aggression.

The use of AI and other multi-domain technologies has had a dramatic effect on the nature of warfare. The Russia-Ukraine war is a recent example of this. A weak country like Ukraine has effectively engaged targets in five different locations, as deep as 4000 kms inside Russia with armed drones on 1 June 2025. Even in Myanmar and Sudan, insurgents and government forces are both using unmanned aerial vehicles and algorithms to conduct ops. Azerbaijan's use of Turkish and Israeli drones along with loitering ammunition shows how effective new technologies can be in achieving results in war. It is most likely that future wars will see the wholesale integration of AI into every aspect of military planning and execution. To carry out the mass drone and missile attack on Israel on 7 October2024, it cost Hamas approximately $100 million. Most of these lethal munitions were intercepted with US and Israel interceptor missiles costing more than $2 billion. This shows that the defensive systems are far more expensive than the attacking rockets and missiles, but these defensive measures have reduced casualties to the civilian population in Israel to the minimum and prevented damage to their military installations. The Iranian and Hezbollah attacks on Israel were similarly countered with these AI led weapons.

Despite the cost, the benefit of superior technology in military conflict is immense. It should however be kept in mind that the Internet has proven to not be a benign tool and using that as a cautionary tale, we must remain vigilant about the impact of the rapid advancements in AI and related technology. For the India-Pakistan-China dynamic, this dimension only adds complexity and new challenges.

CHAPTER 7

Unfolding Dynamics

From the foregoing chapters, it can be inferred that Pakistan is unlikely to relent in its aggressive and intractable conflict with India. By all accounts, China will continue to support Pakistan as a proxy against India. China, with its aim to become a world super-power, is unlikely to change its authoritarianism and confrontational expansionism. For China, coercion using trade and financial clout are a means to achieve world dominance that its leaders desire. As a neighbour to China, India is directly affected by these policies which are belligerent and entirely self-serving. China will do whatever it takes to prevent India realizing its aims in a multi-polar world. As for Pakistan, its policies of remaining inimical to India have brought no advantages and have made the country economically and politically fragile. Maintaining terrorist groups, conducting conventional and sub-conventional wars, and pursuing an arms race are expensive gambles for Pakistan and so are the hiring of lobbyists and anti-India groups in various countries. The outlook for world economies published in *Bloomberg Businessweek* projected India's gross domestic product (GDP) as $3.3 trillion (estimated to have grown to $4.1 trillion in 2024), China's as $14.2 trillion (estimated to have grown to $17.96 trillion in 2024) and that of the US, the largest economy in the world, as $29.17 trillion.[1, 2] Pakistan does not figure in the report, but its GDP is estimated to be one-twentieth that of India. As per the World Bank estimates in 2021–22, the Pakistani economy grew by 3.7 per cent and that of India by 8.5 per cent. Prospects of growth for the Indian economy are expected to be positive going forward. In contrast,

1. *Bloomberg Businessweek*, 19 November 2018–6 January 2019, pp 8–9, and17 January 2022, pp15

2. *Bloomberg Businessweek* 25 January 2021, pp 6

Pakistan's economic growth prospects are unlikely to improve. It continues to have high rates of infant mortality, a growing youth population without suitable employment opportunities and a growing religious and class divide.

Drazen Jorgic, senior correspondent at Reuters, explains the state of Pakistan's economy. He states that Pakistan has had to make hard decisions to stay afloat. It has devalued its currency, and its Rupee had fallen 26 per cent in the last ten months of 2018. Further devaluation of their currency, almost 50%, has been occurring against the US dollar up to 2023. The Pakistan government has raised interest rates to curb inflation. The rate of inflation increased to 30% after the terrorist action against India at Pulwama by Pakistan in 2019 and in January 2024 it was about 27%. After the re-organization of J&K State into two union territories, trade between India and Pakistan was stopped, escalating prices of essential commodities. Pakistan also continues to pay large amounts of foreign exchange for debt servicing. In 2019, the Pakistan government declared that they would raise funds for debt servicing by asking their diaspora to contribute more to get through the financial crisis. Their diaspora did respond, and an, estimated $2 billion was received through remittances to Pakistan in each month in 2020–21. This, however, was inadequate even in the short term to ease the foreign exchange crisis, catering for debt servicing and paying for imports. Pakistan was then forced to return to the International Monetary Fund (IMF) in early 2023 to seek easier terms for servicing its debt. This was only partially accepted because Pakistan did not meet all the requirements set by the IMF. The IMF had asked Pakistan to ensure strict spending limits on new projects and that it would examine its deal with China on CPEC in detail. India has stated that any loans or debt relief granted by the IMF to Pakistan indirectly funds state sponsored cross border terrorism, hence being a member of the governing council of this financial institution it had objected to any further concessions to Pakistan. When the loan of $2.3 billion was to be sanctioned for Pakistan on May 2025, India abstained from voting. The loan has been granted to Pakistan on 9 May 2025.

In an earlier interview on the *British Broadcasting Corporation* (BBC) in 2018, on their program 'Hard Talk', Pakistan's then Finance Minister had stated that they had shared details of CPEC funding with the IMF. The IMF had provisionally granted a waiver of $5 billion out of the $10 billion required for debt servicing to Pakistan at that time.

Saudi Arabia did grant a loan of $5 billion in 2019 for this purpose, but as per an article published in the *Dawn*, Saudi Arabia had also asked Pakistan to return of a $3 billion soft loan granted in 2018. Pakistan has returned $1 billion, but as of December 2023, Pakistan's external debt was $131.6 billion. This includes sums borrowed from China, the Paris Club, IMF and others.

Besides the economic hardship, Pakistan is facing an existential crisis since it ceased to be a liberal society and is dogged by internal strife driven by class, religion and social status. It transformed into a country being run with the support of Islamists, which has not resulted in economic prosperity or unity. Subsidies for fuel and other commodities have made the country dependent on imports, which are supplemented by very few exports. Attempts to lift or reduce subsidies have led to unrest and agitations and they now seem permanently entrenched in Pakistan's economy. Pakistan's financial crisis worsened because of the devastation caused by the disastrous floods in August 2022. In this natural disaster, nearly one-third of the country was water-logged. This affected about one-fifth of the Pakistani population. There had been considerable loss of human and animal life and property. Large-scale devastation occurred in the country's existing infrastructure and there are limited capital reserves to rebuild and reinforce the ageing infrastructure that exists.

In an article published in the *Dawn*, Moeed Yusuf, who was earlier Associate Vice President at the Asia Centre in the US Institute for Peace, wrote about the far-reaching change likely to take place in the India-Pakistan dynamics. He said the economic and military differential between the two countries was growing rapidly and exponentially. Yusuf quoted analysts saying, 'There are regular references to the growing economic and military differential between India and Pakistan. The conclusion is that within a decade or less, Pakistan's window of opportunity to negotiate on Kashmir will shut. The power differential will be unbreachable.' Yusuf further suggests that 'Pakistan must shift focus from geo-politics to geo-economics.' Translated, this means 'abandoning the jihadi factories aimed at India and focus on the economy.' However, the political circumstances in the country have precluded any improvement in the economy thus far. The politicians are self-serving and have no solutions to the financial crisis. Pakistan's terror attacks on India are unlikely to cease till its make-believe parity, which it desires vis-à-vis India, is entirely unattainable due to India's fast-growing economy. Indeed, the military, economic, and political power equation is likely to shift inexorably in India's favour. Economic incompatibility between India and Pakistan, as discussed above, exacerbates competition and makes rapprochement difficult unless there is a rethink by Pakistan.

The tumultuous political situation in Pakistan has been a continual area of concern. Imran Khan, who came to power with the backing of the Army, was unable to sustain his leadership despite the initial support. He attempted to curb inflationary pressures and restore some balance in a failing economy but found it difficult to function independently. Khan had to deal with religious factors, an uncooperative and ambitious political opposition and a very influential Pakistan Army. He was made to evict his close advisor, a Princeton University based economist, Atif Rehman Mian, because the latter belonged to the minority Ahmadiyya sect of Muslims, who are reviled in Pakistan. Imran Khan ultimately tried to play to the gallery to build support for himself by aligning with the Islamists. At that time, General Bajwa, the Army Chief, was re-evaluating options for Pakistan, suggesting a way forward to restore trade with India. Imran Khan did not support this change in the dynamics between the two countries. His supercilious attitude, unhappiness with the Army, or his lack of cooperation on the issue and not adhering to the Army's wishes, coupled with slow economic growth, most likely led to his ouster from power.

Seeing an opportunity to take over the reins of power, the opposition parties in Pakistan's Parliament came together. Along with a few defectors from Khan's party, they introduced a no-confidence motion against him on 10 April 2022, which was a success. In what is a common fate of politicians in Pakistan, Khan was jailed and Shahbaz Sharif, Nawaz Sharif's younger brother, was then appointed as the interim Prime Minister. Prior to national elections, Pakistan had a caretaker government in place. After the elections in 2024 a coalition government has been formed which is headed once again by Shahbaz Sharif of the Pakistan Muslim League-Nawaz.

Use of Religion in Politics

Pakistan is a populous country of many contrasts. It has densely populated cities like Karachi, and in the countryside towards the Durand Line border with Afghanistan the sparse tribal population lives under the yoke of warlords and militant groups. Some of the anti-national groups have their bases and allegiance in neighbouring Afghanistan. The emergence of the TTP, which has a free run in Afghanistan, and other militant groups, poses an existential threat to the internal stability of the Pakistani State. The backward tribal areas provide a stark contrast in a country which does have expertise in the field of IT and cyberspace, a growing defence industry, and nuclear capability. Pakistan's educated population and its institutions of higher learning have the capability to exploit modern technologies and have the potential to create wealth and a stable society. However, grandiose arrogance governs the Pakistani elite, and its Army in particular. The ruling establishment and the Pakistan Army do not want to give up their dominating position in the country. To protect its standing, the military remains insecure and suspicious of politicians who want to change its status and bring the Army under political control. The Army believes that it represents the best of the country and that it is the only institution that binds the entire nation together. In such circumstances, personal misunderstandings are magnified, and even inconsequential or otherwise manageable events can lead to crisis situations of huge dimensions. It is this attitude that, perhaps, sets the Thucydides trap for India. The growing economic inequality between the two countries, as discussed above, should be an awakening for Pakistan's political leadership.

Tahir Malik, a Pakistani journalist who writes in *The Express Tribune* from Lahore, gives yet another version of the Pakistan Army's mindset. He interviewed Army officers after their retirement from service and inferred that the Pakistan Army has a warrior-like background of over 1,400 years, during which period Muslims repeatedly invaded and later ruled over some parts of India, subjugating the population and people of other religions. He speaks of the arrogance in the mind of the Pakistan Army and their belief that a Muslim soldier is superior to others, including a Hindu soldier.[3] Malik does not explain the reasons for this mindset. Perhaps this is motivational speak in the Pakistan Army when morale is sagging, and defeat is imminent. Malik's opinion does not address the fact that in the four wars against India, Pakistan's Army manned purely by Muslims was defeated each and every time. The Indian Armed Forces, which are secular, non-partisan, apolitical, courageous, and patriotic have repeatedly defeated the Pakistan Army. These defeats should have induced caution, encouraged lessons learned, caused introspection, some shame, and even some humility. But in the Pakistani mindset, arrogance overrides all else. Why this arrogance remains after the repeated defeats, and how they continue to propound the theory that the Muslim soldier is superior, defies logic.

It should be noted that prior to British rule, India was not a single entity or a united country. It was a divided whole under the rule of hundreds of major and minor principalities. Rulers of the principalities had their own

---

3. 'How Pakistan Military's Mindset Towards India Works', a presentation by Tahir Malik, recorded on YouTube

methods and agenda in dealing with the Muslim invasions from the NW. As a conglomerate of divided entities, India could not strongly confront these invasions. Tahir Malik further exhorts that in a civilized world, the last instrument to resolve disputes is war. He states that since 1947, Pakistan has not understood this. Malik suggests that there are so many other options to resolve conflicts, such as diplomacy, communications, track two dialogue, cultural exchange, meeting of scholars, people to people contact, investment, youth programs, media conferences, education, tourism, and trade.

Malik implores his countrymen with the question, whether there should be sanity or war? The logic of his arguments cannot be faulted. There is no doubt that Pakistan needs to maintain its Armed Forces for its security needs this is undeniable. However, it does not explain what is stopping Pakistan from embracing a more progressive agenda and maintaining peace with its neighbours. Tahir Malik could perhaps have asked the senior retired Pakistan officers he interviewed, how would they change the mindset in the Pakistan Army, will the Army allow the elected politicians to govern without interference, and how will it do away with the false sense of bravado and arrogance? In January 2023, when Shahbaz Sharif was the interim Prime Minister of Pakistan, he gave an interview to *Al Arabiya*, a Dubai-based news channel. In this interview Sharif averred that Pakistan wants peace with India. Seeing the dire state of his country's economy and the increasing economic differential with India, this statement created hope and did make sense. But these words have been spoken before by others, to no avail.

Until a few years ago, India had a larger population of Muslims than Pakistan. These Muslims had made a conscious decision to remain in India in 1947 at the time of independence. Given this indisputable truth, it is difficult to fathom the reasons why Pakistan wants to be the representative and saviour of Muslims in India. In India, Muslims are at par with all citizens. They are hardworking and as patriotic as any other religious denomination. Muslims in India celebrate Hindu festivals as well as their own and integrate into Indian society with their rich traditions, delectable cuisine and exceptional arts and crafts. In India religious beliefs are usually acquired by birth and the vast country exists as a melting pot of culture, religion, tradition and every kind of diversity. India does follow a Universal Civil Code under which all citizens have rights to caste, creed, and religion. The Indian Constitution gives these rights to all its citizens. There have been incidents of violation of civil rights and the Universal Civil Code at times because of partisan politics and self-appointed vigilantes and indiscriminate display of religious fervor. India may, therefore, not seem to be secular enough to some observers. This discord, however, does not occur in India alone but elsewhere in the world as well, where right wing nationalists are asserting their identity in various ways, including the use of a religious plank. In India's sustained democracy these incidents are unfortunate exceptions in a predominantly peaceful society.

On some occasions, Pakistan has projected certain decisions taken by Indian authorities as anti-Muslim. One example of this is the restrictions in India on holding religious gatherings in public places. There were objections made by the public when parks, roads, railway stations and other common areas that were being used for prayers by large numbers of Muslims. India is a populous country, and public resources and amenities are limited to cater to such a large population. Given this scenario, the objection was justified, and it was clearly a civic matter for the attention of the Indian administration. Politicians in Pakistan chose to elevate this to a contentious issue and added incendiary commentary to what was India's internal administrative matter. Such divisive comments propagated by Pakistan's leadership do stir up emotions in Indian Muslims. Some Muslim groups in India have played politics with this and added fuel to the fire when Pakistan's aim is to cause religious strife in India.

It is worth visiting some interesting facts about India and the origins of the country it is today. Anyone who has lived or traveled in India will find it is an incredible amalgamation of history, culture, people, nature, and diversity. Ancient history depicts India as a peaceful and thriving nation where people from all over the world visited for trade and commerce. India had the largest GDP in the world a few centuries ago. It is also the only country that is home to every religion in the world and India has never invaded a foreign nation. In the past, Muslims from the Middle East came to India to trade in spices, natural resources and artisan crafts. The Muslim invaders whose Mughal Dynasty ruled northern India for several centuries left their influence in architecture, culture, food, and of course religion. Islam as a religion was widely accepted and is still an intrinsic part of many aspects of Indian life. The Cheramaan Juma Masjid, a mosque in Kodangalur Taluk, Thrissur district in the state of Kerala in South India, is, perhaps, the oldest mosque in India. It was built in 629 AD/CE by Malik Deenar, a Persian ex-slave and a companion of Prophet Muhammad, on orders of Cheraman Perumal, the king at that time. The mosque has been renovated from time to time. It still exists as the symbol of tolerance that

India displayed in that ancient period. The state of Kerala has a nearly equal population of Christians, Hindus, and Muslims who live in harmony. It is to be noted that the Indian Armed Forces recruit officers and personnel from all over the country with no bias against any religion. Two infantry regiments recruit troops from the state of J&K, including Muslims from the Kashmir Valley. There are Muslims in every combat arm, combat support arms and services in the Indian armed forces. India maintains a well-trained armed force and some elements of this force are actively involved in UN peacekeeping missions.

Hinduism remains the religion followed by the majority in India. Shashi Tharoor, a member of the Indian Parliament and a former Deputy Secretary-General of the UN, is an author. He has written on the subject, describing Hinduism concisely, in his book, *Why I Am a Hindu*. While explaining the basic tenets of Hinduism, he states that it is a way of life without any fundamentals, with no founder or prophet or any organized church. The Hindu majority in India is accommodative of other minorities, but in neighbouring Pakistan, the reality is quite different. Jibran Nasir, a lawyer and an activist in Pakistan, works for the protection of human rights and against sectarian violence in his country. In an interview on *Al Jazeera* TV, Nasir spoke of radicals hijacking the rights of people. He also suggests that the time has come for Pakistan to reset its relationship with India. Nasir opines that people in his country are desperate for a better future. In the ultimate analysis, Pakistan is at the centre of a conundrum in the region. Aside from its inimical actions against India, Pakistan is also responsible for war and turmoil in Afghanistan which began with its training of the mujahideen to fight King Zahir Shah's Government. Pakistan succeeded partially in creating an Afghanistan like situation in J&K. In addition, after creating militancy in the state, every government in Pakistan has attempted various ploys to bring the Kashmir issue to the attention of the world. After the state of J&K was reorganized by India into two union territories, Pakistan has become even more vociferous on the subject.

Pakistan's Prime Minister Shahbaz Sharif did not fail to highlight the Kashmir issue in his first speech to the country's Parliament. Imran Khan, though a liberal himself, had been exhorting Kashmiris to be ready to wage jihad. He expected this jihad to ensue once the restraints imposed by India in the union territory of J&K were lifted. At one point, Khan even made statements exhorting Muslims of the entire world and those of India to come together to fight a jihad against India's suppression and purported atrocities against the people of Kashmir. There was no response to Khan's rousing rhetoric about a jihad. Perhaps even people in Pakistan realize that such exhortations from the Prime Minister of Pakistan do not elicit peace in the region. In his past life, Imran Khan was a keen sportsman, who was once married to a Jewish lady from the UK. His support of terrorism in Kashmir and the revival of medieval practices there is ironic given his liberal past.

It is relevant here to mention the concept of *Akhand Bharat*, which means an undivided or greater India. The maps of India prior to 1947, under British rule, show the area of Pakistan and Bangladesh as part of India. Afghanistan, Burma, and Sri Lanka were earlier also a part of India. In fact, Afghanistan was ruled by Hindu kings until the tenth century, and it was recognized as a separate country under the Treaty of Gandamak only in 1876. A movement had begun in India, prior to 1947, to keep the country undivided and a call to reunite India to its original past has been invoked from time to time since then. This call is led mainly by Indian cultural and non-political organizations. Some experts even envisage and recommend a confederation between India and Pakistan to bring an end to the conflict, to promote cultural bonds, usher in economic development, and solidarity on major issues. For these protagonists, the Two Nation Theory, the basis for the partition of India, has been a failure from the very beginning. Some individuals even envisage a broader confederation between members of SAARC, like the European Union. In his book *The Spy Chronicles*, A. S. Dulat, the former Director General of the Research and Analysis Wing (RAW), India's intelligence agency, visits the concept of *Akhand Bharat*. Lieutenant General Durrani, ex-Director General of ISI and co-author of this book shares his views on the subject, stating that some in his country call the partition of India a mistake because it has led to problems and the resultant constant state of war. The concept of re-unification can be considered, but as per Durrani, the chances of an Afghanistan-Pakistan confederation are greater than a confederation of India-Pakistan. This rhetoric about *Akhand Bharat* may in fact be exacerbating the insecurity in the minds of the Pakistani establishment and the Deep State.

An Islamist who is deeply indoctrinated in religion, fears that Muslims will continue to be dominated, mistreated, and subjected to terrible atrocities, by non-believers of Islam. Fighting *kuffar*, or non-believers is taught in madrasas and is an existential reality in Pakistan. Another narrative that is propagated is that Muslims are suffering at the behest of Israel and in the neighbourhood of Pakistan, by India. The prolonged Israel-Hamas war, Israeli strikes and offensive into Lebanon to neutralize

Hezbollah, and may create more radicals who harbour insecurities about their religion. Israel has degraded their effectiveness as terrorist organisations operating as proxies of Iran. The launching of air strikes on Iran were intended to destroy Iran's capability in uranium enrichment and in becoming a nuclear power.Israel did strike vital installations and achieved air superiority. This set the stage for the US to join the war on 22 June 2025, as it too launched air strikes on Iran's well known nuclear establishments at Fordow, Natanz and Isfan with its B2 stealth bombers. These bombers carried Massive Ordanance Penetrators (GBUs) each weighing 13000 kilograms. This was supplemented by 75 precision guided missiles and two dozen cruise missiles. After the strikes President Trump declared in a nation wide address that Iran's means of enriching uranium have been obliterated. In contrast the IAEA has assessed that the set back to Iran's enrichment means could be minimal and some analysts have stated it could be significant. Only after inspection of nuclear facilities can the damage be ascertained. The US came out in open support of Israel, a Jewish state that has faced terrorism and wars ever since its creation in 1948, from Muslim nations surrounding it, purely from the point of view of religious fervor and hate. A cease fire was accepted by Iran and Israel. The other aim of the war was to impose caution in Islamic nations and dissuade them from targeting Israel. The US had even hinted at a regime change in Iran. It is because of this incendiary narrative that religion continues to dominate the conversation, and Islam is portrayed as being under threat.

The civilian government in Pakistan practices politics derived from the feudal culture and seeks the support of religious leaders. Feudal landlords and ambitious Army officers all have their own agenda. The problems generated by the proliferation of radical groups are ignored in the tussle for power and supremacy. In Pakistan, the madrasas are now prominent education institutions as government run and private schools are inadequate in number to educate the bourgeoning youth population. The madrasas provide an alternate avenue for education, and students who complete their studies in madrasas often go on to become religious clerics and Islamists, also known as *mullahs*. These *mullahs* sometimes set up their own mosques and madrasas and over the years, millions of children have been taught in these seminaries. This cycle continues and today a substantial youth population in Pakistan must find work without acquiring adequate skills and training. This regression in the youth is bringing a sea change in Pakistan's society and is retarding the country's progress.

An era of fostering ultra radical ideology and facilitating its propagation has become a double-edged sword for Pakistan. Terrorist attacks mounted internally against the Pakistani state are now a frequent occurrence. Examples of this are the unprecedented scenes of unrest and forced entry into military areas in various Pakistani cities. Even the residence of the GOC XI Corps in Peshawar was reported to be attacked by supporters of Imran Khan after he was arrested in May 2023. After this incident in Peshawar, a few erudite and balanced retired senior Pakistani Army officers have come to the realization that such incidents of unrest may recur. They have gone on record to state that this constitutes the greatest threat to the long-term stability of Pakistan. It is widely acknowledged that such incidents of dissent are instigated internally and not by external forces. A similar assessment had been made earlier by General Petraeus, as quoted in a previous chapter. General Musharraf had previously committed 1,50,000 troops to contend with the internal threat posed by TTP and other militant groups.[4] This force included 90,000 regular troops, which meant that nearly one-third of their regular Army infantry units were deployed. These numbers far exceeded the US forces deployed in Afghanistan, which were at a maximum at the time of the surge ordered by President Obama. The Pakistan Army intended to hold onto areas that they had cleared of militants in the Swat Valley and South Waziristan. However, the terrorist groups who were well-versed with the region, managed to withdraw to safer areas. Some of them evaded capture by moving further afield. As per media reports, the Pakistan Army suffered an estimated 9,000 casualties in this operation.

Today, Pakistan grapples with suicide attacks, bomb blasts, and IEDs. These deadly incidents of terrorism are carried out by Pakistani citizens who are anti-establishment. Spokesmen of the military establishment have stated that they themselves have been victims of terrorism. This is perhaps to give the public the impression that the country is combating terrorism. In fact, this is face-saving rhetoric. While completely denying the terrorism it has inflicted on its neighbours, Pakistan is now facing retribution from individuals who it trained and sponsored to cause havoc on its neighbours. This however draws the sympathy of US and other countries for the reason given above.

---

4. *The Unravelling, Pakistan in the Age of Jihad*, by Jon R. Schmidt, pp212

Unravelling the Status Quo

Given the predicament Pakistan faces with its internal strife, it would be prudent to consider a hypothetical scenario where Pakistan's leadership attempts to dismantle the terrorist groups and tries to undo radicalism. This would not be a quick fix and for starters, Pakistan will have to invest heavily in education and slowly wean away students from madrasas. A changed education policy was articulated by the Imran Khan Government on being elected. This policy stated that the curriculum in all the religious seminaries will be modernized and will incorporate subjects that are taught in government-run schools. This would indeed be a positive change towards the education of the country's growing youth population. After the curriculum in madrasas is changed, it will take at least one generation to bring about a change in society.

It is a difficult proposition to bring about such a change in a radical, divided society. However, if this change is successful, the next step would be to find employment for the members of the militant groups. Measures will have to be taken to ensure that these groups do not emerge again under another guise. Their means of finance would need to be identified and blocked, and bank accounts discontinued if they are found to be anti-national. Some terrorists and radicals may voluntarily join mainstream politics and other occupations. The remainder will need training and psychological re-orientation. These measures would require considerable investment and political will. Until this happens, internecine sectarian conflicts will continue within Pakistan. An example of this sectarian strife is the constant targeting of Shias by the Sunni terrorist groups in Pakistan. The Shias receive support from Iran and a jihadi group in Pakistan called Tehreek Nafaze Fiqhe Jafariya (TNFJ) protects their interests. It is worth noting that Mohammad Ali Jinnah, the founder of Pakistan, and Zulfikar Ali Bhutto were both Shias.

It may be that the relationships between ISI and its sponsored terrorist groups do not remain binding in times to come. The LeT, HM and JeM are becoming more powerful by the day as their cadres multiply and spread throughout Pakistan. Upon the completion of their religious studies at madrasas, the youth rejoin their communities, and some get employment at the offshoots of these militant organizations. The leaders of jihadi groups are popular and for unemployed youth the power and glory of being part of such an outfit is quite alluring. It would take considerable political will to break the nexus that these groups have formed with the radicalized population. To remain relevant in Pakistan, these terrorist groups must maintain status quo and pursue terrorism against their primary foe, India.

Employing the jihadi groups to bleed and destabilize India and establish a balance of power through their sub-conventional war is Pakistan Army's strategy and is one of the functions of the ISI. The ISI acts only under policy guidelines of the Pakistan Army or in direct response to orders of their Army HQ. The attack on India in Mumbai by terrorists was one of the most heinous and deadly. The involvement of the LeT in Mumbai on 26/11 had been proven. Pakistan had the opportunity, but it did not make any effort to dismantle the LeT after the attack. Instead, it tried to hide behind the facade that Zakir Rehman Lakhvi, who is the director of ops of the LeT, planned and executed the attack on his own with a select group of terrorists. As per a report in the *Dawn* newspaper, Sajid Mir was the controller of this op. In this way, the government of Pakistan absolved Hafiz Saeed, the head of the LeT and his organization for the terrorist attack. This also absolved the ISI from any blame. Confessions by the collaborator of the LeT, David Headley, during interrogations in the US, and Ajmal Kasab, the sole member of the suicidal group captured alive by Indian police in Mumbai, gave adequate proof of ISI involvement. Kasab, in his confession, gave details of the entire planning and execution process of the LeT. These conclusions were refuted by Pakistan, with claims that the confessions were made under duress. When Pakistan is clearly identified as the perpetrator of terrorist attacks, their modus operandi is usually to vehemently deny involvement, ask for more proof and occasionally carry out token arrests while a mock legal process dismisses the crimes on flimsy grounds.

As discussed, the India-Pakistan political relationship has a history of conciliatory talks, which were followed by violent terror attacks perpetrated by Pakistan. India followed these instances with more appeasement of Pakistan and with more talks, ad nauseam. The peaceful quest towards reconciliation led India to suffer many bloody attacks. The Narendra Modi Government has demonstrated a change in policy and their approach is that a major terror attack would be met with a strong Indian response. On 18 September 2016, four Pakistani terrorists of the group Jaish-e-Mohammed carried out an attack on the administrative base of IA in Uri, J&K. As a result, a retaliatory surgical strike was conducted by Indian Special Forces, across the LOC, to indicate that India would respond in kind and crossing the LOC was no longer taboo. There have been other such surgical strikes and fire assaults by the Indian Army in which specific missions were accomplished across the LOC.

Pulwama Terror Attack

In February 2019, a convoy of Indian security personnel vehicles moving on the Jammu–Srinagar National Highway was subjected to a terrorist attack by the JeM in Pulwama. In this attack 40 unarmed police personnel were killed. This violent and unprovoked assault left the Indian population seething. There was a groundswell of opinion that Pakistan and its terrorist group, JeM, should be taught a lesson. Indian authorities were aware that a JeM training camp was located at Balakot, led by Yusuf Azhar, who is the brother-in-law of Masood Azhar, the head of the JeM. Balakot is approximately 160 km from the LOC inside Pakistan in Khyber Pakhtunkhwa provine. India retaliated with an Air Force strike in Balakot on 26 February 2019. After the Pulwama attack, Indian intelligence learnt that the JeM had moved 300–350 of its terrorists from their holding areas close to the LOC to obviate an attack by Indian ground/air forces. This was further confirmed by communications intercepts from cell phones in Balakot. Targets were pinpointed and monitored by an array of Indian satellites. As per Indian media reports, the IAF employed a combination of Mirage 2000, Sukhoi Su-30MKI, Phalcon AWACS aircraft, mid-air refuellers and precision guided munitions for targeting the terrorist training camp between 3:40 and 3:53 a.m. The IAF Chief spoke on Indian television to confirm that the assigned targets had been hit. Predictably, the Pakistan Army downplayed the strike by stating that nothing of consequence was hit and all that could be seen in the area were a few craters and broken trees. India characterized the air strike as non-military, pre-emptive action against terrorists, not against the Pakistani military. The Indian response was conducted based on credible intelligence that JeM was using the targeted camp to train terrorists. The selection of the target and execution of the plan ensured that there was no collateral damage or casualties to the civilian population. The mobile phones in the specific buildings/areas that were operating did not come on air again after the strike, indicating the targets had been eliminated.

While the Pakistan response was all bluster, the official briefing from India was professional and specific. Pakistan did not allow any of their own or foreign journalists to visit the area after the air strike by India. Pakistan's Foreign Minister called the Indian action a grave aggression and asserted that Islamabad had the right to respond. Pakistan did respond for the sole purpose of demonstrating its rights. The Pakistani Air Force (PAF) came across the LOC to bomb an Indian Army HQ in the Poonch district of J&K. This strike by Pakistan was ineffective as the Indian AF had scrambled its aircraft to interdict the Pakistan AF carrying out the counter strike. The skirmish resulted in the shooting down of an MiG-21 and possibly a PAF, F-16 aircraft. The Pakistani pilot bailed out of his aircraft in POK and did not survive due to injuries sustained and ill-treatment by the local population. Prime Minister Imran Khan was hasty in announcing on Pakistani TV channels that two Indian aircraft were shot down by the Pakistan AF. This was not accurate, as one downed plane belonged to their own air force. The Indian AF pilot, Wing Commander Abhinandan Varthaman, who had engaged the F-16, had also bailed out. He had ejected after his aircraft was hit and his parachute landed in POK. He was captured but later returned to India unscathed. Parts of the Advanced Medium-Range Air-to-Air Missile (AMRAAM) missile fired from the Pakistani F-16 aircraft were recovered by Indian troops in Indian territory and were shown to the US authorities. The debris of the Pakistani air force plane that was shot-down had landed in POK. The US chose not to comment on the shooting down of the F-16 it had supplied to Pakistan. It is worth noting, if true, that the F-16 was engaged and downed by an obsolescent and ageing but upgraded MiG-21.

The Balakot air strike by the IAF has serious connotations. With this counterstrike, India laid out new red lines and executed a mission inside Pakistan. This was a strategic shift which pressured Pakistan to respond. However, by responding hastily to India's riposte, Pakistan continued to demonstrate a belligerent strategy which indicated that it did not wish to change its policy of supporting terror groups who wage the proxy war. The definitive response from India means that it is now harder for Pakistan to justify or succeed in this sub-conventional war. The use of air power by India, in response to Pakistan's sub-conventional attacks, has demonstrated that in future Pakistan can expect severe retaliation from India. This could extend to operational strikes on selected targets anywhere in Pakistan's territory, by any means necessary. In response to Pakistan's aggression, India concomitantly took measured diplomatic steps and also mobilized the opinion of all major international powers against the use of terror. The US National Security Advisor at that time, John Bolton, recognized India's right to self defence. The UNSC condemned the Pulwama attack, recognized JeM's ownership of it and demonstrated total support for India. It could be seen as a shift in the UNSC concerning the state of J&K. In this case, the UNSC clearly separated contested sovereignty claims and human rights issues from the issue of terrorism perpetrated by Pakistan.

By launching a counterstrike, Islamabad catered to its domestic audience to show that it had acted in response to the attack on its sovereignty. This, however, provided a bigger diplomatic arena for India to denigrate Pakistan for the Pulwama attack. India also succeeded in having Masood Azhar declared an international terrorist. China initially tried to stall this request but finally relented. Azhar was sanctioned as an international terrorist by the UNSC. Even Pakistan's allies, Saudi Arabia and the UAE, have condemned the Pulwama attack with full knowledge that the attack took place in J&K and that the attack was been claimed by the JeM based in Pakistan. This now begs the question; despite Masood Azhar being declared an international terrorist, what are the compulsions for Pakistan to continue to provide him sanctuary? There are other individuals, citizens of India, who have been given protection in Pakistan for many years despite being declared as terrorists and wanted by India. What are the compulsions for Pakistan to wage this sub-conventional war? The answers may be in understanding the mind-set of the Deep State in Pakistan. In this instance, perhaps the Deep State and the ISI had decided to attack for two reasons. In August 2018, Pakistan's newly elected Prime Minister, Imran Khan, spoke of his willingness to discuss all issues with India. The suggestion to commence a dialogue with India was unacceptable to their Army, which had to indicate a negative reaction to this statement and reiterate its undisputed primacy in Pakistan. The aim of the attack was also to rattle India when its general elections had been declared.

Pakistan soon found out that decision-making in India was not impacted by the upcoming elections. Unfortunately, once again, the pre-election political climate led to a polarized media. A few published articles and debates in Indian media tried to insist that the IAF strike on the terrorist training camp at Balakot did not hit their intended target and therefore served no purpose. Even some of the intelligentsia in the country provided a negative analysis of India's air strike. Meanwhile the severity of the attack by India was confirmed by Masood Azhar's brother, when he addressed a section of the population in Bahawalpur, the HQ of the JeM in Pakistan. He displayed anger and intense hatred when he, spoke of avenging the Indian attack on their establishment. His rambling tirade can still be found on YouTube. After such a strike, what is of consequence is not the body count. The precedent that was set by India is what matters. India demonstrated its ability and will, to launch a riposte inside Pakistani territory which is of great consequence. In denying that the Indian attack did not destroy any part of the camp is an implicit admission by Pakistan that a terrorist camp existed in Balakot. While India succeeded in violating Pakistan's sovereignty and achieving its mission, Pakistan's response was timid and inconsequential. The Pulwama attack further proved that Pakistan breeds agents of terror inside J&K. Pakistan had been kept on the grey list of the FATF until its removal from the list on 21 October 2022. This was done after a consensus decision of all 39 members, including India. It is noteworthy that India supported this decision. Despite being given a reprieve, Pakistan remains under scrutiny and is being watched for money laundering, financing terror attacks, and financing and proliferating terrorism.

The Baisaran-Pahalgam Terrorist Attack

General Asim Munir, Pakistan Army Chief, had once again referred to Kashmir being the jugular of Pakistan and made anti-Hindu remarks on 16 April 2025, in an attempt to give credence to the two-nation theory. His speech was essentially aiming to show how different are Hindus and Muslims. Soon thereafter on 22 April terrorists from The Resistance Group, an affiliate of LET killed 25 innocent tourists after ascertaining that they were non-Muslims and one pony owner in the meadows of Baisaran, 5 kms from Pahalgam in J&K. Although the security forces and the local population have continued to be targeted by terrorists in shootings in small numbers in past years, this attack was a major one that targeted tourists. An attack had been carried out targeting terrorists in 1995, in which Al-Faran terrorists from Pakistan kidnapped six foreign tourists from Lidderwat area. This had reduced the number of foreigners visiting Kashmir considerably. The Pulwama attack in 2019 discussed above and the Reasi attack on 9 June 2024 on a bus carrying pilgrims were the other major incidents of terrorism. Once again, after the murderous attack at Pahalgam, the Indian population rose up in unison imploring the government to retaliate against Pakistan that continues with its relentless proxy war. There were protests carried out by Kashmiris in Srinagar as well.

The Indian special forces have been silently tracking the the terrorists who perpetrated the Baisaran massacre. According to Indian media, the special forces were able to intercept the coded communications from the terrorists. They were able to discern the messaging system used between the LET and the terrorists. Indian special forces identified the location of these terrorists as being a local shepherd's hut. Intelligence obtained recently indicated that the same terrorists who carried out the murder of toursists were hiding at this location. In a covert operation by the Indian special forces, the three terrorists, including Hashim Musa, a former member of the SSG, were killed. In the recovered items were Chinese encrypted radio sets, night vision devices and Pakistani rations besides personal arms and ammunition. It may have been of more value if one of the terrorists was captured alive. Later, two other terrorists of the same group were purported to have been killed in a gun battle on the outskirts Srinagar.

Pakistan at this time has growing separatist movements in Baluchistan and Khyber Pakhtunkhwa provinces. Its economy is at a critical stage of bankruptcy. The speech by Gen Asim Munir on 19 April 2025 was perhaps the most provocative as if inviting India to start a war. The murder of 26 civilians on 22 April was perhaps planned by the Pakistani establishment and it aimed to draw retaliation from India in order to rally their population around a common anti-India agenda. This attack has united Indian people in support of Kashmiris and has perhaps had a lesser effect in uniting Pakistan. It may even be negative in reducing the support for terrorist within the population of J&K. All political parties in India stated that they would support whatever retaliatory decision is made by the government. The government left it to the armed forces to plan the necessary response to Pakistan's attack. The process of finding the perpetrators of this outrage and inquiring into how the terrorists managed to avoid local security forces and intelligence became a matter for evaluation later. Seeing the prolonged past pattern of terrorist ops against India, the case for apportioning blame on Pakistan was decisively taken. It is reported that Pakistan's LeT that had started seeking satellite photographs of the Pahalgam area earlier from private agencies.

The Indian armed forces took their time in planning the multi-domain ops. Moving and placing of resources at appropriate locations, gaining intelligence from satellites and other sources, coordinating secure communications identifying targets were accomplished prior to launching the riposte on 6 May 2025. Nine terrorist camps were hit out of the 25 identified. The major point to be noted is that new red lines have been drawn for punishing Pakistan for its continuing terrorism and proxy war. The Indian forces struck with precision the HQ of JeM at Bhawalpur and at Muridke, HQ of the LET near Lahore. Pakistan was expected to escalate the conflict, which they did on 7/8 May 2025, with stream of drone swarms, aircraft and missile attacks. The Turkey supplied Bayraktar drones, decoy drones, loitering ammunition Pakistani aircraft and missiles were successfully defeated by employing Akash Teer, a next generation real-time targeting and interception system and other upgraded air defence gun systems. The Akash Teer system has been developed indigenously by India. The success of this system has surely been noted by the US, China, Turkey and Pakistan itself. This is an AI controlled, satellite linked command system. The retaliation from India was immediate on the night of 9/10 May 2025 as Indian drones, loitering ammunition and Brahmos missiles bypassed all Chinese supplied radar systems engaging and putting out of commission early warning radars and 13 military airfields. This was modern multi-domain precision targeting. There were various types of ammunition used based on target selection. The Indian political establishment has sent strong signals that India will henceforth respond in strength to such terrorist attacks. Important messaging from the India political leadership includes the following-

a. Any terrorist act against India will be treated as an act of war. This gives the Indian government the reason to act rapidly and decisively to any future terrorist attack.

b. Talks with Pakistan will take place on the return of Gilgit-Baltistanto India and terrorism.

c. The Indus Water Treaty has been suspended. This is likely to hurt Pakistan.

d. *Op Sindoor* has not ended but it continues.

e. India has been able to control further escalation and has accepted the stoppage of fire. This has been extended for a month.

The reaction from Pakistan JeM and JEI has been that they will avenge the attack by India on their establishments and the jihad against India will continue. The official reaction from Prime Minister Shahbaz Sharif has been that Pakistan would like to start a dialogue with India on the current situation. The talks if started may workout the terms of the ceasefire and also the way forward bearing in mind the stoic remarks of the Indian Prime Minister. The motivation behind the terrorist attack at Pahalgam have been extensively dealt with by analysts. This is the pattern of unremitting hostilities that Pakistan pursues in its proxy war. The conduct of the terrorist attack at Pahalgam, at a time that Vice President of the US was on a visit to India shows that the terrorist attack was executed to draw attention of the world towards Kashmir. The attack was condemned by the UNSC stating that action be taken against terrorist groups. After India's riposte to the escalation by Pakistan there has been considerable discussions generated in the national and international media. It is a moot point but of note that Pakistan has been a loyal ally of both the west and China. In these countries there is the belief that Pakistan has been a victim of terrorism and hence there is some sympathy for this country. In the world of shadow diplomacy there appears to be leverage that Pakistan provides to both the US, its allies and China.

After the stopping of fire on 10 May 2925, it can be educed that the new normal in dealing with Pakistan will be:

a. Despite Pakistan's repeated nuclear blackmail / bluff, counter-action will be taken to conduct ops inside Pakistan in case terrorist attacks are launched by that country on Indian soil. This once again shows that there is space below the nuclear threshold for such actions. This does set a dangerous precedent for future target selection by both countries. While planning such interventions care has to be exercised in gauging that the radical elements in the hierarchy in Pakistan may still initiate the use of nuclear weapons and hence to neutralize these have to be foolproof.

b. The China factor must be carefully understood as supportive of Pakistan in the confrontation with India.

c. The visuals of Pakistani army generals attending the funerals of terrorists show that the line between state and non-state actors is now blurred. The new paradigm could be to strike at the leadership of the terrorist groups that wage the proxy war.

d. India must be prepared for a long haul as Pakistan is unlikely to relent.

Regional Imbroglio

India's deployment of armed forces in the union territory of J&K is intended to defend its territory, contend with infiltration from across the LOC, deal with terrorism, separatism, and radicalism generated by Pakistan. These armed forces also deployed to counter and prevent hostile actions by China. Contending with this complex border security dynamic is part of the ongoing regional imbroglio for India. Pakistan may believe that with a relentless policy of terrorism and by playing the Islamic card, it will be able to wean Kashmir away from India. In Kashmir, Pakistan's aims continue to be to wear down and demoralize the Indian Security Forces, carry out selective killing of minorities, including migrant labour from other parts of the country, and concomitantly enhance the influence of Islamists. As proven so far, Pakistan's strategy will not succeed as Kashmir is and remains an integral part of India. It is rebounding to be an affluent region, with an educated and entrepreneurial population. Indian Security Forces are deployed in J&K to defend an integral part of India. The Kashmiri population has started to realise this. The government of India is resolute in dealing with the Kashmir situation and is handling it according to Indian laws. On a visit to Iran, Imran Khan made a bold statement which was perhaps for the consumption of the international community. He said that there is no place for terrorism in modern society. On his return to Pakistan, Khan was subjected to criticism in the Pakistani Parliament and in the media, for making such a statement. There is clearly no obvious acceptance of such a viewpoint amongst the radical powers in Pakistan.

It is to be acknowledged that terrorists, especially mercenaries, have no concern for the welfare of society. They have no value for human life. They only create strife and internecine conflicts, which retard progress and cause disruption. Their aim is to gain power and introduce medieval practices to subjugate people and in Kashmir and elsewhere, terrorists bear allegiance to no one. In the name of Jihad, these mercenaries act against the civil population, intimidate, kill and create a fear psychosis. They silence dissent and brutally punish any resistance. The terrorist groups operating in the Kashmir Valley burned down a few school buildings to deny children the premises for education. They damaged railway stations, so painstakingly constructed at that altitude, and even destroyed the local assembly buildings known as 'panchayat *ghars*', which house the offices of elected representatives of communities at the grass-roots level. None of this benefits the citizens. It is purely destructive and disruptive.

As mentioned above, in the bloody history of terrorism in Kashmir, the most horrific incident that occurred when six western tourists and their two guides were abducted in the Anantnag district of Jammu and Kashmir on 4 July 1995. About forty militants from Islamist terrorist Al Faran an affiliate of Harkat-ul-Ansar kidnapped the hikers and beheaded Norwegian, Hans Christian Ostrø. An American, John Childs, managed to escape. The rest of the party were missing and are presumed dead. Such heinous acts and the one in Pahalgam on 22 April 2025 would be severely detrimental to tourism, which is flourishing in J&K today. The Indian authorities must not allow the will of Pakistan to prevail. Tourism must be revived in its full form to ensure that life continues as normal in Kashmir. The fragile equilibrium in Kashmir, which has been achieved by the Indian Security Forces and the resilient local population can therefore be undone very quickly by bad actors who only want to impose misery. This is the reason for the dominant presence of the Indian security forces in Kashmir, which continues to help maintain peace and safety in this region. In the fine balance of normal life and impending terrorist threats, Indian Security Forces have made every effort to act in good faith, ensuring civilians are not terrorized, and that undue casualties do not continue to occur in Kashmir. It should be clearly understood that security forces cannot be present everywhere. The intelligence apparatus has to be supported by the people to be effective and obviate dastardly and cowardly attacks on civilians such as the one in Baisaran. The locals could have identified aliens in the area, who were planning the mission. These terrorists would have had communication with their mentors, perhaps sought refuge with the local population, carried out reconnaissance prior to carrying out this horrific act. In this instance the terrorists had chosen a soft target, where there was no presence of security forces and no road link exists. Tourists either undertake a trek to the area or are moved up on ponies. Mobile phone communications do not exist in the area.

As stated above, the support for terrorism within J&K had diminished considerably as conditions of everyday life for people have improved. More than ever before, there is prosperity and opportunity for the residents. In contrast, in Pakistan there is lack of accountability in governance, feudal rule persists, and there is an increasing prevalence of radical Islam. Chronic poverty, lack of opportunities for education and employment, limited growth ventures, military dominance, rampant corruption, election rigging, and a sagging economy are the realities of life in Pakistan. Indian journalists, who have spoken to ordinary Kashmiris, have found that the locals are fed up with the terrorist mercenaries sent by Pakistan. They understand the futility of this terrorism, desire security in their lives and a better future for their families. They only want peace. This is confirmed by the trend of voluntary surrender by local-bred terrorists who have heeded the advice of their families to give up arms. Monetary support from Pakistan has kept the terrorism alive in Kashmir, but Pakistan's influence has been fading in the politics of the state. It should be clear to Pakistan that India will never give up the Kashmir Valley or its rightful claim to the entire state of J&K as it existed prior to 15 August 1947. The 'Mission Zero Terror' announced by the J&K police was partially successful in 2023-24.

Targeting of security forces, pilgrims, attacks on citizens of the state and civilian labour is an issue that still persists and hence the announcement was premature.

The ceasefire in the Kargil War came to effect on 10 July 1999. At this time, it was deemed safe for military envoys of various countries, who had embassies or high commissions in India, to tour the HQ XV Corps in Srinagar and the tactical HQ of 3 Infantry Division in Kargil. The aim of these visits was to receive a briefing about the misadventure perpetrated by Pakistan. These international representatives were given a perspective of the alignment of the LOC and Pakistan's armed intrusion across the LOC. The review was conducted using maps and by directly surveying those areas that were visible on the ground from a stand-off distance. The visiting military officers were given a brief background to the India-Pakistan conflict, the probable reasons for Pakistan to launch the perfidious intrusion across the LOC, the extent and depth of the intrusion and the operational situation as it existed. They also met a Pakistani prisoner of war undergoing treatment in the field Hospital at Kargil. In his memoir, *In the Line of Fire*, Musharraf has averred that most of the casualties suffered by Pakistan's troops in Kargil were inflicted while withdrawing during the ceasefire. He was alleging that Indian forces were attacking Pakistan's troops as they withdrew. This is a gross misrepresentation. In fact, it was evident to the visiting contingent of the military attachés that a peaceful ceasefire was being observed. They also learnt from the prisoner of war about the location where he, along with his unit, was given special training for the ops. This included details on staging forward to a concentration area where their uniforms were withdrawn, and they were issued civilian clothing resembling that of jihadis. The military attachés were also briefed about information obtained from radio intercepts, which confirmed the sagging morale of Pakistan's troops, and their dwindling willingness to continue to hold their remaining positions in the intrusion area. Overall, the Pakistan Army had no results to show after Kargil ops and there are no gains out of terrorism. Why not attempt serious negotiations to end this state of war?

Track 2 diplomacy or back-channel negotiations, which ensued for nearly five years in the nineties, created the conditions that led to the visit of Prime Minister Vajpayee to Pakistan in February in 1999. But despite this visit, tensions again ratcheted up with the launch of the Kargil War. A few years after that tempestuous period, to diffuse tensions, India and Pakistan attempted to negotiate once again and Musharraf paid a visit to India in

2007. Efforts were made to reach another understanding regarding the Kashmir dispute. Pakistan Corps Commanders were consulted about the proposed plan; however, they could not be persuaded despite Musharraf's agreement. This was likely because by then General Musharraf had a weakened standing in Pakistan and also Pakistan made unacceptable demands. The Pakistanis consulted with their proxies in Kashmir about the proposed plan, especially the Hurriyat Conference, but did not find any support. International intervention in the Kashmir dispute has not been attempted by any country or organization since the signing of the Shimla Agreement in July 1972. The US has not been prepared to countenance a role in mediating the Kashmir dispute. It was only during Imran Khan's visit to the US in October 2019 and his meeting at the White House with Trump, in his first tenure as President, that Trump unpredictably stated that he could mediate between India and Pakistan to resolve the Kashmir dispute. Any mediation by a third party would be unacceptable to India. President Clinton did intervene in 1999 during the Kargil War at the request of then Pakistani Prime Minister Nawaz Sharif. However, he did so only after due consultation with Prime Minister Vajpayee. At the Indian Army was poised to eliminate the remainder of Pakistani positions in the intrusion areas, capture more prisoners of war, and, if directed by the political leadership, to take the war across the LOC into Pakistan. Clinton's intervention on Pakistan's behalf resulted in a ceasefire, which came into effect to save democracy in Pakistan and to save Prime Minister Nawaz Sharif from ignominy.

The impasse between India and Pakistan continues and, the other part of the imbalanced equation in this region is China. The latter has played a significant role in assisting Pakistan with its Kashmir policy and has remained inimical to India. After the communist party came to power in 1949, China laid claims to the Northeastern parts of J&K across the Karakoram range, akin to their exaggerated claims on the territory of other neighbouring countries. This was a part of China's expansionist strategy to gain favourable terrain and enabling access into areas that did not belong to them. In many cases, boundaries had not been demarcated between China and its neighbours, which made it easier for China to usurp territory. Pakistan was more than willing to come to an agreement with China since it involved territory that legitimately belonged to India. By giving away thc Shaksgam Valley in a border settlement with China, Pakistan acted as if this part of J&K was part of its own territory. The most important outcome of this relationship was the formation of the China-Pakistan nexus. As discussed, this nexus has serious implications for India's security as it poses a dual threat by China and Pakistan. China had also challenged India's sovereignty in Kashmir by issuing stapled visas to Indian citizens from J&K, thus supporting Pakistan's claim on the state. This issue was resolved after Prime Minister Manmohan Singh took up the matter with the visiting Chinese premier in December 2010. The issue of terrorism, border issues, and Kashmir are not mutually exclusive from the China-Pakistan nexus. The friction is aggravated by the fact that any negotiations between China and India must include the areas of J&K that China is occupying in Eastern Ladakh/Aksai Chin, to which India has a legitimate claim, the CPEC and the Shaksgam Valley. The demarcation of the IB between the two countries is also critical and a formidable challenge. The Chinese claim over the Sakteng Wildlife Sanctuary in NE Bhutan at the Global Environmental Facility Council meeting is another overt hostility. China also questions the sovereignty of India over Arunachal Pradesh, which creates further challenges. As per the EurAsian Times of October 2024, China has built 22 dual use villages within Bhutan's territory. Satellite imagery has shown this development. These villages are connected by roads from the Chinese side and are isolated from Bhutan's nearest habitations. These villages have been set up to coerce Bhutan to come to terms with China and perhaps to gain control of strategic areas. China's sustained threat on India's northern periphery was proven by its unprovoked move forward and its aggressive posturing in April 2020. Pakistan remains China's important partner not only against India but it also assists in dominating the Indian Ocean region via their collaboration in CPEC.

Afghanistan has also had an impact on the India-Pakistan relationship. It has a border with the erstwhile state of J&K in the north and with China in the east, along its Wakhan Corridor, which is 350 km long and 15–65 km wide. This corridor separates J&K from Tajikistan. The takeover by the Taliban and internecine terrorism in that country could influence events in J&K. Since Pakistan continues to support separatists in J&K, it could very well up the ante in J&K with the active participation of the Taliban, if the latter are willing. This scenario appears unlikely as the Taliban have been following their own agenda after establishing their government in Afghanistan. The Haqqani Network has been included in the Taliban Government, much to the chagrin of the US. This Network is known to support Al Qaeda, which is steadily seeing a revival with Osama bin Laden's son at the helm. These militant groups have a mutual understanding from the past as they were earlier based in the tribal areas of North Waziristan in Pakistan. As mentioned, there have been incidents between the border guards of Afghanistan and Pakistan, including live firing across their border. This indicates that the relations between the two neighbours are not entirely friendly. The TPP is based in Afghanistan, and it is a jihadi force that is anti the Pakistan Army and the government. While speaking at the Marghella Dialogue organized by the Islamabad Policy Research Institute, in 2024, Gen Asim Munir referred to the TPP as 'Fitna al Khawarji'. This implies that the TPP had become a hub for terrorist organizations and proxies around the world. The TPP does have quite a few affiliates, and it is linked to the Afghan Taliban and Al Qaeda. The suicide attack on a mosque in Peshawar on 23 January 2023 was initially claimed by the TTP. If the TPP can obtain the active support of the Afghan Taliban, they may then plan to occupy the Pashtun areas of Pakistan for themselves. This could metastasize into a radical Islamic threat to the integrity of Pakistan. The Afghan Taliban also have their network in Baluchistan and provide safe havens to the resurgent Baluch Liberation Army separatists. The situation could escalate if these separatists begin widespread operations in Pakistan.

The Pakistan administration must realize sooner than later, that the AFPAK region is plagued by long-lasting and complex rivalries that are more serious than their rivalries with India. Iran is concerned with the resurgence of the radical Sunni regime in Afghanistan that is supported by Pakistan. They support the Shia groups in the Hazara area and the Northern Alliance. The Baluch Liberation Army, which was raised in 2000, is also known to be covertly located in the border area inside Iran. Pakistan has engaged their hideouts with rocket attacks. There have been reciprocal rocket attacks from Iran onto suspected location of Jaish-e-Adil, a Sunni group that has attacked Iranian border security forces. The Iran-Pakistan border is 900 kms long and is not entirely peaceful. This threat has led to the deployment of a Pakistan Army Corps to guard this border. ISIS has also been active in Afghanistan especially against minorities. This terror groups can spread its influence together with radical Islam into the CARs and from there to Chechnya, Dagestan, and Russia itself. Hence, Russia maintains a considerable interest in the region. The US has maintained surveillance over the affairs in Afghanistan as demonstrated by the drone strike that killed Ayman al-Jawahiri in Kabul. Given the complex ground realities in this region, Pakistan must introspect and reassess its motives. Its actions in the past are the basis of this perpetual state of war and militancy in its neighbourhood, and the root of terrorism within its boundaries. Unfortunately, there is a lack of concern and a lack of understanding in most of the world as to why this region has become a dangerous hot bed of sectarian conflicts. This is a myopic outlook since the conflicts and terrorism in this region have proven to have severe implications.

Emerging Relationships and the China Challenge

The security threat from China is increasing as it develops its 'String of Pearls', which encompass the creation of naval bases and dual-use facilities in the Indian Ocean around the Indian subcontinent. This development is being conducted by China to secure the sea lanes through which its trade passes and to seek area dominance. China's involvement in the Hambantota Port in Sri Lanka, the creation of an artificial island naval base in Maldives, the naval base in Djibouti, the port at Gwadar and the adjacent future naval base at Jivani in Pakistan are particularly of concern. China is also funding the development of the Kyaukpyu Port in Myanmar and the port in Cox's Bazar in Bangladesh. In July 2020, China proposed to Iran that the port at Jask be developed. Jask is near the mouth of the Gulf of Hormuz, one of the seven choke points on the seas of the world. The PLA Navy has commenced sailing surface-armed vessels, submarines, and oceanographic survey ships in the Indian Ocean. According to a report accessed by the *New York Times*, a strategic partnership agreement was signed between China and Iran, which is indicative of China's expanding presence in Iran. China has agreed to spend $400 billion on ports, railways, telecom, and other projects in Iran over the next ten years. One of the projects is the railway line from Chabahar to Zahedan on the Afghan border. There is cooperation between the two countries in defence as well. The sanctions imposed by the US against Iran are of no consequence to China. It is one of the biggest consumers of petroleum products and imports its oil from Iran, Russia and other sources. The cooperation between China and Iran is of concern to India because it also obtains some crude oil and natural gas from Iran. The development of CPEC through POK and Gilgit-Baltistan and its possible expansion in Afghanistan, when viewed in conjunction with the foregoing, shows China's rapidly increasing influence in the area. China's seemingly unstoppable and very aggressive strategies pose a threat not only across land borders but also on the seas, outer space, and cyberspace.

India has observed with concern, the rapid building of artificial islands in the South China Sea and in the Maldives. This is part of a salience of military coercion that China is resorting to without going to war. China's strategy is to make more and more nations dependent on its goods and services, to shift the power balance in its favour. The South America continent has traditionally been in the sphere of influence of the US. However, the US has not paid sufficient attention to the relationships on this continent. China has used this as an opportunity to actively forge relations with south American nations through investments in individual countries and through BRICS. While attending the Asia Pacific Cooperation Forum (APEC) in Peru in November 2024, President Xi Jinping inaugurated the Chancy port. This port will be a commercial hub for shipping to access the vast Chinese market and vice versa. It is likely that Lithium and other raw materials and goods from Chile, Ecuador, Columbia and even Brazil are expected to be shipped to Shanghai and other Chinese ports. This port was developed at a cost of $ 3.5 billion. As per reports, it will also provide facilities for use by Chinese warships. Tony Sage, CEO of Critical Minerals Corporation, has stated that China now controls 87% of the supply chain of rare earth materials in the world. It is in a position to block the supply of rare earths as and when it desires. China's success and its growing self-confidence has created a situation in which the world has acceded to Chinese influence, and it is clearly ascendent in various regions of the world especially in the global south. The US under the Trump administration is making attempts to find and manage its own supply of rare earths and strategic elements. Seeking rare earths from Ukraine, desire to take over Greenland, and hoping to make Canada the 51st state of the US seemed to be part of this strategy. All these announcements by President Trump have come to nought.

China does support Pakistan by way of technology transfer, supply of armaments and in the field of IT, to assist Pakistan with cyber sovereignty. This also impacts the realms of technology and modernization of armed forces. India has been maintaining a neutral stance in affairs relating to Taiwan, Xin Jiang, and Tibet. The use of Gilgit-Baltistan for CPEC, is indicative that the China challenge and threat remains as China has not backed off from its aggressive designs against India. In the past, India has signed several agreements with China, which have not resulted in resolving the border issues. These agreements are:

a. 1993: Agreement to maintain peace and tranquility along the LAC.

b. 1996: Confidence-building measures in the military field along the LAC.

c. 2005: Modalities for implementing confidence-building measures in the military field.

d. 2012: Establishing a working mechanism for consultation and coordination on India-China border affairs.

The question remains, 'Why is the border between India and China still not defined?' India cannot unilaterally do so, if the other side is unwilling to elaborate on its perception of the same. India had not agreed to join China's BRI and refused to attend the summit on the subject in 2017, despite being invited to attend. This was followed by the Chinese intrusion into the Doklam plateau in Bhutan in June 2017, as explained earlier. Consequent to their withdrawal from the area, China moved up a brigade group, which is located at Khamba Dzong, a small township 30 km north of the Bhutan border. India has a Friendship Treaty with Bhutan, signed on 2 March 2007, and Bhutan has independent foreign and defence policies in relation to all countries while it abides by the principle of common security with India. The stand-off at Doklam lasted for 73 days. Observing the geography of the region, it can be understood that the access from the Doklam plateau through Bhutan leads to the plains area of India. It is about 90 kms crows flight distance from the Bhutan-Tibet border to the Bhutan-India border in the Cooch Bihar district of West Bengal. There exists a narrow strip of Indian territory between Bhutan and Bangladesh. Any operation into the area from the north, if successful, would aim to cut off the land link to the seven states of Eastern India from the rest of the country. This area, therefore, has strategic importance, and the move by China to occupy an area in proximity to Bhutan's border, close to the Doklam plateau, provides a firm base for launching ops. The dual-use villages that have been constructed and occupied by the China as mentioned earlier cements their claims on territory and to consolidate their hold in the border areas.

It is essential to analyze why China has resorted to such provocative actions. Why had their troops advanced forward in Eastern Ladakh and disturbed the status quo with India? When President Obama visited India in January 2015, the US had, perhaps, already made plans to contain and contend with China's growing territorial ambitions and power. Obama had prepared a strategy of establishing a pivot in the Indo-Pacific region. India provides an important flank of this pivot; hence, it was perceived important to this strategy. After the standoff in Doklam in June-August 2017, the Indian Government, did try to establish cordial relations with China by organizing one-to-one summit meetings between Prime Minister Modi and President Xi Jinping with Modi visiting China in August 2018 and a reciprocal visit by Xi Jinping to India in October 2019. These informal meetings aimed to prevent war and further standoffs on the IB. Avoiding war is necessary to facilitate the unhampered growth of any country's economy. China has perhaps inferred more than what exists in India's cooperation with the US and has acted to restrain India by carrying out its forward deployment in Eastern Ladakh. In the enhanced deployment of troops on the border, China has forced India to deploy more military resources on the eastern border thereby indirectly helping Pakistan.

China's economic and military growth, coupled with advancements in AI and cyberspace, have given it confidence to pursue its ambitious goals and face multiple challenges head on.

As a part of its political agenda, one of the goals is to disturb the status quo, and counter India's rising prominence in the world. Much like China, India's economic growth, infrastructure development, and modernization have been exponential in the past 20 years. China may also want to dissuade India from playing a significant role in the region, in conjunction with the US and its allies. This could be termed as containment action. When India changed the special status of J&K on 5 August 19, and reorganized it into two union territories on 30 October 2019, it supplemented this move with publication of maps of the erstwhile J&K, which highlighted Indian territory that China and Pakistan occupy. Perhaps this became a pretext for the China to launch the forward deployment and challenge India's claims in J&K. The Chinese had likely assessed that since the deployment of Indian security forces in the area was thin, they would achieve an element of surprise. Consequent to their forward move, China expected a localized reaction from India but were surprised at the stoic determination of the Indian establishment. Militarily, if the Chinese plan was limited, then it may have been to gain moral ascendency, secure and strengthen areas in proximity to the border, deny Indian patrolling in select areas and improve their defence posture. If the plan was strategic, then after this preliminary action, China would require a larger buildup of forces to be deployed at select points along the border. That would, perhaps, create an overall imbalance for it in other theatres. The risk for the PLA, in case of a war, would be considerable, as the outcome of such a war, launched independently or even in collusion with Pakistan, would likely be unpredictable. A defeat would be disastrous for the CCP and Xi Jinping.

This recent standoff between India and China requires further elaboration. The initial phase of forward move in 2020 in Ladakh resulted in the deadly skirmish in the Galwan Valley. The Chinese troops had advanced unopposed approximately up to the areas that Indian security forces patrolled posing an enhanced threat. The patrolling by the Indian Army and Indo-Tibetan Border Police was being carried out periodically up to pre-designated points. A status quo existed. If the Chinese had larger plans militarily, then they may have attempted to extend their advance further with a view to annex the area of the Nubra Valley and the Siachen Sector and link up with the Pakistan-occupied area of Gilgit-Baltistan. This would be a risky op and would probably not remain below the nuclear threshold for India. The Depsang Plains and DBO are areas that must be defended by India to prevent the Chinese from achieving this. If this option is exercised by the Chinese and is successful, it would jeopardize Indian defences in the Siachen Sector. This glacier abuts the Shaksgam Valley and is of strategic importance to India. Indian troops, in a counter move, had occupied the Kailash range on the South bank of Pangong Tso overlooking the Chinese garrison at Moldo on 29/30 August 2020. This area provides the shortest avenue to the Chinese Western Highway. To carry out this op, for the first time, the IA employed troops of the Special Frontier Force (SFF), which is manned by people of Tibetan descent, who were born in India hence are Indian citizens. China also attempted an incursion in the state of Arunachal Pradesh on 9 December 2022 which was repulsed by the Indian Army.

With these actions, China has had activated the entire un-demarcated border with India. As a result, India has embarked on a modernization spree of its Armed Forces, undertaken strategic rebalancing of its defence posture, and decided to forge closer relationships with the US and its allies, wherever their co-operation was felt necessary. India had made attempts at economic decoupling with China, which is a difficult challenge in view of the tie-ups that exist. To defuse tension after the 2020 hostilities, India and China joined a video conference organized by Russia between the Indian National Security Advisor and the Chinese Foreign Minister in 2020 in which both sides stated that they did not intend to go to war. China has taken advantage of the differing perception of the un-demarcated border and has never delineated their claims on any map. China has also not provided a concrete version of the border except very vaguely in the 1959 letter of Zhou Enlai to Nehru. The purported aim was likely an effort to gain more territory with no historical basis. It was a ploy to legitimize ownership of the area through which it had constructed the Western highway, providing depth to this highway in Aksai Chin. Similar claims were made by China with other neighbouring countries. For China this is a low-level conflict, and India remains unclear about the Chinese claims to the border. Therefore, uncertainty prevails.

This offensive action by China can be compared with that of Pakistan in 1999 after the Lahore Declaration. India and its people were not psychologically prepared for an intrusion by Pakistan. Similarly, China's aggressive move in 2020 was unexpected. In hindsight, it can be conjectured that the Chinese had perhaps assumed that India was leaning towards the West. This evaluation was likely based on the analysis and statements on foreign policy in the Indian media. India, it seems has been caught up in the power struggle between the West and China and the latter therefore felt the need for a show of force.

It has been reported that in the standoff in 2020, the PLA had assembled approximately 60,000 troops in Tibet and Aksai Chin for carrying out exercises. They would have prepared to sustain these forces logistically for prolonged periods and equipped them for winter. They utilized these additional troops and adopted a forward posture. China has constructed roads and laid fiber optic cables in the area occupied in order to have assured communications with forward elements. According to a report published on 22 March 2023 by the Center for Strategic and International Studies, the Chinese have constructed a HQ with concrete shelters, a radome and antennae towers on the Pangong Tso, inside the area that they have held since the fifties. Satellite imagery shows numerous shelters for artillery and anti-aircraft systems as well as shelters for armoured personnel carriers and vehicles. Further east and approximately 26 kms from the LAC, is a newly constructed bridge over the Pangong Tso. As is well known, China's ability to develop and build infrastructure rapidly is unmatched. The infrastructure they have created has enhanced their ability to build up forces into forward areas. Eight new roads emanate from their G-219 towards forward areas. The Chinese have developed three dozen airfields and heliports in Tibet and Xinjiang. Initially, the severe winter conditions in the area, the rarified atmosphere at heights above 14,000 ft, the lack of experience of the Chinese in such cold weather warfare, and the casualties to their troops because of altitude and cold, had forced them to thin out troops from depth areas and from friction points or points of contact with the Indian Army. These infirmities have been overcome as troops have got acclimatized to these conditions, are better equipped, and have been provided with shelters. The occupation of the Kailash range by the Indian Army has played a significant part in the psyche of the Chinese. This range was held by the Indian Army in the 1962 war when an epic battle was fought by an infantry company of the 13th Battalion, the Kumaon Regiment, at Rezangla, to the last man and the last round. In case of aggression by the PLA in the region, they can expect more such counter-intrusion ops by the Indian Army. Ever since the Chinese move forward and the buildup by Indian armed forces, several meetings have been held between the representatives of the two countries. This is an indication that neither side wants to escalate the situation, however, this cannot be taken for granted. Trust is at a deficit between India and China and the situation at the border is volatile. This was proven by a scuffle between opposing troops at Naku La on 20 January 2021 in Sikkim and a subsequent one in the Tawang Sector in Arunachal Pradesh in December 2022. The Chinese had made uncompromising statements during the corps commander-level talks ever since. Progress has however been made in defusing tensions, and it appears that the Chinese are now focused on strengthening their foothold in the border areas of Tibet.

At the national level, the reasons for Chinese belligerence are evaluated. Strategies evolve from this analysis and are employed during negotiations. It is quite clear that existing treaties or protocols have proven to be inadequate for maintaining peace and tranquility on the border. In any future negotiations, it may be advisable to establish mechanisms to eliminate the chances of further incursions by either side and avoid skirmishes that may lead to an escalation. A buffer or a no man's land, if agreed upon, may facilitate this. In this buffer, neither side should deploy, patrol, or develop infrastructure. This should logically lead to the eventual demarcation of the LAC. After the ninth round of corps commander-level negotiations, a plan to disengage evolved. A synchronized and phased disengagement had been completed on the North and South banks of Pangong Tso. After this, it is believed that the PLA had fallen back to the west of Sirijap. The Indian Army has agreed to withdraw up to Finger 4 on the north bank of Pangong Tso and from the Kailash range. These actions have created a buffer between the forces which is to be adhered to by either side. Surveillance needs to be maintained to ensure that there is no breach of understanding in the local area. Subsequent negotiations have yielded further disengagements from the Gogra-Hot Springs and Galwan areas. Negotiations have also resulted in an understanding of patrolling in the areas of Depsang and Demchok.

A moot point of interest is the length of the India-China border. China has stated in official media that the length of the border with India is 2,000 km, which disregards the border in Gilgit-Baltistan, Shaksgam Valley and Eastern Ladakh. According to Indian sources it is 4,596 km long. This includes 2,715 km in the western Sector, including Gilgit-Baltistan, the Shaksgam Valley, Eastern Ladakh, Aksai Chin, and part of Tibet. It is 556 km in the central sector and 1,325 km in the eastern sector.

The situation at the LAC with China does justify India's possession of nuclear capability and the need for modernization of its Armed Forces. India and China's nuclear capability will, perhaps, deter a conventional war. Defence preparedness requires long-term planning based on national strategy, threat perception, international situation, and intentions. India must build a stronger anti-missile defence system. With the development of Ahash Teer, S-400 with its upgrades from Russia, the indigenous upgradation of older systems and the Akash air defence missiles this could be achieved for the short and medium term. These defensive anti-missile measures could be overcome, as assessed, in the future by hypersonic missiles, such as the DF-17 missile which has been developed by China. India too, has successfully tested a hypersonic missile on 15 November 2024 which has a maximum range of 1500 kms. China had also in January 2025 demonstrated its sixth generation fighter aircraft and multiplied its air and sea power. Options for acquiring more fighter aircraft by India are being examined. Similar action is being taken to upgrade the capabilities of the Indian Army and Indian Navy.

Indian authorities understand well that China is comparatively technologically advanced and has greater economic and military strength. China has reportedly deployed smart electro-optical infra-red and radio frequency sensors along areas occupied opposite the Indian troops. It is using unmanned aerial vehicles for surveillance and reconnaissance. It has its Bei Dou global navigation satellite system for missile guidance. This system has the ability to establish a three-dimensional panoramic datum of the theatre. It also gives the PLA the ability to maintain surveillance over deployment by India and other nations on its periphery and over supply chains, communication hubs, and headquarters. This itself adds to their capability to wage war both in the virtual and the physical domain.

With China, the dispute over territory can be combined with trust deficit, ideological differences and their quest for world domination. It is also true that China will try and prevent India to rise to become a great power and a competitor. The ongoing stand-off has brought about some lessons for India. One major lesson is that India cannot be complacent and must upgrade to an integrated and effective technological means of surveillance over inimical nations. It must also improve methods of acquiring intelligence, carry out realistic assessment of intelligence and incorporate a real-time reporting system. National intelligence agencies should develop strong relationships with tech companies and select universities for developing technology specific to vulnerabilities to cater for techniques that adversaries may employ. India cannot expect friendly nations to physically join the war against China if ever it does occur. The disputes with China and Pakistan and the vast land and maritime frontiers dictate that India must not delay the upgradation and strengthening of its Armed Forces. To be prepared for war is the most effectual means of preserving peace and this should be based on the national strategy. India should be prepared for a multi-front war. The forward move by China was a deliberate action to achieve psychological ascendency over India. It also conveys the China's broader ambitions and strategic aims.

On the world stage, China aims to build economic and political dominance and limit the influence of American power. Its A2/AD doctrine is designed to interfere with US plans to aid allies in the far east if and when needed. China has strengthened its power matrix and is steadily presenting a fait accompli to the world with its aggressive actions. These include, as already mentioned, the creation of artificial islands in the South China Sea, the building of naval bases in the Asia-Pacific region, aggressive air and naval patrolling, live firing exercises opposite Taiwan, aggressive naval actions in the East China Sea, sanctions against select countries and animosity with India. The countries with islands in the South China Sea do not have the power to stop China from occupying the areas that lie within the 'nine-dash line'.

There is no reasonable explanation as to why China has laid claims on a part of the ocean that is a common waterway of the world. These dash lines were first seen on maps published by China in 1947. These lines along with creation of artificial islands facilitate China to extend its EEZ, encroach upon the EEZs of littoral nations, and gain control of the South China Sea. These actions are clearly detrimental to the freedom of navigation through the seas. China may, perhaps, take similar action to gain control of the East China Sea and the Senkaku Islands, which are claimed by Japan. The US deployed its aircraft carrier groups in the South China Sea. Germany and the UK had deployed their warships to the South China Sea in 2021, and France has deployed its nuclear-powered submarine in the area. Australia has filed another case in the Hague, contesting China's claims. Encouraged by the support of the US, the countries in the littoral who claim the islands in the area may also seek to contest China's domineering posture.

Under President Biden, the US administration has taken measures to strengthen the alliances in the Indo-Pacific. These measures include upgrading the Quad to heads of state level, a US and UK agreement with Australia to build nuclear powered submarines as a part of the Australia,

UK and US security arrangement, tri-lateral summits connecting US with Japan and Philippines, Japan and South Korea have been held, military presence expanded in Australia, Papua New Guinea and Philippines. The US has transferred HEU to fuel nuclear submarines in Australia, a country with no nuclear weapons, thereby setting a precedence and casting aside non-proliferation considerations. The US and its allies collectively have the power to counter the emerging threats from China. The pivot that President Obama desired to create is now in place.

India is a member of The Quad, which has been created

for the purpose of responding to inimical action by China in the seas in the Asia-Pacific region. A significant meeting of Quad representatives was held in Japan in October 2020 to evolve a coordinated response to China. A meeting was also held between foreign and defence secretaries of the US and India on 26–27 October 2020 to discuss the stand-off with China, amongst other matters. The interests of the US and India are aligned at present and defence and commercial ties are stronger. President Biden participated in the G20 summit in India in October 2023 and in a one-on-one discussion with Prime Minister Modi, reiterated the friendly ties and common interests between India and the US. President Trump, in his second term has also articulated friendly overtures towards India. On the face of it, this is indicative that the US desires to have India as an ally. The US itself will not want India to rise to yet another major power that could pose challenges. The threats posed by China were also discussed at the G-7 meeting hosted by the UK in June 2021. In the NATO summit held in the US from 9 to 11 July 2024, it is noteworthy that Australia, Japan, New Zealand and South Korea were invited to attend as observers.

China's relationship with Pakistan has been mentioned throughout this narrative. Despite the friendly nature of this relationship, the CPEC loan to Pakistan could become a problem if the latter is unable to pay back the principal amount to China. In a related assurance, China had indicated that it will defer debt repayment until Pakistan is able to do so. Some analysts in the West have stated that CPEC is being used by China to colonize Pakistan. As far as India is concerned, the CPEC utilizes the area of J&K State that is occupied by Pakistan, and this has strategic implications. Without its occupation of POK and Gilgit-Baltistan, would Pakistan have any value for China? Reports on 15 May 2020 indicate that China and Pakistan have signed agreements for the construction of six hydropower projects in this region on which work has begun. These add more diplomatic and political challenges to the Indian claim over POK and

Gilgit-Baltistan. The available water in Gilgit-Baltistan can be utilized by China to augment its efforts to meet the increasing requirement for silicon crystals and wafers. This capability that China has is of great significance to the world at large. China's initiatives to develop the BRI, String of Pearls, infrastructure development in Tibet, the proposed extension of the same to Nepal, and its suspected aid to insurgencies in India are indicative of China's larger designs in the region.

India is the only country in the region that can challenge China's growing domination. In its Look East Policy, India is in a growing relationship with ASEAN countries, especially with Vietnam and the Quad. It has signed an agreement with the Philippines to supply an unspecified number of BRAHMOS cruise missile systems. Despite the realization by the US that it needs India to counter China and secure the western flank of the Indo-Pacific pivot, the relationship had been marred, at times, by the disruptive foreign policy of the US administration. The Indian Government has cooperated with the US, where there are common national interests, but has charted its own path when interests are diverse. The US continues to impose laws on India, which interfere with relations between India and its friendly nations. For example, Iran provides India with some of its oil and natural gas and also allows a passage to Afghanistan via their Chabahar Port. To obviate sanctions, India had to seek a waiver from the US for purchasing crude oil from Iran. The US has also objected to India's purchase of the S-400 air defence system from Russia. Such pressure tactics seem to be unreasonable impositions on a friendly nation. The delay in the supply of jet aircraft engines to India by GE adds to such consternation. The imposition of 50% tariffs on Indian imports to the US, and verbal support to Pakistan in exploring and devloping its oil reserves, shows the unpredictable nature of Trump's strategy. Whether India can depend upon the support from the US when needed is a matter that needs further assessment. In relation to Pakistan, successive US administrations have provided financial aid to that country and their Army. This continuing financial assistance from the US, shows that while the US supports India on being targeted by terrorists, in its dark foreign policy it becomes silent in supporting anti-terrorist ops. The visit by Gen Asim Munir to the US and a lunch with President Trump was organised when the Israel-Iran war was ongoing in June 2025. It was apparent that the US was preparing to enter this war and hence, once again would seek help from Pakistan to utilise their air bases. This was also to ensure that Pakistan does nothing anti the US in support of its co-religionist nation Iran. This could also be to discourage India from importing oil from Russia. It may be that the US wants to retain influenece and a presence in Pakistan to disrupt the projects undertaken under CPEC, if and when required.

Recipients of aid under the BRI are frustrated with China's aggressive demeanor, rampant corruption, poor safety and the fiscal sustainability of its projects. These factors may have a negative effect on the progress of the BRI. The Chinese economy has been slowing down, and the country is also experiencing a rapid demographic inversion. Chinese investments in India aim to make China's technology and products all-pervasive in Indian life in an innocuous way. Since the China-India episode at the border in April 2020, things have changed. The Indian Government has amended the rules for foreign direct investment to prevent any takeover or purchase of Indian enterprises. Initially, 59 Chinese apps were banned, followed by another 118 to obviate breaches of security. India did not join the Regional Comprehensive Economic Partnership (RCEP) because China would most likely dominate this forum and because it would provide further access to India through commercial links. China is still interlinked with India because of its vast economy and its manufacturing capacity. These linkages are economically valuable for businesses in both countries. Measures that can be taken to improve relations with China are discussed in the next chapter.

Countering the Scourge of Terrorism

As discussed, India-Pakistan relations have consistently been marred by wars and terrorism initiated by Pakistan. After 78 years of becoming an independent country, Pakistan has continued its relentless strategy of bleeding India. This prevents India from getting to terms with its troublesome neighbour. This relentless belligerence does not auger well with Pakistanis who are willing to normalize relations with India and who are moderate in their religiosity. More pressure from other countries, the UNSC and FATF will impose further financial constraints on Pakistan and may force the Pakistani establishment to rethink and curb its hostile actions against India. Despite the financial morass that exists in Pakistan, its leaders refuse to acknowledge the reality. In a statement to the Pakistani Parliament, Imran Khan said that one day Pakistan will loan money to India. Nearly 40 per cent of the Pakistani population lives under the poverty line, so this assertion was made without any basis. If Pakistan embarked on a new path towards reconciliation and began trade and cooperation with

India, it would be beneficial to both countries. In fact, as a partner, India has the means to bail out an economically weak Pakistan from its debt servicing burden.

To face the scourge of terrorism and belligerence, India has been forced to develop a resolute approach to its Pakistan policy. As already discussed, this approach has led to an appropriate riposte to Pakistan's terrorist attacks and strong measures to counter Pakistan's proxy war. It should be clearly understood that Pakistan had managed to convert the Indian union territory of J&K into a zone of conflict. However, even in this proxy war, Pakistan has not been successful. India has countered this adversity through diplomacy, international alliances and deployment of adequate forces to combat terrorism generated by Pakistan and its proxies. One opinion is that a proxy war must be fought with a proxy war. The use of long-range missiles, air power, weapons based in space and autonomous armed drones will perhaps, impose caution on Pakistan. This is quite evident from *Op Sindoor*. Warfare is changing rapidly with the increasing capability provided by autonomous weapons and applications of AI. Ripostes and surgical strikes, although inadequate in curbing terrorism, have had some effect on this unrelenting strategy. India should acquire/develop new and advanced capabilities to wage war and if possible, develop its assets inside Pakistan to be able to target selected facilities and terrorist leaders as and when it wants. This had been done some years ago as stated by B. Raman, retired RAW official in his book, *Kaoboys of RAW*. India's riposte in the 1980s in Pakistan's Sind province, forced Pakistan to call off its terrorist attacks and to stop sponsoring Sikh separatism in Punjab. The turmoil and separatist movements that India could generate in the restive provinces of Pakistan would be a worst-case scenario.

Pakistan does not have much to be proud of since independence. There has been negligible progress in any field, including standard of living, infrastructure, education, poverty alleviation, science and technology, and especially in the economy. The political parties that represent all shades of the Pakistani population draw legitimacy from religion and seek support from the madrasa educated. The moderate and radical clerics are culturally conservative and do not have any capacity to bring about social progress. The liberal elite, for their own safety, engage in realpolitik with the religious heads while hiring foreign security companies for their own protection. They, at times, outdo each other to display animosity towards India, all for the sake of a false sense of patriotism and to seek favour with the powers that be. This is a major contradiction in the attitude of the liberal-minded Pakistani. At times, political leaders in Pakistan have acknowledged the futility of terrorism sponsored by their country. They have mustered the courage to speak out against the proxy war and have made efforts to stop this unrelenting belligerence. Asif Zardari, in his earlier role as President of Pakistan, had declared in an interview with the *Wall Street Journal* that India is no longer his country's arch enemy. He had stated, 'India has never been a threat to Pakistan.' This truly was an extraordinary statement if it was to be considered credible and not mere rhetoric. It was an audacious assessment, perhaps made with the aim of ending Pakistan's decades-long hostility with India. Zardari had realized that the inimical relationship with India was a self-definition of the Pakistani State. He had called Kashmir's separatists as terrorists and had no objection to India's nuclear deal with the US. He went on to state, 'Why should we begrudge the largest democracy in the world getting friendly with one of the oldest democracies in the world?' Zardari had assessed that Pakistan's economic survival was conditional upon better ties and trade with India. He stated, 'There is no better strategy for a nation like us.' Even citizen-level initiatives such as Pakistan-India Peoples for Peace and Democracy have hesitated to outline such a vision of economic cooperation. Zardari's vision of a non-adversarial relationship with India was not supported by their Army but he was astute enough to keep relations with his Army's top brass on an even keel. He gave Gen Kayani, the COAS, an extension of three years to keep these relations mutually amicable. Now that Zardari is President of Pakistan for a second time, will he be able to exert some influence in bringing about a dialogue with India and restore trade? Nawaz Sharif went as far as acknowledging that his country had occupied areas across the LOC in 1999 in the Kargil War and that it was a 'stab in the back' of his counterpart, Prime Minister Vajpayee, after signing the Lahore declaration earlier in the same year. He made this statement a few weeks before Narendra Modi's visit to Lahore for his daughter's wedding. The above examples were opportunities for Pakistan to possibly change course. With inimical actions against India, Pakistan has steadily dug itself into a dire financial crisis.

The Kargil War was launched by Pakistan 27 years after signing the Shimla Agreement. Until then, policymakers in most of the world believed that the Shimla Agreement of 1972 was of consequence and that it would be honoured, preventing future wars between the two countries. The Kargil War violated the provisions of this agreement. Even after India's decisive victory in this war, there have been more serious challenges posed by

Pakistan to India's security. These include the Mumbai massacre, the attack on India's Parliament, and many more examples highlighted earlier. These incidents have only added to the animosity between the two countries. LOC violations and infiltration by terrorists had increased in 2020 and in 2021. Once again, the question is whether a sub-conventional war or terrorism can ever bring about the resolution of the conflict? Possibly to curb Pakistan's hostile intentions, the Defence Minister of India, Rajnath Singh, hinted at a change in the country's nuclear policy. In a tweet, in August 2019, after the abrogation of Articles 370 and 35A and listening to the highly charged rhetoric from Pakistani media and leadership, Singh stated that if Pakistan could use nuclear weapons in the first instance, then so can India. Imran Khan's response to the tweet by Rajnath Singh was an appeal to the world community to intervene to restrain India. This indicates that Pakistan now comprehends that India will utilize its entire range of arsenal in case of a grave provocation or threat to its national security. This is an implied change in India's nuclear doctrine and its overt nuclear status does provide the necessary security guarantees against conventional wars that may be started by Pakistan and China. At the same time, the risk of deploying nuclear weapons is far greater than can be imagined. No rational nation can risk the total unmitigated disaster due to a nuclear war. The exercising of a nuclear option would be a last resort when the very existence of a nuclear-armed nation is at stake or when the security situation is totally adverse. India has for long played the role of a soft state and is a status quo power. It needs to maintain large ground forces to prevent territorial land grabbing. It has withstood wars and terrorist attacks launched by Pakistan, and prolonged tension on the border with China. India will avoid a nuclear conflict and try to counter the provocation by other means unless its security is dangerously affected.

The end to the sub-conventional war and Pakistan initiated terrorism will depend upon various factors. India has demonstrated patience and has the experience to continue to fight jihadis, insurgents, and terrorism for prolonged periods. With the reorganization of J&K, the internal security situation is in India's favour. Besides, it is becoming clear that Pakistan cannot achieve its strategic objectives through the sub-conventional war. Given the poor state of its economy, Pakistan must acknowledge that the terrorists it grooms and funds do not help in economic growth. This form of warfare is a cheap option to bleed India. Arrogance motivates and forces Pakistan's politicians to adopt a belligerent attitude, even though India has supremacy in demography, economics, manufacturing and industrial capacity, military power, and diplomacy. History has shown that war as a means of resolving disputes between India and Pakistan has failed on all counts. In all four wars, Pakistan has been resoundingly defeated and the sub-conventional war, ongoing for years, has not brought about any results.

Rightly so, the priority for the Government of India is to eliminate terrorism from the union territory of J&K and to bring stability to the lives of the population. To achieve this, anti-terrorist ops are being conducted by Indian Security Forces, as discussed earlier. Unfortunately, security forces continue to suffer casualties, and this will continue until the scourge of terrorism is eliminated. The Muslim population in the Kashmir Valley has endured the sub-conventional war, have not migrated from their communities, claimed refugee status or left the area for Pakistan. Why would a Kashmiri have allegiance towards an impoverished and radicalized nation such as Pakistan when there is no oppression by India, and freedom exists. Propaganda by terrorists can stir up emotions in the affected population and unfortunately, International human rights agencies have on occasion favoured terrorists when observing the plight of the locals. Sections of the media, both print and visual, some of which are owned by anti-nationals, anti-government organizations, and terrorists, have been utilized along with social media to spread disinformation. To make the security forces more effective, the Indian Government has allocated special powers through an act of Parliament. These powers are more than justified under the circumstances and the Indian Security Forces have maintained a very high sense of discipline and conducted their operations with restraint. This concerted effort to maintain peace and security in an unstable region is often depicted as being heavy handed in some international media. In contrast, human rights violations and terrorism in the region are not acknowledged as significant concerns by independent watchdogs. Actions by terrorists have included subversion, extortion, abduction, sabotage, violation of women, killing of family members of security forces, killing of tourists, destruction of schools and public property, use of improvised explosive devices (IEDs) and suicide attacks to cause casualties, random elimination of local civilians who do not follow their dictates, ethnic cleansing, attacks on seats of power, massacres in metropolitan cities, sedition, and defiance of the authority of the Government. With these issues to contend with, the Indian Security Forces are deployed in Kashmir with a mandate to stop the human rights violations by terrorists and to protect the Indian citizens from terrorism. It is to be understood that to enact peace in a very turbulent region, India's security forces are deployed not against the Kashmiri population, but in their defence, as a direct response to the terrorism and insurgency from Pakistan.

In an article published in the *Dawn* newspaper, Pakistani journalist, Maqbool Bhatti states that neither extremism nor Pakistan's nuclear arsenal will go away. Similar views are expressed by Shahzad Chaudhary, a retired Pakistan Air Force Officer and now an analyst. They assess that terrorism is here to stay and also suggest that there are enough reasons to reduce tensions with India. They advise this for Pakistan to become more stable, or else, Pakistan may implode or fall prey to radicalism. Despite these obvious realities, there seems to be a bankruptcy of rational thought in Pakistan's leadership about these dire possibilities. It could also be that radicals create a split in the Pakistan Army or that Islamists within the Army may provide terrorists with nuclear materials to make a dirty bomb, train them in nuclear technology, provide clandestine storage for these materials, and even provide them with a functional miniaturized nuclear device. In an impoverished population seeking daily survival and with rampant greed and radicalism prevalent, any such thing can happen. The erstwhile Al Qaeda leader, al-Zawahiri, had once evinced an interest in acquiring nuclear weapons. These are worrisome possibilities for the entire world. In fact, looking back over a few centuries, terrorists have done nothing noteworthy for humanity or contributed to the betterment of life. Their only contribution seems to be a spread of their beliefs, raising fear and animosity to gain control and usurp power, because of which even their own co-religionists and sects within are anti each other and have resorted to killing without any inhibitions. Any homegrown terrorists that exist today are mostly on Pakistan's payroll or are intolerant radicals.

Successive elections for the state assembly in J&K have proven that the mainstream population is democratic and desires to remain in the Indian Union. By a unanimous vote, the elected legislators in the state had accepted the accession of J&K to India in 1953. Those who had boycotted later elections have done so under the dictates of the Hurriyat or threats by terrorists under the direction of Pakistan. They have been left out of the democratic process at their own peril. In June 2020, Syed Shah Geelani resigned from the Hurriyat, and he died on 1 September 2021. The movement that he had built had degenerated into a proxy for Pakistan, an anti-political nihilist and corrupt faction incapable of its actual political purpose.

To pursue their nefarious ends, the terrorist groups from Pakistan have had access to increasingly sophisticated arms and ammunition, explosives, timers, communication devices, even drones and finances. All such munitions are provided by the ISI for use against civilian targets, Indian Security Forces, and state government installations. There are no rules of engagement or a hierarchical structure apparent. The terrorists operate in small mission-specific cells, which are not known to each other so that even if a member of the cell is captured, it does not jeopardize the larger organization. They are lightly armed, operate with stealth, and do not follow a predictable pattern. Terrorism experienced by the citizens of J&K, has in the past forced them to provide support to the terrorists because of fear. Those who did not support terrorists suffered reprisals and were punished ruthlessly. Terror does create a disproportionate effect on a vulnerable society. An effective intelligence grid has now been established by the Indian Security Forces to counter the methods used by terrorists. The aim of this grid is to prevent terrorist attacks and to keep the population safe from reprisals. Intelligence helps in identifying terrorists and reducing their effectiveness. The better the intelligence, the more effective and faster preventive measures can be undertaken. To improve upon intelligence-gathering, Indian authorities have been able to persuade misguided young men in Kashmir, those who had joined terrorist outfits, to surrender. Some of them voluntarily joined as informers, and some have been recruited by the local police. They have brought about positive results in targeting specific cells of terrorists. These means of gathering intelligence can be extended by recruiting undercover agents in every sizeable population center and community.

There are various technical methods that can be employed to gather intelligence in a terrorist environment. Interception and scrutiny of communication from hand-held cell phones, landlines, other communication systems, email, and social media are to be done in real time. Closed-circuit TV cameras can be deployed at certain vulnerable locations. Moles can be placed within terror groups to monitor Internet usage and report mala fide intentions. In terms of the counter-terrorism resolution, Number 1373 of the UNSC, India and friendly countries can share information and act against terrorist organizations. Under its provisions, financial assets and money transfers to terrorists can be monitored and even blocked, the supply of arms, ammunition, and other munitions can be intercepted, and their trans-border movement can also be prevented.

Terrorists unleashed by Pakistan had aimed to achieve domination of Kashmiri communities through an Islamist ideology and fear. This ideology is also practiced by ISIS, Taliban, Al Qaeda, TTP, the anti-India terror groups in Pakistan, and other fundamentalist groups, such as Boko Haram and Al Shabab in other regions of the world. A section of Pakistan's erudite people, such as the late Tarek Fatah, who was a Canadian journalist, had called their mother country a rogue state, and some others have gone to the extent of calling it a nation that is pathologically ill. These are some of the major indications of a conflicted nation. Within Pakistan's boundaries law enforcement agencies, lawyers, and the judiciary are frequently threatened if they fail to obey the diktats of the terrorists and of the Deep State.

Since gaining independence what has Pakistan achieved? It destabilized Afghanistan and installed the medieval Taliban government. Pakistan has also illegally retained and subjugated the part of J&K they occupy and have surrendered the Shaksgam Valley to China. Pakistan also generated a failed insurgency in the state of Punjab in India, generated terrorism and launched wars with India along with continuing its effort to create turmoil in the Indian union territory of J&K. Due to poor governance, Pakistan created conditions for East Pakistan to break away. Therefore, what Pakistan has achieved is, that it is an untrustworthy party in international relations that disregards agreements and treaties and follows its own irreverent agenda. It is a renter nation seeking free money from wherever on whatever pretext, to stay afloat. Pakistan is one of the countries that has keenly propagated the cult of terrorism in the world. With this sobering knowledge, further analysis is required to assess whether there are any prospects of peace between India and Pakistan, and between India and China. This is discussed in the next chapter.

CHAPTER 8

Intransigence and Reconciliation

Abrogation of Articles 370 and 35A in J&K

The solution to the problems that plague India-Pakistan relations does not lie in repeatedly bringing up the J&K issue in international forums or, for that matter, creating anarchy and radicalism in the Kashmir Valley. Pakistan continually adopts an anti-India stance on even perfunctory and inconsequential matters, thereby exacerbating animosity towards India. India, the larger nation, in its magnanimity has attempted on various occasions to discuss the Kashmir dispute with Pakistan along with other issues. This has been to no avail. With no real identity of its own, for Pakistan Kashmir has steadily become its rallying point and its raison d'être. A mercenary nation, Pakistan has compromised with China, by allowing the construction of the CPEC through Gilgit-Baltistan-POK and enabling its exploitation. Pakistan has no other option but to continue its efforts to raise the Kashmir issue for the purpose of obfuscating the fact that it illegally occupies a portion of the state. The population of the state of J&K has come to understand that remaining in India brings prosperity. Hypothetically, if separation of J&K from India were to occur, then they would most likely be drawn or forced into an embrace with Pakistan, an impoverished, radical, and unstable nation. Pakistan's support for terrorism and radicalism is regressive for Kashmiris and will not help in achieving a better future in the progressive modern world. Most residents of J&K – Hindus, Sikhs, Christians, Buddhists, nomads, and even Muslims – in most districts of the Kashmir Valley, Jammu division, and the union territory of Ladakh are not anti-India. The Indian population does not hold any malice towards the Kashmiris who now reside in various parts of the country. A small section of the Kashmiri population has been radicalized and follows the tenets of Wahabi Islam, which is propagated at the behest of Pakistan by JeI. This kind of Islam has attempted to overcome and change the culture of Kashmir, which is uniquely moderate and Sufi in nature. The adoption of radical Islam by a few has led to Muslim moderates, who desired to have a better life away from the threat of radicalism and terrorism, leaving the state of J&K to establish businesses and homes in other parts of India. A few have even migrated overseas.

Articles 370 and 35A had accorded a special status to the state of J&K. These articles were inserted in the Constitution of India on 14 May 1954 by an order signed by the then President of India, Doctor Rajendra Prasad. The Prime Minister of India at the time, Jawahar Lal Nehru, acquiesced to this, perhaps as a compromise with Sheikh Abdullah. Under the provision of these articles, J&K was to have its own constitution, its own judiciary, make its own laws, have its own flag, and decide who are citizens of the state. There was an entry permit required by non-Kashmiri citizens from the rest of India to visit the state. No Indian citizen from outside of J&K was allowed to buy, lease, or own property and set up business in the state. The people of J&K had the freedom to self-govern, they enjoyed internal autonomy except for finance, defence, foreign affairs and communications. This freedom did not serve to improve living conditions in the state, develop infrastructure, or improve the economy. It failed to meet the aspirations of the people in the state. The Modi Government made the decision to abrogate the provisions of Articles 370 and 35A, to remove the special status of the state of J&K.

There are valid reasons for the abrogation of the special status of J&K, and these merit some consideration. Over the years, people have continued to migrate from Pakistan, POK and Gilgit-Baltistan to J&K and to other parts of India. These people either left Pakistan, POK, and Gilgit-Baltistan voluntarily or because of communal strife. In J&K, the migrants total an estimated 750,000. Some of these migrants have moved to other parts of India. Most of this population has been kept stateless by successive state governments under the provisions of Articles 370 and 35A. This was because most of them were non-Muslims, and if they were recognized as state subjects, it would impact the official demography of J&K. These individuals were not allowed to buy property and not allowed to vote because they were denied citizenship in the state. In contrast to this, the Rohingya, who illegally migrated from Myanmar, some reached the state, crossing the entire expanse of India. They had set up camps and shanties in proximity to sensitive Indian Armed Forces establishments. This action by Rohingya, a desperate measure after being evicted from their homes in Myanmar, has not gone unnoticed. The Rohingya refugees, if not surveilled may exacerbate internal security problems. The demography in the Jammu Division has also been undergoing a steady and subtle change. In this area, large tracts of government land, earlier owned by the rulers of J&K, now under state government control, have been allotted to Muslims from other parts of the state. This action by elected governments in the state needed no justification, as there was no embargo for citizens from one part of the state to own properties in other areas of the state, or for that matter, in the whole of India. This had been going on for decades in the state, and the central governments in succession either did not take notice of this or ignored it, having left matters of governance to their own elected politicians. In Ladakh too, the Muslim population from other parts of the state has taken advantage of the matriarchal nature of the Buddhist Ladakhi society.

Another major issue relates to the formation of elected government in J&K. The mainstream politicians that headed successive governments in J&K belong to the Kashmir Valley. No political leader, especially from the Jammu and Ladakh divisions, ever had the majority support of elected members in the State Assembly to head a government. This was likely due to the delimitation of seats in the state that led to Kashmir Valley having 44 seats, the largest number, the Jammu region 37 seats, Ladakh only had four seats, and 24 had been reserved for POK and Gilgit-Baltistan in the legislature. This delimitation required revision as per provisions of the Constitution of India which lays down that delimitation be carried out every ten years. The elected government in the state had even ignored a 2010 ruling by the Supreme Court of India that a delimitation commission be set up for the state as it had become overdue.

Despite having held political power for long periods in the state, and despite its unique special status, as mentioned above, the elected politicians did not serve the population of the state. They failed to provide efficient, competent and transparent administration and allowed corrupt practices and irregularities to prevail. They allowed terrorism to take hold and did not take decisive action against the brutal acts of ethnic cleansing in the Kashmir valley. Infiltration by terrorists from Pakistan increased under their watch and major anti-national activities were also not prevented. In certain parts of the state, the flag of ISIS and Pakistan was flown in place of the state flag and the national flag of India. In some instances, it is believed that politicians may have sought covert support from terrorists, including those who took up arms against their own country and the Indian Constitution, for political expediency. The welfare and aspirations of migrants from Pakistan, POK, Gilgit-Baltistan and nomads in the state was neglected. A report published in the *Economic Times*, a daily newspaper in India, alleged that the political leaders of J&K exploited valley politics for personal gains. The people in the state were disillusioned with this kind of poor governance and corruption, which existed at all levels. Taking advantage of the deteriorating law and order situation, Pakistan exacerbated radicalism and terrorism, and a separatist movement was reborn in the Kashmir Valley. Those seeking 'Aazadi' were some of the disaffected youth and radical Islamists. Politicians, even with a political mandate and the security forces at their disposal, allowed matters to drift and did not curb the violence and insurgency. The APHC was becoming more vocal and seditious, declaring that because they were Muslims, they were Pakistanis. Good governance was required to be ushered into the state.

In 2019, Narendra Modi took office for a second term as Prime Minister of India. His party, the BJP, had established the majority government at the center, and it succeeded in winning a large number of seats in the State Legislature in J&K. In the state elections, some seats were also won by the National Conference, the People's Democratic Party (PDP), and the Congress. Despite a divided electorate in the State, the BJP and the PDP did cobble together a coalition government. This was the first coalition government in the state's history of a Hindu nationalist party and a Muslim party. The central government was observing the developments in J&K and with inputs from the elected members of the State Legislature, they perceived the reality of the situation. The prevalent terrorism, insecurity in the minds of the people, and the call for 'Aazadi' in the Kashmir Valley were on the rise. The killing of 40 CRPF personnel by the Pakistani terror group JeM in the Pulwama district on 14 February 2019 was the final straw. This was an outrage which created anguish in the minds of the entire Indian population. A riposte was carried out by India as described earlier. The BJP, in their re-election manifesto, had stated that the special status accorded to J&K would be revoked. In the rest of India, there was also a strong movement questioning why the state of J&K still retained its special status. With a strong majority in the Indian Parliament, Prime Minister Modi had the mandate to revoke Articles 370 and 35A. Both houses of the Indian Parliament approved the abrogation of these articles and on 23 December 2023, the Supreme Court of India upheld the revoking of Articles 370 and 35A from the Constitution of India stating that these were temporary provisions, and the President of India could revoke them. At the time of revocation of the special status, the state was placed under curfew, and all telecommunications within and from outside the state were blocked by Indian authorities as a precautionary measure. At certain times and in certain areas, the curfew was relaxed. The aim of doing away with the special status of the state was to eradicate sedition and terrorism, provide security to the people, enhance employment opportunities, promote sustainable business development, and improve overall economic conditions in the state.

It should be noted that in the late eighties and early nineties a coalition of political parties formed the central government in India. These were weak partnerships with huge political shortcomings. Political rivalry created conditions for parochial politics and a lack of focus on national interests. At the time when the ethnic cleansing of Hindus took place in the Kashmir Valley, there were mass agitations ongoing in India over reservations for minorities. The state of Punjab had also been in turmoil as it recovered from the insurgency generated by Pakistan. Indian troops were deployed in Sri Lanka as part of the Peace Keeping Force. These complicated conditions in India, coupled with an ineffectual central government had enabled Pakistan's unchecked foray into terrorism in Kashmir and it also allowed radicals to carry out ethnic cleansing of Kashmiri Pandits in the valley. The revoking of Articles 370 and 35A could only be done by a strong, majority government at the center with a will to redress the situation. This change in the status of the state was not immediately accepted by all sections of the population. It did lead to an immediate cessation of hostilities from the Islamists and terrorists in Kashmir. However, it was a resolute step to shake up the status quo and time will tell, about its success in the long term.

The lockdown imposed in the state of J&K after the abrogation of the two articles led to much debate internationally. Without a clear understanding of the circumstances that resulted in the abrogation of Articles 370 and 35A, it was alleged that the human rights of Kashmiris were being violated. At that time, a British Labour Party Member of Parliament (MP), Debbie Abrahams, spoke of human rights violations by India in Kashmir. According to reports in Indian media, Pakistan's ISI interacts with Raja Najbat Hussain, who is the chairman of the J&K self-determination movement in the UK. Hussain, who is on the payroll of the ISI, used his connections with UK MPs, including Abrahams and Jeremy Corbyn, the erstwhile leader of the opposition and a Labour Party MP, to issue statements that these human rights violations should be investigated. There was no attempt to verify the ground realities when these allegations were levelled. The obvious double standards are blatantly troublesome. When actual human rights violations were being committed in the Kashmir Valley and the Kashmiri Pandit community was enduring brutal ethnic cleansing in which hundreds were killed, these events did nor elicit a similar international hue and cry. The current Prime Minister of the UK, Keir Starmer, has demonstrated a more nuanced understanding of the Kashmir issue. He emphasized during a meeting with the Indian diaspora that Kashmir is a bilateral issue and should be resolved peacefully by both neighbours.

The abrogation of Articles 370 and 35A gives J&K a fresh start. Curbs of various kinds imposed in the Kashmir Valley and the Jammu division had been done away with. Mobile phone communications utilizing satellite networks and broadband connections on the Internet have been restored, and landlines are now completely functional. Once these changes were enacted, the Indian Government allowed a tour of Kashmir to two groups of diplomats in embassies or high commissions in Delhi. This was an opportunity for independent observers to interact with the local population and assess the situation in Kashmir firsthand. Chairman of the Kashmir Peace Council, Mohammad Ashraf, has commented that the revocation of Articles 370 and 35A will usher in a new era as it does away with the dynastic-dominated governance that had held power in the state. While in power, these politicians had done very little for the people in the state. Ashraf stated that this new status for J&K would reduce the gun culture and bring in development, investment, and employment. That is what people in the state desire. Ashraf was critical of Pakistan for having occupied the areas of J&K that it continues to hold and terms it illegal. He was supportive of the action taken by the Government of India to revoke the said articles from the Indian Constitution. He further stated that this is the first time that Indian leaders have come forward to embrace the Kashmiri population and that, slowly but steadily, the benefits will start to accrue for the people. He expressed a strong belief that the government would do what the youth of Kashmir wanted. Ashraf was asked in a news program that Article 370 had provided a distinct identity to the people of Kashmiri and if the abrogation of this Article had taken away that identity. He stated that there was no other identity that a Kashmiri has except that he/she is an Indian, and that is what each Kashmiri must accept. He said that the entire population had been feeling distressed and insecure, and their aspirations were not being met. This change was necessary as it is for the better.

The reaction from Pakistan on the abrogation of Articles 370 and 35A had predictably been vociferous and had shown some amount of desperation. In the wake of this legislative change in India, the Pakistan Army held a conference of corps commanders, the real power brokers in their country, to discuss what action should be taken by Pakistan and whether Pakistan should go to war with India. After holding this emergency conference, the senior officers concluded that there would be no result forthcoming from going to war with India. Clearly, and very worryingly, it appears that Pakistan would contemplate going to war with India even when India undertakes administrative measures within its own territory. The rhetoric that has been articulated by the leadership in Pakistan shows that they are unlikely to come to terms with changes instituted by the Government of India. Imran Khan, the Pakistan Prime Minister at that time, called for a solidarity agitation on 30 August 2019, exhorting people in his country to turn out in strength to show their support for the Kashmiri population. This event was not a success due to a low turnout. China also objected to this administrative action by India in tandem with Pakistan. With China's sponsorship, Pakistan was able to have a session of the UNSC convened to discuss the actions by India in the state of J&K. The reaction of the UNSC turned out to be muted as it did not even take the minimum step of issuing a statement after the meeting on Kashmir. The only advice that came out of the meeting was that it was an internal matter of India and that both countries should resolve the issue through dialogue. In 2017, when Pakistan changed the status of Northern Areas, renaming them as Gilgit-Baltistan and bringing the area directly under their central government, there was little reaction from India. If older maps of Pakistan and those printed on their postage stamps of the fifties are examined, these do not show any part of J&K within their country. Pakistan's claim on J&K is a convenient ploy with no historical precedence.

If India forcefully brings up the illegal occupation of POK and Gilgit-Baltistan in international forums and makes the world community aware of the ongoing proxy war, it could cause further damage to Pakistan's agenda. This is not to say that India seeks external intervention. Democracy has prevailed in J&K ever since its accession to India in 1947. A delimitation commission was appointed for four states where it was due, including the union territory of J&K, to ensure that the delineation of constituencies was fair in all these regions. This commission had completed the task and submitted its report on 20 May 2022. There was a delay due to the COVID-19 pandemic. As a result of this commission, Jammu Division has been awarded an increase of 6 seats, Kashmir Valley 1 and 5 seats have been increased for nominees from tribals and others. Citizenship for people who migrated from Pakistan/POK and Gilgit-Baltistan, who reside in the state and were so far stateless, is also being resolved. The screening of the Rohingyas from Myanmar will take some additional time and effort to resolve. A census of Kashmiri pandits evicted from the Kashmir Valley was conducted and they participated in the elections for the legislative assembly in 2024. The central government, under the aegis of the Election Commission of India conducted elections in J&K in September-October 2024 and people of the state participated with great enthusiasm. This is a clear indication that the population in the union territory respects democracy and has accepted their new status. Elections for District Development Councils had been conducted in 2020 in the 20 districts that comprise the union territory of J&K. These elections have ushered in democracy in the union territory, which is a very positive change.

One of the reasons why restrictions were imposed on mobile phone communication and Internet usage in J&K, was that terrorists prevailed by utilizing social media to generate violence. They assembled stone throwers at short notice, conveyed instructions for targeting security forces and civilian targets, reorganized terrorist cells, and allocated missions to them. They even threatened children to dissuade them from attending school. Despite these threats, children undertook school board examinations in March 2020 and the Kashmir Valley has remained calm after the state was reorganized into two union territories. Farmers in the state are being compensated adequately for their produce, and the produce is distributed and marketed to the rest of the country. There are other measures being undertaken under the aegis of the government for building confidence in the population. During the COVID-19 pandemic, Indian security forces were a major support to counter the surge in infections as they provided door to door assistance, distributed personal protective equipment, vaccinated the population, and provided essential medicines and daily needs. Medical teams carried out vaccinations in remote villages. In some areas, they travelled on foot to reach citizens in far-flung areas. This has been appreciated by the people of Kashmir. There seems to be growing cooperation from the population to expose terrorists and separatists and to assist in unravelling their organizations. Insurgency has seen a downturn in the Kashmir Valley.

The democratic governance in the union territory of J&K indicates the central government's goodwill towards the population in the union territory. Terrorist threats to the electorate from participating in the elections were rendered unsuccessful and the election commission of India conducted elections for the legislative assembly in an impartial manner in J&K. Prior to this, to accurately achieve delimitation, the National Register of Citizens (NRC) was brought up to date in the entire country including in Ladakh and J&K. In this process, there was a need to carry out a census of Kashmiri Pandits, who had been evicted from their homes in the Kashmir Valley. This includes those living in refugee camps in the Jammu division and those who have moved out of J&K and resettled in other parts of India. Even their children born after their ethnic cleansing from 1989 onwards needed to be included in the rolls of citizens. All these actions were painstaking and a slow process which was compounded by the spread of the Corona virus and China's hostilities in Eastern Ladakh. With the completion of the population survey, the citizens of India living in the union territories of J&K and Ladakh were accounted for. The delimitation of seats had been done. The free and fair elections conducted in J&K provided opportunities for the youth to take on the political mantle. The National Conference and Indian National Congress have secured a majority of seats in the legislative assembly. An elected government has been formed in the union territory of J&K with Omar Abdullah as the Chief Minister.

With a series of resolute and decisive actions the government of India had indicated that it will not permit terrorism and separatism to surface again in J&K or, for that matter, in any part of the country. Previously, intelligence estimates had suggested that terrorism would revive in the summer of 2020. This did not come to pass. Even the stone throwers and mercenary disruptive mobs have disappeared from Kashmir Valley. There are no longer any curbs on civil liberties and all schools, colleges, and universities, which had been closed temporarily due to the pandemic, opened on 6 August 2020 and are functioning since then. The Government of India ensured that the state was peaceful before conducting the legislative assembly elections. This allowed for a true representation of the will of the people. The democratic election facilitated an elected government to be installed in J&K. Having failed to create a misperception of India's actions, Pakistan again attempted to rake up the issue of human rights in Kashmir. As highlighted before, Pakistan coerced foreign media and politicians to voice concerns about human rights and civil liberty violations by the security forces deployed in the Kashmir Valley. These largely ill-conceived and uninformed opinions were initiated by Amnesty International employees of Pakistani origin and failed to gain any traction. China also convened a second meeting of the UNSC after the state of J&K became two union territories. This effort to cause disruption also was futile. As before, the UNSC advised that it was India's internal matter and stressed the importance of the Shimla Agreement.

As explained, there is a change in the status quo in J&K, and Pakistan's influence has diminished in the dynamic. However, disaffection and frustration in Kashmir and Pakistani-sponsored terrorism are related but independent variables that may continue to exist for some more time. The latter is being eliminated by various means, including with the support of the local population. The amelioration of disaffection requires major efforts and the passage of time. Proper governance, enforcement of the law of the land, security of citizens, fair transactions, elimination of corruption, education and development of skills suitable for employment are a few measures that are being undertaken. The elected government in the union territory has the mandate to work on these aspects. Opportunities for employment are being created with the allocation of government resources and efforts continue to enable a just and safe society. Additional funds have been provided to the union territories of J&K and Ladakh for fast-tracking development and improving infrastructure. Private enterprise is being encouraged in the union territories. Businesses and industries, as they develop progressively, will create job opportunities and bring prosperity. The Home Minister of India has suggested that full statehood can be restored to J&K once the situation is conducive. The Prime Minister of India held a meeting with mainstream politicians from J&K in June 2021 to share his vision for the future and to listen to their suggestions. Demands for the restoration of Articles 370 and 35A were raised by a few politicians. With no basis, these demands smack of petty politics and self-interest. The people of the union territory of J&K desired security, stability and progress in their lives, should hopefully become a reality. The decision by the Supreme Court of India to validate revoking these articles implies that there was no permanence to these articles in the Constitution and doing away with these articles was not illegal. With this change, the J&K region is now at par with the rest of the states and union territories of India. Pakistan has of course retained its inimical stance and asserted that since J&K is a disputed territory, the ruling by the Supreme Court of India is of no consequence.

In the past, tourism, which had been a major industry in J&K and Ladakh, had suffered and had virtually come to a standstill because of more than a decade of terrorism in J&K. Countries noted the threat to tourists and issued advisories to their citizens to avoid travelling to J&K. Prior to the insurgency and threat of terrorism, tourism was a major source of income for the population and visitors traveled from afar to enjoy the pristine natural beauty in Kashmir and Ladakh, which is comparable to the best in the world. Many positive developments have made tourism a vibrant sector in J&K once again. Various religious destinations that are popular with travelers to this region including the Hazratbal Mosque in Srinagar, where the hair of Prophet Muhammad's beard is preserved, the Vaishno Devi Temple, the Amarnath caves and other ancient Hindu temples. Thousands of pilgrims from India and abroad now visit these shrines each year. The hospitality industry, which had shrunk or shut down because of terrorism and the COVID-19 pandemic is now being revived and there is considerable scope for developing and enhancing infrastructure for adventure sports, water sports, high-altitude tours, mountaineering, and hiking. A train service was inaugurated in the Kashmir Valley in 2004, which was a very expensive venture in this mountainous region. India has one of the world's largest rail networks and engineers here are skilled at this tricky construction. A new train line has been extended from Udhampur to Banihal, which is the existing railhead in the Kashmir Valley. This has linked Baramulla in the Kashmir Valley to New Delhi. This again is a remarkable achievement.

With travel and tourism flourishing, all major domestic airlines have daily flights to Srinagar, Jammu, Kargil, and Leh. The Srinagar-Zoji La-Kargil-Leh national highway, which is blocked in winter due to excessive snow and avalanche hazards, is being converted to an all-weather road. The alternate road link, open in summer months only, connecting Manali in Himachal Pradesh to Leh through Rohtang, Baralachla, and Taglangla passes, is also to be made all-weather by the deployment of adequate resources and construction of tunnels and bridges. There is a third road axis under development from Manali, Rohtang Pass to Darcha, Padam, through Zanskar, to Nimu, and Leh. A nine km long tunnel under the Rohtang Pass, which is heavily snowbound in winter, has been inaugurated. The Governor's rule in J&K had fast-tracked development as envisaged. Foreign and Indian tourism and sports companies are encouraged to set up operations in J&K

and Ladakh. In Ladakh, polo and ice hockey are played and are becoming popular. White water rafting and other adventure sports are now available to visitors to Ladakh as well. Movie halls are open in J&K after many years. The Kashmiri handicraft industry, famous for its unique materials and crafts, is getting a boost as its products are being marketed countrywide, showcased abroad and exported. All these developments are generating many business and employment opportunities. Tourism in the area has exceeded all expectations in 2022-2924. This self-imposed restriction of not targeting tourists has come undone with the Pahalgam killing of 26 civilians on 22 April 2025. Whether tourists will still continue to visit Kashmir and how will the tourism and other ancillary industries be affected only time will tell. The start of the pilgrimage to Amarnath, cavesthrough Pahalgam and Baltal in large numbers has brought cheer to the local population and the tourists are displaying happiness in visiting Kashmir. These are positive indicators that the tourism industry will revive in J&K

Similar to the rest of India, J&K has an up-to-date and modern education system offering various disciplines and subjects. Despite living in a disturbed area for many years due to Pakistani terrorism, Kashmiri youth have continued to achieve higher literacy. And during the period of unrest, economic growth and employment have been considerably better in this region in comparison to Pakistan as a whole. As business, industry, and tourism develop, there is a need to train the youth, including women, in various professional skills, to facilitate employment at all levels of business. Industrial Training Institutes are being revitalized, and new ones are being established. As reported in Indian media, there is a collaboration between the J&K Entrepreneurship Development Institute and the Entrepreneurship Development Institute of India, Ahmedabad. These institutions are intended to train 10,000 youth in batches to help them acquire suitable skills to join and sustain businesses and facilitate access to starter finances. Literacy, training and scientific knowledge will continue to promote careers.

The recent pace of development and progress in every aspect of life in J&K is quite heartening. There are seven new industrial estates being set up in the Kashmir Valley. Proposals to set up industrial units amounting to Rs 81122 crores have been received from industrial houses in India and abroad. Approximately 2250 acres of land have been allotted for setting up industrial parks. EMAAR, a major investor from Dubai plans to establish health care projects and construct a mega mall on the outskirts of Srinagar. About a thousand entrepreneurs have started businesses with small, micro and medium enterprises. This is just the start of the development process. With these multi-faceted developments and ease of doing business it is likely that the union territories of J&K and Ladakh will become business and tourist hubs. It is now up to the elected government in J&K to give further impetus to the development that has been ongoing under President's rule in J&K. Given this rapid progress begs the questions: Why would the people of J&K desire to join Pakistan? What does Pakistan have to offer them? Why should the local population allow terrorists to carry out dastardly acts such as the one in Pahalgam that will likely have an adverse impact on business and industry?

Is Peace Possible?

Indian diplomacy has been very effective at negating the anti-India propaganda periodically unleashed by Pakistan. After the short war in May2025, Pakistan has managed to disturb the status quo and has somehow garnered support from quite a few countries in the world. They are playing the victim stating that their country had nothing to do with the terrorist attack at Pahalgam. The global debate on apportioning blame has definitely shifted in India's favour. The Resistance Force, which is an affiliate of the LET, had initially claimed responsibility for the attack, later reneged from it stating that their web site had been hacked and the admission was inserted onto their website. Despite this there has been some focus on bringing the perpetrators to justice. Three of them have been identified. India has acted carefully after due preparation to strike at the leadership of the terror groups in response to the terror attacks. Continued diplomacy and sustained efforts will ensure that Pakistan is back in the grey list of the FATF. Pakistan has been loyal to the US in assisting in their ops and ventures in Afghanistan, joining alliances such as CENTO and SEATO and has made China their main patron through its nuclear cooperation, common foreign policy and CPEC. The US and China are able to influence opinions in many nations around the world. It appears that the Kashmir issue has once again received unprecedented recognition and some nations are once again hyphenating India and Pakistan together. The presence of a Turkish submarine in Karachi harbour during this short war is itself significant. The targeting of thirteen air force bases inside Pakistan, especially the Nur Khan air base, near Rawalpindi has sent strong signals to Pakistan that India can attack any targets of its choosing it deems fit in any future engagement. If Pakistan had continued with the ops there may have been very significant degradation of their air force and other military assets. New Delhi may then have been compelled to strike deeper into Pakistan including on sites of political and military significance. Better sense prevailed and it was the DGMO from Pakistan Army who sought the ceasefire which came into effect on 11 May 2025.More on this subject is discussed later.

As far as India is concerned, the reorganization of the state of J&K into two union territories, J&K and Ladakh, had become essential. This was a move to prevent and defeat foreign terrorists infiltrating J&K and to stop the utilization of modern communication and social media to conduct propaganda and disruptive terrorist ops. Active engagement from the local authorities and oversight from the Indian Government remain in place. The aim for India is to denigrate and defeat the cult of terrorism, and clearly highlight that all the legislative actions taken are to preserve the sovereignty and integrity of the country and to uplift the population of J&K. These actions will ultimately serve to strengthen democracy and maintain India's sovereignty. Any disaffection that may still being felt by the population is being mitigated by measures taken in consultation with the union territory of J&K. The positive developments that are occurring in the state have helped to eliminate any misgivings about the status of this region as an integral part of India.

India's key role during the COVID-19 pandemic is note-worthy. This pandemic created a crisis in the whole world, and India was no exception. As infection spiked uncontrollably, there was initially a paucity of medical resources and limited availability of vaccines to cope with the sudden massive upsurge. An initiative taken by India in the initial stages to counter the spread of the virus was noteworthy and is pertinent to India-Pakistan relations. To coordinate the anti-pandemic measures in the SAARC region, India had organized a virtual meeting of heads of government through video conferencing on 14 March 2020. All heads of government except Pakistan's Prime Minister, Imran Khan attended the conference. He deputed a junior minister to join the conference. The aim of the conference was to set up a COVID-19 emergency fund, create a common research program to tackle epidemics, share knowledge, capacity, and resources, and evolve a common strategy to deal with the pandemic. It was in this spirit that India had called the conference. Pakistan's junior minister, speaking at the conference, raised the Kashmir issue, asking India to lift the lockdown in the state. This shows how churlish and petty Pakistan can be about maintaining their single-point agenda, even when there are bigger issues at hand. The pandemic was taking a toll on humanity worldwide and the other heads of state and Prime Minister Modi ignored the petulant comments of the junior minister from Pakistan. The attending heads of state made specific requests to India for assisting their countries in combating the Corona virus. India, as is well known, was successful in developing its own Corona virus vaccines. Being the largest manufacturer of vaccines in the world, India was able to meet the requirements of SAARC nations for vaccines and personal protection equipment. Pakistan was not included in this effort. Vaccines and other medicines were also provided to countries that desired to source them from India. The foreign minister of Nepal was in New Delhi in January 2021, requesting vaccines for his country. Afghanistan had received 6 million doses of the Astra Zeneca vaccine made by the Serum Institute of India. Some 87 countries were provided vaccines manufactured in India free of cost. At a time when the world was facing dire circumstances, an opportunity existed for Pakistan, through its Prime Minister Imran Khan, to display solidarity with the efforts to deal with the pandemic. Instead, Imran Khan boasted of training 10,000 terrorists to fight in Kashmir. Rather than request India for the vaccines, Pakistan reached out to the WHO to supply them under the COVAX program. Ironically, Pakistan could possibly have received Indian-made vaccines routed through the WHO. The support provided by the Indian security forces to the entire population of Kashmir countered the absurd point raised by the Pakistani junior Health Minister in the video conference. It seems Pakistan cannot be a positive contributor even in a global crisis and it is evident that the animosity with India is very unproductive for Pakistan. This friction and mindless belligerence have not been and will not be of any political, diplomatic, financial, or territorial benefit.

While Pakistan languishes in a self-made morass, India is participating in various global forums to address the problems facing the world at large. India continues to contribute to stopping environmental degradation, reducing the effects of global warming, the resultant climate change, and contending with economic inequalities. Further, it contributes to ending conflicts, participates in peacekeeping in conflict zones, and assists in mitigating the destruction caused by natural disasters. India will continue to fight the scourge of terrorism under the provisions of the UN resolutions. The UN embodies the collective will of the nations of the world to deal with problems and crisis situations. It needs to be understood that the UNSC was created to deliberate and take decisions on preventing wars, mediate in case of outbreak of war, disarmament and other situations referred to it. At the time of its creation, the UN had 51 members, and the UNSC had five permanent members with veto powers and six more elected members. The membership of the UN has grown to 193, whereas the UNSC remains as it was 78 years ago. There are many nations who aspire to become permanent members of this council. A two-thirds majority of the members of the general assembly, which translates to 129 votes, is required to achieve any reforms to the UN council. The reform would also need to be ratified by five permanent members of the security council. To realize its full potential internationally, India has made a bid to become a permanent member of the UNSC. India has already received the support of the US, having been endorsed by President Obama during his visit to India in November 2010, by France, and Russia as a permanent of the UNSC. It needs to convince the remaining two permanent members of this organization to receive their endorsement. At present, there is also a major stumbling block to the reform of the UNSC by the African Union. This Union, comprising 54 members of the general assembly, are opposed to the reform. Their condition is that Africa should be given two permanent seats in the UNSC. If India desires to become a permanent member of the UNSC, it must resort to considerable and consistent international diplomacy. This is necessary to convince a maximum number of members and groups within the UN General Assembly of the contributions that India is making towards conflict avoidance, resolution, and so on to get their support. Among the current lot of permanent members, China may still not endorse India for membership of the UNSC. It may want to seek some advantages in relation to CPEC/BRI and over the disputed LAC/IB with India, or it may not support India at all. The UK will require convincing of its own even though it is becoming favourable towards India. This is discernable from debates in the UK Parliament and from statements of their Prime Minister. In the elections held for temporary membership of the UNSC in June 2020, India was elected as a member, obtaining 184 votes out of 193. This large percentage of favourable votes showed India's acceptability in the UNSC. This was also mentioned by Khawaja Asif, a former minister of Pakistan, during a debate in the parliament of his country.

India has now positioned itself centre-stage in the global discourse. It has been proven that India is ready to share responsibility in the global system. India taking on the responsibility of the chairmanship of the G20 in 2022 is an example of its accepted status. The successful conduct of the G20 summit in September 2023 by India bears testimony to its elevated status in world forums. Some analysts have assessed that the UN must change with the times. If the UN does not reform, then forums such as G7, G20, BRICS, SCO and formal treaty organizations such as NATO may arrogate powers to themselves. Today, the G20 is the major macroeconomic forum in the world. The African Union is now a member of this forum.

India is in a strong position to foster closer relations with its neighbours in the SAARC region and to assist in their development. These countries are Afghanistan, Bangladesh, Bhutan, Maldives, Nepal, Pakistan, and Sri Lanka. Bangladesh has adopted an anti-India stance after their Prime Minster Sheikh Haseena was forced to flee the country and seek refuge in India. Globally, nations that traditionally were enemies, such as France and Germany, are now allies. Nations are not destined to be enemies forever if each country considers reasons for developing better relations in today's world. This is an opportunity for India to ensure that the SAARC countries remain friendly through diplomacy, financial aid and other means. A case in point is the indirect economic assistance provided to Sri Lanka. India has taken measures to alleviate Sri Lanka's economic problems by offering them $4 billion in the form of currency swaps, loan deferrals, and lines of credit. Following this, Sri Lanka was able to negotiate its debt restructuring with the EXIM Bank of China, paving the way for the IMF to assist this island nation with a bailout package. After the visit of President Mohammed Muizzu of Maldives in October 2024, India gave $1.4 billion aid to alleviate their debt burden with China. Most countries are realizing India's enhanced global stature and that India desires to extend a hand of friendship. The invitation by Canada to Prime Minister Modi for the G7 summit in Alberta from 17-19 June 2025 shows the importance of India in world affairs. This facilitated Modi to restore the tenuous relationship with the host country, brief G7 leaders on the reasons for India to launch Op Sindoor and discuss matters of common interest. In South Asia, however, domestic insecurity is intensified due to the meddling of one or more neighbours.[1] This refers to the India-Pakistan relations, the Afghanistan conundrum, the security threat from China, and perhaps, the Big Brother syndrome. Insecurity is also created by some select countries who manipulate events and politics, and who do not want to see India rise and become a regional power.

Pakistan will continue its unrelenting hostilities with India till Pakistanis and their deep state stop believing that they can persist in bleeding India

1. *Shooting for a Century: The India-Pakistan Conundrum* by Stephen Cohen

through a thousand cuts. This rivalry has only served to elevate the role of their Army and undermine civil society. Ideologically motivated hardliners in the Pakistan Army such as Lt Gen Hamid Gul, who headed the Military Intelligence and the ISI, have led the charge. After retiring from Army service, he declared that he would expect his country not to be based on Islam but then supported Pakistan's allegiance to the Taliban and the Haqqani Network. There are many other senior officers with radical views. Gen Qamar Bajwa, Pakistan's previous COAS, has spoken publicly of his desire to eliminate the embrace of extremist ideology.[2] Whether this succeeds is questionable.

Pakistan's Persistently Inimical Policy

The growing differential of power between India and Pakistan perhaps causes greater insecurity for Pakistan. In its bid to counter India, Pakistan indulges in wasteful expenditure while its population remains mired in poverty and lacks reform. Problems are compounded by the uneducated or partially educated youth from madrasas with radical motivations and no avenues or skills for employment except to work as labour, unskilled artisans or become jihadis. Many leaders of terrorist groups that nurture madrasas, continue to preach vitriolic hatred against other nations, especially India. Terrorists who were trained in Pakistan, who had joined the mujahideen in the war against Soviet occupation of Afghanistan and who returned to their home countries had followed this cult of violence. This pattern has thus spread far and wide in the world. Pakistan, in a way is exhausting itself, as imposing terror does very little to correct the economic and military imbalance vis-à-vis India. If the ISI loses control over the terror groups it supports, these rebel outfits may perpetrate their own random attacks on India, which will have grave implications. An example of this incendiary rhetoric is a statement by the LeT in June 2020, threatening to blow up the Taj Mahal Hotel in Mumbai once again. The creation of The Resistance Force is yet another means to wage the proxy war against India.

To contend with terrorism, India has to undertake whatever measures necessary to do so. Enhancing its intelligence capabilities within Pakistan, maintaining surveillance over terrorist groups and infiltrate them, putting

---

2. 'Pakistan Army is so insecure that any remark on it sends it into a tizzy', an article by Husain Haqqani, Director for South and Central Asia at the Hudson Institute, Washington DC

a further economic squeeze on Pakistan and a pro-active diplomacy are essentials. The major surprise has been that the Taliban government in Afghanistan has come to the support of India in *Op Sindoor.* This could be that Afghanistan is connected to India through history and in civilization. India has all along continued to support the people of Afghanistan even after the Taliban takeover in their country. These links if developed further will be useful in India's strategy against Pakistan. India has to try and get Pakistan on the grey list if not the black list of the FATF.

Going back in time a little, in an assessment given by GOC HQ XV Corps in Srinagar, in February 2020, while addressing the visiting diplomats and the Press Trust of India, he had stated that the Pakistani launch pads in POK are at full strength of terrorists waiting to be infiltrated across the LOC into J&K and that they had been trained and given weapons and other munitions. Pakistan has also made a few attempts to send weapons and drugs to terrorist cells controlled by ISI inside India using drones and balloons. Intelligence estimates in September 2023 indicated that there were more than a dozen well-dispersed launch pads across the LOC that had terrorists awaiting induction into J&K. *Op Sindoor,* launched by India and diplomacy connected to it are indicative of growing animosity between India and Pakistan. Is the latter amenable to change course in its relationship with India? This remains an open question.

General Bajwa, the previous COAS, had been given an extension in service for three years, and he retired in November 2022. In December 2020, he had remarked that the Kashmir issue must be resolved with India in a dignified manner. He further stated that there is a need to bury the past and move on to unlock the full potential of South Asia and Central Asia. He, perhaps, had a change in his thinking and concluded that the sub-conventional war against India was unlikely to achieve its strategic objectives. This was, perhaps, an opinion that was not acceptable to then Prime Minister Imran Khan. The latter, for political expediency, had started leaning towards the radical anti-India elements for support. Imran Khan took the decision to not to resume trade with India. He had suspended the two-way trade after the abrogation of articles 370 and 35A by the government of India. It is well known that the civilian leadership in Pakistan must have the backing of their Army to initiate a peace dialogue with India. With tensions rising, a conciliatory move came about when the DGMOs of both Indian Army and Pakistan Army issued a joint statement agreeing to strict observance of all agreements and ceasefire along the LOC with effect from 24/25 February 2021. This had brought about calm that India had desired all along in the trans-LOC region. The ceasefire did not hold and trans LOC firing was resorted to by Pakistan together with the deadly terror attack on 22 April 2025. A ceasefire was once again asked for by the DGMO of Pakistan Army on 10 May 2025 that suspended the trans-border firing. The DGMOs agreeing to a stoppage of firing does not determine policy, this will be done by the political leadership.

It can be seen that India has been an unwarranted victim of terror attacks and infiltration and has been caught in undesirable conflicts with China and Pakistan. The ceasefire along the LOC, that has been extended for a month gives time to formulate policy and further direction after examining various options. The successor to Imran Khan, Shahbaz Sharif, as the interim Prime Minister, has attempted a somewhat conciliatory approach towards India. His statement to the media in Dubai spoke of lessons that Pakistan had learnt. To quote, 'We have fought three wars with India, and it only brought misery, poverty, and unemployment for the people. My message to the Indian leadership and Prime Minister Narendra Modi is that let us sit down at the table and have serious and sincere talks to resolve burning issues like Kashmir.' Sharif did not miss the opportunity to mention Kashmir as the 'burning issue' and ignored the need to resume bilateral trade and address economic issues. He also mentioned that the UAE can play a part as a facilitator. This statement underscores his lack of sincerity. Did he attempt to deliberately ignore that negotiations between India and his country are subject to the provisions of the Shimla Agreement? Sharif's office further added that no talks could be held until India reversed its illegal action of 5 August 2020, the day on which the Indian Government abrogated the special status of J&K. With India, it is pretty much the same stalemate. An economy in crisis could be reason enough for Pakistani politicians to have a dialogue with India. Learning from nations such as Singapore and those devastated in the second world war, Pakistan could choose a path of progress and pursue economic prosperity. Japan and Germany are also examples of nations who have experienced a progressive turnaround. Pakistan, as stated earlier has the sympathy of other major nations who are scared that nuclear Pakistan may fail. There are some obvious and simple steps that Pakistan could begin with. The international community needs Pakistan to implement the promises made to the FATF. India needs Pakistan to start dismantling the terrorist groups in the country, stop its terrorist attacks and support to separatists within Indian borders. If it does not take these corrective steps, this country is headed for further penury and economic distress. Even with the establishment of the Taliban government in Afghanistan, the situation for Pakistan is not quite stable. The Taliban must know that Pakistan is not able to provide any support. Pakistan has limited means to prevent violence and terror inside its borders. The attack on a police station in Karachi by the TTP on 16 February 2023 is a symptom of this malaise. India grows stronger economically, diplomatically and militarily and will not compromise on its vital interests. It will continue resolute efforts to persuade Pakistan to stop threatening peace.

Existential Threats and Reconciliation with China

China has slowly but steadily developed into a strong and assertive authoritarian nation after the takeover by the communists in 1949. Mao Zedong was the Chairman of the CPP at that time. His philosophy that 'political power grows out of the barrel of a gun' is being practiced by the current regime of Xi Jinping. The CPP, under Xi's chairmanship has become a powerful entity promoting nationalism, and China is no longer hesitant to flex its economic and military muscle. The expansion of organizations such as BRICS and other groups representing the world's south are perhaps created to counter the liberal international order formulated by the US and western democracies. China's path forward in the 21st century is based upon extension of the state's power rather than pluralism. It is bent upon redressing the humiliation it was subjected to by European and Japanese colonialism. Every day and in every way, China, is endeavouring to gain more and more power and wealth.

India, a strong, populous nation in China's neighbourhood, is directly impacted by China's quest for dominance. This implies differing levels of threats and different levels of conflict. By simply thwarting China along the unsettled border, India will not be able to achieve durable peace. In his statement after the second summit with Prime Minister Modi at Mamallapuram in India, Xi Jinping had declared that China and India have entered a new phase of sound, friendly developing relations. This statement notwithstanding, six months later, the Chinese commenced their belligerence and incursions into areas patrolled by Indian security forces. This indicates the true nature of Chinese irredentism and strategy and brings into focus the trust which is lacking between the two countries. China has waged war with nine of its neighbouring countries, including India, over border disputes. In all cases, it has made exaggerated claims on territory. China has attempted to enforce its perceptions of the borders through the use of Armed Forces or financial coercion. It presents a *fait accompli* by surreptitiously occupying territory that it considers its own but is disputed, with considerable strength of its PLA. With the disputed border, China has shown no inclination to define its perception of the border thus avoiding resolution. The countering of surreptitious and inimical actions by China, requires political will, consensus within various political entities, understanding and coordination with friendly countries, preparation and employment of large amounts of resources of the nation including armed forces. This complex dilemma prevents any permanent resolution of the conflict. Protocols and agreements meant to avoid conflict have not guaranteed peace with China. The ongoing border standoff in Eastern Ladakh and deadly scuffles between opposing troops and untenable claims across the IB and in Bhutan pose serious threats to India's security and territorial integrity. China continues to resort to the strategy of a protracted, open-ended conflict.

After the confrontation on the Indo-China border in 2020, there are about 50000 to 60000 troops with armaments from both countries are deployed opposite each other and remain on alert. This enhanced militarization has the potential to spark a larger conflict. Further clashes after the deadly clash in June 2020 have been avoided with meetings between local commanders on the ground and at the political level. After over four years of negotiations a partial agreement on patrolling along the LAC has been set up as per statement of the Indian Foreign Secretary. The Chinese Foreign Ministry has acknowledged that progress has been made in the discussions but has not committed on the details of the agreement reached. Leaving the facts murky, the Chinese have not explained whether the agreement covers the entire border or just the hotspots in Eastern Ladakh. India should continue to remain wary and carefully analyze the Chinese intentions. It appears that both countries have understood each other's viewpoint and have been able to reduce differences in the prolonged negotiations. At the time of writing, there is no clarity on the time frame for the agreement to be implemented. It is hoped that this agreement should end the standoff that occurred after the Galwan clash. The LAC, it needs to be understood, divides the area of physical control by both sides and does not depict territorial claims. Each side should hereafter ensure adherence to the deal reached to prevent any breaches. It may be that because of a rethink by the Chinese the situation has improved. Chinese authorities, while dealing with the border issue, have stated that the LAC cannot be defined as it will create more disputes. If that is so, then so be it, perhaps those disputes can also be resolved through negotiations. The importance of the most recent agreement should therefore not be overstated and unnecessarily felicitated. It is not a prelude to a broader détente between India and China because of the geo-political situation that exists. China's growing presence in the Indian Ocean and its friendly relations with Pakistan and use of Gilgit-Baltistan for its strategic purposes are unresolved challenges. China's claim line can be discerned at the negotiating table only if they are willing to do so. If the ongoing negotiations are broadened, it may become possible to deal with the differences on the entire border, especially in Arunachal Pradesh and Ladakh which China claims and Aksai Chin that India claims.

The above agreement notwithstanding, in recent years, China seems to have shown a disinclination to resolve the border issue. They have adopted a threatening attitude, strengthened their defensive posture in areas which they have advanced up to. Simultaneously they are settling their citizens in proximity to the Indo-Tibetan and Bhutan-Tibet border. In so doing the Chinese are cementing their occupation of Tibet and of territory they claim. These new developments enhance the threat from this country. The summit meeting that has taken place between Modi and Xi Jinping on the sidelines of the BRICS summit in Kazan, Russia, on 23 October 2024 may result in further negotiations and reduction of tensions.

The signing of the Indo-US nuclear deal under President Bush, the positive visit by President Obama to India, and the visit by President Biden in September 2023 during the G20 summit and the optics of the same were no doubt noted by China. A perception of a growing partnership between India and the US is evident with agreements on sharing intelligence and India's participation in the Quad naval exercises. The locating of IAF presence in Tajikistan at Gissar and Farkhor, friendly relations with Russia and with countries such as Mongolia, Vietnam and Philippines have perhaps shown that India will pursue its own interests and are not meant to be threatening to China. Traditionally, India has remained non-aligned, but China may perceive that India is playing both sides. This is actually not the case. India maintains its long-term policy of neutrality and correspondingly takes suitable measures to protect its own interests.

The terrain in the Tibetan plateau gives China an advantage. It is not as rugged as on the Indian side of the border. China has developed infrastructure in Tibet and Xinjiang that connects these areas to its hinterland, which provides China enhanced capability to rapidly switch forces. If the Indo-China conflict is to be defused, then it is imperative that India prevails upon China to begin with the disengagement in the remaining areas of contact. Once this is achieved, then talks on the de-escalation and reduction of force levels can be pursued in all sectors of the border.

China is far more powerful in most fields of the power matrix as compared to India. China began its development much earlier; however, this does not imply that India is far behind. To enable the economy to grow, the Indian Government allowed the defence budget to shrink in real terms and simultaneously, Prime Minister Modi tried to come to an understanding with Xi Jinping through bilateral summits, to prevent war. Despite the cutback in defence spending, India does have the ability to inflict massive harm on the Chinese. Further caution between both sides can be imposed if India ensures that it speaks from a position of strength without being unduly provocative in order to avoid exacerbating tensions. This notwithstanding, in the ultimate analysis, India has to be prepared to contend with various shades of Chinese belligerence on its own. India should systematically and critically examine the key tenets and develop an understanding of Xi Jinping's philosophy. His way of thinking and his methods have led China to attempt to gain supremacy in the world. His thoughts are encapsulated in 'tianxia' vision, a Sino-centric world order. Xi's aim seems to be to recreate China's premodern supremacy from a few centuries ago. Like President Trump's slogans, Make America Great Again (MAGA) and America First agenda, Xi too is making endeavours to bring China to the peak of power, and influence and be the strongest country in the world. This philosophy guides the Chinese grand strategy.

India is surely not the main adversary of China, but India is part of China's vision to dominate the world. India must therefore be prepared to deal with China in every aspect of the power matrix. India aims to ensure that it exercises self-reliant and pursues its policy of *Make in India*. It also aims to diversify its supply chain so that it is not entirely dependent on China for essential finished products. India could become an alternative global source for various goods and services. Gaining further technological capability – in AI, as well as in software and hardware and modern defence armaments are also important ways for India to contend with any contingencies created by China. The success of Indian offensive and defensive weapon systems in *Op Sindoor* would have been noted by China, Turkey and most world powers The possibility of a limited war will continue to exist until the border issue is resolved. India must do what it takes to keep strategic plans updated, manufacture and acquire defence systems, continue public debate and rally its people in the interest of national security. The national media, which is now very powerful in India, should support this agenda.

The visit by Prime Minister Modi to Russia and Ukraine earlier in 2024, his participation in the BRICS summit, and India's foreign minister's participation in the SCO summit held in Pakistan in July 2024 may have been noted with concern by the west. The US knows that India is an important part of their politico-military strategy in the Indo-Pacific and hence would like to continue to have an understanding with India's leadership. Alternatively, the US may once again prop up Pakistan as a centerpiece of its strategy seeing the close relationship it has developed with China. Relations between the US and China have become increasingly adversarial, with continuing disputes on freedom of seas, trade, theft of intellectual property by China, and support to Russia in their war in Ukraine. Due to the trade war with the US and its embargo on the export of sensitive items and technology, China has accelerated its drive for technological self-sufficiency and innovation, especially in AI. The investment by US private companies in China are huge and it will be impossible to extricate enterprises from China entirely. The US is attempting to re-establish manufacturing at home and seek alternate supply chains in which India should figure prominently.

The US has found the expansionist policies of the CCP unacceptable, especially in the Far East, where China is consolidating its hold on the South China Sea, and it also continues to threaten Taiwan. This is part of Chinese strategy to flex its growing military power. Sailing of Chinese warships through the open seas of the Taiwan Straits, fighter aircraft intrusions into Taiwan's airspace, and warnings by Xi Jinping to the PLA to prepare for war are examples of this intimidating policy. Whether China will employ military power to block the sea routes through the South China Sea and assimilate Taiwan by use of armed force, possibly risking a world war, is still an open-ended scenario.

In the G7 meeting in June 2021, President Biden enunciated a plan for 'Build Back Better World' (B3W). As part of this plan, the G7 countries had committed to spending $500 million in developing countries to combat climate change and facilitate better healthcare, gender equality, and digital technology. The success of this initiative is unclear, whereas in comparison, China has plans to spend $3.7 trillion on its BRI project in which more than 150 countries are participating. It is likely that Afghanistan will also join the BRI. They have asked the Chinese to develop a land link to Xinjiang through its Wakhan Corridor. China has been wary of the Taliban as they wield Islamic influence on the Uyghur population in Xinjiang province. To obviate any support to Uyghur separatists from the Taliban and also to develop an alternate route to the CPEC, China has brought Afghanistan into their sphere of influence.

India does not brandish an ideology of domination like the US and China. However, it has an ascendant economy and tremendous goodwill across the world. The death of Indian soldiers in the Galwan Valley clash on 15 June 2020 brought about a change in the India-China relationship. There has been a lasting groundswell of anti-China sentiment in India. Using lessons learned in the confrontation with China, India has strongly expressed its stand on various matters in the ongoing negotiations. India is wary of the threat and understands the need to remain strictly transactional in dealing with China. It is also becoming apparent that strategic autonomy is meaningless unless India is militarily strong to contend with the threat posed by its neighbours. Without military power, diplomatic leverage would not work, and military power can only be enhanced if the country is economically strong. India remains the only democracy in the region that can resist and counter China's domination and belligerence. This is its strength.

In the ongoing series of talks about the LAC between military and diplomatic leaders of India and China, the aim has been to de-escalate the situation along the entire border. As mentioned earlier, a partial agreement on patrolling has been a step in that direction. Further dialogue must continue to address the entire Indo-China border or else, incidents, such as the one in Tawang sector in Arunachal Pradesh, will continue to occur. Notwithstanding the partial understanding reached in the negotiations, China seems to be in no hurry to resolve the border dispute. India on the other hand has been quite accommodative of the Chinese in attempting to defuse the tensions on the border. Indian troops that had moved forward and occupied the Kailash Range on the south bank of Pangong in the standoff in 2020, were withdrawn thereby setting a precedent towards resolving the ongoing impasse in eastern Ladakh. India has clearly stated that the border issue cannot be separated from trade and economic linkages. India and China both need investments to foster mutual enhanced economic growth. The Chinese are still very willing to invest in ventures in India's vibrant economy. There were at least 45 proposals by Chinese companies to establish manufacturing in India, which were given tacit approval by the Indian Government in 2020–21. While approving such projects, India has made sure that sensitive areas of the economy, such as 5G communications, are not open to Chinese acquisition.

The Chinese public posture indicates that the country wants to build trust with India and peace along the disputed border, while its official media at times is skeptical of relations with India. Future projections of economic growth for India and China show that the India's growth rate will exceed and to be higher than that of China. The IMF had estimated that the Indian economy would grow by 9 per cent in 2023, but it actually grew by 8.24 percent, whereas China grew at 5.4 percent. These growth rates are likely to be lower in 2024-25 for both countries. This is still not an indication that India's economy will catch up to the Chinese economy even in the long term. It also does indicate that India will have the financial means and resources to grow in all fields of power matrix. Trade and commerce assist China in its quest for achieving world domination and this is likely to remain their focus. India authorities understand this and continue to strive to achieve self-sufficiency in strategic areas, adapt to changes in supply chains and position India as a manufacturing alternative for the world. At present China is still the dominant manufacturing base of the world.

While contending with the China, India must continue to maintain its relationship with the US and other friendly nations. The visit by the Prime Minister Modi to Russia in July 2024 highlights that India also desires to sustain its friendly ties with Russia. Acquiring a strong backing from friendly countries, sharing of intelligence, emergency procurement of sophisticated military hardware as and when required, and posing counter threats to China remain key priorities for India. It also has to strengthen its capability to undertake countermoves across the border and the Bay of Bengal to put China at a strategic disadvantage, if required. China is vulnerable to strategic interdiction of its trade. India must develop sufficient power to interfere with Chinese trade that passes through the Malacca Straits and the CPEC. The launching of a fourth nuclear powered submarine and successful test of a hypersonic missile shows that India has considerable expertise in developing modern equipment for three-dimensional warfare. India's competition with China is geo-strategic, because of divergence in ideology and political systems. With its ports along the Indian Ocean and investments in Suez, Haifa in Israel, Seychelles, Madagascar, Mauritius and even in Myanmar, India does have considerable influence. Chinese animosity remains existential and for any permanent resolution, this animosity needs to turn into cooperation one day. For India, there is a need to maintain political dialogue, rebuild trust and understanding, and keep a firm commitment to solving the border issue.

Pakistan's Intransigence Revisited

The cessation of fire after four days of ops along the LOC and IB with Pakistan during *Op Sindoor* has come about as India did not want further escalation. India has to be prepared to deal with a bigger threat than that posed by Pakistan alone. To preserve its resources for the major threat from China and the possibility of a two-front war, the ceasefire was a judicious decision. In any case the aims set for *Op Sindoor* have largely been accomplished. Briefly, the aim was to carry out reprisals against the outrage by Pakistani terrorists, killing twenty-five tourists and a pony owner in Pahalgam. If the power balance is to be roughly evaluated then it can be visualised that the extensive and sensitive active border with China requires considerable resources to manage the threat. This would leave near parity on the western border in the strength required to deal with Pakistan. The balance can be upped with the adoption of superior technology in weapon systems, better intelligence, and training. It is clear that the Pakistan armed forces found themselves at a disadvantage during *Op Sindoor*. China however has developed newer and more lethal means to wage war. Their newer weapon systems are AI driven and have lethality not seen earlier. As of now China has perhaps not made available their latest weapon systems to Pakistan. To keep India under check and to ensure continuity of the India-Pakistan hostilities China will provide Pakistan with upgrades to their war fighting means. This is evident from the offer that China has made to sell 40 of their fifth-generation fighter aircraft, the J35A, at 50% concessional rates to Pakistan. Similarly other nations such as Turkey that saw their Bayraktar drones defeated by India would surely be scrambling to make improvements in its algorithms. The visit by Prime Minister Shahbaz Sharif soon after the cessation of fire in May 2025 to Turkey, Iran, Azerbaijan, and Kyrgyzstan, may be for various reasons but it shows the urgency that Pakistan has for garnering support of these Muslim nations. It was an urgency driven visit to seek better weapon systems. During the engagements in *Op Sindoor,* both countries are likely to have had losses. Pakistan's airforce has suffered losses as their airforce seemed to have been grounded after night 9/10 May 2025. This was because of the losses, targeting of their AWACS air craft and ground based air defence radars. Having achieved what it had to, the government of India and its armed forces will be carrying out appraisal of the politico-military lessons learnt in *Op Sindoor*. These are a subject of a separate study. Suffice to say that preparedness to wage a successful war has to evaluate the capabilities of adversaries and have better technological armaments to cater for all contingencies. India surely has surprised most of the world with its advancement in acquiring new means of waging war. Further progress is required to meet the fast-changing modes of technology being used in weapon systems both defensive and offensive. A few military lessons that are evident are:

a. Armed drones including decoys and loitering munitions are an essential part of combat. The use of unarmed aerial vehicles in probing air defence radars and weapon systems to activate these will assist in targeting these accurately.

b. To engage in sustained conflict adequate stocks of weapon systems have to be catered. Indigenous capability to produce weapon systems, drones, modern aircraft and AI driven targeting systems have to be developed or enhanced.

c. Upgradation of weapon systems by improving the capability of existing ones and replacing those which have become obsolete with new technologies is essential to keep ahead of capabilities of inimical nations. This requires constant evaluation by the armed forces, communication with the political leadership and approval.

d. Combat aircraft will have to operate with impunity outside the effective range of air defensive missile systems unless there are improvements in their technology, early warning suites, stealth characteristics, speed and other evasive means.

e. Endeavour has to be made to jam the functioning of alien satellite clusters being used by inimical nations to wage war. Drones, loitering ammunition and combat aircraft that have satellite links need to be countered. This would deny automatic targeting means to the enemy.

f. The environment in a sub-conventional war will remain to be chaotic. It is essential to have better intelligence at all levels especially at grassroots to prevent targeting of citizens and security forces. Terrorists can only be successful if they have collaborators within the local population. Local spies, sleeper cells, local terrorist outfits operating on behalf of their mentors in Pakistan are enemies of the nation. Those aliens who have illegally entered India could also be assisting inimical forces hence they need to be identified and action initiated to verify their credentials, detain them and deport or jail them. The media can assist in this in many ways.

g. With superior technology India has displayed advantage in its capabilities. It is clear that wars can be of short duration and more devastating. This should bring caution in the adversaries especially Pakistan.

h. Terrorist groups will henceforth spend more time and resources on concealment within their country. Terrorists carrying out attacks on Indian soil will be better trained, adept in covering their tracks after an attack thus making it difficult for intelligence to unearth the outrage.

It has been proven that the terrorist groups from a vital component of Pakistan's means to wage the sub-conventional proxy war. At the cost of repetition, it can be stated that there is blurring of lines between state and non-state actors who pursue war for Pakistan. The terrorist groups have grown in influence in Pakistan as their cadres have multiplied exponentially over the last five decades since their creation. Some of these cadres have been recruited in the Pakistan Army as well. With the terror groups clearly displaying their wrath against India, they have reiterated that there is likely to be no let-up in their ops against India. Terrorism is likely to stay.

The killing of innocent civilian tourists in Pahalgam has affected the tourism industry in most of the region. This is perhaps for the first time that a terrorist act in Kashmir has created an aversion for Pakistan's proxy war in the minds of the local population. There have been mass protests against Pakistan's terrorism in Srinagar as it directly affects their means of earning. Tourism was booming in the state. Be that as it may, it will take some time for the hurt caused by the Pahalgam outrage to subside. Tourism should once again regenerate in Kashmir despite the terror threat. It should be remembered that a peaceful situation can easily be disturbed anytime by terrorists. The Pakistan hierarchy should understand that it does not have superior technology to fight a short duration war and surely it cannot sustain a protracted war unless it is propped up by support from other nations. The granting of $ 2.3 billion loan by the IMF to Pakistan during Op Sindoor is a case in point. Saudi Arabia and UAE have also given 3 billion $ to sustain Pakistan. Indirectly most of these funds will go towards procurement of weapon systems for their armed forces. Pakistan will surely build up its war fighting potential in the near future.

The 35 years of proxy war, with numerous terrorist attacks on India, have not changed anything in Pakistan's favour. Pakistan's nuclear blackmail has not worked and may not work in the future. Under these uncertain circumstances the prospects of war flaring up between these two nuclear armed nations remains a matter of concern for the world. Once there is a flare up, there is immediate advice rendered by friendly nations to start a dialogue and put a stop to military action. During *Op Sindoor*, the US did endeavour to talk to both India and Pakistan and claimed that it was responsible for bringing about the ceasefire. This was not entirely true. India had stated clearly that it was the Pakistan Army that sent messages to stop the fire. India, has the policy that it will under no circumstances accept third party mediation in negotiations with Pakistan. At the time of writing both countries have adopted a hardline approach. The Pakistani political leadership has promoted Gen Asim Munir to field marshal's rank, to show that they stand by their army even if circumstances are adverse and to reinforce their false claim of victory. In the current hostilities Pakistan army has managed to disturb the status quo.

The UNSC and major countries of the world except Turkey and Azerbiajan had condemned the killing in Pahalgam. On India's retaliation the support changed into diplomatic efforts to stop escalation. The effort by India to carry out reprisal were determined and purposeful. They were planned and executed to hit selected terrorist camps to demolish the facilities at these terrorist camps. There was no intention to harm any civilians and did not target Pakistan's military or civilian areas. India reacted to the terrorist attack in the manner of its own choosing and this was an escalation compared to the strike at Balakot where only one strike was carried out. The media in both countries went into an overdrive. Its importance in influencing international and national opinions exists. The Indian Defence Minister has called Pakistan a rogue state. Pakistan is not at peace within its own boundaries and will not allow its neighbours to live in peace. The purported leak of fissile material from nuclear facilities in the Kirana Hills is alarming as well. If this were true, the leak could have occurred while nuclear weapons were being assembled or it was an accident. It is a matter of conjecture what really happened there. Hence India's appeal to bring in the IAEA to ensure safety of Pakistan's nuclear arsenal.

If Pakistan were to adopt a cooperative attitude it could exploit its geographical location for the growth of trade, tourism, and transit. It is located at the crossroads of Central Asia and South Asia and China and the

Middle East. India too would have many advantages if Gilgit Baltistan and POK were part of J&K. India would then have direct access to Afghanistan and central Asia to enhance prospects of trade and transit through its sea ports.

Pakistan's relationship with India will, perhaps, continue as per its first-ever security policy, which was enunciated by Imran Khan on 14 January 2022. In this policy, it was clearly reiterated that Pakistan will continue moral, diplomatic, political, and legal support for the people of Kashmir. India can, therefore, expect terrorism sponsored, abetted and conducted by Pakistan to continue as was apparent with terrorist incidents in J&K in 2024-25 and Pahalgam. Pakistan's policy, however, expresses an interest in establishing peace with India and also builds legitimacy for its Army. This can only happen if a deliberate change occurs in Pakistan's strategy towards India. Unless this re-orientation in policy occurs, the FATF, UNSC, and others will bear more pressure on Pakistan if it continues to nurture terrorist groups and perpetuate terror. To reduce terrorism, Nawaz Sharif made an attempt to dismantle the terrorist groups when he was the Prime Minister of Pakistan, prior to the general elections in his country in July–August 2018. As per some reports, he had directed the Army to prepare plans for the dismantling the jihadi groups. Plans made were shelved as radical groups were forewarned and most of their leaders went underground. Nawaz Sharif was thereafter not allowed to contest elections for reasons already mentioned.[3] While speaking to Indian journalists during the SCO summit in July 2024, Nawaz Sharif once again expressed hope for resuming dialogue and trade with India. Will the Deep State permit this? The decisions that emerge from the co-relations between politicians and the Deep State in Pakistan are not easy to decipher or predict.

During his visit to China in February 2022, Imran Khan discussed the Kashmir dispute with Xi Jinping. In their discussion, some relevant advice seemed to have been rendered by Xi Jinping. He is believed to have stated that Kashmir was a dispute left behind by history and that it should be resolved based on the UN charter, UNSC resolutions, and bilateral agreements. He further advised that this should be resolved peacefully and not with unilateral action, such as the Kargil War, as that may complicate the situation. If this advice was rendered, it should have been taken seriously as this country is currently mired in extremely serious economic difficulties and is subject to

3. *The Unravelling: Pakistan in the Age of Jihad* by Jon R. Schmidt pp 222

terrorism internally from the TPP, BLA and others. These matters should be the priority for Pakistan. Xi Jinping however, failed to mention that disputes with India should be resolved in terms of the Shimla Agreement of July 1972. And China is itself unwilling to resolve the border dispute with India even though these disputes have been left behind by history. Pakistan would likely be of less strategic value to China if it did not retain POK and Gilgit-Baltistan.

It is to be understood that India cannot ignore Pakistan. As an immediate neighbour, Pakistan has remained persistently inimical, takes an undue interest in Indian internal affairs, continues with the sub-conventional war against India and retains POK and Gilgit-Baltistan illegally. The US and the Western nations cannot ignore it, as it provides them diplomatic access to China, Afghanistan, Iran and Central Asia. Pakistan's practice of nurturing terrorist groups, using terrorism as an instrument of state policy and its nuclear capability need to be monitored and India has to enhance its defence capability, given the animosity of its two neighbours. In India, politicians and diplomats have failed to make any headway with their counterparts in Pakistan, because the dialogue process has always been thwarted by their Deep State. Hence further pressure from India is necessary to create conditions to force Pakistan to carry out meaningful negotiations.

India is continuing to try to ensure that J&K is free from the scourge of terrorism. The radical religious practices and thoughts that Pakistan has imposed on a small section of the population are likely to persist in J&K for some time. There are however some positive changes apparent in J&K, seeing the peaceful prayers conducted during Ramadan at the Hazratbal Mosque in Srinagar and the participation by the electorate in the elections for the legislative assembly and Indian parliament in 2024. The Kashmiri Pandits who were forcefully evicted from their homes need justice and intolerance against these people should ebb. In the Pahalgam attack tourists have been made victims after discerning their religion. This is an example of religious intolerance. Was the attack carried out with the approval of the political leadership or was it purely planned by and executed by the deep state? Eventually the answer to question should emerge. Violence of this kind would once again affect tourism drastically as stated earlier. If that were to happen, it would most likely alienate the local population from terrorist groups. There is still much to be done to win over the population of Kashmir who have kept their emotions restrained. It is the people who have provided support to terrorists in carrying out the attack.

This has to change to ensure that terrorists find it difficult to survive. The election process has perhaps assuaged their feelings as this allows the common Kashmiri folks to express themselves and pursue their interests. Considerable geo-political and demographic changes have taken place in the area, and to undo these would be quite difficult if not impossible. With Pakistan the intractable conflict is historically entrenched. Pakistan's attitude and behaviour, even etiquette can be seen as quite predictable. The unchanging pattern of which is reflected in criticism, competition, suspicion and above all, a trust deficit. After thirty years of war, the Treaty of Westphalia brought peace among the warring nations of Europe. Surely, this model can be adopted by India, Pakistan, and even China to bring peace. Will Pakistan ever change? Hope should be maintained to come to terms for the resolution of conflicts in this region. After all, India and Pakistan are the born from a common heritage, and share an indelible, incredible history.

Explanatory Notes

Hindutva	It is the predominant form of the Hindu religion and, in a sense, Hindu nationalism. It is based on the concept of a homogenized majority of Hindus and their cultural identity. This concept has fascist undertones but is more so a form of conservatism. It is propagated by Hindu nationalist organizations. This ideology was based upon the perceived vulnerability of the Indian religion, its values, culture, and heritage.
Upanishads	These are a collection of Sanskrit texts of religious and philosophical nature written in India, probably between 800 BCE and 500 BCE. These include spiritual teachings and ideas of Hinduism, some of which are shared with the religious traditions of Buddhism and Jainism. They are known as Vedanta, the last parts of the Vedas.
Vedas	These are the oldest scriptures of Hinduism that deal with meditation, philosophy, spiritual knowledge, ceremonies, and sacrifices.
Nasidya Sukhta	This is the 3500th verse of the Rig Veda, which describes Hinduism.

Bibliography

Bergen, Peter *United States of Jihad*, Investigating America's Home-grown Terrorists. Crown Publication. 2013

Talibanisation, Negotiating the Border, between Terror, Politics and Religion. 2013

Bose, Sumantra *Transforming India*, Challenges to the World's Largest Democracy. Harvard University Press. 2013

Brown, Vanda Felbab *Aspirations and Ambivalence, Strategies Realities of State Building*, published by Brookings Institution. 2013

Chandler, Michael *Countering Terrorism*, published by Reaktion Books Ltd. 2007

Clinton, Bill *My Life*, published by Vintage House, Random House Inc. 2004

Cohen, Stephen *Shooting for a Century, The India Pakistan Conundrum*, Brookings Institute Press. 2013

Cole, Juan Engaging *The Muslim World*, published by Palgrave McMillan. 2009

Dulat, A. S., *The Spy Chronicles, RAW, ISI and the Illusions of Peace*, published by Harper Collins. 2018

Falk, Richard *The Path to Zero, Dialogue on Nuclear Dangers*, Paradigm Publishers, Boulder, Colorado, USA. 2012

Gall, Carlotta *The Wrong Enemy, America in Afghanistan*, Houghton Mifflin Harcourt, Boston. 2014

Gopal, Anand *No Good Men Among the Living, Taliban and the War through Afghan Eyes* (Pulitzer Prize nominee) Gupta, Amit Global Security Watch India, published by Praeger, an imprint of ABC-CLIO, LLC. 2014

Gul, Imtiaz *The Most Dangerous Place, Pakistan's Lawless Frontier*, published by Penguin Books, New York. 2009

Haynes, Susan *Nuclear Proliferation by China*, University of Nebraska Press. 2016

Katz, Mark *Leaving Without Loosing: The War on Terror after Iraq and Afghanistan*, John Hopkins University Press. 2012

Khanduri, B.C. Field Marshal KM Cariappa: *Life and Times*, Lancer Publication. 1995

Johnson, Rob *A Region in Turmoil: South Asia Conflicts since 1947*, published by Reaktion Books. 2009

Malik, V.P. Kargil From *Surprise to Victory*, published by Harper Collins Publishers New Delhi 2006

Madhok, *Balraj Kashmir: The Storm Center of the World*, published by A Ghosh, Houston, Texas, USA. 1992

Markey, Daniel *No Exit from Pakistan America's Tortured Relationship with Islamabad*, published by Cambridge University Press. 2013

Mawyer, Martin *Twilight in America; The Untold Story of Terrorist Training Camps Inside America*, published by Christian Action Network. 2012

Musharraf, Parvez *In the Line of Fire*, published by Free Press, New York. 2006

Paul, T.V. T*he Warrior State, Pakistan in the Contemporary World*, published by Oxford University Press. 2015

Ralph Peters *Spies Lies and Terrorists In (Not Much) Disguise*

Robinson, Linda *Tell Me How this Ends*, Google Books. 2010

Polk, William *Crusade and Jihad*, published by Yale University Press, New Haven USA. 2018

Raman, B. *Kowboy's of RAW*, published by Lancer Publications Atlanta. 2013

Rashid, Ahmed *The Anarchic Republic of Pakistan*, William B. Eerdmans Publishing Company, Cambridge, UK. 2012

Saikal, Amin *Zone of Crisis, Afghanistan, Pakistan, Iran and Iraq*, published by IB Tauris & Co London. 2014

Schmidt, John *The Unravelling, Pakistan in the Age of Jihad*, published by Farrar, Straus, Giroux, New York. 2011

Schofield, *Victoria Kashmir in Conflict India Pakistan and the Unending War*, published by IB Tauris & Co Ltd, London. 2003

Singhal, D.P. *India Afghanistan a Study of Diplomatic Relations*, published by South Asian Publishers. 1982

Tellis, Ashley Asia in the Second Nuclear Age, published by the National Bureau of Asian Research. 2013

Verma, Kunal *The Long Road to Siachen*, published by Rupa Publishing Pvt Ltd New Delhi. 2010

Wirsing, Robert *Kashmir in the Shadow of War, Regional Rivalries in the Nuclear Age*, published by M.E. Sharpe Inc. 2016

Wolpert, Stanley *India and Pakistan Continued Conflict or Cooperation*, University of California Press. 2010